Genesis

A Commentary for Children

Herein is Love
COMMENTARY SERIES

Genesis

A Commentary for Children

Nancy E. Ganz

ISBN 0-9723046-0-6 (previously ISBN 0–9688830–0-1)

Shepherd Press
PO Box 24
Wapwallopen, PA 18660
www.shepherdpress.com
(800) 338-1445

Graphic Layout & Design: Tobias' Outerwear for Books (www.tobiasdesign.com)
Production: Andrew MacBride

Cover Artwork: Nicora Gangi—www.machairastudio.com
Cover landscape is from her original pastel entitled "I Set My Bow." God said,
"I have set My rainbow in the clouds, and it shall be the sign of the covenant
between Me and the earth" (Genesis 9:13).

Unless otherwise noted, Scripture is taken from the Holy Bible,
New International Version (NIV), © 1972, 1976, 1984 by the
International Bible Society.

Manufactured in the United States of America

Dedication

This book is lovingly dedicated to:

James Dale Turnbull, my father,

Margaret Jean (Scott) Turnbull, my mother,

Norman John Turnbull, my godfather, and

Isabella Archer (Turnbull) Brooks,
my godmother and dear Aunt Tibbie.

Acknowledgements

There is one person who has helped me and loved me from the moment he met me, and that is my husband and pastor, Dr. Richard L. Ganz. I thank him for his enthusiastic support of my work.

I would also like to acknowledge two men, whom I consider dear friends, though long deceased, whose work has continually instructed and inspired me in my study of God's Word. They are Matthew Henry and John Calvin.

I also thank the many pastors, elders and friends in the Reformed Presbyterian Church, who have encouraged me to continue in this labour of love.

I give a special thanks to Stas Jesionka for his technical expertise and Nicora Gangi for her beautiful art, which now adorns my books as well as my home.

CONTENTS

INTRODUCTION

Why Did I Write This Book?

I wrote this book to teach children about the LOVE of God. When I was a child I learned about the God of wrath in the Old Testament. When I came of age I was confirmed in the church, even while I rejected this God in my heart — but at the right time, on the day appointed for me by God, at the age of twenty-one, the Lord brought me to Himself and I embraced this God with faith. I placed my trust in Him to forgive my sins and rescue me from death. He was not a God of wrath, but a God of LOVE and Grace. It has grieved me that my heavenly Father should be so maligned, especially in the eyes of little children. God's great LOVE pours forth from the very beginning of the Bible, from the opening words in Genesis, to the closing words in Revelation. God's great SALVATION is proclaimed throughout the Scriptures — and that is how my heart was turned to Him, by seeing this salvation unveiled in the Old Testament. I discovered that the Bible was not a collection of unrelated short stories and it was seeing this unity of the Scriptures that brought me to faith. I came to a saving knowledge of Christ through the Gospel of Moses and the last shreds of unbelief were ripped from my eyes by the proclamation of John the Baptist. He was the voice calling out in the wilderness who finally reached my heart: "Behold the Lamb of God, who takes away the sin of the world!" I beheld Jesus, because I understood for the first time about the Lamb of God in the writings of Moses. This Messiah had been announced from the beginning. I had not understood what manner of Man He was, because I had not been taught all that had been written beforehand concerning Him. Jesus said, "How foolish you are, and how slow of heart to believe all that the prophets have spoken . . . And beginning with Moses and all the prophets, He explained to them what was said in all the Scriptures concerning Himself" (Luke 24:25, 27). How foolish we are not to teach our children about Christ the way He taught about Himself! How foolish we are not to begin where He began, with the writings of Moses! It is the Old Testament writings about which this is written: "From infancy you have known the Holy Scriptures, which are able to make you wise for salvation through faith in Christ Jesus. All Scripture is God-breathed and is useful for teaching" (II Timothy 3:15, 16). I believe that knowing the Old Testament from their earliest days will make our children wise for salvation through Jesus Christ. Our children must see the LOVE of God from the beginning; they must see God's plan of SALVATION unfolding from the beginning, if they are going to place their trust in Him. "HEREIN IS LOVE: not that we loved God, but that He loved us and sent His Son as an atoning sacrifice for our sins" (I John 4:10). The work of God's Son was proclaimed to us from the very beginning.

I decided to write this book when I was sitting in the National Arts Centre Theatre in the capital of Canada. The National Ballet Company of Canada was performing *The Nutcracker* and I was thinking, "The world takes a silly little story like this and tells it to the children so beautifully and meaningfully that they remember it for the rest of their lives. The church takes the most beautiful and meaningful story ever told—the salvation of God's people—and somehow turns the most exciting events and amazing facts in all human history into unimaginably boring lessons. How is this possible?" It was that thought in that moment which motivated me to write this book in this way.

There was also a very practical reason for this book. I needed Bible lessons for teaching. In 1980 my husband, Dr. Richard L. Ganz, was called to plant a church in Ottawa, Canada. I found myself responsible for the Sabbath School of that new work. What materials were available for teaching children the Scriptures? I was disheartened by what I found. Most Sunday School material was so uninteresting and so uninspiring that I could barely read through the lessons myself. The great theme of Scripture—God saving a people for Himself—was somehow lost in these lessons and what emerged was the repetitive message: "Be good. Do this. Don't do that." Of course children must be taught right from wrong, but without faith, works are dead—and they cannot bring a child to life. "It is by grace you have been saved, through faith . . . not by works" (Ephesians 2:8, 9). All the accounts in the Scriptures, all the stories of the Bible, are there to strengthen our FAITH in God. "These are written that you might BELIEVE" (John 20:31). Every lesson should encourage the children to believe—to believe in God's Word, to believe in God's LOVE. I became aware that in most Sunday School lessons the focus was wrong. These lessons focused on what we should do, instead of focusing on what God had done. Their emphasis was upon our works, rather than upon God's Grace. What does the Bible say about teaching our children? "We will tell the next generation the praiseworthy deeds of the Lord, His power, and the wonders He has done . . . He established the Law in Israel, which He commanded our forefathers to teach their children . . . Then they would put their trust in God and would not forget His deeds, but would keep His commands" (Psalm 78:4, 5,7). Works follow faith. Keeping His commands follows putting their trust in God. And how do they come to put their trust in God? It is by us telling them "the praiseworthy deeds of the Lord."

> *O Lord, my God, how many are the wonders Thou has done!*
> *How many are the gracious thoughts, which Thou to us has shown!*
> *No one can sort and set them out. None can compare to Thee!*
> *If I would tell and speak of them, they could not numbered be.*
> *I never have within my heart concealed Thy Righteousness.*
> *I Thy Salvation have declared and shown Thy Faithfulness.*
> *Thy Mercy great, Thy steadfast LOVE, I ever have revealed,*
> *And from the congregation great Thy Truth have not concealed.*
>
> Psalm 40:5, 10, The Book of Psalms for Singing, 40C

In this book, in these lessons, I have humbly endeavoured to begin this task, the task of telling the children of God's wonders, the task of declaring to them God's righteousness, SALVATION and faithfulness, the task of revealing to them God's Truth, His great Mercy and His steadfast LOVE.

For Whom Did I Write This Book?

I wrote this book for the children, praying that, step by step, it would bring them ever closer to Christ. It was written to encourage them, lesson by lesson, to put their trust in God, to believe in His promises, to rejoice in His salvation. It was also written for any adult concerned about this most vital ministry—the teaching of our children.

I have used these lessons for many years with real success. I have taught many different classes of children of varying ages. What I have discovered is that most people underestimate the ability of children to understand the Word of God. They also underestimate the power of the Word of God to pierce through the hearts and minds of our little ones. The Truth will captivate them, without any gimmick. It takes a very short time for my little students to realize that they are in a class involved in serious learning. They listen carefully. I have had large classes of eight-year-olds weeping with grief as I teach through one lesson, then laughing with joy as I teach another. I have had parents say to me, "We can't get our child to read a book or to show much interest in anything, but he races home after your class to read the Bible!" I have had mentally challenged children in my classes. They may not understand everything, but they listen attentively and, to my surprise and delight, answer the most important questions correctly! The children I have taught over the years have written me letters, thanking me for teaching them about God. These many children have taught me something very important: These little people, these small saints in the kingdom of God, don't want fluff. They want the pure milk and the good meat of God's Word— and we cheat them and starve them if we give them anything less than that. By God's Grace, may we never stand in their way to the LORD; may we never cause them to stumble.

Where Did I Write This Book?

It was difficult for me to find a place to write this book. We had four children, all home-schooled. My pastor/ husband's study was in our home, which meant there was not a spare room in the house. We had a thriving new work, with people constantly visiting our home. I was becoming desperate. There was no longer a quiet moment anytime or a quiet corner anywhere. At last I retreated to the hayloft of our log barn. At first I used to write sitting on a bright-red, antique, horse-sleigh, with a clipboard and pen in hand, but when the Canadian winter struck and the temperatures dipped below −40 degrees F., I could not work, not even with double mittens. However, there was a small dark grain room in the barn. With the help and skill of our friend, Stas Jesionka, we converted this into a study for me. We added windows, insulation, a heater, and eventually a computer. It is the most wonderful room in the world. It overlooks the farmlands of the Mississippi Valley in Ontario, Canada. In winter I trudge through the waist-deep snowdrifts in the barnyard. In spring I walk by the sheep with their little lambs. In the autumn the barn loft is filled with hundreds of bales of hay. A narrow pathway, with walls of hay towering on each side, is left for me to walk to my study. One of my little pupils, who had been visiting our farm, reported to her parents: "My Sunday School teacher works inside a haystack!" Yes, at times all you can see of my room is a small wooden door under a huge mound of hay. It is my favourite place to go to be with God, to study His Word and to proclaim His praises.

May the LORD Himself bless my work for Him.

THE WORD OF GOD

T he world is filled with books, countless millions of books. Have you ever been to a big library? There you can see thousands and thousands of books, stacked up shelf upon shelf, lined up row after row, stored in room beside room. There are books from the floor to the ceiling. There are books from one end of the room to the other. A small child could get lost among all those books!

There is one book, which is very special, different from all the other books in the world. Do you know which one that is? Yes, the Bible! Do you know what makes the Bible different from any other book? Perhaps you would answer that it's a book about God, but there are many books about God — and many of them are not true. Perhaps then you would answer that the Bible is a true book about God, but if you looked in a good church library you would find many true books about God, written by righteous men who knew Him. However, the Bible is unique even among those books. What then makes the Bible different? The Bible is the only book on the face of the earth whose author is God. All the other books are words that people have written. All the other books come from the minds of men and women, but the Bible comes from God! The Bible is God's Word.

Words can be used in different ways. Here are three different ways of using words:

1) **Writing**—People use words in writing. We can write words on paper with a pen; we can embroider words onto material with thread; we can carve words into wood with a knife; we can type them on a computer screen with a keyboard; we can print them on a sidewalk with chalk; we can scratch them onto a stone with a nail; we can make words in the snow with an icicle; we can press them into the sand with our fingers, etc. There are many different ways that we can write words.

2) **Speaking**—People also use words in speaking. We can whisper words; we can scream words; we can giggle words; we can sing words. There are many different ways that we can speak words.

3) **Thinking**—This is a third way that people use words. In our minds we think in words. We often pray this way, speaking silently in our hearts to God.

God has made people like Himself, for God also uses words in these three ways:

1) The Word of God in the mind of God, that is, the Wisdom of God, was there "from eternity, from the beginning, before the world began . . ." (Proverbs 8:23). This form of God's Word was "the first of His works," before He created anything (Proverbs 8:22). The universe and everything in it (including you, including me) exist because of the Word of God, because God *thought* of us. "How precious to me are Your thoughts, O God! How vast the sum of them" (Psalm 139:17)! "How great are Your works, O Lord! How profound Your thoughts (Psalm 92:5)!

2) The Word of God was also spoken. "We understand that the universe was formed at God's command" (Hebrews 11:3). "Long ago by God's Word the heavens existed and the earth was formed " (II Peter 3:5). We exist, the world and everything in it exist, because God *spoke*. "He commanded and they were created" (Psalm 148:5). And from the beginning God spoke to men, for God graciously "reveals His thoughts to man" (Amos 4:13). The LORD spoke at various times in various ways for various reasons. Sometimes

He whispered in a still small voice. Once God spoke from a burning bush. Sometimes He thundered from a mountaintop. Occasionally God sent angels as His messengers to proclaim His Word. Usually though, God spoke His Word through men called prophets. These men "spoke from God as they were carried along by the Holy Spirit" (II Peter 1:21). A prophet of God was asked: "Who are you?" He answered, "I am the voice . . ." (John 1:19–23). God most often used the voices of men to speak His Word to the world.

3) God's Word was also written. One time God wrote His Law, the Ten Commandments, on tablets of stone. These stones were inscribed by the finger of God. Another time the fingers of a human hand suddenly appeared out of nowhere in the air and this hand wrote on the wall three terrifying words. It was a message from God. But usually God wrote His Word by using people. He used earthly hands to write heavenly words; He used human minds to express divine thoughts. God used men like Moses and Malachi, Matthew and Mark. He commanded them to write—and they wrote. They did not write their own words; they wrote God's Word. God's Word became their words and their words became God's Word. The Bible is the book that God *wrote* for us, using human agents.

Some people say there is no God. Others say that God may be there, but we can't know, for God is silent. They say God has nothing to do with us. These people are wrong. From eternity God has been there and from the beginning God has communicated with us. God's Word has been spoken to man and God's Word has been written for man. Isn't it amazing that what God said thousands of years ago thousands of miles away has not been lost?! Neither has it been destroyed! Many angry men and wicked kings have tried, but they were the ones who perished and vanished. The Word of God remained. "The Word of the LORD endures forever" (Isaiah 40:8). God preserved His Word throughout the ages and scattered His Word throughout the nations. His Word has been copied millions and millions of times. God's Word has also been translated, so that people all over the world can read the Bible in their own language. (The Bible was originally written in Hebrew and Greek, which are different languages with different alphabets. If someone had not translated the Bible for you, knowing your ABC's would be of no help to you at all, for you would not have been able to read God's Word. But the LORD made sure that his message would reach you!) God has not been silent. His voice has gone out into all the earth and His Words to the end of the world.

God did not keep or hide Himself from us. One way that God gave Himself and showed Himself to us was in His Word. In the Bible God told us everything we need to know about Him. In the Bible He gave us everything we need to know about faith and life. In the Bible God told us how we can be with Him now . . . and forever. In His great LOVE for us, God gave us a very precious gift—His Word! The Word of the LORD is more precious than silver or gold, for it brings us life. We cannot live by bread alone; we live by every Word that proceeds out of the mouth of God. The Word of God is the Word of Life and the Word of Truth. It is a very great treasure and must be kept carefully by us. Where should we store this treasure? We must store God's Word in our hearts. How can we do this? We can store God's Word in our hearts by listening to it, by reading it, by studying it, by thinking about it, by saying it, by writing it, by singing it, by memorizing it—and by living it! It is not enough to hear God's Word or to know God's Word or to say God's Word. You must also *obey* God's Word! You must *live* God's Word! (That is one other way that words can be used. You can think words and you can say them and you can write them, but you can also do them. For example, you can think, "I want to go outside and play." You can say to someone, "I want to go outside and play." You can write a note: "I want to go outside and play." Or, you can go outside and play! You can actually do it!)

If you treasure God's Word in your hearts, you will have it forever, but it will also overflow to others. Out of this treasure you have stored in your hearts, God's love and truth and life will flow to other people. If you have treasured God's Word in your hearts, it will be part of you, in what you think and speak and write . . . and do! It will be a blessing for you and for others all the days of your life. God's Word will guard you and guide you until you reach heaven, until you see the Living One, who is called "The Word of God" (Revelation 19:13).

Who is this Person called the Word of God? It is Christ Jesus, our Lord. You see, God did one more thing with His Word, something that we cannot do with our words. We can think and speak and write and live our words, but God caused His Word to become flesh. "In the beginning was the Word, and the Word was with God, and the Word was God. He was with God in the beginning . . . And the Word became flesh and made His dwelling among us" (John 1:1, 2,14). God's Word became a Man, who walked in this world with us. God sent this Man to us, who was the Word of God incarnate. He was the highest expression of God's Word and the greatest expression of

God's LOVE. "Herein is love: not that we loved God, but that He loved us and sent His Son as an atoning sacrifice for our sins" (1 John 4:10). "For God so loved the world that He gave His one and only Son, that whoever believes in Him shall not perish but have eternal life" (John 3:16).

The teacher's guide for this lesson starts on page 408.

IN THE BEGINNING, OUT OF NOTHING

- Genesis 1:1
- Colossians 1:15–20
- Hebrews 11:3

Everything in our world has a beginning. A giant oak tree begins as a tiny acorn. When it first begins to grow, it is just a little green shoot, barely visible above the earth, but after many years of growing it becomes a full-sized tree, so children like you can climb up in its branches and sit among its leaves or jump down to play in its shade and gather the little acorns on the ground below. Where do these acorns come from? They come from the oak tree. And where does the oak tree come from? It comes from an acorn . . . but long long ago, there were no oak trees in the world; there were no acorns. There was nothing!

Everything in our world has a beginning. A tall bright sunflower begins as a small grey seed. When it first begins to grow, all you can see are just two tiny leaves unfolding above the ground, but after many weeks of growing it becomes a flower taller than you are, with a face fatter than yours. Birds can perch on its stalk and peck at its seeds. Where do these seeds come from? They come from the sunflower. And where does the sunflower come from? It comes from a seed . . . but long long ago, there were no sunflowers in the world; there were no seeds. There was nothing!

Everything in our world has a beginning. A big brown toadstool, which pops up overnight, begins as a spore smaller than a speck of dust. Little white threads grow from this speck. Then a small button appears. Next the toadstool's cap slowly opens up like an umbrella. Finally millions of microscopic spores fall from the gills and float away to make more toadstools. These spores come from the toadstool and the toadstool comes from a spore . . . but long long ago, there were no toadstools; there were not even specks of life called spores. There was nothing!

Everything in our world has a beginning. A white squawking chicken begins as a fluffy yellow chick, which hatches from an egg. Have you heard this riddle: "Which came first, the chicken or the egg?" Chickens come from eggs and eggs come from chickens . . . but long long ago, there were no chickens; there were no eggs. There was nothing!

Everything in our world has a beginning. A green jumping frog begins as a small black polliwog wriggling from an underwater egg. Where do these eggs come from? They are laid by an adult frog . . . but long long ago, there were no frogs; there were no polliwogs; there were no eggs. There was nothing!

Everything in our world has a beginning. A butterfly hatches from a cocoon. The cocoon is made by a caterpillar. The caterpillar hatches from a tiny insect egg no bigger than a dot on a piece of paper. Where does this egg come from? It is laid by the butterfly . . . but long long ago, there were no butterflies; there were no eggs, not even the ones the size of dots. There was nothing!

Everything in our world has a beginning. You had a beginning! Only a few years ago you were a little baby. Your parents remember the day you were born. That special day, your birthday, is celebrated because it marks your beginning in the world. Before that, you were a tiny person living and growing and playing within your mother's womb. At the very beginning of your time there, you were so small that you couldn't be seen without a microscope. Your mother didn't even know you were there! And before that, you didn't exist. Where did you come from? You came from your mother and father. Where did they come from? They came from their mothers and fathers, your grandparents. And where did your grandparents come from?

They came from their mothers and fathers, your great-grandparents . . . but long long ago, there were no mothers; there were no fathers. There were no people at all. There was nothing!

Everything in our world has a beginning. The world itself had a beginning. Before that time even the world did not exist. There was nothing, absolutely nothing! There was not even a speck of dust, let alone a spark of life. This is hard for us to understand, because the world we see now is so vast and so full. Where did everything we see come from? The answer to this question is written in our hearts. Everybody knows the answer, but not everybody likes the answer or says the answer. Where did everything come from? The answer is also written in the Bible. It is given to us in the very first words on the very first page of the very first book of the Bible. "In the beginning God . . ." (Genesis 1:1). God was there in the beginning. God was there before the beginning. God was there without a beginning. That is also difficult for us to understand. Because everything in our world has had a beginning, because we ourselves have had a beginning, it is hard for us to understand that Someone had no beginning, that God was always there. God is eternal. He had no beginning; He will never end. The LORD is the One who is "without father, without mother . . . without beginning of days or end of life" (Hebrews 7:3). God was there in the beginning. God was the beginning!

Many brilliant people, such as scientists, have tried to figure out how the world began, but the best they can do is guess and suppose and imagine—because they were not there. No people were there in the beginning. No human beings were present at the opening ceremonies of the universe to report what happened, but God was there and He has revealed to us the truth about the beginning of the world. In His Word, in the first book of the Bible, in the book called Genesis, a great proclamation is made: "IN THE BEGINNING GOD CREATED THE HEAVENS AND THE EARTH" (Genesis 1:1). Again and again the Bible declares that the LORD God is "Maker of heaven and earth" (Psalms 115:15; 121:2; 124:8; 134:3; 146:6). God made everything that we see. The Bible says: "By faith we understand that the universe was formed at God's command, so that what is seen was not made out of what was visible" (Hebrews 11:3). God did not make the heavens and the earth out of something; He called them into being out of nothing. "He commanded—and they were created" (Psalm 148:5).

In the beginning God, (God the Father, God the Son and God the Holy

Spirit)—in the beginning this one God, created the heavens and the earth. "There is but one God, the Father, from whom are all things . . . and one LORD, Jesus Christ, through whom are all things" (I Corinthians 8:6). Concerning the Son of God we read, "By Him all things were created: things in heaven and on earth, visible and invisible . . . all things were created by Him and for Him. He is before all things, and in Him all things hold together . . . He is the beginning" (Colossians 1:15–20). We also read this about Jesus: "He was with God in the beginning. Through Him all things were made; without Him nothing was made that has been made. In Him was life . . ." (John 1:2–4). Again the Scriptures claim that "the world was made through Him" (John 1:10). Jesus said, "I am the Alpha and the Omega, the First and the Last, the Beginning and the End" (Revelation 22:12).

God has revealed to us in our hearts and in His world and in His Word that He is the LORD, the Creator of heaven and earth. Knowing that, knowing that all things come from Him, we should love God. We should obey God and worship God. We should trust God. His praises should be upon our lips:

> *You are worthy, our LORD and God*
> *to receive glory and honour and power,*
> *for You created all things.*
>
> *Revelation 4:11*

The teacher's guide for this lesson starts on page 410.

THE FIRST DAY

- **Genesis 1:1–5**
- **Isaiah 45:6**
- **I John 1:5**
- **Revelation 21:23; 22:5**

In the beginning God created the heavens and the earth. What did God's newly-formed world look like in the beginning? If you could go back to that first day, what would you have seen? You would have seen nothing, for there was a darkness so deep that no human eye could penetrate it. But God saw what He had made and God has revealed to us in His Word what the world was like in the beginning. God says that the earth was a vast and dark waste of water. If you could have seen it then, if your eyes could have pierced that original darkness, you would not have recognized this earth, which is your home and native land, for then it was a place without shape and without form. There was nothing solid, nothing firm. Not even a tiny patch of ground, not even a tiny grain of sand, could be seen. There was only water; the world was only pure, cold, black, dead . . . water! These waters were empty. They were sterile. They were void of any life. Not even a microbe existed in them. God tells us in the Bible that "the earth was formless and empty, and darkness was over the surface of the deep . . ."

In the beginning the world was a desolate darkness, a suitable dungeon for demons perhaps, but not a habitable home for humans. Human beings need light. They want light. Do you like to be left alone in a dark room at night? It may be scary, but at least you have some light, for a thin crack escapes under your door or a pale moon glows through your window or a street lamp reflects on your wall. It may be dark, but you are not in total darkness. Total darkness is a terrifying experience! Once I went on a tour of some underground caves. We walked down . . . down . . . down . . . beneath the earth where no ray of sun shone. At the deepest and darkest place the guide switched off all the lamps to give us the experience of total darkness. There was not so much as a pinpoint of light anywhere. We could not see anything, not even our own hands held right in front of our faces. Our eyes strained through the blackness to see something, the outline of anything, but it was in vain. There was absolutely no light. I was afraid I would begin screaming, but I controlled this fear with two comforting thoughts: First of all, I was not alone in the darkness. I knew that God was with me, that my family was with me, (for I could feel two little girls clutching my hands tightly,) and that there was a guide leading the group. No, I was not alone, although I could see no one. Another comforting thought was this: The awful blackness would last only a few moments. The guide knew that people soon panic in total darkness. He knew that an inexplicable terror grips human beings in unbroken blackness, so after the allotted three minutes had slowly elapsed, he restored the light. It is possible to experience total darkness here on the earth, like the darkness in the beginning.

In the Bible God speaks of another darkness, the "outer darkness"—the darkness of hell, where there is weeping and wailing and gnashing of teeth (Matthew 8:12; 22:13; 25:30). This darkness lasts forever. In this outer darkness there is no comfort in God's presence, for God is not there in the eternal blackness of hell. The Bible tells us that God "dwells in unapproachable light" (I Timothy 6:16). "God is light and in Him there is no darkness at all" (I John 1:5). When the wicked are cast into hell, they are cast away from God, who is the source of all light. This outer darkness, this utter darkness, is part of the torture and torment of hell.

On that first day the world began in darkness, but it was not a kind of hell, forsaken in outer darkness. True, there was not a glimmer of light or life anywhere in the world; there was not one sparkle of light upon its waters, nor one wriggle of life within its waters, but we read in the Bible that

God was there! The One who is Light, the One who is Life, was there with the world. We read that "the Spirit of God was hovering over the waters." God had not abandoned His creation. He was there, caring for it, hovering over it like a protective parent.

This was just the beginning! The new-born world was not designed for eternal death or everlasting darkness. No, God was preparing it for a long history and a glorious destiny. God was preparing it for the pinnacle of His creation—human beings! So God said, "Let there be light," and there was light! God saw that the light was good. This was God's first good gift to the world and to us—light! There were no people yet to see that light or feel it or rejoice in it or thank God for it, but God saw the light which He had made and God saw that it was good.

Did you ever wonder what kind of light it was that shone on the earth on that first day? Was it the strong bright blaze of the sun? Was it the soft faint glow of the moon? Was it the twinkling light of the stars? No, they did not shine upon the earth on that first day. It was not the daylight or the night-lights which we know. It was some other kind of light, a mysterious kind of light, which we cannot explain. I used to wonder if it was the light of God's own glory, in which He bathed the new-born earth. In the Bible we read that the Holy City coming down out of heaven "does not need the sun or the moon to shine on it, for the glory of God gives it light . . . There will be no more night. They will not need the light of a lamp or the light of the sun, for the Lord God will give them light . . ." (Revelation 21:23–22:5). I also used to wonder if during those first three days the earth was surrounded by a green glow of light like the emerald rainbow which encircles the throne of God in heaven. (See Revelation 4:3.) But I think it was not the light of God's presence which appeared on that first day, because the light of God's glory is eternal light, having no beginning and having no end. The light which shone on the earth on the first day had a beginning. God created it. He called it into existence out of nothing. This was not the light of heaven; it was the light of earth, brought into being by God for the purpose of giving light to the world. God declares, "I am the LORD and there is no other. I form the light and create darkness" (Isaiah 45:6).

From that very first day, God has been giving light to the world. It has been an enduring gift, one that has lasted thousands and thousands of years. A day has not passed in which there has been no light. It is a daily demonstration of God's LOVE. Every moment of light is a blessing, a very great blessing, for which we should praise God. From the beginning of time God has been giving light to the world and in the fullness of time God sent another Light to the world, because the world was trapped in the darkness of sin and death. God so loved the world that He gave His Son. He was "the true Light which, coming into the world, enlightens every man. He was in the world, and the world was made through Him . . ." (John 1:9, 10). Jesus, the Son of God, said, "I am the Light of the world. Whoever follows Me will never walk in darkness, but will have the light of life" (John 8:12). He was God's greatest gift to the world. Herein is love: not that we loved God, but that He loved us, and sent His Son—the Light of the world!

On that first day there was one other gift that God gave to the world. Do you know what it was? Time! Did you ever consider that God created time? Did you know that time had a beginning? Did you know that time will have an end? The stream of time has been flowing since that first day, but on the last day this stream of time will be swallowed up in the ocean of eternity. This was how God created a time-structure for man's existence: God separated the light from the darkness. He named the light "day" and the darkness "night" and He caused them to follow one another in a regular succession. Both day and night belong to God. He made them both— and He made them for us. He made day and night for human beings. He ordered our time. He numbered our days. He gave us a time to be awake and a time to sleep, a time to work and a time to rest. First He made darkness; then He made light.

And there was evening, and there was morning—the first day.

The teacher's guide for this lesson starts on page 412.

THE SECOND DAY

- Genesis 1:6–8
- Psalms 147, 148
- Jeremiah 51:15–16

On the first day God *created* the light and He *separated* the light from the darkness and He *named* the light "day" and the darkness "night." On the second day God continued His work, His work of creating and separating and naming. God said, "Let there be an expanse between the waters to separate water from water." And it was so. God named this expanse "sky." Now the earth was not only covered with water below the sky, but the earth was also encircled with water above the sky. What do we call this water that is above the sky? Yes, you have seen it. It doesn't look like the water which we drink, nor is it like the water in which we swim. The water above us is in a different form. It is not a liquid, but a vapour—and we call this state of water "clouds." The new-born world was wrapped by God in a blanket of clouds! Out of these clouds God would send all kinds of strange things to the earth: drops of water, flakes of snow, balls of ice, storms of wind, crashes of thunder, flashes of fire. All of them would glorify the LORD. "Praise the LORD from the heavens, praise Him in the heights above . . . Praise Him you highest heavens and you waters above the skies. Let them praise the name of the Lord, for He commanded and they were created . . . lightening and hail, snow and clouds and stormy winds fulfilling His Word . . . Let them praise the Name of the LORD, for His Name alone is exalted. His splendour is above the earth and the heavens . . . Praise the LORD" (Psalm 148:1, 4,5, 7,8, 13)! "Sing to the LORD with thanksgiving . . . He covers the sky with clouds; He supplies the earth with rain . . . He sends His command to the earth; His Word runs swiftly. He spreads the snow like wool and scatters the frost like ashes. He hurls down His hail like pebbles. Who can withstand His icy blast? He sends His Word and melts them; He stirs up His breezes and the waters flow . . . Praise the LORD" (Psalm 147:7, 8,15–17, 20).

In between the waters, in between the blue liquid of earth's vast ocean and the white vapour of earth's cloud cover, God gave an invisible gift to the world. He created something, without which human beings could not live. Without it there would be no life at all on the earth. What God created that day, you cannot see, but you can catch it and hold it—with your lungs! Take a deep breath. There, you have caught some air! Your lungs will take oxygen out of the air and your heart will pump that oxygen to all parts of your body. You cannot live without the oxygen, which is in the air. When people drown or suffocate or choke, they die because they cannot get any air with its life-giving oxygen. That was what God made on the second day of creation: earth's atmosphere. God called into being this marvellous, mysterious air for His creatures to breathe. What a wonderful gift to the world. As far as we know, there was no other planet in the universe which was given this precious gift of a life-sustaining atmosphere. Instead, many of the planets were surrounded by poisonous gases. When astronauts travel in outer space in their rocket ships, they must take oxygen with them to breathe. Even if you went to earth's nearest neighbour—the moon—you would have to take some of earth's air with you or you would die. But God gave air to the earth; He created it on the second day, so that there would be life.

On that second day there was no human being in existence to take a deep, delicious breath of that purest and freshest of air. There was not yet a human voice that could praise God for the breath of life. But the Son of God was there. "He was with God in the beginning. Through Him all things were made; without Him nothing was made that has been made" (John 1:2, 3). Both the Eternal Son, Who is "the Wisdom of God" (I Corinthians 1:24), and the Holy Spirit, Who is "the Spirit of Wisdom" (Ephesians 1:17), could say with Wisdom: "I was there when . . . God marked out the horizon on the face of the deep, when He established the clouds above and fixed securely the fountains of the deep . . . I was the craftsman at His side. I was filled with delight day after day, rejoicing always in His Presence . . ." (Proverbs 8:27–30). The triune God—Father, Son and Holy Spirit—delighted together in the work of that day.

And there was evening, and there was morning—the second day.

The teacher's guide for this lesson starts on page 414.

THE THIRD DAY

• **Genesis 1:9, 10**
• **Psalm 95:1–5**

O n the third day God continued His work because the world was not yet ready for man. Although there was now light for man to see and air for him to breathe, there was still nowhere for him to be! Man could not hover above the water as God's Spirit did; nor could man walk upon the water as God's Son did. No, man needed a firm place upon which to stand. So God continued His work. First He separated the water that covered the earth. God said, "Let the water under the sky be gathered to one place, and let dry ground appear." And it was so. "O LORD my God, you are very great . . . The waters stood above the mountains, but at your rebuke, the waters fled; at the sound of your thunder, they took to flight. They flowed over the mountains; they went down into the valleys, to the place you assigned for them. You set a boundary they cannot cross; never again will they cover the earth" (Psalm 104:5–9). God spoke—and the waters of earth's one vast ocean listened. The waters obeyed the command of the LORD, flowing to the places that He had appointed for them. And now the surface of the earth, which had been buried beneath the waves, appeared! God called this dry ground "land" and the gathered waters He called "seas." And God saw that it was good.

The earth would be a good home for man. When God fashioned the earth on this third day "He did not create it to be empty, but formed it to be inhabited" (Isaiah 45:18). God was preparing the world for human beings. Now there was land! Oh, how wonderful was that first sighting of land! How the angelic hosts in the heavenly realms must have rejoiced at its appearing! Now there was a place for people to live! There was firm dry ground awaiting them, where their feet could stand . . . and walk . . . and run . . . and dance with delight! Now there was a place for people to rest and to sleep, where they could lie down upon this earth and look up towards heaven. Now there was a place for people to kneel before the LORD and worship Him: "Come, let us sing for joy to the LORD . . . Let us come before Him with thanksgiving . . . For the LORD is the great God, the great KING above all gods. In His hand are the depths of the earth, and the mountain peaks belong to Him. The sea is His, for He made it, and His hands formed the dry land. Come, let us bow down in worship. Let us kneel before the LORD our Maker, for He is our God" (Psalm 95:1–7). That third day God was extending His dominion. He was creating for Himself and for His creatures a new domain—the dry ground, the many lands, the vast regions of this beautiful earth!

The earth was no longer formless; it was no longer empty. On that third day God shaped it and formed it and filled it with all kinds of treasures. God made man's home a place of titanic and exquisite beauty, a place that would be interesting and exciting for him to live. God made snow-capped mountains for man to climb, rugged coastlines for him to explore, mighty canyons for him to discover; God made wind-swept deserts for man to cross, fertile valleys for him to farm, and rushing rivers for him to ford; God made the gentle hills for people to wander, the turbulent seas for them to master, and the placid lakes for them to sit beside and wonder. All these gifts God gave to the world—and more.

Beneath the surface of the earth were rocks and gems and jewels. There were rubies, sapphires, diamonds, emeralds! There was gold and silver and bronze. Underground, God filled the earth with the splendour of all kinds of hidden riches, making this world a vault of priceless treasures. And above ground, God filled the earth with the majesty of many horizons. Who has seen them all? The Son of God was shown their grandeur in an instant. He saw all the landscapes of all the world; He saw all the wealth of all its king-doms, but no other man has had such a view. In an entire lifetime, we be-hold only a few of our world's spectacular scenes and only a fraction of its immense wealth.

But on that third day, God saw what He had made. From the mightiest mass of mountain to the tiniest grain of sand, from the most magnificent cluster of jewels to the most ordinary clod of mud, God saw what He had made—and God saw that it was good.

The teacher's guide for this lesson starts on page 416.

GREEN!
GLORIOUS GREEN!

- **Genesis 1:11–13, 29–30**
- **Psalm 96:11–13**
- **Matthew 6:25–34**

O n that third day there was no man to leave a footprint on the newly firmed land or a fingerprint on a newly found stone. There was not a single human being to see the spectacular view of even one of those newly formed horizons. There was not one earthly voice raised to God, praising Him and thanking Him for all His works most wonderful. Earth's only sounds were the crashing of waves upon the sands of vacant beaches and the moaning of winds among the rocks on lonely mountains. The earth, though beautiful, was still barren. There were vast areas of land, stretching for thousands of miles, but that land, although it was good land, was brown and bare. The whole world was a wasteland. There was not a living thing anywhere, not even a single blade of grass. Then God said, "Let the land produce vegetation . . ." and it was so. God spoke—and the land obeyed! God brought forth out of the earth, plants; out of soil which contained no seeds, God brought forth plants of every kind! By His command, they came into being. Each little plant was a miracle of life . . . from God, who is Life. Each little plant was an expression of love . . . from God, who is LOVE. The LORD filled the earth that day with good gifts to delight man and to glorify Himself. Even the tiniest flower was created to be a joy for man and praise for God. On that third day, when plants sprouted and blossomed everywhere, there was yet no man or woman to rejoice in them, but the earth was surely full of God's praise!

On that third day the LORD lavished the land with the lushness of life! God clothed the bare, new-born earth with a garment of green. Green! Glorious green! There is something about that colour which is soothing to the human eye and pleasing to the human heart. There is something about it which is invigorating and inspiring. It is the colour of life! If you have ever been in a desert region for a long time, then you know there is nothing more beautiful than sighting the green of an oasis. It is the sign which says: LIFE! Once I travelled for many days through an arid area known as the "badlands" or the "wastelands." Why do people call these deserts "bad" and a "waste" of land? It is because nothing grows there except for a few prickly cactus plants. When I first saw these lands, they were strangely beautiful to me with their towering red rocks and swirling dust devils and shimmering heat waves and tumbling brown weeds, but after many hours and many miles of this bold red landscape, with its painted hills and vermilion cliffs and majestic canyons, it was a relief and a delight to drive past the small green patch of a humble homestead, where animals were grazing and a garden was growing and an orchard was thriving. I will never forget what a welcome sight that green land was. Green! Glorious green! It is a gracious gift from God.

Can you imagine how dismal the earth would be without any plants or flowers? Perhaps you can if you live in a country that has long winters. Let me tell you a story about a little girl who loved flowers. They were her favourite thing in all the world, but she lived in a part of Canada where snow covered the ground for many months of the year. Her birthday was on the Ides of March, which is the very middle of that month, but by the time her birthday arrived each year it was not a happy one for her, because she was starving for flowers. She would look out her window, but the only thing growing in the garden were the drifts of ice and snow. One year her parents took her to the great "glass gardens" in a nearby city—and there the spring flowers were blooming. How she loved that place . . . and oh, what a happy birthday it was! Just to step inside the door and breathe was wonderful, for the scent of the blossoms was exhilarating. The little girl pranced from flower to flower, delighting in the bright petals and sweet perfume of each one. She would have been perfectly content to live in that glass house with all the flowers, but of course she had to leave to go home with her family. However, every year she asked for a certain birthday present. Can you guess what it was? Yes, it was to go back to those green houses to spend her birthday among the blossoms. (Can you guess who that little girl was? Yes, it was I.) Even a little child, like you, knows that a flower is a very special gift. One little flower can make a person smile—and God gave us a whole world of flowers so that smiles and songs would be upon our lips, so that joy and thanks would be within our hearts.

When God adorned the earth with plants and flowers on that third day, it was not just to make the world look and smell more beautiful. God had another purpose for the plants. Do you know what it was? God made the plants for His creatures to eat! To every living creature, both man and animals, God gave the green plants for food. Although they did not yet exist, a feast was awaiting earth's creatures. Before God created them, He provided for them. There were grasses for the sheep, leaves for the koalas, corn for the racoons, bananas for the monkeys; there were nuts for the chipmunks, berries for the bears, carrots for the rabbits and seeds for the gerbils. For every kind of animal, God created food to eat. And for the man and woman, God gave every plant and tree on the face of the whole earth. He said to them, "They will be yours for food." Luscious red strawberries, juicy orange peaches, sweet purple grapes, bright green kiwis, huge golden pineapples—there was a world full of delicious foods for human beings to taste and eat! There was a world full of good gifts for them, blessings from a loving God!

On that third day God created an abundance of goodness for man to see and smell and taste. As if all this were not enough, God also created every plant and tree with a hidden treasure in it. When God brought them into being, He said, "Let the land produce vegetation: seed-bearing plants and trees on the land that bear fruit with seed in it according to their kinds." What was that hidden treasure? Seeds! God made the plants with seeds, so that they could reproduce themselves, so that there would be a never-ending supply of food upon the earth.

Think of the apple tree, the "common" apple tree. It's a green leafy tree with pink perfumed blossoms and round red apples. It is beautiful, fragrant and delicious. It also holds a treasure. Cut an apple in the middle, crosswise. Inside you will see two stars, holding the precious seeds, the forgotten jewels of the apple tree. From those tiny brown seeds can grow more apple trees. Is this not marvellous in our eyes?

As the third day ended there were no people to see what God had done. At that time there was no human being in existence, who could say, "Yes, what you have made is marvellous, O LORD!" There was, however, a soft applause from the earth, as millions of leaves rustled and grasses whispered in the wind their praise to God. And the dusk of that day was thick with the fragrance of earth's new flora, an aroma pleasing to the LORD. The little flowers bending in the breezes bowed before Him. Their silent beauty gave glory to the Creator; without saying a word, they spoke of Him. God saw that it was good.

And there was evening, and there was morning—the third day.

The teacher's guide for this lesson starts on page 418.

THE FOURTH DAY

- **Genesis 1:14–19**
- **Psalm 19:1–6;**
  148:1–6
- **Isaiah 40:25, 26**

T here was darkness and there was light. There was evening and there was morning. Three nights and three days had passed, but we do not understand how, for God had not yet made the heavenly bodies to shine upon the earth, not even the most important one for us—the sun. The earth is dependent upon the sun for light, but that was not always so. The plants are dependent upon the sun for life, but that was not always so. The earth was for a time bright and green without the sun. Perhaps God was trying to teach us, even in Genesis 1, even in the very first chapter of the very first book in the Bible, that all things are dependent upon Him, that Light and Life come from the LORD! God does not explain for us how plants could grow without the sun or how the earth had day without the sun. God does not explain it for us to understand; He simply records it for us to believe. Day light and plant life existed, not by natural causes, but by the Supernatural Cause of all things, by the Word of God, by the LORD! We are confronted with the unsettling reality of miracles from the beginning.

Once more God spoke. He said, "Let there be lights in the expanse of the sky . . ." and it was so. God made earth's sun and moon and stars. God made comets and meteors and asteroids. God made worlds beyond our world—planets with twelve moons, planets with bright rings, planets with red storms. God made pinwheels spinning in space, called galaxies, in which our world was no more than a dot among millions of stars burning bigger and brighter than our sun. God filled the universe. It was so vast and so full that man could not see its end nor count its stars. Even with mega-telescopes, man's eyes could not see the limits of the universe. Even with mega-computers, man's mind could not calculate the number of celestial bodies. But God could. The Bible says that "He determines the number of the stars and calls them each by name" (Psalm 147:4). Although man is now able to explore beyond the earth in the regions of outer space, he will never be able to fathom the immensity or the mystery or the beauty of this universe. It is beyond his understanding. God made it thus, for His own glory and for man's delight. There will always be some new wonder or splendour in the heavens for humans to discover. There will always be some new star to excite man and exalt God. The heavens declare the glory of God! And man is without excuse if he does not do so also, for since the creation of the world God's invisible qualities—His eternal power and divine nature—have been clearly seen, being understood from what has been made. The sun and moon and stars all point beyond themselves to the One whose radiance far surpasses theirs. The LORD is exalted *above* the heavens! His glory is *beyond* the skies. When an astronaut returns to the earth from his travels and claims, "There is no God!"—he lies. When he says, "I have been into the heavens, and God is not there!"—he lies. The universe is filled with the evidence of God's existence. Only a fool ignores it. What God has made testifies to the truth and only a fool denies it. "The heavens declare the glory of God; the skies proclaim the work of His hands. Day after day they pour forth speech; night after night they display knowledge. There is no speech or language where their voice is not heard. Their voice goes out into all the earth, and their words to the ends of the world" (Psalm 19:1–6). The heavens proclaim that the LORD is God—and their voices, though silent, are louder than the lies of men.

The Bible tells us other reasons why God made the sun, the moon, and the stars:

1) God said, "Let there be lights . . . to separate the day from the night." There is always "day" upon the earth and there is always "night" upon the earth. While one side of our globe experiences light, the other side experiences darkness. What divides day from night is the light from the sun. At any particular point on the earth, day begins when the sun first appears and it ends when the sun disappears. Earth's day and night depend now upon the sun. Earth's 24-hour cycle is also in relation to the sun. If the earth was rotating all alone in space, man could not mark the beginning or the ending of each rotation. The sun becomes earth's point of reference.

2) God said, "Let them serve as signs to mark seasons and days and years." The length of earth's days are determined by the sun. Earth's months are measured by the moon. It takes the moon approximately one month to orbit the earth. Earth's seasons are determined by the tilt of the earth in relation to its revolution around the sun. The cold winter months are caused because there is less sunlight, because we are tilted away from the sun; the warm summer months are the opposite, having more sunlight because we are tilted towards the sun. Earth's years are determined by the length of time it takes this planet to revolve around the sun. It takes 365 days for the earth to complete its elliptical orbit around the sun, one year. (If you lived on another planet, such as Pluto, a year would take 90, 520 days and you would have to wait 248 years between each birthday!)

3) God said, "Let them be lights in the expanse of the sky to give light on the earth." God made two great lights to shine upon the earth—the sun to govern earth's day and the moon to govern its night. God also made the stars, so that their faint, far-away light would reach the earth. God set them all—the sun, the moon and the stars—in the expanse of the sky to give light on the earth for us.

The sun, the moon and the stars—these were God's good gifts to the world on the fourth day of creation. They were heavenly gifts from our heavenly Father. They were demonstrations of His great LOVE. "I will praise you, O LORD . . . for great is your love, reaching to the heavens; your faithfulness reaches to the skies. Be exalted, O God, above the heavens; let your glory be over all the earth" (Psalm 57:10, 11).

On the fourth day of creation there was a new glory over all the earth. Starlight twinkled in the heavens for the first time and moonbeams danced upon the waters. For the first time there was a sunrise upon the earth, when the white clouds of the misty morning turned purple and pink, crimson and gold, followed by a huge fiery red ball rising slowly on the horizon. For the first time the earth was bathed in the brightness of a new kind of light—sunlight! Once again the appearance of the earth was completely changed. Now, on this fourth day, it glistened and glowed with the light of the sun. God had wrapped the earth in glorious garments, the heavenly hues of celestial lights. Now spectacular sunrises and sunsets would revolve *unceasingly* around the earth. Somewhere on earth the sun would always be rising; somewhere it would always be setting; and somewhere the sun would always be shining, sparkling on earth's waters to turn dewdrops into diamonds and oceans into gold. Now rainbows would appear in the mists of the waterfalls. Now the leaves on the trees would shimmer in the forests. Now shadows would appear and disappear everywhere on the face of the earth. On that fourth day there was yet no man or woman in all the universe to feel the warmth of earth's sun. There were no human beings to see the splendour of the sun's first day or the moon's opening night. But God saw what He had made, and God saw that it was good.

And there was evening and there was morning—the fourth day.

The teacher's guide for this lesson starts on page 420.

THE FIFTH DAY

• **Genesis 1:20–23**
• **Psalm 104:24–31**

By the fifth day God had given many good gifts to this world, but there were yet no living creatures. Not one moved on the face of the land or in the skies above or in the seas below. The fields and the forests moved in the wind, but nothing moved in them. Not one creature scampered in their branches or galloped through their grasses; not one wriggled on a leaf or slithered round a stalk. No, not a creature was stirring, not even a mouse. Neither was there any movement in the skies, except for the wind-blown clouds; nor was there movement in the seas, except for the wind-tossed waves. There was a stillness in the world as it waited for God to continue His creative work.

Earth's vast oceans were empty, but once again God spoke. He said, "Let the water teem with living creatures . . ." Thus God created the great creatures of the sea and the small ones. God created every living and moving thing with which the water teems. He made millions of different kinds of underwater creatures. He made the adorable seahorse and the beautiful starfish; He made the pretty goldfish, the ugly catfish, the funny boxfish. God made the terrifying sharks and the electrifying eels; He made the glittering jewelfish and the sputtering spitfish. He made the lovely little "dragons," the friendly dolphins and the happy humpback whales. He made fighting fish and kissing fish. Some He made as colourful "rainbows;" others were as graceful "angels." He made the tiny creatures, like the loveable little polliwogs. God also made the sea monsters, like the giant jellyfish, the eight-armed octopus, the sharp-pointed swordfish, and the mightiest of all earth's creatures—the great blue whale! This whale could swallow a man whole as if he were a mosquito. Beside this whale a dinosaur was a mere dwarf! God clothed his sea creatures with skins and scales, spots and stripes, spines and shells—and He clothed them in every size and shape and colour. Like the stars in the sky, there were so many fish in the sea that they could not all be named or numbered by man. Even now, in our time, thousands of years later, man is still discovering "new" fish, ones that his eyes have never seen before, ones that his lips have never named before. Now that human beings have built submarines, they can dive deeper and deeper into the oceans' depths, enabling them to see more and more of God's sea creatures. But in the beginning, on that fifth day, it was God who saw them. He saw them all, even the ones in the darkest places in the deepest oceans, and God saw that they were good. Because they were good, God blessed them, saying, "Be fruitful and increase in number and fill the water in the seas . . ." and it was so. God's blessing was upon them and they began to multiply, reproducing themselves and filling the world's oceans and lakes and rivers and ponds with their life.

Once I visited a zoo in Switzerland. On one of its small buildings there was a sign which read, "*La Maison des Poissons,*" which means "The Fish House." It didn't sound very interesting and I wasn't going to bother to go inside, but I have always been grateful that I did. What a remarkable place it was! *La Maison des Poissons* was filled with an impressive collection of living, moving, sparkling creations—hundreds of tiny tropical fish, all exquisitely beautiful and graceful and colourful, all of them giving glory to the One who made them, the LORD of Life, the LORD of LOVE! I was amazed by these little creatures. I was awed by this handiwork of God. How had I missed the fact that this kind of beauty existed? How had I never before appreciated this good gift from God? But it was not too late—and I learned something very important that day, on that visit to the zoo, in that House of Fish. I learned that even the lowliest and littlest creatures are magnificent creations and that the waters of the world are filled with a hidden host of witnesses, who glorify the LORD. Though they swim silently in the sea, even the tiniest tropical fish testifies to the majesty of the Almighty. Even a fish could turn the heart of a person to search for the LORD!

On the fifth day God gave the world another good gift. Until that day the only sounds in the world were the splashing waves and the sighing winds and the rustling leaves, but now on this fifth day God would bring the most wonderful sounds to the earth. God said: "Let birds fly above the earth across the expanse of the sky." So God created the incredible winged creatures that soar through the air—singing! When man arrived in the world, there would be music to greet him! God made man's home filled with the sounds of singing. From that fifth day, the dawn of every new day would begin with the song of a single bird, joined by another . . . and another . . . and another . . . rising in a crescendo to a chorus— hallelujah chorus—to the LORD! The singing of the birds in praise of God began on that fifth day and it has never ceased. From dawn to dawn to dawn, from east to west around the world, the LORD's praises have been sung and gloriously proclaimed by His little winged creatures.

A man who loved God, a great defender of the faith, once said, "When you listen to a nightingale, you are hearing an excellent preacher." This man's name was Martin Luther and he was saying that this bird's song was so beautiful that it argued eloquently for the existence of God. Who can argue with a nightingale? Only a fool answers its song by saying, "There is no God."

Another man, who hated God, a great destroyer of the faith, was puzzled by the extraordinary beauty of a peacock feather. This man's name was Charles Darwin. He proposed that all living creatures, including humans, were not created by God. He believed that life was a cosmic accident, a chance occurrence, and that earth's creatures came into being through a process of natural selection called "evolution." But the peacock feather perplexed Darwin. He could not explain to himself or anyone else how a peacock feather could have just happened. "How could it have evolved," he wondered, "since it had no purpose?" But we know the answer to his question. This feather was designed by God for this great purpose: to glorify Himself! God also made the peacock feather to delight man and instruct him. A peacock feather points very clearly to the hand of the One who "painted" it! Who but a fool would dare to deny God before such evidence? It seems that a great giant of unbelief, even a Philistine like Charles Darwin, could be felled by a single feather!

There is one more person to discuss, an ordinary person. She lived all alone in a little room in the centre of a big city—a noisy, dirty, ugly city. Because it was the middle of winter it was cold and dark, and because she did not believe in God, her life was as bleak as the winter. Even her dreams were filled with despair. Still, every morning, she got up and went to her work through the sloshy busy streets. One day she saw something that made her stop. It was a simple sight, just a flock of little brown sparrows hopping and chirping on the sidewalk. They weren't singing like nightingales, and they weren't parading like peacocks, but there was something about them that was comforting and reassuring. What was it? A little chirp of cheer in the never-ending noise? A little hop of happiness in the meaningless motion? A little creature of God's in a man-made metropolis? Whatever it was, those plain brown sparrows helped the young woman. Who was that person? It was I, many years ago, before I believed in God.

Don't ever think that birds are unimportant. God gave them to people as a gift, a good gift. For thousands of years people have been blessed by birds: They have been cheered by their songs, impressed by their beauty, inspired by their gliding and flying and soaring through the air. A great poet once wrote, "Oh, that I had the wings of a dove! I would fly away . . ." (Psalm 55:6).

But long ago, on that fifth day of creation, it was God who delighted in these works of His hands. It was God who delighted in the graceful swan and the gentle dove. It was He who loved the big-eyed owl and the long-legged stork. God observed the beauty of the quetzal's tail, the toucan's beak, the cardinal's crown. It was God who watched the peacock spread his fan. He was the One who saw the little hummingbird sipping nectar from the flowers. God watched the pink flamingo wading through the waters, the green parakeet hopping on the branches, and the giant ostrich racing across the grasslands. God also noticed the small sparrow pecking in the dust. Yes, on that fifth day it was God who saw the birds and He saw that they were good. He blessed them, saying "Let the birds increase on the earth"—and they did. They built their nests and laid their eggs; they hatched their chicks and fed their young—and filled the earth with their soaring and their singing to the glory of God!

And there was evening and there was morning—the fifth day.

The teacher's guide for this lesson starts on page 422.

Frog

Lesson 9

THE SIXTH DAY

- Genesis 1:24, 25
- Psalm 50:10, 11
- Isaiah 11:6–9

It was the sixth day, the last day of God's work. There were creatures swimming in the sea and flying in air, but there were not yet any land creatures moving along the ground. On this day God created the animals. He said, "Let the land produce living creatures . . ." and it was so. From the dust of the earth God made all the living creatures that move along the ground. He made each one according to its kind: Some were insects; some were reptiles; some were mammals—and each category of creature could be divided into many subcategories. God created millions of different species of animals, but each one had its own place and was related to its own kind, according to the design and order that God created.

On this sixth day there was a new energy and activity upon the earth, as countless creatures began living and breathing and moving by the Will and the Word of God. Now bright butterflies were fluttering above the flowers; tiny busy ants were tunnelling in the ground; spiders were spinning silvery webs across the branches. Now glistening green frogs hopped through the grasses;

heavy tortoises trudged along the sand; clever multi-coloured snakes scampered over the rocks. Now there were fat funny hippos wallowing in the water; there were graceful deer leaping through the woods; there were kangaroos bouncing across the plains. Now mischievous monkeys swung by their tails and striped zebras galloped across the land and enormous elephants waved their long trunks through the water, splashing and spraying each other happily and noisily in the world which God had made for them. "He did not create it to be empty, but formed it to be inhabited" (Isaiah 45:18)— and now the earth was inhabited with every imaginable kind of creature . . . except for one.

What happened on that sixth day was miraculous! These marvellous creatures did not evolve naturally over millions of years. No, they came into being suddenly, in one day, perhaps in an hour or in an instant—by the command of God. It was a supernatural work! God said, and it was so. God spoke, and it was done. From the earth, from the dust of the ground, God brought forth life. How could it be that from dust God created the roar of the lion and the squeak of the mouse? How could it be that from dust came the soft fur of the rabbit and the sharp quills of the hedgehog? How could it be that from dust came the mighty movement of the great monsters and the fragile flight of delicate lacewings? How could it be? With God, nothing is impossible!

God saw that the animals He had made were good. Every one of them glorified their Creator. Every one of them would be friends for the beings whom God would make last of all. Not one of these creatures was too small or too big, too tame or too wild, for these two great purposes: to glorify God and to benefit man.

Animals are man's fellow-creatures upon the earth. You know what it's like to have an animal friend, don't you? Have you ever had a little ladybug walk along your arm? Have you ever kept a chirping cricket in a cage or a glowing firefly in a jar? Have you ever had a butterfly perch on your finger? Do you know what it's like to have a small striped chipmunk eat out of your hand? Have you ever felt the warm rough tongue of a kitten on your nose? Have you ever cuddled a soft furry gerbil next your cheek? Perhaps you know what it's like to have a woolly white lamb follow you or to have a big friendly dog run beside you? Perhaps you've been greeted by a goat, shaken "hands" with a seal, been hugged by a monkey or kissed by a kangaroo. Do you know what it's like to ride on the back of a horse or a camel or an elephant? Have you ever had an animal that you loved very very much, a special animal friend that came to you when you called and snuggled with you when you were lonely and played with you when you were happy? Having such a friend is wonderful, isn't it! That's one reason God made them. God made these creatures for us to love and to help—and God made these creatures to love and help us. Animals were a wonderful gift of God to the world on that sixth day—and they were a wonderful gift to man. That good gift would be there when man arrived. They would be waiting for him—and they would not have to wait long.

The teacher's guide for this lesson starts on page 424.

A CREATURE IS CROWNED

• Genesis 1:26–28
• Psalm 8

On that same day, the sixth day, when God made all the land creatures, He made one more creature of the earth—the one for whom all the others had been made. On the sixth day God made the first human beings, a man and a woman, and God crowned them as rulers over all the other creatures of this world. Why? Why did God choose them? They were not the largest of earth's creatures; no, that honour belonged to the great blue whale, who could swallow a man whole! They were not the strongest creature in the world; an elephant could crush a man easily under its feet! They were not the fastest creature on earth; that gold medal belonged to the cheetah, who could leave a man in the dust far behind him! Human beings did not have the fierce roar of a lion or the sharp teeth of a tiger, nor could they fly through the air like a bird or swim through the sea like a fish. If it was a question of beauty, surely the zebra with its stripes or the leopard with its spots would win the contest for the crown. However, long before any of these creatures could make a claim upon the crown, even before the foundation of the world, God knew whom

He would choose. The creature whom God would create and appoint to rule this world would be unique, different from any other creature in heaven or on earth. God would create a being who was spiritual, like the angels in heaven, but also physical, like the animals on earth. God would make a new creature, one who was both body and soul. God would make a creature whom He called "man." God would make this creature both male and female—and they would reign.

From the beginning this creature called "man" was different from all the other animals:

1) Man's privileged position as the final creation set his kind apart as the pinnacle of God's work. All that came before the man and woman was in preparation for them.

2) There was a notable difference in the way God made man. With every other created thing on earth God simply said, "Let there be . . ." and it was so. God said, "Let the land produce . . ." and the land brought forth plant and animal life according to God's command. But now God said, "*Let us make man . . .*" When God said "us"—to whom was He speaking? God the Father, God the Son, and God the Holy Spirit were in consultation together for the creation of man. God spoke to Himself, that is, the Three Persons of God spoke among themselves to make the man and woman. There was a conference of the Holy Trinity for this final and most special work. This time there was affection as well as authority in the Voice that spoke the Word. It was with LOVE, Infinite LOVE, that God spoke the words: "Let us make man."

3) We read in the Bible that "the LORD God formed the man from the dust of the ground and breathed into his nostrils the breath of life, and the man became a living being" (Genesis 2:7). God drew very close to man when He created him and very close to the woman when He created her (Genesis 2:27). God did not simply speak; He did not command them into existence from a lofty distance. No, there was intimate contact between these two creatures and their Creator. The hands of God fashioned them and the breath of God quickened them. Of all the millions of creatures upon the earth, which other one was thus touched by the Almighty God? There was none. What made the man and woman different from all the other animals was their unique connection to the LORD! It is our special connection to God that makes us human.

4) When God said, "Let us make man . . ." He did not stop there. He added these incredible words: "*Let us make man in our image, in our likeness . . .*" The pattern for man's being came not from the animals, but from God. Most people believe that humans are just other animals. Because we have a similar shape, many people believe that we are descendants of apes. Once, when I was visiting the monkey house at a zoo, I read this sign on the gorilla cage: "You are looking at your great, great, grandfather." But that is not true. We are not the grandchildren of gorillas. We are the children of God! We come from Him. Human beings are similar to the animals because we are all creatures of the earth; we are all made of the same substance — the dust of the ground. Both human beings and animals are of the earth, earthy, but there the likeness ends, for human beings had a most glorious beginning, different from all the other animals. The man and woman were created in the image and the likeness of God Himself! Humans were not created to be like gorillas; they were created to be like God! The Bible declares, "God created man in His own image; in the image of God He created him; male and female He created them."

5) When God said, "Let us make man in our image, in our likeness . . ." He did not stop there either. He continued: "Let us make man in our image, in our likeness, *and let them rule.*" God set the man and woman above earth's other creatures to rule them. He said, "Let them rule over the fish of the sea and the birds of the air, over the livestock, over all the earth, and over all the creatures that move along the ground."

So God created the man and the woman in His own image. God blessed them and said to them, "Be fruitful and increase in number. Fill the earth — and subdue it." They both were commanded to subdue the earth. They both were commanded to rule. God said to them, "Rule over the fish of the sea and the birds of the air and over every living creature that moves on the ground."

On the sixth day God saw the man and the woman, the creatures whom He had crowned with honour and glory, the creatures whom He had made to rule over all the earth. God saw them; He saw all that He had made, and it was not just good. It was very good.

And there was evening, and there was morning — the sixth day.

The teacher's guide for this lesson starts on page 426.

THE IMAGE OF GOD

• Genesis 1:26–31; 5:2

We read in the Bible, "God said, 'Let us make man in our image, in our likeness' . . . So God created man in his own image, in the image of God He created him; male and female He created them." Thus God gave man (male and female) a very great gift, one which was given to no other creature on earth, the image of God. Men and women were created in God's own likeness. The pattern God used for people was Himself! And by this God gave human beings a special connection to Himself, one far surpassing the Creator/creature relationship, which God had with earth's animals. There was a special link of love between God and these creatures whom He had made like Himself. With them there was a special relationship. God had a special affection for the man and the woman. God loved them with a special love. That love was demonstrated from the very the beginning, when what was bestowed upon them and within them was the gift of God's own image.

How were people made to be like God? Do we look like God? No, for God does not have a body. "God is spirit" (John 4:24). We have bodies, which we can see, but God is invisible. No one has seen God. Then how were we made in the image and likeness of God? It was not in our outward appearance, but rather in our inward nature, that we were made to be like God.

Here are some of the ways in which the man and woman were made to be like God:

1) When the LORD God formed the man from the dust of the ground, He gave him a body, but God also gave him a soul. God breathed into him, so that God's Spirit would be part of him. When God made man, He made him a spiritual being. God is spirit, and those who bear His image are spiritual.

2) God said, "Let us make man in our image, in our likeness, and let them rule . . ." The Sovereign LORD made man (male and female) to rule, just as He Himself rules. The great King of kings and LORD of lords made man a king and a lord also. God is King over all the earth, but He created and appointed the man and woman to rule under Him. God gave the man and the woman dominion over all the earth. God blessed them and part of that blessing was the command to subdue the earth and rule over all its inhabitants. God blessed the man and woman and said to them, "Rule over the fish of the sea and the birds of the air and over every living creature that moves on the ground." Human beings, who were both body and spirit, were created to subdue both physical and spiritual beings. Not only were they made to rule the animals, but they were created with the capacity to conquer angels.

3) "Holy, holy, holy is the LORD God Almighty" (Revelation 4:8). When God created man in His own image, when He created them male and female, He created them holy. God graciously gave them His goodness and holiness and righteousness. "I will proclaim the name of the Lord and praise the greatness of our God! He is the Rock. His works are perfect and all his ways are just. He is a faithful God who does no wrong, righteous and upright is He" (Deuteronomy 32:3, 4). God is upright and "God made mankind upright" (Ecclesiastes 7:29). God created the man and woman in His own image. Thus they were created good, just as God is good. They were created perfect, just as God is perfect. God made them like Himself. Human beings were "created to be like God in true righteousness and holiness"

(Ephesians 4:24). In the beginning there was no evil in human beings. There was not even the slightest tendency in them towards evil. Every inclination of the thoughts of their hearts was only good, continually. In the beginning God's judgement upon the man and the woman was that they were good, "very good."

People were created in the image of God, to be a reflection of the glory of God. "The heavens declare the glory of God" and so also "the earth is full of His glory" (Psalm 19:1; Isaiah 6:3), but in the beginning it was the man and the woman, the ones created in God's image, who most clearly and brightly and purely shone with the glory of God. As they stood upon the earth, bearing God's image, they bore a true witness to the existence and the excellence of God. What a great tragedy it was when the man and woman lost the clearness and brightness and pureness of that image by their sin!

Man was created in the image of God, but he was not God. At the appointed time, however, there was born into the world a Man, who was the *full* "radiance of God's glory and the *exact* representation of his being" (Hebrews 1:3). The God of heaven, who is Spirit, became flesh and lived upon the earth, being found in appearance as a man. "Although He existed in the form of God, although He was in very nature God . . . He made Himself nothing, taking the form of a servant, being made in the likeness of men . . ." (Philippians 2:6, 7). How extraordinary that man was made in the likeness of God and that God then took for Himself the likeness of man! Jesus Christ—"He is the image of the invisible God . . . for God was pleased to have all His fullness dwell in Him . . . In Christ all the fullness of the Deity lives in bodily form . . ." (Colossians 1:15, 19 & 2:9). God anointed Jesus with the Holy Spirit. To Him God gave the Spirit without measure. No man has seen God at any time, but when Jesus was upon the earth, people who saw Him said, "We have seen His glory, the glory of the One and Only, who came from the Father, full of grace and truth . . . No one has ever seen God, but God the One and Only, who is at the Father's side, has made Him known" (John 1:14, 18). Jesus Himself said, "Anyone who has seen Me has seen the Father" (John 14:9).

The teacher's guide for this lesson starts on page 428.

THE GIFT OF LIFE

- **Genesis 2:7**
- **Job 10:8–12; 33:4**
- **Psalm 139:13–16**

On the sixth day the LORD God formed the man from the dust of the ground and breathed into his nostrils the breath of life, and the man became a living being. God had filled the world with good gifts for man, but this was the most precious gift of all to him—the gift of life! Human life did not happen by chance. Human beings were not an accident in the universe, the ultimate evolution of an inexplicable one-celled speck of life. No, human life was a most gracious and glorious gift given by God. We read in the Bible that the LORD God was the One "who created the heavens and stretched them out, who spread out the earth and all that comes out of it, who gives breath to its people and life to those who walk on it" (Isaiah 42:5). In God "we live and move and have our being" (Acts 17:28). He is the LORD of Life and He made us alive in Him. We cry out: "The Spirit of God has made me; the breath of the Almighty gives me life" (Job 33:4).

People are precious. There is nothing more valuable on the face of the earth than a human life. When there is an earthquake and buildings tremble and topple to the ground, people search frantically through the rubble and ruins . . . for what? For gold and silver? For gems and jewels? No, the desperate search is for something more valuable than these; the search is for human bodies, ones that are still breathing, still moving, still living. In such a disaster every attempt is made to rescue human beings and to save human lives. It would be a wicked society if such attempts were not made. Woe to the society where life is cheap, where human lives have no value, where people spit upon the precious gift that God gave—life!

Have you ever thought how wonderful it is to be alive? Have you ever thanked God for making you? Have you ever thanked Him for giving you life? Have you ever thought how wonderful it is to be a human being? Think about the body God gave you. You have eyes that can see, ears that can hear, mouths that can speak. You have fingers and hands and arms that can do and make all kinds of things. You have toes and feet and legs that can run and jump and dance. You have lungs that can take oxygen out of the air and hearts that pump blood to all parts of your body, even when you're sleeping. You have bodies that can learn to swim underwater or somersault through the air or twirl on the tip of a toe. The human body is most amazing in the tasks and feats it can perform! Think about the mind God gave you. You are able to think and plan and dream. God gave us brains that can reason, design, create, understand, remember, calculate, communicate, imagine, etc. Think about the soul God gave you. You are a human being, which means you can experience joy and sorrow. You can laugh and you can cry. As a human creature you are able to love; you are able to hope; you are able to trust. Think about what you are and who you are. You are a most amazing creature! Take care of yourself. Take care of your body, your mind and your soul—for they are all precious gifts given to you by God. Be careful with the life that God has given you and be thankful to Him for it. Rejoice as you sing and pray the words from this psalm: "O LORD . . . I praise you because I am fearfully and wonderfully made! Your works are wonderful; I know that full well" (Psalm 139:14). Rejoice in the life that God has given you—and in the God who gave it to you. He knows you; He knows you in the very core of your being. Nothing about you is hidden from Him. He knew you before you were born, before you ever existed. You can say, "O LORD, you have searched me and you know me . . . You have laid your hand upon me . . . You created my inmost being; you knit me together in my mother's womb . . . My frame was not hidden from you, when I was made in the secret place. When I was woven together in the depths of the earth, your eyes saw my unformed body. All the days ordained for me were written in Your book before one of them came to be" (Psalm 139: 1, 5,13–16).

God gave us life! What should our response be to the One who gave us life? We should serve the LORD with all that we have and all that we are. We should serve God with our entire beings! Moses told us what we should do. So did Jesus. They said, "Love the LORD your God with all your heart and with all your soul and with all your strength and with all your mind" (Deuteronomy 6:5 & Luke 10:27).

On the sixth day the LORD God formed the man from the dust of the ground. God did not use nuggets of gold or lumps of silver. He did not use the powder of pearls or the dust of diamonds. God did not use sparkles from the stars or pebbles from the moon. No, the LORD used dirt, ordinary dirt, to make the man. Such were the humble beginnings of the human race — and such we still are. We are of the earth, earthy. Our bodies are clay vessels. Without the life that God breathed into us, without His Spirit, we are merely clods of dirt or lumps of clay. Have you ever seen a human body that has no life? It is useless — open eyes that do not see, silent lips that cannot speak, empty hands that do not move, rigid legs that cannot walk, a heart as cold and still as stone. But a statue was not what God created. No, God made man a living being. The LORD God breathed into the man's nostrils the breath of life — and the man became a living being. His body was formed from the dust of the earth, but his life and soul came directly from God Almighty. The human spirit and the life of man testifies to the existence of God. "We have this treasure in jars of clay to show that this all-surpassing power is from God and not from us" (II Corinthians 4:7).

Why did God make man? God made man for the same reason He made everything else. The heavens declare the glory of God; the earth is full of his praise. Man was also created to glorify God and praise the One who made him. The LORD speaks of His "sons" and "daughters" ". . . whom I created for my glory, whom I formed and made" (Isaiah 43:7). God speaks of his people, "the people I formed for myself, that they may proclaim my praise" (Isaiah 43:21). We are God's workmanship, created to do good works. What are these good works that we must do? We must believe God. We must obey God. We must worship God. Holy, holy, holy is the LORD God Almighty — and we too must be holy. His praises must be upon our lips. "You are worthy, our Lord and God, to receive glory and honour and power, for you created all things, and by your will they were created and have their being" (Revelation 4:11). Every human being has a purpose on earth. Each one of us was given life for a reason. Our purpose on earth is to glorify God! Our reason for life is to praise the LORD!

L'chaim! That is an expression which celebrates LIFE. It is an acknowledgement that life is good, but does it acknowledge that the Giver of life is good? Our celebration should be in the LORD, who gave us the good gift of life. To Him be the glory forever and ever! Amen.

The teacher's guide for this lesson starts on page 430.

THE GIFT OF A GARDEN

• **Genesis 2:4–17**
• **Revelation 2:7; 22:1–3**

The study where I work is an old grain room inside a barn that is piled with bales of hay. The windows of my room overlook a vast valley, where one sees fields and farms for many many miles. Through the centre of the valley runs a river and all along its banks grow trees. Beyond the valley in the distance are wooded hills that are still wild. The view changes with the seasons: In spring one sees the rich brown earth, ploughed into furrows and raked into rows and planted with seeds. In summer the many fields look like a patch-work quilt. Some of the patches are masses of pink clover blossoms; others are stripes of lush green corn stalks; some are waves of golden wheat swaying in the wind; others are dotted with the purple flowers of alfalfa plants. In the autumn, the scene changes again when the crops are harvested. Everywhere one sees the hay stacked in fields of stubble. Next comes winter, but even then one sometimes sees evidence of the crops when the withered corn stalks are left standing in their rows with the white snow falling thick between them.

Much of the earth is now like this view from my window—a

landscape cultivated by man—but in the beginning it was not so. There were no orchards, no fields, no gardens, no groves—for there was no man to work the ground and no rain to water the earth. However, springs of clear water bubbled up out of the ground and flowed in streams over the surface of the earth. At that time the whole world was an immense untouched, unscratched domain where plant and animal life flourished in an unending jungle. This was the overwhelming world in which man was formed; this was the overwhelming world in which he found himself.

No man had cultivated the earth, but the LORD Himself planted a garden. It was called the Garden of Eden, which means the "Garden of Delight." The LORD made this special place in the world for the creature he loved so much—the man whom He had formed. Now the whole world was more beautiful than any flower garden that we could make or even imagine and the whole world was more bountiful than any grove of fruit trees that has ever flourished by our hands or in our dreams, but God gave the man even more than the whole world, that beautiful and bountiful world. God gave the man a gift inside a gift, a garden inside a garden, a paradise inside paradise! Man was given the Garden of Eden! God took the man from the place where he stood alone in the whole wide world and placed him in that perfectly prepared place of pleasure—the Garden of Eden.

In those beginning days, the whole world was filled with wonderful trees, but the most exquisite ones and the most delicious ones God caused to grow in that garden. The Bible says, "The LORD God made all kinds of trees grow out of the ground—trees that were pleasing to the eye and good for food." God also put there in the middle of the garden two extraordinary trees, that grew nowhere else in the whole world. One was the tree of life. The other was the tree of the knowledge of good and evil.

Man was indeed a special creature to be given these two trees in his garden. Remember, man was not like the other animals. Man was a spiritual creature, as well as a physical one; he had a soul as well as a body. It was not enough for him to have the fragrance of the flowers for his nose to smell or the beauty of the blossoms for his eyes to see. He needed more than taste for his tongue and food for his stomach. He was not an animal. He needed food for his soul as well. Man could not live on "fruit" alone; he also needed the Word of God, so the LORD provided for him a spiritual tree, a tree with a command, a tree that enabled man to live by every Word that proceeds out of the mouth of God. God's command to the first man, to the only human being upon the earth, was this: "You are free to eat from any tree in the garden; but you must not eat from the tree of the knowledge of good and evil, for when you eat of it you will surely die." By these Words of God the man was given a choice. Man could choose to believe God and obey Him or man could choose to disbelieve God and disobey Him. In the giving of that command, God bestowed upon man yet another gift—the gift of freedom. Man, although he was created good, was not forced to be loyal to God. The LORD did not make a robot, unable to resist a command. No, the LORD created a being who was not only good, but also free. It was within man's range of "freedom" to rebel against God, but it was also within his range of freedom to remain loyal to the LORD!

In the beginning man was free, free to choose for God or against God. The man's freedom was meaningful and his choice was consequential, because he was choosing between life and death. The choice stood before him in the centre of the garden. One tree was the tree of life; the other was a tree of death. The choice was clear. Obedience to God would bring blessing and life; disobedience would bring cursing and death. It was the first time that God said: "I have set before you life and death, blessings and curses. Now choose life, so that you and your children may live and that you may love the LORD your God, listen to his voice, and hold fast to Him, for the LORD is your life . . ." (Deuteronomy 30:19, 20).

Thousands and thousands of years have passed from that beginning time. The Garden of Eden has vanished, but we also have a choice before us, symbolized by a tree. This tree stands forever in the centre of the world and in the centre of human history. The tree that stands before each one of us is the cross! On that cross was nailed the Son of God to pay for our sins, that we might have everlasting life. The first man and woman in the world had to choose between life and death—and so do we. We, their children, must also choose between life and death. The Bible says, "Whoever believes in the Son has eternal life, but whoever believes not the Son will not see life, for God's wrath remains on him" (John 3:36). Jesus Himself said: "God so loved the world that He gave His one and only Son, that whoever believes in Him shall not perish but have eternal life" (John 3:16). Again the Bible says, "He who has the Son has life; he who does not have the Son of God does not have life" (I John 5:12). The command of the gospel is to believe. "Believe in the Lord Jesus, and you will be saved" (Acts 16:31). Have you obeyed this command? Do you believe God's Word? Have you trusted in

Jesus? If the answer in your heart and on your lips is "yes"—then you have life. But if the answer is "no," if you have not obeyed the gospel and if you have not believed in the Lord Jesus, then you are still dead in your sins. "Whoever does not believe stands condemned already because he has not believed in the name of God's one and only Son" (John 3:18). The choice is before you. Which will you choose? Belief or unbelief? Obedience or disobedience? Life or death?

The teacher's guide for this lesson starts on page 432.

THE FIRST WEDDING

- **Genesis 2:15–25**
- **Matthew 19:3–6**
- **Ephesians 5:22–33**

When the LORD God put the man in the Garden of Eden, he was given the responsibility to work it and take care of it. That was another gift from God—work! Is work a gift? Yes! Do you know what it is like when you are bored, with nothing to do? Do you know what it is like when you are interested and excited, with some very important and pleasant task to do? What God gave the man in the "Garden of Delight" was a delightful duty. Man was given work that would give him great pleasure. It was work that would fulfill him in every way. The man was of the earth, earthy, and he would love to work with the earth. (We have experienced that love of the earth also. After the long winter months, when the ground, which has been frozen solid and covered with snow, is finally released from its cold bondage, one of the joys of spring is just to see the patches of brown earth again and to breathe in the fresh fragrance of the soil. It is an honour then to have dirty hands as we happily work the ground in the garden and feel the fine earth between our fingers.) In the Garden of Eden the first man knew, far better than we do, the joy of working with the earth. The LORD God put him there to work it and take care of it—and like everything else that God gave to man, it was good for him. It was for his blessing. This work would make the man very happy.

The LORD entrusted the Garden of Eden to man's care. Part of that care was the physical work, work that exercised his body, the work of his hands with the soil. Another part of that work was spiritual and involved man's soul. Man had to take care of the Garden of Eden by guarding it. There was evil in the universe. In realms not visible to man there were spiritual forces of wickedness. The evil had not penetrated this earthly paradise yet, and it was man's responsibility to guard the garden from it. Sin could not enter the world . . . except through man. He must guard the garden; he must guard himself. The LORD God commanded the man, "You must not eat from the tree of the knowledge of good and evil, for when you eat of it, you will surely die." The world was filled with life and everything in it was good, but sin and death were lurking just beyond the garden's gate.

God mentioned the presence of evil and the threat of death. Immediately thereafter He said, "It is not good for the man to be alone." The man needed someone to help him with this work. The man needed someone to help him guard the garden from sin and death. The man needed someone to stand with him against the assaults of an unseen enemy. So God said, "I will make a helper suitable for him." God knew that He had one more being to make. God knew that there was a final act of creation before this day ended. God knew that something, someone, was still missing from the earth. He knew that the man was alone and that this was not good, although the man himself might not have realized it yet. God wanted the man to experience his need, so that he would exult in both the provision for this need and the Provider of it. Let the man rejoice in the helper God would give to him and let the man glorify the LORD who gave her to him!

So the LORD brought all the beasts of the field and all the birds of the air to the man. God, who was the man's LORD and King, had named him man (which in the Hebrew language is "Adam" and probably comes from the word "adamah," which means "ground"). Adam, who was the lord and king of earth's creatures, now gave names to them. Whatever Adam called each living creature, that was its name. Perhaps the LORD brought the beasts and birds to the man in pairs—the lion and the lioness, the buck and the doe, the ram and the ewe, the bull and the cow, the rooster and the hen, etc. Perhaps Adam saw at that time that each animal had a mate. Perhaps, as all these creatures filed past him two by two, Adam began looking for his mate among them, a creature who was like him, but there was none. No adequate helper, no suitable partner, was found for the man. Now Adam realized that he was alone. He was alone in his home and in his work. He was the only human being in the whole world, in the entire universe. Oh, what an awful loneliness must have ached in Adam's heart! Not even a whole world of friendly animals or myriads of holy angels could take away that loneliness.

Adam did have animal friends to be sure. Beautiful birds flew around him and alighted upon him, singing their sweet songs to him. Large spotted leopards rubbed up against him purring, and licked his hands with their rough tongues. Furry little mice scampered around his feet and squeaked to him. In the beginning all of earth's creatures were friends with Adam. They knew the man, who was their king, and they loved him. Adam also knew them. He had named them and he loved them. But for the man there was no creature like himself, one who walked as he walked or talked as he talked. With the animals Adam had a friendship and a kinship—but not a partnership. The LORD was also in the garden with the first man. The LORD walked with him and talked with him. The LORD was surely his Friend! Adam also had a kinship with God and a fellowship with Him, but that was not a partnership either, for God was his Maker and his Master. The man was not God's equal and the animals were not man's equal. There was no one like him, equal to him, a partner for him. Adam was alone.

The world was not yet completed. Even Adam was aware now that someone was missing. Although Adam had been given the whole world, he was in need. He needed a person like himself. He needed a partner, a helper. The LORD God saw this and for the first time during the six days of creation God said, "It is not good." In the account of creation we read again and again, "God saw that it was good . . . God saw that it was good . . . God saw that it was good." Now we read that the LORD God said, "It is not good!" "It is not good for the man to be alone. I will make a helper suitable for him," a helper corresponding to him. So the LORD God caused the man to fall into a deep sleep. God did not need Adam's input. "Who has understood the mind of the LORD, or instructed Him as his counsellor? Whom did the LORD consult to enlighten Him, and who taught Him the right way?" (Isaiah 40:13, 14). The answer is: No one! God did not need the man's help in anything—and certainly not in an act of creation! God alone knew the perfect person for the man and so God caused Adam to fall into a deep sleep. While he was sleeping, God took one of the man's ribs. Then the LORD God made a woman from the rib he had taken out of the man.

God had saved the best gift for man until the last! What an amazing crea-ture this woman was! Like the man, she too was touched by God and formed by Him. She too was intimately connected with the LORD, but she was also intimately related to the man. She was formed from him and out of him. She was not made from the dust of the earth, (as was every other creature,) but she was made from dust double-refined. She was made from a bone, from one of the man's ribs. She was taken from his side, from close to his heart, that they might love one another and be near one another, standing side by side and walking hand in hand, all the days of their life together. She was the one whom God had formed to be the man's partner and helper.

As He had done with all the other creatures, God brought this last one to Adam too. What would he think? What would he say? When Adam saw her, he was overjoyed at the sight of another person like himself. What he said are the first human words recorded in the Bible. He said, "This is now bone of my bones and flesh of my flesh . . ." He recognized at once that she was like him. There was another human being in the universe, so close to him that she was one with him; she was of the same substance, "bone of my bones and flesh of my flesh." But the man also realized that she was differ-ent from him. God had not given him an exact replica of himself. No, God in His LOVE and wisdom, compassion and understanding, had given him a better gift. The person God had created for his partner was not only the same; she was also different! Adam first recognized the sameness, then the difference—and so he named her with a different name than his own. He was taken from the earth, "adamah"—and so his name was Adam or MAN, but she was taken from the man. He said, "She shall be called WOMAN, for she was taken out of the man."

"Man is the head of the woman . . . for man did not come from woman, but woman from man; neither was man created for woman, but woman for man" (I Corinthians 11:3, 8,9). "Adam was formed first" (I Timothy 2:13). God placed that honour upon the man. His headship was part of God's per-fection in the Garden of Eden, evidenced by the fact that he was the one who named the woman. The man was honoured by being formed first, but the woman was honoured by being formed last. She was given that honour by God. She was God's final work. She was the pinnacle of the pinnacle of creation. She was the crown of creation and "the crown of her husband" (Proverbs 12:4). The Bible says that "the woman is the glory of man" (I Corinthians 11:7).

God honoured them both! He created them both, male and female, in

His own image. One was created first; the other was created last. One was the head; the other was the crown. God loved them both and God gave them to each other as an expression of that love. They belonged to each other. They were a gift to each other, a very good gift given by God.

How happy Adam must have been! The LORD had provided everything for him—a friend, a partner, a helper, and more than all of these, a WIFE! The first marriage on the face of the earth took place in the Garden of Eden. It was a perfect wedding in a perfect place. The bride and groom were clothed in the beauty of holiness, for they knew no sin. Being robed in righteousness, they had no need of other clothes. Their marriage was made in heaven. They were united by God Himself, who said, "The two shall become one flesh." The LORD pronounced his benediction upon their union. God blessed them and said to them, "Be fruitful and increase in number and fill the earth." That was one of God's wedding gifts to them—the blessing of children. "Behold, children are the LORD's good gift; the fruit of the womb is his reward" (Psalm 127:3). This blessed union between the man and the woman would bring more people into the world. The angels were not given such a gift. They do not marry, nor can they produce more of their own kind. God also blessed the man and the woman with dominion over the earth, saying, "Subdue it. Rule . . ." That was another wedding gift from God—the whole world! God also gave them a bountiful banquet, not just for their wedding day, but for all their days. God said, "I give you every seed-bearing plant on the face of the whole earth and every tree that has fruit with seed in it. They will be yours for food." God withheld no good thing from the man and the woman whom He loved.

That sixth day, when the man and the woman were created and married, was indeed a blessed day. The man did not have to spend even one night alone upon the earth. As evening came and the darkness deepened, his wife was beside him. They loved each other perfectly. As the day ended, God saw all that He had made—the heavens and the earth and all that they contained. He saw the man and the woman, their marriage and their love for one another. God saw all that He had made—and it was very good. The sixth day alone of all the days of creation received this pronouncement: very good! The LORD's work of creation was complete. It was perfect.

And there was evening, and there was morning—the sixth day.

The teacher's guide for this lesson starts on page 434.

THE SEVENTH DAY, A HOLY DAY

- **Genesis 2:1–3**
- **Exodus 20:8–11**
- **Deuteronomy 5:12–15**
- **Isaiah 57:2, 20, 21; 58:13, 14**
- **Mark 2:27, 28**
- **John 5:17**
- **Hebrews 4:1–11**
- **Revelation 21:1–7**

T he sixth day ended. God's work was completed. The heavens and the earth in all their vast array were finished. There was nothing to add and nothing to take away from God's creation. It was very good. It was perfect. The excellence of what was made testified to the Excellence of the One who made it. The creation glorified the Creator! God was pleased with his work . . . and He rested. The Bible says, "By the seventh day God had finished the work He had been doing; so on the seventh day He rested from all his work. And God blessed the seventh day and made it holy, because on it He rested from all the work of creating that He had done" (Genesis 2:2, 3). God set apart this day, the seventh day. There were six good days that went before it, and on the sixth day when God saw all that He had made, it was very good — but it was the seventh day alone that God blessed. God blessed the seventh day and made it holy. It was a day of rest and peace, called the Sabbath Day.

God made this blessed day for the creature whom He loved so much. The Lord Himself declared, "The Sabbath was made for man" (Mark 2:27). This day of rest and peace was a gift to the man and the woman, another gracious gift from God. The LORD could have made the heavens and the earth in a twinkling or in a millennium, but He made it in six days and rested on the seventh, so that people could have a pattern. Human beings, from the very beginning, were given an example of how they should live. It was to be a life of working for six days and resting for one day, which was following the pattern that God established from the first. "Be imitators of God" (Ephesians 5:1) is the command given to us. We were created to be like Him.

Days in the Bible are counted from evening to evening. When the sixth day ended, the evening of the Sabbath Day began. That evening was the beginning of the seventh day for God, when He began resting from all the work of creating that He had done. It was the seventh day for God—but the Sabbath was the first full day for man. That first Sabbath eve must have been the most beautiful evening that ever passed upon this earth. Everything was new. Everything was good. The man and his wife were experiencing their life in the world for the first time . . . and it was wonderful! But most wonderful of all, as they walked beneath the glorious sunset sky and through the thick fragrance of the flowers at dusk, was the fact that the LORD their God walked with them. He was there in the garden in the coolness of that Sabbath Eve. Most wonderful of a whole world of things most wonderful, was that the LORD God was with them! Surely their first night on earth, which was the Sabbath, was one of rest and peace—for God was with them.

It is probable that the first faint light of dawn and the first glorious sunrise that the man and woman ever saw, were those belonging to the seventh day, the Sabbath. Their first hopeful and joyful experience of a new day was on a holy day, a blessed day, the Sabbath Day! It would be their first full day upon the earth. They began their life in the world, not with work, but with rest. They had not earned this rest by working for six days. No, it was a gift to them from God. They entered into this rest by God's grace, not by their works. What a blessed beginning for the human race with important lessons to learn right at the start! God's rest and peace were gifts of grace, not wages for work. Their primary work was to worship the LORD; their first priority was not their own labours, but rather, it was to rest and rejoice in the LORD and in the works that He had already accomplished. The reason the man and the woman were created was to glorify God and enjoy Him forever. The very first day of that forever, the man and the woman spent in the presence of their God, enjoying Him and glorifying Him, as they were meant to do. God made this seventh day a holy day for the creatures who were created to be holy for the purpose of worshipping their God who was Holy, Holy, Holy. That first Sabbath day in the Garden of Eden, was a glimpse of heaven on earth, when God's people, though they were only two, praised Him perfectly.

> *You are worthy, our LORD and God,*
> *to receive glory and honour and power,*
> *for you created all things . . .*

> *Revelation 4:11*

The Sabbath was not just a pattern for man to follow on earth; it was also a picture for him of heaven. "Those who walk uprightly enter into peace; they find rest as they lie in death" (Isaiah 57:2). We read in the Bible that by the seventh day God had finished the work he had been doing. What was the work He had been doing? Yes, it was the work of creating. We read that God rested from all "the work of creating" that He had done. But did God stop working altogether? Was there any other work that He was doing? We read in the Old Testament that the LORD, who watches over us, neither slumbers nor sleeps (Psalm 121: 3, 4). In the New Testament Jesus Himself said, "My Father is always at His work to this very day, and I too am working" (John 5:17). God's work of creating was finished by the seventh day, but his work of caring for his people and saving his people was just beginning. Very soon sin and death would enter the world—and then there would be no rest or peace for man. "The wicked are like the tossing sea, which cannot rest, whose waves cast up mire and mud. There is no peace," says my God, "for the wicked" (Isaiah 57:20, 21). But, "God so loved the world that He gave his one and only Son, that whoever believes in Him shall not perish, but have eternal life" (John 3:16). Jesus Himself said, "Come to Me, all you who are weary and burdened, and I will give you rest. Take my yoke upon you and learn from Me . . . and you will find rest for your souls" (Matthew 11:28, 29). Jesus also said, "Peace I leave with you; my peace I give you" (John 14:27). When we believe in Jesus, we enter into God's rest and peace. It is a Sabbath-rest for the people of God, because we rest from the work of trying to save ourselves. We rest in God's salvation. We rest in the work that the LORD finished upon the cross. When Jesus gave up his life to pay for our sins, His work of salvation was completed. Jesus said, "It is finished" (John 19:30)—and with that, He bowed His head and gave up His spirit. The Sabbath Day then changed from the seventh day to the first day of the week, when Christ rose from the dead. Christ's resurrection was a new beginning for mankind. Man's new life, in which he was a new creation, was beginning on a new Sabbath. Now we celebrate, not only the completed work of creation; we also celebrate the completed work of salvation!

Thus we follow God's command: Remember the Sabbath Day by keeping it holy. We set aside one day in seven to rest in and rejoice in the great works of God, which He has done for us. We honour our God, our Creator and our Redeemer, by remembering to keep His day, the LORD's Day, holy. We look back at God's work, His work of creating and His work of redeeming, which is finished . . . and we also look forward. We look forward to the new heavens and the new earth; we look forward to our final rest and greatest peace, when we will be with the LORD forever. Once more God will say, "It is done" (Revelation 21:6)—and his work for us will be finally finished.

Have a happy and a holy LORD's Day! Good Sabbath to you all!

The teacher's guide for this lesson starts on page 436.

WAR IN HEAVEN

God saw all that He had made, and it was very good. The glory of the LORD filled the earth. Every creature that had breath gave praise to God. The man and the woman worshipped Him in perfect holiness. There was not even a shadow of sin in their hearts. What shone from within them was the radiance of righteousness. In the beginning, everything in the world was beautiful.

But that was in the beginning. Sadly, a change occurred. Now much of what is in the world is ugly and evil. Look in any newspaper. There you will see photographs recording the wretchedness and wickedness of the human condition. And if there were cameras that could photograph the human heart, you would not find what God made; you would not see thoughts that were only pure and good and true. No, there inside the human heart you would see a cesspool of filth and a whirlpool of sin that would make you vomit. Of all the millions and millions of human beings that now live upon the earth, "there is none righteous, no not one" (Romans 3:10), although the first two humans were created "very good."

What happened? God created perfect people, but what happened to this righteous race? How did earth's population become polluted and corrupted to the very core? How did a world that was once so wonderful for man become so sorrowful? What happened? To answer these questions we must go back to a time before the beginning.

Before God created the world with its inhabitants, God created angels, multitudes of angels who lived in the heavenly realms. We know this heavenly host existed first, because they witnessed the creation of the world and worshipped God for His most wonderful work. The LORD says that when He laid the earth's foundation man was not there, but "the morning stars sang together and all the angels shouted for joy" (Job 38:7). In heaven there are still "thousands upon thousands of angels in joyful assembly" (Hebrews 12:22) worshipping God. Heaven is filled with the sound of God's holy angels, a host "numbering thousands upon thousands and ten thousand times ten thousand," singing praises to the Lord (Revelation 5:11).

God created the angels to be powerful spirits and celestial beings. God made them to be like "gales of wind" and "flames of fire" (Hebrews 1:7). A man, to whom God revealed the sight of many angels in heaven, described the appearance of one of them. He testified: "I saw another mighty angel coming down from heaven. He was robed in a cloud, with a rainbow above his head; his face was like the sun, and his legs were like fiery pillars" (Revelation 10:1). What heavenly splendour! These celestial creatures were so magnificent that if an earthly being (such as you or I) saw one, we would be tempted to fall down at the angel's feet to worship him. However, if he was a holy angel of the LORD, he would quickly rebuke us saying, "Do not do it! I am a fellow servant with you . . . WORSHIP GOD" (Revelation 22:8, 9). "Praise the LORD from the heavens. Praise Him in the heights above. Praise Him, all His angels. Praise Him, all His heavenly host . . . Let them praise the Name of the LORD, for His Name alone is exalted. His splendour is above the earth and the heavens . . . Praise the LORD" (Psalm 148:1, 2, 13, 14)! These mighty angels were created, like us, to praise and worship and glorify the LORD. They were also created to be servants of God. "Praise the LORD, you His angels, you mighty ones . . . who obey His Word. Praise the LORD, all His heavenly hosts, you His servants, who do His will" (Psalm 103:20, 21). The angels were created to praise the LORD and serve the LORD, but they were also appointed to help us. "For surely it is not angels whom God helps" (Hebrews 2:15), but rather it is flesh and blood humanity whom

God helps and loves and saves! "Are not all angels ministering spirits, sent
to serve those who will inherit salvation" (Hebrews 1:14)? The angels were
created by God and for God (Colossians 1:16), but the LORD graciously uses
this heavenly host of angelic beings to serve us and help us, who are but lowly
creatures of the earth. How great is the LORD that our heavenly Father has
for us!

The angels were created to praise and serve the LORD in heaven, but
many of them were not content with the exalted position that God had given
them. They rebelled against the LORD. They used their God-given gifts of
freedom and brilliance and power to treacherously revolt against their Creator, Who had so graciously and gloriously blessed them. Although these
angels knew God, (knew of His greatness and goodness with a clarity and
proximity unknown to us, for they dwelled with God in heaven), they neither glorified Him as God, nor magnified Him as LORD. They exchanged
the truth of God for a lie, and worshipped and served created things (that
is, themselves or other angels,) rather than their Creator, Who is blessed forever. Thus there came to be a host of other angels, an army of evil spirits,
who were opposed to God and everything good. They became demons and
devils, "the powers of this dark world" and "the spiritual forces of evil in the
heavenly realms" (Ephesians 6:12). The Bible says: "God did not spare these
angels when they sinned, but sent them to hell, putting them into chains
of darkness to be held for judgement" (II Peter 2:4). Again we read: "The
angels, who did not keep their positions of authority, but abandoned their
own home—these God has kept in darkness, bound with everlasting chains
for judgement . . ." (Jude 6). These traitorous angels lost their heavenly
home; they were banished forever from the grace of God, being condemned
and imprisoned forever in their own wickedness. Wander where they would,
they were locked in darkness, dragging their chains after them, with no way
to escape their sin or their doom. How great was their fall! How wretched
was their state! By their own apostasy, they lost their true majesty. Now all
they could do was masquerade as angels of light, pretending to be what they
had eternally lost.

Although these dark angels were both chained and doomed, they continued their futile fight against God. If "an evil man is bent only on rebellion" (Proverbs 17:11), how much more is an evil angel! Refusing to relent
or repent, being bound forever in the blackness of their own souls, these
demons displayed, by their unceasing animosity towards God, His righteous

judgement upon them. Although they were hurled into hell, there was "war in heaven" (Revelation 12:7) and battles on earth, for "our struggle is not against flesh and blood, but . . . against the spiritual forces of evil in the heavenly realms" (Ephesians 6:12). Involved in this war were two great angelic armies. There were "legions" of evil spirits fighting against God and there were "legions" of holy angels fighting for Him (Mark 5:9 & Matthew 26:53). Human beings did not escape involvement in this cosmic clash between good and evil.

Leading the hosts of hell, as well as leading astray the whole world, is the chief of the fallen angels, called the "Prince of Darkness," the "Prince of Demons," the "Prince of this World" (John 12:31; 14:30). This evil spirit is known by many names in the Bible: He is called the Devil and Satan, because, (as the Greek and Hebrew words mean,) he is an accuser, a slanderer, an adversary. He is called our Enemy: "Your enemy the devil prowls around like a roaring lion looking for someone to devour" (I Peter 5:8). He is called the Evil One: "The whole world is under the control of the Evil One" (I John 5:19), for he is "the spirit who is now at work in those who are disobedient" (Ephesians 2:2). He is called the Tempter (Matthew 4:3), who entices men to sin. There is no truth in the devil: "He is a liar and the Father of Lies" (John 8:44), the Deceiver "who leads the whole world astray" (Revelation 12:9). He is the "Angel of the Abyss, whose name in Hebrew is Abaddon and in Greek Apollyon," which means Destroyer or Destruction (Revelation 9:11). He is the Dragon and the Serpent, "the great dragon" and "that ancient serpent called the Devil or Satan" (Revelation 12:9).

The devil is also alluded to as Lucifer.[1] Lucifer means the Shining One or the Morning Star, because he was created as a bright and brilliant heavenly being, (although now he only masquerades as an angel of light.) God gave this so-called Lucifer an exalted position among the heavenly host, but he was not content, because he was still a servant of the Most High. This angel wanted to be the one most high himself! Lucifer was not content being a ministering spirit, whose purpose was to worship God and whose service was to obey Him. No, he wanted to be the one worshipped and the one obeyed. In the pride of his heart, Lucifer envied God and hated God. He wanted to be the King of kings and the LORD of lords himself. He wanted to sit upon the throne of God and take for himself the glory and honour and power, which God alone is worthy to receive. He was not content to be an angel; he wanted to be like God! He said in his heart, "I will make myself like the Most High" (Isaiah 14:14). So he rebelled against God and a multitude of the heavenly host joined him in that rebellion—but "God did not spare these angels when they sinned" (II Peter 2:4).

Thus there were angelic and demonic beings, who existed before this world and beyond this world in the invisible spiritual realms. They were already there in the beginning days of the earth. Although the devil had lost his place and power in paradise, although all the angels who sinned were confined in dungeons of darkness where hell was now their home; nonetheless, both the holy angels of heaven and the evil demons of hell had access to the earth. The war was still being waged; the battle ground had simply shifted and extended to include another part of God's dominion. Earth became the new war zone. At some point in time here on earth, Satan began "roaming through the earth, going back and forth in it" (Job 1:7 & 2:2). The Bible tells us that "the devil prowls around like a roaring lion, looking for someone to devour" (I Peter 5:8).

In those first early days, what did Satan find as he roamed and prowled around this world? He must have found all kinds of creatures with bodies of flesh and blood. These creatures were not as the angels, who were powerful spirits, beings like "gales of wind" and "flames of fire" (Hebrews 1:7). No, these animals of the earth were weak and dumb, bound to the earth like clods of clay and despicable in the eyes of this evil angel. Satan also found another creature, a male and a female, who were made of flesh and blood like the other beasts, but these two also had spirits, as well as bodies. This odd pair, who were a mixture of both heaven and earth, were called man and woman. They did not shine like other spirits. They had neither the glory of God nor the light of angels. To Lucifer, the Shining One, they would have been miserable and contemptible creatures indeed, made out of the mud as they were, except that their beings shone with the beauty of holiness. They were children of God, both pure and good, and they reflected the light of the LORD. How Satan hated that light! He hated holiness and he hated these humans! He must snuff out their light, which shone so clearly, not only in this new world, but in the entire universe. Yes, this "Prince of Darkness," the devil, must snuff out their light, but how?

The Son of God, when He walked upon this earth, told men and women about this evil angel. He said that from the beginning the devil was "a murderer" and "a liar" (John 8:44). "The devil has been sinning from the beginning" (I John 3:8). From the beginning then, from those early days when everything was beautiful and everyone was good, there was also an invisible being, called the Evil One, roaming and prowling back and forth throughout the earth. There was a murderer and a liar on the loose. There was a spoiler and a destroyer lurking beyond the shadows in the unseen realms. But he could do nothing; he could harm no one. He could not shrivel so much as a blade of grass, for this was not yet his domain. It had been given to another. He had no power in this world, for all authority had been given to the man and woman. They had been given rule over all the earth. It belonged to them, and they belonged to God, not Satan. No, he was not yet the ruler of this world. It all belonged to God and to the righteous rulers whom God had appointed under Him. The only way this evil angel could conquer the world was to conquer them. The only way Satan could take control of this world was to take control of the man and the woman. The only way Satan could become "the prince of this world" was to destroy its God-appointed monarchs. All Satan had to do was make the man and woman fall. All he had to do was make them sin, make them eat from that forbidden tree, and they would surely die!

Satan was experienced in this line of work. Had he not enticed multitudes of heaven's angels to rebel against God? If he could lead legions of angelic beings to follow him, why not these weak little worms of the earth as well? How could they possibly stand against an angel, who was so much stronger and more powerful than they were? Of course, on their own they could not. If they were alone in this battle, against Satan and his army of demons, they were surely and hopelessly and eternally lost—but, thanks be to God, they were not alone! God was with them! They could be strong in the LORD and in His mighty power. In that way they could take their stand against the devil's schemes. But would they? When the day of evil came, would they turn to the LORD and trust in Him? When the day of evil came, would they stand or would they fall? That day, the day when they would be tested and tempted, was coming soon.

The war in heaven is a battle on earth. It is a war between the Holy One and the Evil One, a battle between good and evil that sweeps the entire span of earth's history. The Bible, from beginning to end, from Genesis to Revelation, speaks of this battle. In this war Satan is continually, definitively, and ultimately defeated. Satan's "casting out" and "hurling down" seems to be a past-present-future event, which has happened, which is happening, which will happen:

We see in the beginning that the serpent is cursed by God; he is cast to the dust and waits to be crushed (Genesis 3:14, 15).

We see in the proclamation of the gospel that the demons are cast out and the devil is hurled down. Jesus said, "I saw Satan fall like lightening from heaven. I have given you authority to trample on snakes . . . and to overcome all the power of the Enemy; nothing will harm you. However, do not rejoice that the [evil] spirits submit to you, but rejoice that your names are written in heaven" (Luke 10:18–20).

We see Satan defeated when the Son of God triumphed over the powers of darkness by his death on the cross (Colossians 2:15). Just before His crucifixion Jesus said, "Now is the time for judgement on this world; now the prince of this world will be driven out" (John 12:31).

We see Satan defeated at the ascension of Christ, when there was war in heaven. "Michael and his angels fought against the dragon, and the dragon and his angels fought back. But he was not strong enough, and they lost their place in heaven. The great dragon was hurled down—that ancient serpent called the devil, or Satan, who leads the whole world astray. He was hurled to the earth and his angels with him . . . Now have come the salvation and the power and the kingdom of our God, and the authority of His Christ. For the Accuser . . . has been hurled down" (Revelation 12:7–10).

We see Satan defeated through the perseverance of the saints. "They overcame him by the blood of the Lamb and by the word of their testimony; they did not love their lives so much as to shrink from death" (Revelation 12:11).

We see Satan defeated at the end, when the Son of God, the Son of Man, comes on the clouds of the sky, in power and great glory, with thousands upon thousands of his holy angels to judge the wicked (Matthew 16:27; Jude 14), who are cursed and cast into the lake of fire prepared for "the devil and his angels" (Matthew 25:41). In the end we see the dragon, that ancient serpent, who is the devil or Satan, thrown into the lake of fire, where he will be tormented for ever and ever (Revelation 20:10).

From the beginning this evil spirit was roaming and prowling through the world, but before his arrival, before the battle ground was even prepared, we read of God's Holy Spirit hovering over the unformed earth. The LORD was watching over the world in the darkness of the beginning before time began. We do not know exactly when Satan entered the scene, but he was there in those early days. When the man and woman were walking on the earth, they could not see this evil spirit wandering through their world, but God could. Satan's invisible movements were never hidden from the eyes of God. The LORD was watching over His people. He was not only watching everything; He was controlling everything too, for "the LORD reigns" (Psalm 97:1)! Yes, "the LORD reigns" (Psalm 99:1)! "The LORD is the great God, the great King above all gods" (Psalm 95:3)! Satan could not take one step upon this earth, beyond what God permitted. The LORD had an eternal plan for this world. It would be here, on earth, that God would utterly defeat the Evil One and it would be the seed of the woman, the Son of Man, who would utterly destroy him. God would use these humble creatures that He loved so much. He would use the man and the woman in the destruction of his archenemy. He would crush Satan under their feet (Romans 16:20). God would be glorified on earth, and nothing, NOTHING, not even the most evil or the most powerful angel in the universe, could stop God from being glorified in heaven and on earth. One day multitudes of human beings would join myriads of angels in the worship of God. Together they would raise their voices in a shout of triumph and worship, that would drown out the roar of the enemy forever. The shrieking of the demons and the wailing of the wicked would be silenced by the overwhelming sound of God's praises. Like the peals of crashing thunder and the roar of rushing waters, would be the sound of the righteous rejoicing:

> *Hallelujah!*
> *Salvation and glory and power*
> *belong to our God . . . Hallelujah!*
> *For our Lord God Almighty reigns.*
> *Let us rejoice and be glad and give Him glory!*
> *Hallelujah!*
>
> Revelation 19:1–7
>
> *The LORD has established his throne in heaven,*
> *   and his kingdom rules over all!*
> *Praise the LORD,*
> *all you His servants, you who fear Him,*
> *both small and great.*
> *Praise the LORD,*
> *you His angels, you mighty ones, who do*

His bidding, who obey His Word.
Praise the LORD,
all His heavenly hosts, you His servants, who do His will.
Praise the LORD,
all His works everywhere in His dominion.
Praise the LORD, O my soul . . .
Praise the LORD, O my soul . . .
Praise the LORD, O my soul.

Revelation 19:5 & Psalm 103:1, 2, 19–22

Notes

1. There is one other name by which Satan is known—and that is Lucifer. It comes from the following passage of Scripture:

How you have fallen from heaven, O Morning Star, [O Lucifer], Son of the Dawn! You have been cast down to the earth, you who once laid low the nations! You said in your heart, 'I will ascend to heaven; I will raise my throne above the stars of God; I will sit enthroned on the mount of assembly, on the utmost heights of the sacred mountain. I will ascend above the tops of the clouds; I will make myself like the Most High.' But you are brought down to the grave, to the depths of the pit" (Isaiah 14:12–15).

It is clear from the context (Isaiah 14:3–23) that this passage is referring directly to a human and historical ruler, the king of Babylon. However, it seems this passage is also a thinly veiled allusion to Satan, from which we can better understand the nature of his sin and his fall. Although there is controversy surrounding this passage, I believe that it is a double exposure, which reveals Satan, as well as the king of Babylon.

1) Lucifer means "Shining One" and "Satan himself masquerades as an angel of light" (I Corinthians 14:33).

2) Elsewhere in Scripture the angels are referred to as "morning stars" (Job 38:7), but in particular, Satan is referred to as "a star that had fallen from the sky to the earth" (Revelation 9:1). This passage continues: "The star was given the key to the shaft of the Abyss. When he opened the Abyss, smoke rose from it like the smoke from a gigantic furnace. The sun and moon were darkened by the smoke from the Abyss . . . The people, who did not have the seal of God on their foreheads . . . had as king over them, the Angel of the Abyss . . ." whose name is Destruction (Revelation 9:1–11). This Angel of the Abyss is the same one who "holds the power of death, that is, the devil" (Hebrews 2:14).

3) The language in Isaiah 14:12–15 is very similar to that of Revelation 12:7–9. Compare:

> The dragon and his angels . . . lost their place in heaven. The great dragon was hurled down—that ancient serpent called the devil or Satan, who leads the whole world astray. He was hurled to the earth and his angels with him. (Revelation 12:7–9)

> How you have fallen from heaven, O Morning Star, O Lucifer, son of the dawn! You have been cast down to the earth, you who once laid low the nations! (Isaiah 14:12)

4) By examining the "seed of the serpent" (Genesis 3:15) and his "brood if vipers" (Matthew 12:34; 23:33), we can learn something about the serpent himself. These "snakes," who are the offspring of Satan, reflect quite accurately the image of the one who fathered them. The apostle John referred to them as "the children of the devil" (John 3:10). Jesus Himself testified that their father was the devil when He said, "You belong to your father, the devil, and you want to carry out your father's desire" (John 8:44). The apostle Paul, "filled with the Holy Spirit" spoke from God when he said to a false prophet, "You are a child of the devil and an enemy of everything that is right! You are full of all kinds of deceit and trickery. Will you never stop perverting the right ways of the Lord" (Acts 13:10)?

   The wicked princes of this earth are very much like their wicked father, the Evil One, the "Prince of this World." The Word of God, by revealing to us the desires deep within the souls of these wicked rulers, is also unveiling for us what was in Satan's heart, for they reflect the devil's own desires. The king of Babylon was not alone in his hope and his boast, when he said in his heart: "I will ascend to heaven; I will raise my throne above the stars of God . . . I will make myself like the Most High." Many other kings have viewed themselves as divine rulers. For example, this is what the Sovereign LORD says to the king of Tyre: "In the pride of your heart you say, 'I am a god; I sit on the throne of a god . . .' But you are a man and not a god, though you think you are as wise as a god . . . By your wisdom and understanding you have gained wealth for yourself . . . and because of your wealth your heart has grown proud . . . Because you think you are wise, as wise as a god, I am going to bring foreigners against you, the most ruthless of nations . . . They will bring you down to the pit and you will die a violent death . . . Will you then say, 'I am a god' in the presence of those who kill you? You will be but a man, not a god, in the hands of those who slay you . . ." (Ezekiel 28:1–10). These rulers of the earth were simply following "the ruler of the kingdom of the air," by giving expression to the thoughts and desires of the evil spirit at work in them (Ephesians 2:1–3).

Can we not see the rulers of this world carrying out the devil's desire? "The dragon stood in front of the woman who was about to give birth, so that he might devour her child the moment it was born. She gave birth to a son, a male child, who will rule all the nations . . ." (Revelation 12:4, 5). Consider Pharaoh's order concerning the Hebrew babies: "Every boy that is born you must throw into the Nile . . ." (Exodus 1:22). Consider Athaliah, who attempted to murder all the sons of David and "proceeded to destroy the whole royal family . . ." except one (II Kings 11:1–3). Consider Herod, who "gave orders to kill all the boys in Bethlehem and its vicinity, who were two years old and under" (Matthew 2:16). Was this not the dragon, working through these earthly evil rulers, as he circled ever closer in his attempt to devour the Christ Child, Who was the King?

5) The king of Babylon in particular is a type of Satan. This earthly ruler was a dark shadow depicting the real ruler of the dominion of darkness. Ultimately, it is the devil himself who rules "Babylon the Great . . . the mother of the abominations of the earth" (Revelation 17:5). Just as the king of Salem is a type of Christ, foreshadowing the "Prince of Peace" (Hebrews 7:1–3), so the king of Babylon is a type and a shadow of Satan, the King of Chaos and Confusion.

6) It is not surprising that the Lucifer of Isaiah 14:12, desires to raise his throne above the stars of God and make himself like the Most High, for the Kingship of Christ and the worship of Christ has always been the focus of Satanic assault. The devil himself has been the great impostor and pretender to that throne, desiring all peoples and nations to fall down and worship him (Revelation 13:4, 8). Satan tempted the Son of God Himself, the true King and only Heir to the throne of God, to bow down and worship him (Matthew 4:9). Note also that it is at the ascension of Christ, when the Son is "snatched up to God and to His throne" that all hell breaks loose in heaven: "And there was war in heaven. Michael and his angels fought against the dragon and the dragon and his angels fought back. But he was not strong enough, and they lost their place in heaven. The great dragon was hurled down—that ancient serpent called the devil, or Satan . . . He was hurled to the earth . . . (Revelation 12:5–9).

7) It seems that Satan tempted the first two human beings with the evil that was in his own heart: the desire to be like God, the desire to rule as God.

The teacher's guide for this lesson starts on page 438.

THE DAY OF EVIL

- **Genesis 2:25**
- **Isaiah 59:2**
- **John 8:44**
- **Ephesians 6:10–18**

We do not know which day this evil day was or when exactly it occurred. It is possible that Satan was already roaming and prowling through the earth on the seventh day, that first Sabbath Day, but that he was unable to attack or destroy the rest and peace graciously given by God to the man and woman on that blessed day. However, one wonders if that invisible angel was already spying on them. Did he hear their worship of God? Did Satan hear the sound of those two human voices singing praises to God in the garden? Did he hear the Law of God, the commandment concerning the tree, proclaimed by the man to his wife? Did he hear them repeat that Word of God together and make a commitment between themselves never to taste its fruit or even to touch it? Did Satan hear the man and woman speaking to the LORD in the garden in the cool of the day, talking to Him face to face as to a Friend? Yes, no doubt this evil enemy of God heard all those things and was enraged. Satan did not want one creature in the entire universe to worship God. Satan wanted all beings to do his will and obey his word. Satan wanted the man and woman to bow down and worship him, but what he heard and saw was their worship of God. How Satan hated God and how he hated the sound of His praises! There was yet a heavenly host who worshipped God; there were still multitudes of angels in heaven who adored the One whom Satan despised . . . and now, two more voices had been added to that throng. These two newly created beings, called humans, also loved the LORD. And these two were not like the angels in heaven. No, these two humans could make more of their kind . . . more and more and more. These two could form a multitude! Had not God Himself commanded them to fill the earth? Soon this new world, like heaven, would be filled with the sound of their voices praising God. Satan must stop such a thing from happening! He must stop this adoration of God before one other human being came into existence. He must act quickly! He must stop this plan of God immediately. He must silence their foolish praises, but how?

He would try to kill them, of course, for Satan was a murderer from the beginning. He did not care about these creatures, who were so fearfully and wonderfully made. No indeed, he hated them almost as much as he hated God. Those two humans were created in the image of God and when Satan looked at them, he was reminded of the One in whose likeness they were made. Satan hated them, because he hated God. He must kill them, but that would not be easy. They were protected by God. They were united to the LORD by a bond of love, not by their frail love for Him, but by God's own great LOVE for them. The LORD was with them and He would not allow Satan to touch so much as a hair upon their heads, much less allow him to strangle those throats from which God's praises poured. No, Satan could not harm them because they were wrapped securely in the LOVE of Almighty God. How could Satan reach them?

Satan was also a liar from the beginning. If he could lie and tempt these creatures to sin against God, then their sin would divide them from God. If Satan could deceive and entice these humans to rebel, then their treason would separate them from God. They would become God's enemies. They would no longer be sheltered by God's LOVE; they would be exposed to God's wrath. Satan knew, firsthand, that no evil can dwell with God. God's holiness cannot abide with wickedness. If God did not spare Satan or the legions of heavenly angels who followed him, did these two miserable creatures of the earth think that they could escape? No, God Himself would execute them for their rebellion. God's own hand would crush them like insects crawling from the earth, and Satan would not have to lift even a finger to grind their life into the dust. Their praises of God would be silenced in death, buried with them in the grave forever. All Satan had to do was lure them with his lies to ensnare them in sin. Then he could sit back and watch them die. The LORD was their life. Apart from their God, these human creatures would simply shrivel up and die. Satan had only to lead them to this certain death. They would choose it for themselves and God would grant it to them. Then they would surely die!

Satan's scheme was to separate these human beings from the LOVE of their God. He could destroy them, if he could divide them; he could divide them, if he could deceive them. Satan was a liar and a murderer from the beginning. The devil held a three-pronged weapon in his hand: Deception! Division! Destruction! He also had many flaming arrows to shoot at these two innocent children of God. What defence had they? We read in the Bible that the man and the woman were naked. Did God leave them alone in the garden — unarmed, unprepared and unprotected — to face this evil and powerful angel? No! God had equipped them for the battle. They had been given the full armour of God, so that when the day of evil came, they could stand their ground and not fall. They wore no clothing, but they were robed in righteousness. The armour given to them by God was holiness. The LORD had also given them a great shield, with which they could extinguish all the flaming arrows of the Evil One. It was the shield of faith. Their trust in God would protect them from any arrow their adversary aimed at them. The man and woman had also been given a weapon — a sharp, double-edged sword, called the sword of the Spirit, which is the Word of God. God Himself had handed that sword to the man. Now the man must use it to guard the garden, himself, his wife and the whole human race. With that one commandment, the man could conquer angels. But it wasn't enough to hear it or know it or say it; the man must do it! Finally, he must be strong in the LORD, trusting in God's mighty power. He must not lean on himself or on his wife; he must rely on God. He must turn to God for help at all times, especially when the day of evil arrived.

It would come very soon, for what Satan had to do, he must do quickly.

The teacher's guide for this lesson starts on page 440.

THE SERPENT

- Genesis 3:1–5
- II Corinthians 11:3, 14
- Revelation 12:9

Satan worked out his battle plan quickly, but carefully. He would have just one chance for a surprise attack. If it failed, the humans would be on their guard. Satan must make his first strike be the fatal one. He would have no better opportunity to make these creatures fall, for they were new in the universe with no experience of war. They had not yet been strengthened or seasoned in their resistance to God's enemy. Since the man and woman had never stood their ground in battle, this first chance was Satan's best chance to make them fall.

Part of Satan's scheme to deceive them was to disguise himself. He would present himself as one of the creatures whom the man and woman ruled. The humans loved and trusted and delighted in their subjects, knowing that all the animals of the earth were gifts given to them by God. All of these creatures were declared by the LORD to be good. Thus the man and woman would not suspect harm or evil or treachery from any of these beloved beasts. This was a very devious part of Satan's design. He would not come to them as he was, as a heavenly being, as an angel superior to them, for that might alert and alarm the humans. No, Satan would come to them as an earthly being, as an animal inferior to them—and so put them at ease and off guard. He would not go to them directly or honestly; he would disguise himself as a familiar friend and speak to them through a favourite pet. But which animal should Satan choose? He chose the serpent, for it was more crafty then any of the wild animals the LORD God had made. It already may have impressed the man and woman that it was a clever creature and thus they would seriously consider what the serpent had to say—and that was what Satan wanted: a hearing. So Satan entered the serpent.

The next step in Satan's plan was to watch and wait. Now Satan, who was embodied in that serpent, could walk boldly and visibly through the Garden of Eden—watching and waiting for the right moment to strike! The man and woman were unaware of the presence of this evil being, for he looked like an ordinary snake. They had no reason to suspect this creature, but rather they had reason to admire him for his wisdom and beauty. There was nothing unnatural about this snake in the garden, and no doubt the man and the woman grew accustomed to seeing him there. How many hours or days or weeks the serpent waited we do not know. How many times he spoke to the man and woman or how many times he went to the tree in the middle of the garden, we do not know. But the day of evil did dawn and the hour of darkness did come and the moment to strike did occur. Satan was ready.

Now that ancient serpent, the devil, did not strike with poisonous fangs to pierce the skin. Oh no, Satan's poison was much more deadly. He attacked with venomous words to cloud the mind, to pierce the heart, to kill the soul. Satan had been watching and waiting for the woman to be alone near the tree and now he spoke. The serpent said, "Did God really say, 'You must not eat from any tree in the garden?'" It was a simple question, spoken sweetly by a cunning creature, who was already twisting God's Word and confusing God's command. Did God say they must not eat from any tree in the garden? No, of course not. The woman knew God's Word and she knew that this was not true. She had authority over this creature. She had the right and the responsibility to correct his error. She answered the serpent's question by saying, "We may eat fruit from the trees in the garden, but God did say, 'You must not eat fruit from the tree that is in the middle of the garden, and you must not touch it, or you will die.'" The woman was not ignorant of God's provision; they were free to eat from every tree in the garden . . . but one. Nor was she ignorant of God's command. She knew that the penalty for disobedience was death, that God had said, "In the day that you eat from it, you shall surely die."

But now the serpent declared to the woman the exact opposite. He said, "You surely shall not die." Satan was no longer questioning or twisting or confusing God's Word; he was now openly denying it and boldly opposing it. "You surely shall not die." These were the first false words ever spoken to human ears. The woman was alone when she heard this lie.[1] She was not talking to a little snake; she was talking to Satan himself, the prince of demons, the most powerful of the evil angels. She had been created to rule animals and trample serpents and conquer angels — but not by herself or in her own strength. Beside her husband, relying upon the mighty power of the LORD, yes, she could face this adversary and take her stand against the devil's schemes; but alas, she was alone when she was assaulted. The Bible says, "Though one may be overpowered, two can defend themselves. A cord of three strands is not quickly broken" (Ecclesiastes 4:12). But when the battle began on earth, when Satan's first deadly arrow was shot, the woman was by herself. She should have cried to her husband or called on her God for help. She had an instant to do so, an instant to flee, before the awful onslaught of flaming arrows came flying towards her. If the lie that the snake spoke, shocked or stunned the woman, puzzled or perplexed her, terrified or horrified her, you can be sure that Satan would not give her even one second to sort it all out. No, that ancient serpent struck immediately . . . again and again and again. Satan's words, which were his weapons, flashed quickly and viciously from the forked tongue of the snake.

The serpent said, "You surely shall not die, for God knows that in the day you eat from it your eyes will be opened, and you will be like God, knowing good and evil." With these words Satan attacked the very core of the connection between man and God — which was God's LOVE for them. The serpent struck at the very heart of the relationship in order to divide God and his people, in order to bring about death. If you want to kill, you go for the pulse of life, which is the heart — and that is what Satan did. The serpent's words attacked God's LOVE for the man and the woman . . . and thus he attacked their faith in God. With these words Satan made it seem that God had withheld something good from the man and the woman. It was a lie! The LORD had just given them the whole world and everything in it. God had not withheld any good thing from them, but Satan was now suggesting that God was not so good, nor so great. He was suggesting that God was not so bountiful, nor so powerful. Satan suggested that God had crippled and blinded the man and the woman, created them in that state and condemned them to remain in it by his command, because He was afraid of what his creatures would become. Satan was assailing the woman with doubts about God. Satan cast doubts, not upon the existence of God, but upon His character. The woman's trust in the LORD was being tried. Satan was ripping away the great shield of faith, which protected her.

The serpent said, "You surely shall not die, for God knows that in the day you eat from it your eyes will be opened, and you will be like God, knowing good and evil." Satan, that angel of light, cast a very strange and evil glow not only upon the LORD, but upon the man and woman themselves. Satan made it seem that human beings were not good the way they were created, that they were missing something. God had declared them "very good," but Satan suggested "not good enough." God had created them perfect, but Satan implied they could be better. Satan was stirring up doubt and discontent in the woman's heart about her own life! Her life, which was a most precious and gracious gift from God, was now coming under attack! Would she believe God? Would she have faith, not only that God was good, but that she was good? If she was to withstand this assault, she must trust God. She must take up the shield of faith, with which to extinguish all the flaming arrows of the evil one.

The serpent said, "You surely shall not die, for God knows that in the day you eat from it your eyes will be opened, and you will be like God, knowing good and evil." With one sentence, with one potent barrage of words, Satan had denied the Word of God, cast doubt on the character of God and stirred up discontent with the life given by God—but none of these attacks would necessarily lead the woman to disobey God. Disbelieving God would not ensure disobeying God. But the serpent was more crafty than any of the wild animals, and Satan was the most crafty of all the dark demons. Satan was the master of intrigue. Among those words of doubt, distrust and discontent, he mixed a fatal dose of desire. His words, which were his arrows, were tipped with poison. Satan was able to stir up the desire to disobey. Had he not led legions of angels to revolt? Satan added enticements. He offered temptations. When the serpent had finished speaking, when Satan had shot his last flaming arrow, the woman would want to disobey God. Her heart would be inflamed with the desire to eat the forbidden fruit.

The woman must not yield to the temptation! She must follow the commands of God, not the desires of her heart. She must obey the Word of God, not the lusts of her flesh. She must take a firm stand now against her own self.

Notes

1. It is generally understood that the woman was alone during this time of temptation. However, it could be argued that Adam was present with her, that he also heard these lies of Satan, for Scripture records that the woman "gave some to her husband, *who was with her . . .*" (See Genesis 3:6.) If Adam stood next to his wife listening and then watching to see what would happen to her, and not intervening out of love for his wife and his God—how culpable a creature he was! Other Scriptures also suggest that Adam was not deceived as the woman was, but that he entered into rebellion against God knowingly and willingly.

The teacher's guide for this lesson starts on page 442.

THE FIRST
TEMPTATION

- Genesis 3:4–6
- Matthew 4:1–11
- Luke 4:1–13
- James 1:12–15

S atan, speaking through the serpent, tempted the woman to eat the fruit, which God had commanded, "You must not eat from the tree of the knowledge of good and evil, for in the day that you eat from it, you shall surely die." Satan said to the woman, "You surely shall not die, for God knows that in the day you eat from it, your eyes will be opened, and you will be like God, knowing good and evil." Satan removed the fear of death and replaced it with a lure. There were three enticements that Satan used to ensnare the woman in sin:

1) Satan promised that, on the day she ate the forbidden fruit, she would not die, but rather, *her eyes would be opened.*
Satan lied. Her eyes were already opened. God had given the man and the woman the incredible gift of sight. He had given them eyes that were open to see a world full of goodness. They had eyes that could see the glory of God all around them. Everything their eyes beheld filled them with happiness and thankfulness. But now Satan tempted the woman with the thought that

there was more to see, that there was a whole other world of things to which she was blind. Satan implied that there were things her eyes did not see and her mind did not know. That was true. The man and the woman had seen nothing evil, nothing ugly, nothing sinful, nothing shameful. Their minds knew none of these things, and it was God's blessing on their lives that these things were kept from them. But now Satan tempted the woman to go beyond herself and to go beyond the boundaries and barriers that God had set for her eyes. Satan aroused the desire in her to see more . . . more than God had given, as if God had withheld something good from her.

Now was the time to exercise faith! The woman must trust in the LORD; she must trust in God's LOVE for her. She must trust that God's commands were for her benefit. She must believe that what God said was true and right and just. She must believe that what God withheld from her, was not worth holding. It was God to whom she must cling. It was the Word of God, the Sword of the Spirit, which must be tightly grasped by her. It was the LORD and his Law, which she must hold close to her heart. She must hold onto them . . . for dear life! She must not let go of all that was good. She must not listen to the lies and empty promises of the serpent.

2) Satan promised that, on the day she ate the forbidden fruit, she would not die, but rather, *she would be like God.*

Satan lied. She already was like God. The man and the woman had been created in the likeness of God. The LORD had graciously bestowed upon them His own image. No other creature on earth was given that gift. The man and the woman were holy, just like the One who is HOLY, HOLY, HOLY. The man and the woman had been given holiness, and so they already were like God. But now Satan tempted the woman with the thought that there was another way to be like God, a way which God had withheld from them because He was jealous to keep his exalted position for Himself. Satan suggested they could be like God in His independent sovereign rule. Why should God reign? Why should He be supreme? Why should God alone determine right and wrong? Why should He alone give the commands for others to obey? Satan suggested to the woman that equality with God was a thing to be grasped and so he infected her heart with the same evil desire that was within him—the desire to be like God, the desire to be God!

Now was the time to exercise faith, not only a trusting faith, but a yielding faith. The woman must submit to the Law of God because He alone was

LORD. Her faith must be one that humbly acknowledged that the LORD is God and there is no other. Now was the time for the woman to remember that God alone was Almighty, Creator of heaven and earth, and she was but a creature, who owed both life and love to Him. Yes, now was the time to love the LORD her God with all her heart and with all her soul and with all her strength and with all her mind. She must not listen to any creature, (whether animal or angel or even her own husband,) who would attempt to turn her against her Creator.

3) Satan promised that, on the day she ate the forbidden fruit, she would not die, but rather, *she would know good and evil.*

Satan lied. She already had the knowledge of good, which was given to her by God. She could not gain wisdom by disobeying God; she could only lose it. "The LORD gives wisdom, and from his mouth come knowledge and understanding" (Proverbs 2:6). By obeying the Word, which came from the mouth of God, the woman already had wisdom, knowledge and understanding. "The fear of the LORD is the beginning of wisdom, and knowledge of the Holy One is understanding" (Proverbs 9:10). The woman's fear of the LORD, her fear of disobeying God, was wisdom and her knowledge of God was understanding. She was not lacking in knowledge. God says, "Be wise about what is good, and innocent about what is evil. The God of peace will soon crush Satan under your feet" (Romans 16:19, 20). Evil was not part of the curriculum in the education God wanted for his blessed and beloved creatures. But Satan presented this knowledge of evil as if it was an advantage of which God had deprived them. Satan was so crafty. He twisted the name of the tree, which God had given as a warning for the man and woman, and he turned it instead into a luring. What God intended as an either-or choice, Satan presented as an all-inclusive option, risk-free. God presented the man and woman with a choice: good *or* evil, blessing or cursing, life or death. Satan promised them the knowledge of both good *and* evil . . . at no cost. Satan tempted the woman with knowledge, a knowledge forbidden to her by God. She was a creature who knew nothing of evil, although perhaps now she had a sense that there was something other than "good" in the world. The serpent, who was just an animal, seemed to know more about this thing called "evil" than the man or woman did. How had he obtained this knowledge? Why couldn't she have it too? Thus Satan aroused in the woman a desire to know not only good, but evil as well.

Now was the time to exercise faith by turning to God. This was the first exposure to evil that a human being had ever experienced. If this encounter to Satan's evil presence alarmed the woman or if this exposure to Satan's wicked promises confused her, if she was suddenly aware that there was something other than "good" in the world and if there was something she sensed that she did not understand, now was the time to turn to God! The LORD says, "If anyone lacks wisdom, he should ask God, who gives generously to all without finding fault, and it will be given to him" (James 1:5). If the woman thought she was lacking in wisdom, she had only to turn to her God for help, and she would have received instruction from the LORD Himself concerning the mystery of evil.

But would the woman respond with faith? Would she raise the great shield of faith to protect herself from all the fiery arrows of the Evil One? Would she stand firm in her faith against this assault? Would the woman stand or would she fall?

The teacher's guide for this lesson starts on page 444.

THE FALL

- Genesis 3:6
- Isaiah 59:12, 13
- John 8:44
- Romans 1:18–22, 25
- 1 Timothy 2:14
- James 1:14–15; 4:7, 8
- 1 John 2:15–17

S atan's words aroused a desire in the woman to eat the forbidden fruit, but everything else argued against it:

1) The whole world presented itself as evidence of God's LOVE. All things in heaven and on earth testified to the goodness and greatness of God . . . except the words of this serpent. Everything that the woman saw was irrefutable proof of the power and honour of God. Where could she turn her eyes and not see the clear demonstration of God's mercy and God's glory? The earth was full of His praise. In this way God had made Himself known to her. The truth about God was plain for her to see. Since the creation of the world God's invisible qualities — His eternal power and divine nature — were clearly seen, being understood from what had been made, so that she was without excuse. Even while the serpent was whispering his lies, the whole world was declaring the truth. The LOVE of God was all around her, even as the serpent was tempting her.

To eat the forbidden fruit was to disregard the witness of the whole world!

2)   Everything within the woman also argued against eating the forbidden fruit . . . except for this unfamiliar desire, which the serpent had ignited. Her body and mind and soul must have warned against disobeying God. Her entire being was created to glorify God and enjoy Him forever. She was a creature who knew how to love the LORD perfectly, with all her heart and soul and strength and mind. She also knew God's perfect LOVE for her. That love of God was within her, even as the serpent was tempting her.

To eat the forbidden fruit was to disregard the witness of her own self!

3)   Countering the suggestion of Satan was the express command of God. The woman had God's Word, spoken by her own beloved husband. She had for her standard the Law of the Lord! That law was perfect and that commandment was holy, righteous and good. The woman was not without a mighty support as she faced this insidious temptation. The serpent had assaulted her with his words, which were like flaming arrows, but the Lord had armed her with His Word, which was sharper than any double-edged sword. To counter Satan's attacks, the woman had been given the Sword of the Spirit, God's own Word. That Word had been written on her heart. It was in her mind and on her lips, even as the serpent was tempting her.

To eat the forbidden fruit was to disregard the witness of God's Word!

The woman should have called upon the LORD for help. She should have fled to her God; she should have run to her husband, but instead of fleeing from the temptation, she moved towards it.

1) The first step towards the fall was just a few millimetres. Scripture records that it was the movement of her eyes. Now she looked at the forbidden fruit. It was not wrong for her to look at it, but at this time — in the hour of temptation and on the day of evil — it was a very foolish and dangerous thing to do. When the woman looked, what did she see? The woman saw that the fruit of the tree was good for food and pleasing to the eye. There was nothing unusual in the appearance of this tree at all. It looked like all the other trees that God had planted in the Garden of Eden, "trees that were pleasing to the eye and good for food" (Genesis 2:9). There was nothing about the tree itself which warned her to stay away. There was only God's Word. The tree's appearance did not repel the woman. Just the opposite! It was attractive to her, like all the other good trees in the garden. It appealed to her sense of sight. But the woman had not been created to live by sight alone. All the other creatures of the earth survived by their senses, but human be-

ings were made to live by faith, by every Word that proceeded out of the mouth of God. The woman's eyes told her one thing, but her heart must have warned her to flee.

There was something else the woman saw. She "saw" that the fruit of the tree was desirable to make one wise, although her eyes did not perceive this. No, her ears had heard this from the mouth of the serpent, and the woman believed his words. The woman had shifted, not only her eyes, but also her thoughts. She was making a very important decision based not on the Word of God, but on the words of someone else. With the new information that the woman had received, she reasoned in her mind that the fruit of this tree was desirable for gaining wisdom. But the woman had not been created to live by reason alone. Human beings were created to live by revelation, by the Truth revealed to them by God. Human beings were required to make moral decisions by faith, trusting in the Word of God—even if His Word went against their own thoughts and judgements and reasonings. The woman's mind told her one thing, but her heart must have fluttered a warning to flee.

2) The woman moved closer to her downfall. This movement was but a stretch of her arm and a twist of her hand. The Scripture records that she took some of the fruit. She was now holding it, touching it. Had she disobeyed God's command by touching the fruit? No, God had said, "You must not eat . . . or you will surely die." She had not yet broken God's Law, although she believed it was wrong. She had just told the serpent that God said she would die if she touched it. Now she touched it—and nothing happened. She actually held a piece of the fruit in her hand—and all was well. She felt fine! But we are not to live by our feelings. We are to live by faith, in spite of how we feel. How unreliable are our feelings! But God's Word is a sure guide, which leads us not astray. The woman's feelings told her, "All is well. Everything is fine." Yet her heart of hearts, on which was written the Law of God, must have been beating: WARNING, warning, WARNING, warning, WARNING, warning!

3) The woman did not listen to the Word of God. Nor did she respond to the warnings of her heart. She also ignored the proof of God's Truth and LOVE all around her. The woman made the final movement, which brought about her fall. The Scripture records the awful words that she ate. She ate the fruit, which the LORD God Almighty had commanded, "You must not eat."

4) The movement of the fall continued. The woman, who was now a sinner, acted according to her new nature. Once her lips had uttered only words of truth, for she was created like God, the God who is called "Faithful and True" (Revelation 19:11), but now she was another creature, one who followed in the footsteps of the father of lies. She had been created a child of God, but now she had become a child of the devil and she acted accordingly. Her lips now spoke the serpent's lies. The voice that the man loved was the voice that brought Satan's temptations to him. The creature whom he cherished and honoured and adored above all others, was the very one whom Satan used to destroy him. Adam trusted his wife. She had been given to him by God Himself, for God was the Father of this bride. She was a creature who was good, declared by God to be "very good"—and she had helped him from the beginning. He had full confidence in her. She had brought him good, not harm, all the days of her life. The words she had always spoken to him were wise and good, words marked by faithfulness (Proverbs 31:11, 12, 26). Adam had no reason to suspect her of treachery against himself or God. But he was without excuse, for he had a standard by which to measure the words of his wife to see whether they were true or false. He too had the same three reliable witnesses, that argued loudly and clearly against the words he was now hearing. The whole world, his own self and the Word of God all refuted what the woman was saying. Most importantly, Adam was the one who had received the command of God directly. Adam had heard God's own voice say to him, "You must not eat from the tree of the knowledge of good and evil." The Law of the LORD was plain, and he must not break that law. If he did, he knew the consequences, for God Himself had warned him, "You will surely die." The sound of the LORD's voice and the Word that God had spoken were carefully and powerfully imprinted upon his memory. Adam had not forgotten; nor was he deceived. Adam knew what God had said and he knew that it was true, but he chose to listen to the voice of his wife rather than the Voice of his God. The woman urged him to eat; she gave him some of the fruit, but she had no power to cause him to sin. The man was free. The choice was his own.

5) The Scriptures record the man's terrible choice: "He ate it." The man chose to obey the voice of a creature, rather than the Creator, who is blessed forever. The man exchanged the truth of God for a lie. He rebelled against God. The man fell. He too became a sinner.

That was the tragic fall of the first human beings. That was also the fall of the entire human race. The first man, Adam, was the head of the whole human race and in him all men became sinners. His fall brought down all humanity. His fall included every human being on earth, (except the one who would be born to save them.) It all happened so quickly, so easily. There were just five little steps from God to Satan, just five little steps from heaven to hell:

She saw.

      She took.

            She ate.

                She gave.

                     He ate.

Just five short steps and it was finished. The human beings had fallen. They had rebelled against God. Satan had accomplished his work. He had lost the war in heaven, but he had won the battle on earth. He was now its ruler. Satan had silenced the praises of God on this planet. The humans no longer worshipped the LORD in truth, nor glorified Him with joy. Their mouths poured forth lies and they hid from the presence of God. It was a great victory for Satan. He had silenced them with sin and soon God would silence them with death. God would surely keep his Word and their graves would not pour forth God's praises. Satan had conquered on earth. His lies had prevailed over God's Truth. He had won! Satan must have shrieked with evil laughter. There must have been a resounding roar from the hordes of hell as they revelled in their triumph. The host of heaven must have wept and God Himself must have grieved. And the man and the woman, what did they do? They tried to hide themselves, for now they felt shame and fear.

The teacher's guide for this lesson starts on page 446.

THE WORD FULFILLED

- Genesis 3:7
- John 3:3–8
- Romans 5:12–14
- Romans 6:18–23
- Ephesians 2:1–5

Satan's Word

Satan promised the first man and woman great gain if they ate the forbidden fruit:

1) *Satan promised that their eyes would be opened.* The Bible records that they ate the fruit and "then the eyes of both of them were opened." But what had their eyes been opened to see? What they saw was their own nakedness and wickedness. Before the fall they had been clothed in holiness, robed in righteousness—but when they sinned these glorious garments fell from them, as surely as your clothes fall to the floor—and they were left with nothing. Before the fall they needed no covering, for they were creatures who were good, very good. They had nothing to hide about themselves. They had no guilt; they knew no shame. But now their eyes had been opened by sin, which is the way Satan opens eyes, so now they experienced guilt and shame. Suddenly they felt exposed. Instantly they realized they were naked. That was what their eyes had been opened to see—their nakedness and wickedness—

because that was what they had become. Without holiness, they had been stripped bare! Because of their sin, they felt ashamed. They wanted to hide themselves and cover themselves, so they sewed fig leaves together to make clothes.

Oh, how Satan had deceived them! They had gained nothing. They had lost everything. If only they had believed God's Word and obeyed God's Law. We read in the Bible that "the commandment of the LORD is pure, enlightening the eyes" (Psalm 19:8). Satan's words had only brought them darkness and blindness. How Satan had lied!

2) *Satan promised that they would be like God.* He incited them to rebel against their Maker and their Master. He enticed them to assert their own wills against God's will. He tempted them to break God's Law, to submit no longer to it or to the One who had given it. Satan presented God's Law as a burden to be cast aside and God's Rule as a bondage to be overthrown. Satan promised them freedom. Were they now free? No, by yielding to Satan's suggestions, they had surrendered themselves and the world to his rule. They were now servants of Satan and slaves of sin. Had they become like God? No, they had become fearful, miserable creatures, filled with sin and covered with shame. Did they now act like the great and glorious God? No, the first "divine" act by these two new "gods" was a pitiful one indeed! They tried to hide themselves by sewing together some leaves and by cowering in the bushes.

Oh, how Satan had deceived them! They had not gained independence. They had gained nothing. They had lost everything. They had not become like God; they had become unlike God. If only they had believed God's Word and obeyed God's Law, then they would have continued in the happy freedom wherein they were created. They would have freely walked on this earth and ruled this world; they would have lived their lives and loved their God with abundant joy. It was by keeping God's commands that they had freedom. It was by obeying God's commands that they remained like God. The Bible says that when we trust in God's Word and hope in God's Law, when we follow His commands and delight in His decrees, then we have freedom (Psalm 119:41–48). It is God's Truth that sets us free (John 8:32). Satan's words had only brought them bondage. The man and the woman, who represented the entire human race, were prisoners of Satan. They were slaves of sin and servants of wickedness. They were no longer free to be holy. They were no longer able to be like God. How Satan had lied!

3) *Satan promised that they would know good and evil.* What he offered them was wisdom and knowledge, but "the fear of the LORD is the beginning of wisdom, and knowledge of the Holy One is understanding" (Proverbs 9:10). By not fearing the LORD, by disobeying God's Word, the man and woman had lost the very foundation of wisdom and knowledge. Before the fall they knew good, because they were good. Now they knew evil, because they were evil. God had created the human race and declared it to be "very good," but now that goodness was lost. Soon God would say about the human race: "There is no one righteous, not even one; there is no one who understands, no one who seeks God. All have turned away. They have together become worthless; there is no one who does good, not even one . . . there is no fear of God" (Romans 3:10–18).

Oh, how Satan had deceived them! The human race had not gained wisdom; they had lost it. Seeking to become wise, "they became fools . . . They exchanged the truth of God for a lie" (Romans 1:22, 25). "Their thinking became futile and their foolish hearts were darkened . . . Since they did not think it worthwhile to retain the knowledge of God, He gave them over to a depraved mind . . ." (Romans 1:21, 28). They had gained nothing. They had lost everything. If only they had believed God's Word and obeyed God's Law. We read in the Bible that it is the LORD's command, which gives wisdom unto men (Psalm 19:7). Did the first man and woman want to know something that was hidden from them? They should have asked God, for He alone is the one who reveals mysteries, for "wisdom and power belong to Him . . . He is the One who gives wisdom to the wise . . . He is the One who reveals deep and hidden things" (Daniel 2:20–22). Eating the forbidden fruit had not made them wise; it had made them fools. Oh, how Satan had lied!

Satan promised the man and the woman great gain, but his promises proved empty and brought them great harm. All Satan's words were fulfilled in a way which led to their destruction.

God's Word

God also promised something to the man and the woman if they ate the fruit which He commanded them not to eat. What had God promised them? Death! The LORD said, "You must not eat from the tree of the knowledge of good and evil, for in the day that you eat from it, you shall surely die." Did God keep His promise? Did God fulfill His Word?

On that evil day, after the man and woman ate the fruit, they were still alive, weren't they? The answer is yes—and no! It is true that they were still standing, but now the weight of sin was upon their shoulders, slowly crushing them. They had begun to die. It is true that they were still breathing, but now each breath was taken with "a certain terrifying expectation of judgement" (Hebrews 10:27), as they faced the wrath of the Almighty and the raging fire that consumes the enemies of God. They were still breathing, but each fearful breath was bringing them closer to their final gasp, for they had begun to die. It is true that they were still moving, but now everything they did was tainted with sin and every move they made was hindered by their bondage to the fear of death. They no longer moved freely or joyfully upon the earth. Their bodies were burdened with sin and their spirits were shackled with death. Although they were still moving, they had begun to die. *Death* had begun its reign.

"Through one man sin entered the world, and death through sin, and so death spread to all men, because all sinned" (Romans 5:12). Adam had set in motion the mechanism of death and like a huge harvester it would cut down everyone in its path, sparing no one, not even those first two humans from the beginning, who had been formed by God's own hands. And death would cut down all their children after them—millions and millions and millions of human beings! Death was like a great machine that was now running, churning, devouring. The first two humans had flicked the switch "on," but were they able to flick it "off"? No, only the hand of God could stop the advance of death once it had begun. The moment the man and woman sinned, was the same moment the wheels of death began to turn. Disobeying God's command—that is, *sinning*—was the fatal switch that set death in motion. Now human beings were dying creatures.

The fact that they did not instantly stop standing and breathing and moving, the fact that they were still living was God's grace! I'm sure Satan thought that they would die immediately. I'm sure he thought that by the end of that evil day, he would see the man and the woman turned to dust again.

But Satan did not know God's LOVE, nor did he understand God's mercy. The first man would live upon the earth for 930 years . . . by God's loving kindness. Then he would die . . . by God's righteous judgement.

The man and the woman lived for hundreds of years after they sinned, but they also died on the day that they ate the forbidden fruit. The Word of

God was fulfilled faithfully. What God promised came to pass perfectly. God said, "In the day that you eat from it, you shall surely die." God spoke the truth. On that day, in that instant when the first man and woman rebelled against God, they did die. They experienced immediate death. When they sinned against God they were separated from Him, and apart from God there is no life. Separation from God is death. On that day human beings became dead beings, spiritually dead. When little babies would be born upon the earth, they would be born dead; they would be born separated from the life of God. All human beings (except for one) would be born dead in their transgressions and sins. They would have to be reborn or born again or born of the Spirit, if they were to have life. The human beings God had created in the beginning, Satan had successfully destroyed. A new creation was necessary. A new man was in order.

On that dreadful day when sin entered the world, death followed immediately. The first humans became dead and dying creatures. They experienced instant death. They also experienced a long slow death, a drawn-out dying that took hundreds of years. Just as God had promised, they received death as the payment for their sin. The world, which once had been filled with life, was now filled with death. The man and the woman experienced death that day; death awaited them at the end of their years; and, unless God intervened, death lay beyond the end . . . forever.

The Bible speaks of three kinds of death:

1. *SPIRITUAL DEATH*—which is separation from God. Unless God rescues us from this, we never know life all the days we spend upon the earth. We are dead, even though we are alive.

2. *PHYSICAL DEATH*—which is the separation of body and soul, when a person's heart stops beating, his lungs stop breathing, his brain stops thinking, his limbs stop moving, etc. This is when a person's soul leaves his body, and the body returns to dust again.

3. *ETERNAL DEATH*—which is separation from God forever. It is called the second death. It is the eternal imprisonment of the soul in hell.

God said, "In the day that you eat from it, you shall surely die." Satan said, "You shall surely not die." God's Word proved true, but it seems that Satan won. His lies brought death to the world. The human beings, whom

God loved, had been destroyed. The earth would swallow them and silence them in their graves. The dust of death would not sing the praises of God. Oh evil day, oh tragic fall, in which God's enemy seemed to triumph!

But, thanks be to God, *death* was not the final word! From before the beginning, from before the foundation of the world, God had a plan. A mere angel could not stop the plan of God. From the beginning, it was the LORD's good pleasure and great purpose to send His beloved Son to destroy the works of the devil:

1) Satan promised the first man and woman that their eyes would be opened, but he brought darkness and blindness to the world. Jesus said, "I have come into the world as a light, so that no one who believes in me should stay in darkness" (John 12:46). The Bible says that Satan, "the god of this age, has blinded the minds of unbelievers, so that they cannot see the light of the gospel of the glory of Christ, who is the image of God" (II Corinthians 4:4). This gospel would be preached to the whole world "to open their eyes and turn them from darkness to light, and from the power of Satan to God, so that they might receive forgiveness of sins and a place among those who are sanctified by faith . . ." (Acts 26:18) — faith in the Saviour sent from God.

2. Satan promised the first man and woman freedom; he promised that they would be like God, but he brought them into the bondage of sin. Jesus was sent "to proclaim freedom for the captives" (Isaiah 61:1). Jesus said, "I tell you the truth, everyone who sins is a slave to sin . . . but, if the Son sets you free, you will be free indeed" (John 8:34, 36). Jesus was the One sent to save his people from their sins. Through faith in Christ "you have been set free from sin and have become slaves to righteousness . . . When you were slaves to sin, you were free from the control of righteousness. What benefit did you reap at that time from the things you are now ashamed of? Those things result in death! But now that you have been set free from sin and have become slaves to God, the benefit you reap leads to holiness, and the result is eternal life. For the wages of sin is death, but the gift of God is eternal life in Christ Jesus our Lord" (Romans 6:18–23). The Bible says: "It is for freedom that Christ has set us free" (Galatians 5:1).

3. Satan promised the man and woman knowledge, the knowledge of good and evil, but the truth of God was lost, suppressed by their wickedness.

What Satan brought to mankind was the foolish and futile thinking that leads to depravity and death. But there was One coming, about whom it was prophesied that "the Spirit of the LORD will rest on Him—the Spirit of wisdom and understanding, the Spirit of Counsel and of power, the Spirit of knowledge and of the fear of the LORD—and He will delight in the fear of the LORD" (Isaiah 11:2, 3). It was Jesus, who would restore to the world the knowledge of God. To all who believed, He gave that same "Spirit of wisdom and revelation" (Ephesians 1:17)—that we might know God better. By faith we must seek "the full riches of complete understanding, in order that we may know the mystery of God, namely, Christ, in whom are hidden all the treasures of wisdom and knowledge" (Colossians 2:2, 3). The Son of God was sent from heaven to destroy the works of the devil. The knowledge lost would be restored; one day the knowledge of God would cover the earth—a mighty victory through Jesus Christ our Lord!

Sin and death were the works of the devil that Christ came to destroy. Jesus said, "I have come that you might have life—and life abundantly" (John 10:10). The Bible says: "God so loved the world that He gave his one and only Son, that whoever believes in Him shall not perish, but have eternal life" (John 3:16). "The wages of sin is death, but the gift of God is eternal life in Christ Jesus our Lord" (Romans 6:23). God's plan of salvation from the beginning, from before the foundation of the world, was to rescue us from the dominion of darkness and bring us into the kingdom of His beloved Son, in whom is redemption, the forgiveness of sins. This mighty rescue from sin would eternally bring glory to God. Death would be swallowed up in victory, to the praise of God's glorious grace!

But on that evil day, when the man and woman were hiding in the garden sewing fig leaves together to cover their nakedness and wickedness, they knew nothing of this Saviour, for He had not yet been promised to them. They knew nothing of God's greatest gift to the world, for He had not yet been given to them. They knew only of their shame and sin as they awaited God's judgement. They did not yet have hope in the Son of God for eternal life. They did not yet have hope in this promise, for God had not yet revealed it to them. They had no knowledge of the victory of Christ. They knew only defeat and despair. They were pitiful, naked creatures, lost and without hope in the world. They did not have the comfort in their sin, which we have in Christ—that by faith in the Son of God, we are clothed once again in holiness, this time in the perfect and eternal righteousness of our

Lord Jesus Christ. They could not yet sing the words, which the people of God now sing:

> *I delight greatly in the* LORD;
> *my soul rejoices in my God. For He has clothed*
>   *me with garments of salvation*
> *and arrayed me in a robe of righteousness.*
>
>   Isaiah 61:10

The teacher's guide for this lesson starts on page 448.

DIVISION, DIVISION, DIVISION, DIVISION

- Genesis 3:8–19
- Isaiah 59:2, 12, 13
- Colossians 1:21

I n the beginning God created the heavens and the earth. At the end of the sixth day, when His work was finished, God saw all that He had made, and it was "very good." Each thing by itself was good and everything together was good. There was a beautiful harmony in the world at that time. There was peace between God and man. The LORD saw the first two human beings and He was well pleased with them. God loved the man and the woman, and they loved God. Their greatest delight was to be in the presence of the LORD. This was very good. Also, the man and the woman loved one another. It was a great joy for them to be together. This too was very good. The man and the woman also loved their world and their work. The earth was a blessing for them, bringing forth all kinds of good things—and the man and the woman were a blessing for the earth as they joyfully tended it with love and care. This was also very good. At that time, during those days in the beginning, there was peace on earth. This peace was everywhere, even in the hearts of the first two human beings.

Then the woman and the man sinned—and there was no longer peace:

1. There Was No Longer Peace Between Man And God

There was division. The first two human beings had sided with God's enemy, that evil angel of old, Satan. They listened to the lies of the serpent; they disobeyed the Word of the LORD. Their sins made a separation between them and their God. Their sins were nothing less than rebellion and treachery against the LORD. They had not remained loyal to the God who had loved them and blessed them. Without a cause, they had become God's enemies. They no longer considered God their friend and God no longer considered them friends. That special relationship between God and man was broken. Through sin, Satan had brought about division. This separation between man and God is sometimes called "the great divorce."

Can we see evidence of this division in the world around us? Yes. God seems to be far, far, far away from people and their problems. He no longer walks with them or talks with them, the way He once did in the Garden of Eden. Because people cannot see God's face or hear God's voice, they say that God does not exist. If they did see Him and hear Him, they would still hate Him. There are millions of people in the world today who ignore God or despise God. Millions of people worship gods of their own imagination. Surely these vast numbers of people are separated from the LORD. They have absolutely no relationship with Him. It was broken long, long ago in the Garden of Eden by the first two people.

The Bible records that this separation took place immediately, on the very day that the man and woman sinned. When the man and his wife heard the sound of the LORD God as He was walking in the garden in the cool of the day, they did not run to meet their friend, as they had done on earlier, happier days. No, they did not look forward to walking and talking with God as they once had in that blessed beginning. Now they were afraid to be with God. Now they dreaded meeting Him. Instead of hurrying into the LORD's presence, they hurried to hide from Him. The Bible says they hid from the LORD God among the trees of the garden. Of course, God knew where they were hiding. He also knew why they were hiding, but God had a few questions that He wanted them to answer. He called to the man, "Where are you?" Adam answered, "I heard You in the garden and I was afraid . . ." Fear! It was a new feeling for the man. The man continued speaking, "I was afraid, because I was naked; so I hid." Nakedness! That was not something new, for the man had always been naked. In fact, the man was not naked now. He was wearing clothes made from fig leaves. However, in the presence of God he still felt naked. Nakedness was a new feeling. When God questioned Adam, he did not bare his soul to God. He was still trying to hide. He did not tell God why he felt afraid and naked. He did not tell God what he had done; he did not confess his sin. So the LORD continued to question him, asking, "Who told you that you were naked?" There was no answer. God then asked, "Have you eaten from the tree that I commanded you not to eat from?" The man quickly shifted the blame from himself. He blamed the woman (and God) for his sin. He said, "The woman that You put here with me—she gave me some of the fruit . . ." Adam did not admit that it was his fault, but finally he did say, " . . . and I ate it."

It was now the woman's turn to be questioned. God said to her, "What is this you have done?" Her excuse was the serpent. She said, "The serpent deceived me, and I ate." We can see the effects of sin from the very beginning, when it first entered into the lives of human beings. Their relationship to God had changed. They no longer trusted God. They were afraid of Him. They tried to hide from Him. They did not openly and honestly confess their sins. They did not quickly and humbly ask for pardon. Their hearts were already hardened by sin. Already they were trying to avoid God and cover sin. And God's relationship to them had also changed. No longer was God pleased with these creatures upon whom He had bestowed His great LOVE. No longer did He delight in them. God was grieved by them. God was angry with them. These human beings no longer stood in His grace and favour; now they stood in His wrath and judgement. The LORD, who had given the man and the woman every good thing, who had given them gracious gift upon gracious gift and blessing upon blessing, now gave them something else. To the woman God said, " . . . with pain/sorrow/toil you will give birth to children." Bringing children into the world, which should have been her greatest joy, would now become very difficult for the woman. God also said to her, "Your desire will be for your husband, but he will rule over you." Marriage, which should have been a great comfort and delight to her, would also become very difficult. To the man God said, "Cursed is the ground because of you; with pain/sorrow/toil you will eat of it all the days of your life. It will produce thorns and thistles for you . . . By the sweat of your brow you will eat your food until you return to the ground, since from it you were taken. For dust you are and to dust you will return." The man's work would become very difficult for him too. Before they had sinned, God had blessed their life and work by saying, "Be fruitful and multiply; fill the earth and subdue it." But now that work would be filled with drops of sweat, tears of grief, cries of pain. Their life and their work would be very hard, and then they would die. God Himself, the LORD of LOVE, was the judge who pronounced their sentence. For the first man it was 930 years of hard labour and then death.

Man would hate God because of this severe sentence upon his sin. He would blame God (not himself) for the hardness of his life and the sureness of his death. He would hate God because of the toil and grief and pain in the world. Satan had brought about the division he desired. There was no longer peace between man and God.

2. There Was No Longer Peace Between People

There was division. At this time there were only two people in the whole world, only two in the entire universe. They were in the deepest and closest relationship possible for two human beings. They were a married couple, in which the two had become one—and yet they were divided. There were only two people in existence, who were united in marriage, but even they were separated by sin!

Can we see evidence of this division between people in the world around us? Yes, it is everywhere. Everywhere people are hating each other and fighting each other. Anywhere there are people you will find them harming each other; you will find them lying and stealing and killing. This very day there are wars happening in the world, where people are slaughtering other people. Hundreds and thousands and millions of people are killed in the wars on earth. But you do not have to travel to a war-torn country or a crime-filled city to see the division between people. Walk into any house; examine any family, and you will find brothers and sisters quarrelling or fathers and mothers fighting. It is a sad truth that even families are divided. Sometimes the strife is so severe that the husband and wife are separated, then divorced, and the family is torn apart. This tragic division between people began very long ago in the Garden of Eden by the first two people.

The Bible records that the sin of the first man and woman immediately caused a separation between them. Before the fall, we read in the Scriptures that "the man and his wife were both naked and they felt no shame" (Genesis 2:25). Their relationship was open and honest, in which they hid nothing about themselves. They communicated freely; they loved perfectly. However, after they sinned, their eyes were opened and they realized they were naked, so they sewed fig leaves together and made clothes for themselves. At that moment the man and the woman began to hide from each other. They could no longer stand before one another unashamed. Sin had so quickly caused such a deep division in their once happy union. Now the man could no longer trust the woman. Her love for him had failed. She had not helped him, but harmed him. Her words had become Satan's words, tempting him and enticing him to sin. And the woman could no longer trust the man. His love had also failed. Before God he did not try to plead her case or cover her sin; he did not try to protect her or intercede for her, but rather, he exposed her and condemned her. His words had become Satan's words, blaming her and accusing her before God. The trust was gone. The love was marred. Their perfect partnership, their beautiful relationship, was destroyed by sin. Marriage would remain upon the earth, but only fleeting shadows of its blessedness would appear. God said that now the woman would long to be loved by her husband, but he would rule over her. Or perhaps she would try to rule over her husband and there would result a strangely intimate struggle for power. Marriage would be difficult. It would often become a battle. So great was the division that sin brought between people, that even between a husband and wife there would not be peace. The separation caused by sin would effect every human relationship upon the earth, even between two people who had become one.

3. There Was No Longer Peace Between Man and His World

There was division. Man was no longer one with nature. He was no longer peacefully and joyfully "at home" in his environment. No, that happy harmony had been destroyed by sin. Now the earth was at war with him and it had become a dangerous place for him to be. His dominion over the earth would be with great difficulty and his work in the world would be filled with woe. The whole creation would be groaning under the curse of sin, and man also would be groaning and sweating and weeping as he struggled just to stay alive for a few years. At the end the earth would swallow him. At death the grave would devour him.

Can we see evidence of this war between man and his world? Yes, we encounter it every day. When we have weeds in our garden or burrs in our hair, when nettles sting our hands or thorns scratch our legs, when poison ivy blisters our skin or plant pollens itch our eyes and block our noses—all these little annoyances remind us that the earth is cursed because of man's sin. When a squirrel runs from us or a dog growls at us or a horse kicks us— they are reminders that the friendship between man and the animals was also broken in the beginning because of man's sin. Even a simple sunburn shows us that on a lovely summer day we have to be careful in this world. Our whole environment is often against us. The plants, the animals and the elements are often our enemies. We could be in the most beautiful place on the earth, perhaps camping in the woods by a lake, but we would not find perfect peace there (or anywhere) in nature. Swarms of mosquitoes would certainly bother us; bees could sting us or snakes bite us; wolves might frighten us or a bear attack us. Unless we brought our own supplies, food would be scarce, starvation a threat; the water could also make us sick. In addition, the wind and the rain, the cold and the snow, would all threaten to destroy us. Do you need more evidence that there is a war between man and his world? Pick up a newspaper and read about all the natural disasters on our globe: floods, famines, droughts, fires, plagues, earthquakes, blizzards, hurricanes, tornadoes, volcanoes! In all these things people are killed— sometimes by the thousands. The earth often destroys man and man often destroys the earth. Man pollutes earth's water and contaminates the air; he levels earth's forests and slaughters its animals. The tragedies of this war are all around us. It has been raging for a very long time, for thousands of years, from the time when sin entered the world through the first man.

The Bible records that when the man and woman sinned they sought some sort of refuge in the earth. They sewed coverings for themselves from leaves and they hid from God among the trees. But the plants of the earth were not adequate to cover their sin or hide them from God. The earth could not provide that kind of shelter for the man and woman. In fact, God now cursed the ground because of the man's sin. "Cursed is the ground because of you," said God to the man. "Through pain/toil/grief you will eat of it all the days of your life. It will produce thorns and thistles for you and you will eat the plants of the field. By the sweat of your brow you will eat your food . . ." No longer would the plants of the earth yield their fruits freely for the man. Now he would have to work hard for his food, ploughing and sowing and reaping, if he wanted enough to eat. No longer would his life be happy and easy—and at the end of his hard labour God said, "You will return to the ground, since from it you were taken; for dust you are and to dust you will return."

4. There Was No Longer Peace Between Man and Himself

There was division. He no longer had peace within himself. His mind was confused; his heart was troubled; his soul was distressed. Man would experience a war within himself, as if he were divided against himself. A kind of schizophrenia (that is, a split self) became the common condition of man throughout his days. Then this uneasy relationship to himself would finally culminate in death, the final division of his being. Death would be the ultimate separation of his self, when his body and soul would be torn asunder, one left to rot in the earth and the other to receive its eternal reward.

Even though you are children, I am sure you have already experienced this sense of separation in yourselves. Have you ever felt "torn apart" inside? Have you ever felt confused or troubled or distressed? To feel "at peace" with oneself is perhaps easier for a child than an adult. Perhaps it isn't.

This inner division was also a result of sin. Man's soul was rent in the very moment of his disobedience. The Bible records that as soon as the man tasted the forbidden fruit, he realized he was naked. The man was ashamed of his own self; he was ashamed of his own body. Never before had he felt this way about himself. At best, he was embarrassed, feeling a strange awkwardness in himself about who he was. At worst, he now utterly despised himself. This too was the result of his sin.

The teacher's guide for this lesson starts on page 450.

HOPE

It seems that Satan won the battle on earth. "OPERA-TION SEPARATION" was successful. Satan had divided, and so he had conquered. Sin had separated the man from his God and now death would reign upon the earth. Through one man sin and death had entered this world. God had created a world of peace, beauty and harmony, a world which was filled with love and laughter and the abundance of LIFE. But Satan was now the prince of this world and he brought to it a new "order" of things—the pain of sin, the chaos of evil, the dust of DEATH. In Genesis 1, we read of blessing. Again and again we read concerning God's creation: "It was good . . . it was good . . . it was good." Everything that God gave was "very good." But in Genesis 3 the serpent appears, leaving behind him a trail of words describing misery. Now, "cursed is the ground!" Now, "thorns and thistles!" Now we read of fear and shame. Now the words, echoing through the generations of man: "I was afraid . . . I was afraid . . . I was afraid." Now, "toil, grief, pain." Now the sweat and the tears and the blood of all mankind, soaking into the earth. Now, the grave. Now, dust.

God's Word to man was: "Dust you are and to dust you will return." Dust to dust. Now, death.

Was there no hope for man? What about the other tree, the tree of life, which was also in the middle of the garden? Perhaps the man and woman could escape death if they ate the fruit from this tree? No, for the LORD God said that the man "must not be allowed to reach out his hand and take also from the tree of life and eat, and live forever." So the LORD God banished the man from the Garden of Eden. God drove him out. God forced him into the world to work. Afterwards, God placed angels in front of the garden and a flaming sword flashing back and forth to guard the way to the tree of life. No man or woman would ever be able to find their way back to the Garden of Eden. It was gone from the world of men. It was as invisible as the angels who guarded it. Nor could anyone ever find that tree of life to steal its fruit. It was no longer on the earth. Man could not grasp eternal life for himself. It was beyond his reach. Man had already made his choice. He had not chosen life; he had chosen death. He had eaten the fruit connected with God's promise, "You will surely die."

Was there no hope then for man? Yes, there was. God! Although man had made himself an enemy to God, his only hope and his only help were still in God. Satan's plan had been to destroy the man and woman by dividing them from God. This he had done. Their sins had surely separated them from God. But Satan's plan would ultimately fail, because Satan did not understand the LOVE of God. Satan underestimated the greatness of God's grace, the measure of God's mercy, the fullness of God's forgiveness. Satan did not understand that God would save His people from their sins. This LOVE of God was demonstrated towards the man and woman in the Garden of Eden, even when the forbidden fruit was fresh upon their lips. These are the ways that God showed His LOVE for the man and woman:

1) God called to the man when he was hiding. God is the Good Shepherd, who searches for His lost sheep. God did not allow the man to hide, but drew him out. The man was lost in his sin, but God found him. God loved him.

2) God did not curse the man or the woman. He punished them, but He did not curse them. Their labours were made difficult. The ground was cursed because of the man, but they themselves were not cursed. The serpent was cursed. The LORD God said to the serpent, "Because you have done

this, cursed are you above all the livestock and all the wild animals! You will crawl on your belly and you will eat dust all the days of your life. And I will put enmity between you and the woman, and between your seed and hers; he will crush your head, and you will strike his heel." Out of all the creatures on earth, the snake would now be cursed, forced to slither along the ground without legs. Human beings would hate the snake above all other creatures, hunting it and killing it with a vengeance. The snake could only strike at a person's heel, but it could have its head crushed by them. Thus the snake was cursed. At the same time Satan, "that serpent of old," was also cursed. But the man and the woman were not cursed. God still loved them.

3) God placed a very great honour upon the man and woman, even after their fall into sin. The LORD promised that they would be involved in the destruction of Satan. God would be pleased to use human beings, the humble of the earth, to fight against this evil angel. The war on earth had not ended. It had just begun! Satan had not eliminated the human race. By God's grace the woman would have children and by God's grace these children of hers would be enlisted into the LORD's great army to fight against Satan here on earth. The LORD said to Satan, "I will put enmity between you and the woman, and between your children and hers." Satan had used the woman to bring forth destruction, but God would use her to bring forth salvation. Satan's triumph over the man and woman was not complete, because one day they would triumph over him. They would crush the serpent; God would trample Satan under their feet. The LORD was not finished with mankind. God still had a great work for them to do. God still loved them.

4) God gave the man and the woman a very great gift that day. It was a promise. God promised that the seed of the woman would crush the head of the serpent. One day a child would be born; one day a son would be given, who would utterly defeat Satan. God repeated this great promise again and again throughout the history of man. Again and again God promised that a Saviour would be sent to destroy the works of the devil. But here in the garden, on the very day they sinned was the first time that God spoke to the man and the woman about His Plan and His Promise to save them. Although they had suffered a terrible defeat, God had in store for them a great victory. The seed of the woman, the Son of Man, was coming to save them! This was God's Word; this was God's Promise; this was God's Plan, from the beginning, because God loved the man and the woman.

5) "The LORD disciplines those He loves" (Hebrews 12:6). God punished the first two people for their sin. Rebellion against God was a serious offence. Treason against the LORD was a capital crime. Will not the judge of all the earth do right? God justly sentenced these traitors with a hard life and a sure death. However, God was merciful in this punishment. He did not sentence them to an immediate or eternal death. No, even in this punishment God sought to benefit these enemies. The Bible says that "God disciplines us for our good, that we may share in his holiness" (Hebrews 12:10). The end God had in mind for human beings was not their destruction, but their glorification. God disciplines us for our good, and for His everlasting praise! This discipline, of course, would not be pleasant for them, but painful—a pain designed to drive them back to God. Perhaps as the man and woman faced the difficulty of their discipline, they would turn to God for help. Perhaps they would hope in God for rest. Perhaps they would trust in God for life. He still loved them, even while they were enemies deserving His judgement.

6) The Bible records that the LORD God made garments of skin for Adam and his wife and clothed them. What a kind, loving and merciful God! He did not send them naked from the garden; He did not send them naked into the world. The clothes they had made for themselves—fig leaves stitched together—were not enough. So God clothed them. God provided the covering they needed. The Bible does not tell us what kind of animal skins God used. What do you think? A zebra or giraffe or leopard had beautiful skins that would have made beautiful clothes. A mink or a mole or a rabbit would have made very soft clothes. The tough leather of a rhinoceros or the hard scales of a pangolin or the sharp quills of a porcupine would have provided the best armour for the man and woman. But I think the LORD made them sheep-skin clothing, not because of the way these woolly clothes looked or felt or protected, but because of what it would teach them: God would provide a lamb to be a covering for sin.

On that dreadful day, the day when Adam and his wife disobeyed God, there was a physical death in the Garden of Eden. It was not the death of the man or the woman, for they continued to live—but there was a death. One of earth's beautiful creatures died. It stopped breathing; it stopped moving. Its blood was poured out. Its blood was shed on behalf of the only two people in the world. A lamb was killed in order to cover their sin. The man and the woman deserved to die on that day, but it was a lamb that took their place. Its death was a substitute for their death. The death of that lamb was the first faint shadow pointing to what God would do one day far in the future. One day another Lamb would be sacrificed to provide a covering for man's sin. "Herein is LOVE: not that we loved God, but that He loved us, and sent His Son as an atoning sacrifice for our sins" (I John 4:10). Behold Jesus! Behold the Lamb of God, who takes away the sin of the world! That Lamb was slain from the foundation of the world. It was God's plan of salvation from the beginning. Even on that first day of sin so long ago, God began to show mankind just how much He loved them . . . and what it would cost to save them! "This is how God showed His LOVE to us: He sent his one and only Son into the world that we might live through Him" (I John 4:9). Yes, God still loved the man and woman that day, more than they could ever understand.

7) God guarded the tree of life from man, and in so doing, God guarded man from himself. God protected man from eternal evil. Imagine how awful it would be if human beings, who were now evil beings, lived forever! God, in His infinite wisdom and mercy, would not allow such an atrocity to occur. There was an end to a man's wickedness. He would not have to endure himself forever. Thankfully, eternal life could not be grasped by anyone; it could only be granted by God, and with it God graciously would give holiness, a holiness from heaven. This righteousness would be by faith, from beginning to end. Man could not achieve this righteousness, any more than he could cover his own sin or grasp eternal life. It was God's work completely. Man's only hope was in God. So, God's LOVE for His creatures was seen even in this: that the tree of life disappeared from the earth. However, the hope of eternal life had not vanished. It was in God, the God of LOVE, the God who still loved His people.

One day God's own Son would say to mankind: "To him who overcomes, I will give the right to eat from the tree of life, which is in the paradise of God" (Revelation 2:7). How could a person possibly overcome that great dragon called the devil? How could a person possibly overcome that ancient serpent called Satan, and so eat from the tree of life? If the first man and woman, who were perfect, could not stand against him, how could any other person ever do so now—and not only resist him, but also overcome him? The Bible gives this answer: "by the blood of the lamb" (Revelation

12:11). That Lamb of God was Jesus Christ, Who poured out his precious blood on the cross to save us from sin and death and the power of Satan. To overcome Satan and to eat from the tree of life, you must have faith in Jesus and His death on the cross. You must accept the covering for sin which God has provided for you. That covering for sin is the blood of His own dear Son. Do you believe this?

In many ways God showed the man and woman that He still loved them. On that most dreadful day, the day when the man and the woman disobeyed God, He gave them a very great gift. God gave them hope. God gave them His Word and His Promise that a Child would be born to the woman—a Saviour, who would crush the serpent, Satan. God showed them that a Lamb would be slain, who would cover their sin. On that day of death, God gave them the most precious gift of all: God gave them the hope of life in Christ Jesus our Lord.

Did the man and the woman take that hope into their hearts? Did they trust the Word of God? Did they believe the Promise of God? I think they did for two reasons:

1) Adam did something that showed he had faith. He gave his wife a new name. Once before he had called her "woman." Now he named her Eve. That name meant "LIFE." He could have named her "DEATH," as a constant reminder of what she had done and what was before them, but Adam named her after the hope that was in his heart, the hope that God had given them. Adam named her Eve/Life, because she would become the mother of all the living. From her would come the whole human race and from her also would come the Living One, who would proclaim to the world: "I am the resurrection and the life. He who believes in Me will live, even though he dies" (John 11:25).

2) Adam and Eve accepted the protection provided by God. They allowed themselves to be clothed by God. They did not reject the covering that God provided for them. They did not insist upon the coverings they had made for themselves. No, they knew they needed God's help.

Then Adam and Eve were expelled from the garden by God. As Adam set out into the world, a world of darkness and death, he had Eve/Life by his side, and in his heart he had hope in the Child who would come forth from her. Adam and Eve set out into a cursed world, a world of toil and grief and pain, but God sent them forth with a word of hope. A Child was coming to save them from sin and death. They were cast into the darkness with a glimmer of hope, which was their glimpse of the Saviour. From so far away they could see but a faint light of His coming, yet it was enough to give them the encouragement to endure. Also, Adam and Eve did not go naked into the world; they went forth clothed by God.

Satan was successful in separating the man and woman from God through their sin, but he did not know that God would bring them back to Himself through a Saviour, Jesus Christ. "And who shall separate us from the love of Christ? Shall trouble or hardship or persecution or famine or nakedness or danger or sword?" All these things the man and woman and all their children after them would face. Could these things separate them from the love of Christ? No, in all these things they would be more than survivors. "In all these things we are more than conquerors through Him who loved us. For I am convinced that neither death nor life, neither angels nor demons, neither the present nor the future, nor any powers, neither height nor depth, nor anything else in all creation, will be able to separate us from the love of God that is in Christ Jesus our Lord" (Roman 8:35–39). Satan could not win because, although he could triumph over the love of man, he could not triumph over the LOVE of God.

> *Sing to the LORD a new song,*
> *for He has done marvellous things;*
> *His right hand and His holy arm*
> *have got for Him the victory.*
> *The LORD has made known His salvation*
> *and revealed His righteousness to the nations.*
> *He has remembered His LOVE and His faithfulness . . .*
> *All the ends of the earth have seen*
> *the salvation of our God.*
> *Shout for joy to the LORD, all the earth.*
>
> *Psalm 98:1–4*

Yes, the victory belonged to God! Satan did not win. Sin and death did not triumph. "Death has been swallowed up in victory . . . Thanks be to God! He gives us the victory through our Lord Jesus Christ" (I Corinthians 15:57).

The teacher's guide for this lesson starts on page 452.

THE STAND

- Matthew 3:16–4:11
- Mark 1:9–13
- Luke 3:21, 22; 4:1–13
- Romans 5:12–21
- 1 Corinthians 15:45–58

The Bible records for us the terrible fall of the first man. We read how Adam was tempted and fell into sin. We also read that through the disobedience of this first man, sin and death then spread to the whole human race. But there is another Adam in the Bible. Do you know who He is? He is called the last Adam. We read in the Bible how this second man was also tempted by that ancient serpent, Satan—yet this last Adam stood firm. He did not fall. He did not sin. The Bible records for us the wonderful stand of this second man. Through his obedience there was hope for the human race, hope for righteousness and life!

The first man, Adam, was from the earth; this second man, the last Adam, was from heaven. Because God so loved the world, He sent His one and only Son from heaven. God the Son, (who was with God before the creation of the world and who was God from all eternity,)—He became a man, a real man, and lived on the earth among us. He was a real person living in a real place. His name was Jesus. His country was Israel. He was born as a baby in Bethlehem; He grew as a child in Nazareth;

He was baptized as a man in the Jordan River like many other people. But when this man Jesus was coming out of the water, some very extraordinary events occurred, which happened to no other people; no, not to one other person on the face of the earth. After the baptism of Jesus, while He was praying,

1. Heaven was opened.
2. The Holy Spirit of God descended on Him in bodily form like a dove.
3. A voice came from heaven saying: "You are my Son, whom I love; with You I am well pleased."

Long ago in the Garden of Eden, God had looked upon the first man, Adam, and was pleased with him also, but that pleasure soon changed to anger because of the first man's sin. All the sons of Adam, all the men born into the world after him, were also corrupted with sin . . . except for this man, because He was not just a son of man; He was also the Son of God! The LORD said, "This is my Son, whom I love; with Him I am well pleased." Although Satan had tempted this man for many years, He had not sinned. Thus God was pleased with Him. But now was the time for this second man to be severely tested. Now was the time for Satan's all-out attack upon Jesus. Would He, the last Adam, stand or fall?

Immediately after the Divine declaration: "You are my Son, whom I love; with You I am well pleased"—immediately after these words, Jesus was sent by the Spirit into the desert, where he was tempted by the devil for forty days and forty nights. There were no people in that lonely region. There were only wild animals and wicked angels roaming back and forth, prowling through the desert and the darkness, looking for prey to tear into pieces. In this wilderness, where jackals howled and demons shrieked, Jesus faced Satan . . . alone. It was an epic battle, in which Christ and Satan fought each other one-to-one in single combat. During this time Jesus ate nothing. No doubt, He was watching and fasting and praying that He would not fall into temptation, that He would not fall. At the end of the forty days of fasting, Jesus was hungry. Now was the right time for the serpent to strike. It was the moment for which Satan was waiting. The man Jesus was experiencing extreme hunger. He was completely weakened from lack of food. Now was the right time for Satan to strike, to shoot his worst fiery arrows . . . one . . . then another . . . then another.

The First Temptation

The tempter came to Jesus and said: "If you are the Son of God, tell these stones to become bread." Jesus was hungry, so hungry that He was in danger of dying. There was no food in this wilderness. Would it be wrong for Him to command the stones to become loaves of bread? The Son of God was able to perform such a miracle. Very soon in his ministry He would change water into wine, so why not now change stones into bread? Delicious bread! Was it wrong? Was it breaking one of God's commandments? This was a tricky temptation. How crafty was the serpent! How subtle was this Satan! The first Adam had also been tempted with food. The first Adam had stood in the height of his strength, knowing not hunger; he stood in a garden full of good fruit and full of God's grace—yet he had been lured into sin with a piece of food, which had clearly been forbidden by God. So quickly, so easily, the first Adam fell. Could the second Adam stand? This second man was weak from hunger in a wilderness without food. The visible evidences of God's goodness were gone. He was starving in a wasteland, experiencing the pain of the curse. He had no clear commandment to not do this, no Word from God to help Him in this temptation. Or did He? Jesus knew the Scriptures. He knew the words that Moses had written in the wilderness to the Israelites: "Remember how the LORD your God led you all the way in the desert these forty years, to humble you and to test you, in order to know what was in your heart, whether or not you would keep His commands. He humbled you, causing you to hunger and then feeding you with manna . . . to teach you that man does not live on bread alone, but on every Word that comes from the mouth of the LORD" (Deuteronomy 8:2, 3). Jesus also knew the Psalms. All his life He had sung these songs from the Scriptures. They were in his heart from his earliest days. He knew how the Israelites had rebelled against God in the desert, not trusting that God could provide food for them. The words in God's song book were sobering, strengthening, words: "They continued to sin against Him, rebelling in the desert against the Most High. They wilfully put God to the test by demanding the food that they craved. They spoke against God saying, 'Can God spread a table in the desert . . . Can He also provide food? Can He give bread too? Can He supply meat for His people?' When the LORD heard them He was very angry . . . *for they did not believe in God or trust in His deliverance.* Yet God gave a command to the skies above and opened the doors of the heavens; He rained down manna for the people to eat, and gave them the grain of heaven. Men ate the bread of angels; He sent them all the food they could eat" (Psalm 78:17–25). Did Jesus trust in his heavenly Father? Yes, He did! Jesus trusted that God in heaven would provide food for Him. Jesus believed in God's deliverance. If Jesus commanded the stones to become bread, it would be sin. It would be an act of unbelief. It would be a sign of distrust in God. The LORD loved Him. Jesus had faith in that LOVE. Besides, Satan was not only tempting Jesus; he was taunting Him: "If you are the Son of God, prove it!" Jesus did not have to prove it to Himself. He had God's Word, spoken to Him from heaven: "You are my Son, whom I love . . ." God's Word was sufficient for Jesus. God said it; He believed it. He did not have to prove that He was the Son of God to Himself and He certainly did not have to prove it to Satan, except by resisting all his temptations. No, although Jesus was starving, He would not listen to Satan. Although He was near death, He would not command the stones to become bread. He would trust in God to deliver Him. He would believe in God's Word. He would live by God's Word. The righteous shall live by faith. So, when the devil said to him, "If you are the Son of God, tell these stones to become bread," Jesus answered, "It is written: 'Man does not live on bread alone, but on every Word that comes from the mouth of God.' "

Oh, that the first Adam had answered thus! But praise be to God, that the second Adam did! He defeated Satan with these words. With the Sword of the Spirit, with the Word of God, Jesus conquered his opponent in the first major battle. Later in his ministry, Jesus said, "My food is to do the will of Him who sent Me and to finish His work" (John 4, 34). What was God's will? It was to crush the serpent. What was God's work? It was to destroy the works of the devil. Satan tempted Jesus with food, not knowing that Jesus' "food" (that is, the thing by which He lived,) was to obey the Father and to defeat the devil. In this first attempt, Satan lost. Jesus did not yield to the temptation. The son of man did not sin; the Son of God could not sin. The second Adam stood his ground. He took his stand for God and He took his stand for us.

The Second Temptation

Jesus trusted God. By lifting that great shield of faith, He had quenched the first fiery arrow of the Evil One. But oh, how subtle was the serpent! Satan would now use that faith to form a new temptation. He would use this man's trust in God to bring about his fall. Jesus had repulsed Satan's attack with Scripture. He had resisted Satan with the Sword of the Spirit, which is the Word of God. But oh, how cunning was this demon! Satan himself would now use God's Word to tempt the second man. With that holy weapon, the Sword of the Spirit, Satan would strike against the Son of God. Satan would use God's own Word against God's own Son. He would try to lure this last Adam to his death by the very Words of the God in whom He placed His trust.

This time it was not the Spirit, but the devil, who chose the place of battle. The Spirit had led Jesus into the desert, but now the devil took Jesus to the very heart of Israel, to the holy city, Jerusalem, to God's temple. Jesus was brought to his Father's house in the city which He had always loved. "Oh Jerusalem, Jerusalem!" The devil took Jesus to the most sacred spot on the face of the earth, to the most blessed place in the Saviour's heart, and there Satan had him stand on the highest point of God's temple. Then the tempter said to him, "If you are the Son of God, throw yourself down, for it is written: 'He will command his angels concerning you, and they will lift you up in their hands, so that you will not strike your foot against a stone.' " Jesus trusted the LOVE of his Father, as He had demonstrated in the first temptation, so now Satan was saying, "Yes! It is good that you trust God, and here is a way you can show how much you trust Him. Throw yourself down from the top of the temple. God will surely protect you. You believe in God's deliverance, don't you? Then take a great leap of faith and prove it. Here at the temple in Jerusalem, here in the sight of all Israel, show how much God loves you. Show how much you trust God. Throw yourself down to a sure destruction—to show God's sure salvation! If you are the Son of God, prove it; since you are the Son of God, show it. Hurl yourself from the top of the temple and let men and angels see God's great deliverance! Let all the world know that you are the Son of God. Let them see how great your faith is and how great your God is!" Then Satan gave his words a holy glow from the light of the sacred Scriptures. He used God's Word to tempt Jesus. Knowing how Jesus believed God's Word and obeyed God's Word, knowing how Jesus in the first temptation had stood upon the firm foundation of "*it is written*," Satan now enticed Jesus with those same words. "*It is written*," said Satan. "He will command his angels concerning you, and they will lift you up in their hands, so that you will not strike your foot against a stone." Satan quoted from the Psalms, from the Praise Book of God, which Jesus loved. All his life, in his home and in the synagogue, Jesus had sung those songs in the worship of God. And now He was hearing Satan speak from Psalm 91, words written about the Messiah, words written about Himself. Psalm 91 speaks of the man who says of the LORD, "He is my refuge and my fortress, my God, in whom I trust." This psalm promises protection for the man who trusts God: "No harm will befall you; no disaster will come near you . . . The Most High, even the LORD, will command his angels concerning you to guard you in all your ways; the angels will lift you up in their hands, so that you will not strike your foot against a stone . . . 'Because he loves Me,' says the LORD, 'I will rescue him; I will protect him, for he acknowledges My Name. He will call upon Me, and I will answer him; I will be with him in trouble, I will deliver him and honour him. With long life will I satisfy him and show him my salvation' " (Psalm 91). Satan was saying to Jesus, you believe God's Word? Don't you believe that God can rescue you and protect you? Don't you believe that God will deliver you and honour you? Don't you trust what God says, that He will show you His salvation? Of course you do, so throw yourself down from the temple, Jesus, for this Word is written about you. God will surely command His angels concerning you and they will lift you up in their hands. Hurl yourself down, for no harm will befall you. God's angels will set you gently and safely upon the ground. Surely you have faith in the promises of God, don't you? Surely your hope is in the LORD, isn't it? If you are the Son of God, then you must obey what is written about you. Since you are the Son of God, you must fulfill the Word concerning you. Glorify your Father in heaven; glorify Him here on earth, here in this holy city, here at the very entrance to your Father's house. Throw yourself down and prove that you are the Son of God, the Son who believes in the Father, the Son who obeys the Father's Word." This was the thrust of Satan's attack. This was how he attempted to push Jesus from the pinnacle of the temple. This was how Satan tried to make the second Adam fall. But Jesus knew the Word of God; He knew the entire Word of God. He knew the words that Satan had omitted from Psalm 91, words which spoke of the Messiah's work: "You will trample the serpent." Jesus knew what He had been sent to do. It was not to hurl himself from the top of the temple as a sensational, wonder-working, miracle-making Messiah. No, his work was to quietly crush the head of the serpent— and that was how He would glorify God! That was how He would demonstrate His faith! That was how He would obey the Scriptures! Satan said, "It is written." Jesus answered, "It is also written . . ." Again Jesus fought Satan's attack with the Word of God. Again Jesus quoted from the Book of Deuteronomy. He said, "It is also written: 'Do not put the Lord your God to the test' "

(Deuteronomy 6:16). Jesus trusted God's Word; He did not have to prove it. Jesus trusted God's LOVE; He did not have to test it. Jesus knew how the Israelites had sinned in the desert. Although God had promised to be with them, although He had said to the Israelites: "I will take you as my own people and I will be your God" (Exodus 6:7) — they did not believe God's Word. They quarrelled with God; as soon as there was trouble they tested God by saying, "Is the LORD among us or not?"(Exodus 17:7). The Israelites had seen God deliver them again and again and again, yet, when there was no water for the people to drink, they doubted. They wanted proof that God was with them. God's Word was not enough. They wanted something new, something more. They wanted another sign, another wonder, another miracle. God must prove His LOVE for them. Otherwise, they refused to trust in Him. So Moses called that place Massah, which means "Testing," because there they tested the LORD, demanding that God prove that He was with them. Later Moses warned the Israelites: "Do not test the LORD your God as you did at Massah." It was wrong to test God. It was sin. The LORD had brought his people into the wilderness to test what was in their hearts. It was not God who must pass their test; it was they who must pass God's test! Would they believe their God? Would they obey their God? That was the test for them, and now that was the test for Jesus. Did He trust God's Word, without having to prove God's Word? Did He trust God's LOVE, without having to test God's LOVE? Yes, He did! Jesus believed what God said: "You are my Son, whom I love." God's Word was sufficient for Him. He did not have to throw himself from the top of the temple to show what great faith He had. He did not have to have angels rescue Him to show what great LOVE God had. No, He simply had to believe and obey God's Word; He did not have to test it or prove it. He would not do such a thing! "Do not put the Lord your God to the test." With those words Jesus, the last Adam, withstood the second temptation. He did not fall into sin. He did not fall to his death. He did not fall. This second man did not waver through unbelief, but took a secure stand upon the unfailing promises and enduring commands of the LORD Almighty.

The Third Temptation

Satan had successfully tempted the first man Adam with the desire to be like God. Satan had tempted him to act like God, to exert his own will, to determine for himself what was right and what was wrong, to live independently — rather than simply and humbly obeying the commands of God.

But now Satan faced another Adam, who was not falling for his temptations. Although this last Adam was the very Son of God, Satan could not entice Him to "be like God" or to boldly act like the Son of God. This second man had a humble spirit. This man, Jesus, although He was in very nature God, did not consider equality with God something to be grasped, but made himself nothing, taking the very nature of a servant" (Philippians 2:6). Satan could not tempt the Son of God to make stones into bread. Why? Because He humbled himself, remaining a man, who entrusted himself to God. The Son of God had answered, "Man does not live by bread alone." His answer to Satan was that He would suffer as a man, behave as a man, wait as a man, trust as a man . . . and stand against Satan as a man. It was the seed of the woman, who would crush the head of the serpent. It was the Son of Man, who would defeat Satan! When Satan tried again to tempt Jesus, this second time to arrogantly test the Word and the Love of God, he came up against the same righteous humility. This second man was truly a servant, and He would do nothing from selfish ambition or vain conceit. This second man would patiently entrust Himself to God, waiting for God to exalt Him at the proper time. How could Satan cause this man to fall?

We read in the Bible that again the devil chose the place of battle. The devil took Jesus to a very high mountain. Perhaps for this temptation it was the pinnacle of the world, the highest spot on the face of the earth. This time Satan did not say, "If you are the Son of God . . ." He did not say, "Since you are the Son of God . . ." No, since Jesus appeared as a man and presented himself as a man, and refused to be anything other than a man, then this time Satan would deal with him as a man. Yes, this Jesus had humbled himself and taken the form of a man—a weak man, a poor man, a servile sort of man, who had absolutely nothing in this world. Perhaps Satan could make this man loath his humiliation. And this was just the beginning of it. What lay ahead for this man to endure was a far worse humiliation. And why was this man willing to suffer so. There had been a joy set before him. There had been a kingdom promised to him. Well, Satan could make promises too. The first Adam had chosen to believe Satan's promise, rather than God's. Perhaps the second Adam could be enticed to make a similar choice. Perhaps Satan could cause this last man to despise his humiliation, dread his crucifixion, and doubt his exaltation. This third temptation would be Satan's worst assault upon Jesus. Here, on the heights of the earth, Satan would attempt to cast him down to the depths of hell—which was only a very short distance. All Jesus had to do was bend his knees and bow his head to Satan.

The devil took Jesus to a high mountain and there they faced each other again. The Son of God had set aside his glory to become a man, but even as a man he had no beauty or majesty in his appearance to commend him. In fact, as he stood before Satan at this moment, he was a most miserable specimen of humanity. He was starving; he was not much more than a skeleton about to collapse. He was a man of sorrows, a man who was suffering, a man acquainted with grief. I believe that when Satan came before Jesus with this third temptation, Satan came in all his glory. He presented himself as Lucifer, the Shining One, the angel of incredible beauty and brilliance, majesty and might. We read in the Scriptures how good men, strong men, were so awed by angelic splendour, that they fell down at their feet to worship them. (See Revelation 19:10 & 22:8.) What Satan was about to suggest was not unreasonable. Men bowed before heavenly splendour and millions of people bowed in worship before the pomp and power of earthly kings. What Satan was about to suggest was not unusual. He was, after-all, the power of darkness. He was the prince of demons. He was the ruler of this world. He was the god of this age. Great was his empire! Great was his worship! And great was the reward he would offer to this one impoverished man, if he would but do the same.

From the top of that mountain, the devil showed Jesus a vision conjured from the pits of hell. In an instant, Satan showed this lowly man all the kingdoms of the world and all their splendour. It could all belong to Jesus. It was his for the bending. "All this I will give you," said Satan, "if you will bow down and worship me. I will give you all their power and glory, for it has been given to me, and I can give it to anyone I want to. So, if you worship me, it will all be yours." On that high mountain, Satan made his magnificent offer. But the LORD had also promised the world to His Son. God said, "I have set my King upon Zion, upon my holy hill." It was written in God's Word, in the Book of Psalms. Perhaps Jesus brought to mind these Words of the LORD: "He said to me, 'You are my Son; today I have become your Father. Ask of me and I will surely give the nations as your inheritance and the ends of the earth as your possession. You will rule . . .'" (Psalm 2:6–9). The offers appeared to be the same; both the devil and the Father promised to make him king of the whole world. So far, there was no great temptation. Whose word would you believe? Whose offer would you take? Surely only a fool would listen to Satan.

However, there was in Satan's offer a terrifyingly real temptation, because neither the devil nor the Father were offering the world to Jesus for free. There was a cost for this kingdom. There was a price that had to be paid. What Satan required from this man was a little show of homage—just a slight bending of his body. It was not a difficult thing, was it, to show this simple sign of respect? It was, after-all, a relatively minor exercise in humility. It was not an unreasonable request, was it, that before the kingdom was given to this man, he should bow down and give the appropriate worship to its present ruler? Satan was the god of this age and the prince of this world, so let this mere man humbly acknowledge it! That was Satan's price: worship. What was the price that God required? Jesus knew what it was. God required the breaking of his body; God required the shedding of his blood. God required his death, even death upon the cross. God required that he offer himself as a sacrifice for sin. Jesus was a man; he did not want to face this. Later in his life, in a garden called Gethsemane, the soul of Jesus was overwhelmed with sorrow as this hour came near to him. At that time he fell with his face to the ground and cried out in anguish to his Father to let this cup—the cup of his crucifixion—be taken from him. And that was exactly what Satan was now offering him! He was offering Jesus a way to bypass this dreadful death. He was offering him the kingdom . . . without the crucifixion. He was offering him the crown . . . without the cross. He was offering him the promised and blessed exaltation . . . without the cursed humiliation. The hissing of that ancient serpent could be heard on this hilltop of temptation: "You surely shall not die." Satan was showing Jesus another way, an easier way, to inherit the kingdom—a way which avoided the cross!

It was a real temptation, yet the soul of that righteous man must have instantly recoiled in horror and attacked in anger. This time Satan was urging an obvious act of hideous sin. To worship Satan was totally rebellious. To worship Satan was utterly blasphemous. It was breaking the first commandment: You shall have no other gods before Me. It was breaking the foremost commandment: You shall love the LORD your God. Jesus loved God, more than anything, more than the whole world, more than his own life. To serve God was what Jesus desired, above all else. Yes, Jesus wanted to inherit the kingdom, but he wanted the kingdom of God. What value was any kingdom, even the kingdom of the whole world, if it was without God? What would it profit a man to gain the whole world and to lose his own soul? Jesus knew that the path God had appointed for him was death, but he believed in God. He believed that God would also give him life! Like the righteous men who went before him, Jesus could cry out in faith: "Though God slay me, yet will I trust in Him" (Job 13:15). Satan tempted Jesus with the most splendid reward ever offered to any man, promising him the wealth of the whole world. All power and honour and glory Satan offered to Jesus. How many thousands of the sons of men had sold their souls to him for so much less! Yet this man did not fall. Nor did he waver. There was not so much as a flicker of interest or a spark of lust in his righteous soul. When Satan showed him all the kingdoms of the world and said, "All this I will give you, if you will bow down and worship me"—Jesus said to him, "Away from me Satan!" It was a direct command, spoken by the Son of God, but it was also a direct command, spoken by a man. Yes, it was a man answering an angel; it was a man ordering the prince of demons. This was not the glorified Son of Man, whose eyes flashed like fire and whose voice broke like thunder and whose face was like the sun shining in all its brilliance. No, Satan was looking at a son of man, who seemed even less than a man. Yet it was this second man, in the weakness of his famished frame, who commanded, "Away from me, Satan!" Again Jesus stood upon the Scriptures, driving back the devil with the Word of God. Satan said, "Bow down and worship me." Jesus answered, "It is written, 'Worship the LORD your God and serve Him only'" (Deuteronomy 6:13).

Satan was beaten. The last Adam had stood his ground. He had not bowed before Satan. He had not fallen. It was the first time in the history of the world, that any man had been able to resist the devil. There was a great victory won that day, although the eyes of men saw it not. When Jesus said, "Away from me Satan!"—he had to obey, for there was a new king standing in this world. When this King spoke, not only the wind and the waves, but also the angels and the demons, had to obey Him. When Jesus said, "Away from me, Satan!"—the devil had to leave.

We read in the Bible that the devil left Jesus, but angels came to him. Yes, now God did send his angels to rescue him. They would not have come, if he had hurled himself from the top of the temple, but now they came, because he had stood his ground. Jesus had entrusted himself to his Father's care, and that trust was not in vain. Just as God had sent ravens to feed Elijah in the wilderness, now God sent angels to minister to Jesus. He had trusted that God would provide food for him in the desert, and now he was given grain from heaven by the hands of angels.

The Final Temptation

When Jesus commanded, "Away from me, Satan!"—the devil had to obey. He departed from Jesus and never again did they meet face to face in combat, but this was not the end of Jesus' temptations. We read in the Bible that the devil left him for awhile, "until an opportune time." There were many times to tempt this man during his ministry and there was one perfect time to tempt him. Satan would use the lips of men to say his words. Sometimes Satan would speak to Jesus as he had spoken to the first Adam—through the voice of a beloved friend. The best example is after Peter confessed to Jesus, "You are the Christ, the Son of the Living God." Right after that great confession, Peter became a stumbling block to Jesus by rebuking him and dissuading him from the cross. Jesus said to Peter, "Get behind me, Satan!" Jesus knew from whom this temptation really came. Satan was always waiting for an opportunity to trap Jesus. He used the people with whom Jesus had contact. Throughout his ministry many were the tests and trials of the Son of God, but there was one final temptation, when the Christ took his last stand against the devil. This final temptation, which was hurled at Jesus again and again and again by the mouths of many different men, occurred at a place called Golgotha, which means "The Place of the Skull." This time Jesus was tempted in Satan's territory, the domain of death. It was also Satan's hour, when the power of darkness and the prince of demons ruled. It was the opportune time; it was the time for which Satan had been waiting. It would be the worst test, the supreme trial, the ultimate temptation!

The man Jesus was in great distress. Within the last few hours he had been betrayed by one of his disciples and denied by another of them. All his friends had abandoned him. Jesus had been cursed and slapped and punched by the elders of Israel. He had been flogged with a whip on his back and beaten with a stick in his face by the soldiers of Rome, who also stripped him, spat on him, mocked him, and crushed a crown of thorns upon his head. He was falsely accused in the court of the Jews and unjustly sentenced in the court of the Gentiles. He was led through the streets of Jerusalem as a common criminal. At Golgotha nails were pounded through his hands and his feet. Thus impaled upon a cross, he was lifted up for all to see. What did people see? They beheld a broken man, whose body was so bruised and bloodied that all who passed by were appalled at him. "His appearance was disfigured beyond that of any man and his form was marred beyond human likeness." He no longer looked like a man. Those who saw him were repulsed by the sight. "He was despised and rejected . . . scorned by men and abhorred by the people." Jesus said about himself, "I am a worm and not a man." This was the Jesus that Satan now faced—a worm! The glorious Son of God had been reduced to a wretched worm! This was the opportune time; this was the hour for which Satan had been waiting . . . for thousands of years. Not only would Satan have the pleasure of seeing the Son of God suffering on the cross, but he thought he would also see this man sinning upon the cross. Surely this was Satan's hour, when he would triumph over God! Was this not the moment when the serpent would certainly crush the seed of the woman and kill the Son of Man?

It was Satan's final temptation. It was the man's last stand. Here, Jesus planted his feet (and his hands) firmly upon the cross. Here, at Golgotha, the battle of the ages would be won or lost. The last Adam was hanging on the cross, dying—and Satan was there also, tempting. It was not a direct confrontation. No, Satan would speak through the creatures whom God loved. He would use human voices to bring hell's message to the Saviour in his agony. His own people, the lost sheep of the house of Israel, over whom He had wept and prayed, would be the ones who tempted Jesus with the devil's favourite opening words: "If you are the Son of God . . ." Person after person walked by the cross and hurled insults at the dying man: "Save yourself! Come down from the cross, if you are the Son of God!" The elders and teachers and priests also mocked him: "He saved others," they said, "but he cannot save himself! He's the King of Israel! Let him come down from the cross, and we will believe in him! He trusts in God. Let God rescue him now if he wants him, for he said, 'I am the Son of God.' " The robbers, who were crucified on either side of him, also taunted him: "Aren't you the Christ? Save yourself and us!" All Israel—commoners, rulers, criminals—joined in the chorus: "Save yourself!" Every segment of society was represented, even the Roman soldiers, who sneered: "If you are the King of the Jews, save yourself!" Once again, and this time repeated over and over and over, in an attempt to wear him down, this temptation was hurled at Jesus. It came from every direction: "If you are the Son of God . . . if you are the King of Israel . . . if you are the Chosen One . . . if you are the Christ of God . . . if you are the King of the Jews . . . *Save yourself! Come down from the cross!*" It was a real temptation. Of course Jesus wanted to come down from cross. Of course he wanted an end to his agony. The cross was a terrible form of torture, an excruciating means of death. Jesus was a man and he experienced the cross as a man, a dying man: "I am poured out like water. All my bones are out of joint. My heart has turned to wax; it has melted away within me. My strength is dried up and my tongue sticks to the roof of my mouth. I am laid in the dust of death . . ." *Come down from the cross!* It was a real temptation, because he had the power to come down from the cross. Yes, he was a son of man, but He was also the Son of God. He was the King of kings and the Lord of lords. All heaven and earth, all men and angels, were at his command. One word from his dying lips and the angels of heaven would lift him from the cross (Matthew 26:53). Just one word, and he could save himself. *Come down from the cross!* It was a real temptation to silence these evil men surrounding him. Why should he hang before them on a cross, suffering under their taunts and withering under their stares, when He could stand before them in all his strength as the King of Israel and the Son of God? Let them bow down and worship their King and their God! Why should He hang upon this cursed cross, dying—and dying for them. *Save yourself!* Look at this human race! Both Jews and Gentiles were banded together against the LORD, united in their hatred of Christ. There they took their stand against him at Golgotha. There an evil assembly of mankind encircled him . . . like charging bulls, like roaring lions, like snarling dogs delighting in the slaughter and the spilling of his blood. These were the depraved creatures for whom he was dying. Why should he save them? *Save yourself!* For this time God would not rescue him. This time God would not answer him. It pleased the LORD to crush him. It was God's will to make him suffer. This time God would not deliver him from death. Save yourself! For there was no one to help. God would not save him. On the cross Jesus cried out, "Eloi, Eloi, lama sabachthani?"—which means, "My God, my God, why have you forsaken me?" His suffering soul was grieved within him, as he silently prayed to his God: "Why are you so far from saving me, so far from the words of my groaning? O my God, I cry out . . . but you do not answer." No, this time, there would be no answer, for God had hidden his face from him. This time, he truly was forsaken of God. *Save yourself! Come down from the cross!*

But Jesus did not save himself. He did not come down from the cross. He did not yield to Satan's final barrage of temptations. Jesus remained on the cross until he said: "It is finished." With that, he bowed his head and gave up his spirit. He had been faithful unto death, even that agonizing death upon the cross. He was laid in the dust of death, but he had not fallen there. No, he had stood his ground against Satan to the very end. Jesus died, just as he had lived—

without sin. As he hung on that cross, despised and rejected by men, Jesus did not forsake them. He did not abandon the human race to the sin and death that they deserved, but rather, he loved them. He poured out his life for them that they might be saved! Although men reviled him as he hung on the cross, Jesus did not revile in return, nor was any deceit found in his mouth. Although men heaped insults and abuses and curses upon him as he was dying, what did Jesus say? "Father, forgive them, for they know not what they do." His words were words of blessing to the end. Although Jesus died a violent death, being crucified by the hands of wicked men, yet he harmed no one. By the Sword of the Spirit, by the words from his mouth, he could have called down fire from heaven to consume his enemies, but the wrath of God was poured out upon him instead. He offered himself as a sacrifice for sin and he was consumed in our place. Jesus was faithful in his LOVE for mankind to the very end and he was also faithful to God. Although Jesus was forsaken of God, he himself did not forsake God. Jesus trusted in his loving heavenly Father through the suffering to the bitter end. He recalled how he had been cast upon God since his birth, and he would not forsake God now in his death. Jesus continued to cry out to his God for help. He did not cease to hope in God, not even when he hung dying on the cross, not even when he knew that he had been forsaken by God. He cried aloud, "My God, my God, why have you forsaken me?" In his heart he also cried out, "O LORD, be not far off. O my Strength, come quickly to help me. Deliver my life . . . Rescue me . . . Save me" (Psalm 22:19–21). Jesus trusted in the LOVE of his Father, even as his life was being poured out on the cross. His dying words were words of faith and trust and hope in his God. Jesus called out with a loud voice, with the last of his human strength, "Father!" Yes, God was still his Father, though He had put His Son to death. "Father," cried Jesus, "Into your hands I commit my spirit." When he had said this, he breathed his last. Jesus was dead, but he had remained faithful to God till the last moment of his life. It was finished. Jesus had stood against the devil and had not yielded to sin. Jesus had kept all of the commandments throughout his life. He had not broken one, not even the least of them. In him, there was no sin. Throughout his death, he had also remained perfectly righteous. He kept the two greatest commandments, loving both man and God until the end. Satan was defeated! He was utterly vanquished by this last man, this second Adam, who would not yield to sin, not once through his life, nor through his death. Jesus remained perfectly righteous. He passed the test and stood the trial, even during the final and most awful temptation.

Come down from the cross. Save yourself. Then we will believe in you.
But it was not coming down from the cross, but staying on it until the end,
that brought about faith. When one of the Roman soldiers, who had nailed
Jesus to the cross, saw how Jesus died, he praised God and said: "Surely this
was a righteous man . . . Surely this man was the Son of God." *Come down
from the cross. Save yourself. Then we will believe in you.* But Jesus gave his
tempters a greater sign that he was the Son of God, the Christ, the King of
Israel. It was not his coming down from the cross, but his coming up from
the grave, that declared whom He was. The resurrection of Jesus was the
great confirmation on earth of the great declaration from heaven: "This is
my Son, whom I love; with him I am well pleased."

> *All you who fear the LORD,*
> *Praise Him! . . .*
> *Honour Him! . . .*
> *Revere Him!*
> *For the LORD has not despised or disdained*
> *the suffering of his afflicted one.*
> *He has not hidden his face from him,*
> *but has listened to his cry for help . . .*
> *All the ends of the earth will remember*
> *and turn to the LORD*
> *and all the families of the nations*
> *will bow down before Him,*
> *for dominion belongs to the LORD*
> *and He rules . . .*
> *Future generations will be told about the LORD.*
> *They will proclaim His righteousness . . .*
> *for He has done it!*

> *Psalm 22:23, 24, 27, 28, 30, 31*

Yes, the LORD did it! He defeated Satan. He crushed the serpent. He
died on the cross to pay for our sins and rose from the dead to proclaim His
righteousness. Blessed be the name of the LORD . . . forever!

The teacher's guide for this lesson starts on page 454.

GRACE AND FAITH

G olgotha was for Jesus a place of death, where the wrath of God was poured out upon Him. However, if we look at Christ hanging on the cross and *believe* — Golgotha is for us a place of life, where the grace of God is poured out upon us. It is for us the place of our salvation. Three years before Golgotha, Jesus said about Himself: "The Son of Man must be lifted up [on the cross,] that everyone who believes in Him may have eternal life. For God so loved the world, that He gave His one and only Son, that whoever believes in Him shall not perish, but have eternal life. For God did not send His Son into the world to condemn the world, but to save the world through Him" (John 3:14–17).

The world was already condemned to death. Through one man sin had entered the world, and death through sin, and in this way death spread to all men, because all sinned. The first Adam brought sin and death to the whole world. The first Adam passed on a sinful nature to all the people who came after him. All his children were born into this world dead, dead in their sins. We, like all the rest of the human race, were by nature objects of wrath, because we, like all the rest, were subjects of sin. When Adam fell into sin, the whole human race fell with him. Adam, because of his disobedience, was condemned to death by a holy and angry God. That condemnation fell upon the entire human race. We all were condemned to death, because we all were corrupted by sin. We all inherited the sin of the first man. This sin separated man from God. All men were separated from God and were under the same sentence of death. We were all alienated from God—enemies—because of our evil behaviour, springing from our evil nature. God said, "You shall surely die! Dust you are and to dust you shall return!"

But there was another Word from God. It was a word of hope, a word of life and a word of truth—which required a response of faith. If God's Word proved true: "You shall surely die"—then how much more can we trust God's Word: "You shall surely live." The Son of God declared to man the way, the only way, to be saved. Jesus said: "The Son of Man must be lifted up, that everyone who *believes* in Him may have eternal life" (John 3:15). Jesus said: "Whoever *believes* in Him shall not perish, but have eternal life" (John 3:16). Jesus said: "Whoever *believes* in the Son has eternal life, but whoever rejects the Son will not see life, for God's wrath remains on him" (John 3:36). Jesus said: "I tell you the truth; whoever hears my Word and *believes* . . . has eternal life and will not be condemned. He has crossed over from death to life" (John 5:24). Jesus said: "My Father's will is that everyone who looks to the Son and *believes* in Him shall have eternal life, and I will raise him up at the last day" (John 6:40). Jesus said, "I tell you the truth: he who *believes* has everlasting life" (John 6:47). Jesus said: "I am the resurrection and the life. He who *believes* in Me will live, even though he dies; and whoever lives and *believes* in Me will never die. Do you believe this?" (John 11:25, 26).

Do you believe this? God could not say it more plainly or more clearly. We must have faith in Jesus! We must believe in the Son of God!

Jesus did the work that God appointed for him. Jesus obeyed the will of his Father in heaven. He went to Golgotha. He was nailed to the cross. He was lifted up for all to see. His body was broken. His blood was shed. He poured out His life unto death. That was what God required of Jesus—obedience unto death, even death upon the cross. But what does God require of us? What is the work that we must do? The Jews asked Jesus that same question. They asked, "What must we do to do the works God requires?"

This was Jesus' answer to them and to us: "The work of God is this: to *believe* in the One He has sent" (John 6:29). To believe—that is God's will for us! To trust the gospel message—that is God's work for us! Jesus took his stand upon the cross, but we take our stand upon the gospel. The Bible says; "By this gospel you are saved, if you hold firmly to the word preached to you." What is this word? What is this gospel, on which we take our stand and in which we put our trust. It is "that Christ died for our sins according to the Scriptures, that He was buried, that He was raised on the third day according to the Scriptures . . ." (1 Corinthians 15:2–4). This is the gospel truth, which is to be obeyed by being believed.

When we are born into this world as human beings, there is a law at work in us. It is the law of sin and death. Unless we are born again, we will surely die. We come from Adam. Our bodies come from Adam's body, for flesh gives birth to flesh, but after a short time, which is barely more than a breath, this body dies and this flesh perishes. Our bodies were taken from the earth and they return to the earth, where they will rot in the grave. Dust returns to dust. Unless we are born again there is only death, only the dust of death. Jesus said, "You must be born again!" He said, "I tell you the truth, no one can see the kingdom of God unless he is born again . . . I tell you the truth, no one can enter the kingdom of God unless he is born of the Spirit. Flesh gives birth to flesh, but the Spirit gives birth to spirit . . . You must be born again!" If we are born again, we are set free from the law of sin and death. What is then at work in us is a new law—the law of the Spirit of life! It is the Holy Spirit, the Spirit of God, the Spirit of Christ, which works in us. We are in Christ and He is in us. "If anyone is in Christ, he is a new creature!" But how can we be born again? How can we become a new creature? How can the Spirit of Life begin to work in us? The answer is: "All this is from God" (II Corinthians 4:18). It is God's gift. It is God's grace. The Bible says: "Because of His great LOVE for us, God, who is rich in mercy, made us alive with Christ, even when we were dead in sins. It is by grace you have been saved" (Ephesians 2:4, 5). We cannot save ourselves, nor can we give birth or life to ourselves, but we can believe in God. We can believe in the power and mercy of God to do this for us. We can trust in God's LOVE. God saves us by His grace, working through our faith. "It is by grace you have been saved, through *faith* . . ." (Ephesians 2:8). We must believe! *Believe in the LORD Jesus Christ and you shall be saved.*

At Golgotha Jesus took his stand against the devil. There on the cross

Jesus defeated Satan. There the Son of God destroyed the works of the devil. He conquered sin and death. It was a great victory for Christ—and it was a great victory for us. "Thanks be to God, who gives us the victory through our Lord Jesus Christ" (I Corinthians 15:57). Jesus took his stand on the cross, and it is there that we must take our stand, *by believing in the Son of God*, who poured out His life to save us from sin and death. Stand firm then. Let nothing move you from this faith, even when the whole world is against you. The Bible says: "Everyone who believes that Jesus is the Christ is born of God . . . Everyone born of God overcomes the world. This is the victory that has overcome the world—*our faith!* Who is it that overcomes the world? Only he who *believes* that Jesus is the Son of God" (1 John 5:1–5).

The teacher's guide for this lesson starts on page 456.

GRACE AND PEACE

In the beginning there was peace in the world, but Satan brought division . . . everywhere! In the beginning there was peace between man and God, but man's sin brought about separation between them. There was no longer peace on earth; there was war. Man no longer stood happily in the grace of God; he cringed miserably under the wrath of God. Sinful man on earth was at war with the Holy God of heaven—and God was at war with him. They were enemies, separated by sin.

Long ago, by the prophets of old, the LORD promised that a Child would be born and a Son would be given, who would restore the peace. "And He will be called . . . Mighty God . . . PRINCE OF PEACE" (Isaiah 9:6). Again it was prophesied that out of Bethlehem would come "One, who will be ruler over Israel, whose origins are from ancient days, from days of eternity . . . And He will be their *peace*" (Micah 5:2–5). It was promised that Someone was coming from heaven, who would be like the rising of the sun, "to shine on those living in darkness and in the shadow of death, and to guide our feet into the path of *peace*"

(Luke 1:79). In the fullness of time, when this Child was born, God sent heavenly messengers to proclaim the joyous news. A host of angels appeared and announced what had been so long lost: PEACE ON EARTH! God and man were separated by sin, but now this Child had been born, this Son had been given, to bring men back to God. The Bible says: "There is one God and one mediator between God and men—the man Christ Jesus" (1 Timothy 2:5). Jesus Himself said: "I am the way . . . No one comes to the Father except through Me" (John 14:6). Holy, holy, holy is the LORD God Almighty. Sinful man cannot come near to such a holy God, but Christ "came and preached *peace* to those who were far away . . . For through Him we have access to the Father . . ." (Ephesians 2:17, 18). The Scriptures teach that God "reconciled us to Himself through Christ" (II Corinthians 5:18).

How does Jesus make peace between God and men? It is our sin that separates us from God; it is our sin that drives us far away from Him, so that we are without hope and without God in the world. But Jesus has dealt with our sin. "Now in Christ Jesus you who once were far away have been brought near through the blood of Christ" (Ephesians 2:13). It was on the cross that Jesus reconciled us to God, because it was there that He took away our sins. The Bible says: "He was pierced for our transgressions; He was crushed for our iniquities. *The punishment that brought us peace was upon Him.* By His wounds we are healed . . . The LORD has laid on Him the iniquity of us all" (Isaiah 53:5, 6). Jesus bore our sins. He paid the penalty for our iniquity. God's wrath was poured out on Him, and He died in our place. It is hard to understand exactly how our sins were removed, but it is not hard to understand "that was how God showed His LOVE to us: He sent His one and only Son into the world that we might live through Him. This is LOVE: not that we loved God, but that He loved us and sent His Son as an atoning sacrifice for our sins" (1 John 4:9, 10). Do we trust in this love? Do we believe in this sacrifice for our sins? Do we have faith in this Son whom God sent? If our answer is "YES" then we have been justified. To be justified means God has declared us to be "NOT GUILTY." We are considered to be blameless of sin. Our sins are no longer counted against us. We are no longer condemned because of our sin. We are considered to be righteous—because of Christ's work for us upon the cross and because of our faith in that work. Our trust, our belief, our faith is credited (or counted) as righteousness! The Bible says that "God will credit righteousness for us who believe in Him, who raised Jesus our Lord from the dead. He was delivered over to death for our sins and was raised to life for our justification. Therefore, *having been justified by faith, we have peace with God through our Lord Jesus Christ,* through whom we have gained access by faith into this grace in which we now stand. And we rejoice in the hope of the glory of God . . . While we were still helpless, Christ died for the ungodly . . . God demonstrates His own LOVE for us in this: While we were still sinners, Christ died for us. Since we have now been justified by his blood, how much more shall we be saved from God's wrath through Him! For if, when we were God's enemies, we were reconciled to Him through the death of His Son, how much more, having been reconciled, shall we be saved through His LIFE! Not only is this so, but we also rejoice in God through our Lord Jesus Christ, through whom we have now received reconciliation" (Romans 4:24–5:11).

If we remain in our sins, we are separated from God now and forever. We do not rejoice in God. No, we fear God! All our lives we cringe before Him, with a terrifying expectation of judgement. Like the first Adam, we try to hide from God. We ignore God; we deny God; we despise God. But we do not rejoice in God. Perhaps in our fear we try to appease God, but in spite of all our efforts, we know we are dying under God's wrath. We cannot rejoice in God, because of our sin. Sin blocks our way to God. Sin blocks our love of God. Sin blocks our joy in God. Sin separates us from God. But in Christ Jesus, what can separate us from the LOVE of God? Nothing! In Jesus, our sins are removed. Christ broke the barrier, and now, through Him, we have access to God. In Christ, we no longer cringe under God's wrath; we are able to stand in God's grace! "Having been justified by faith, we have *peace with God* through our Lord Jesus Christ, through whom we have gained access by faith into this grace in which we now stand. And we rejoice . . ." (Romans 5:1, 2)! Yes, once again we can glorify God and enjoy Him! "We rejoice in God through our Lord Jesus Christ, through whom we have now received reconciliation" (Romans 5:11). This was God's plan from the beginning to bring us back to Himself. God was pleased, through Jesus, "to reconcile to Himself all things . . . by making *peace* through his blood, shed on the cross. Once you were alienated from God and were enemies in your minds because of your evil behaviour. But now He has reconciled you by Christ's physical body through death to present you holy in His sight, without blemish and free from accusation—if you continue in your faith, established and firm, not moved from the hope held out in the gospel" (Colossians 1:19–23). Imagine! If we believe, we are presented to God as holy! In the sight of God, whose judgement is true and right, we are holy! By Christ's death for us upon the cross we have been made holy! We have been cleansed from every spot and freed from every charge of sin. "There is therefore now no condemnation for those who are in Christ Jesus" (Romans 8:1). By faith in the Son of God, we are stripped of our wickedness and clothed in His righteousness. When we put our faith in Jesus, we are made holy, just as He is holy. We are new creatures in Christ, being conformed to the image of God's Son. We are recreated in the image of God, bearing the likeness of the Man from heaven, even our Lord and Saviour, Jesus Christ.

There is no greater blessing in all the world than to be reconciled to God! Our sins separate us from God, but there is hope. The Bible says: "Blessed is the one whose transgressions are forgiven, whose sins are covered. Blessed is the man whose sin the LORD does not count against him . . ." (Psalm 32:1, 2). Our sins lie heavily upon us, crushing us into the grave. What can we do with them? Who will lift the weight of their filth from us? God alone can rescue us. We must turn to Him for help and mercy and forgiveness. We read in the Scriptures that without the shedding of blood, there is no forgiveness. We also read that it is the blood of Jesus, God's Son, which purifies us from all sin. In God's Word, the LORD makes this promise to us: "If we confess our sins, He is faithful and just and will forgive us our sins and cleanse us from all unrighteousness" (1 John 1:7–9). If we are wasting away because of our sin, if we are dying because of our iniquity, then we must say: "Have mercy on me, O God, according to Your unfailing LOVE; according to your great compassion, blot out my transgressions. Wash away all my iniquity and cleanse me from my sin. For I know my transgressions; my sin is always before me. Against You, and You only, have I sinned and done what is evil in Your sight . . . Surely I was sinful at birth, sinful from the time my mother conceived me . . . Cleanse me, and I will be clean! Wash me, and I will be whiter than snow . . . Blot out all my iniquity! Create in me a pure heart, O God, and renew a steadfast spirit within me. Do not cast me from Your presence or take your Holy Spirit from me. Restore to me the joy of Your salvation . . ." (Psalm 51:1–12). We must confess our sins to God—and then our joy in the LORD will be restored. We have this testimony in the Bible: "When I acknowledged my sin to You and did not cover up my iniquity, when I said, 'I will confess my transgressions to the LORD'—then you forgave the guilt of my sin" (Psalm 32:5). If we confess, God will forgive. That is the great promise throughout the Bible, which we must believe and obey. "Blessed is the man whose sin the LORD does not count against him . . . Many are the woes of the wicked, but the LORD's unfailing LOVE surrounds the man who trusts in Him. Rejoice in the LORD and be glad, you righteous; sing, all you who are upright in heart!" (Psalm 32:1, 10, 11). Rejoice because our sins are forgiven! Rejoice, because we are blessed! Rejoice, because we have *peace with God* through our Lord Jesus Christ!

The first Adam brought sin and death, but the last Adam (Jesus) brought righteousness and life. The first Adam brought fear and separation from God, but the last Adam brought joy and reconciliation to God. Through the disobedience of the first man there was condemnation, but through the obedience of the second man there was justification. Through one act of wickedness by the first Adam, many were made sinners, but through one act of righteousness by the last Adam, many were made saints. Praise be to God! Although sin reigned in death, how much more did grace reign through righteousness to bring eternal life through Jesus Christ our Lord!

" 'Peace! Peace to those far and near,' says the LORD. 'But the wicked are like the tossing sea, which cannot rest, whose waves cast up mire and mud. There is no peace,' says my God, 'for the wicked' " (Isaiah 57:19–21). " 'Let them come to Me for refuge,' says the LORD. 'Let them make peace with Me; yes, let them make peace with Me' " (Isaiah 27:5). How? For those who have come to God believing, for those who have come to God confessing their sins and receiving forgiveness, there is peace. Jesus said to his disciples, "Peace I leave with you; my peace I give to you" (John 14:27). After Jesus' crucifixion and resurrection, each time He appeared to his disciples He blessed them with these words: "Peace be with you . . . Peace be with you . . . Peace be with you" (John 20:19, 21, 26). What was this peace that Jesus gave to those who believed in Him?

1. It was peace with God.
2. It was peace with one another.

For those who believe in Jesus, "there is one body and one Spirit . . . called to one hope . . . one LORD, one faith, one baptism, one God and Father of all, who is over all and through all and in all." Because of this oneness, Christians (in the one Bible they all believe) are urged: "Make every effort to keep the unity of the Spirit through the bond of peace" (Ephesians 4:3–5). "Be of one mind. Live in peace. And the God of love and peace will be with you"(II Corinthians 13:11). Jesus Himself left this commandment for Christians: Love one another! Christians are also commanded to "make every effort to live in peace with all men" (Hebrews 12:14). Christ commands his disciples to love even their enemies. In a world filled with hatred, the Christian is to be a person filled with love, because God has poured out His LOVE into our hearts. For those who are lost in the hatred of this world, the Christian can be like a light, shining in a dark place.

3. It was peace within them.

Their hearts and their minds would be guarded by the peace of God. In the world they would surely have difficulties, but they need not be troubled or afraid, for Christ had overcome the world. Their hearts and minds could trust in Him and rest in Him—and be at peace for God surely keeps in perfect peace the one who trusts in Him. This is the LORD's promise.

Again and again, throughout the New Testament, we read this blessing for believers:

Grace and peace to you from God our Father and the Lord Jesus Christ. (Romans 1:7; I Corinthians 1:3; II Corinthians 1:2; Galatians 1:3; Ephesians 1:2; Philippians 1:2; 1 Thessalonians 1:1; II Thessalonians 1:2; Philemon 1:3)

Grace and peace be yours in abundance. (I & II Peter 1:2)

Grace and peace from God the Father and Christ Jesus our Saviour. (Titus 1:4)

Grace, mercy and peace from God the Father and Christ Jesus our Lord. (I & II Timothy 1:2; II John 1:3)

Now may the Lord of Peace Himself give you peace at all times and in every way. The Lord be with all of you . . . The grace of our Lord Jesus Christ be with you all. (II Thessalonians 3:16, 18)

The teacher's guide for this lesson starts on page 458.

A CHILD IS BORN, A SON IS GIVEN

- Genesis 4:1–5
- Hebrews 11:4
- I John 3:11–15
- Jude

A dam and Eve had been driven out of the garden and into the world by God. The ground was cursed and their life was hard because of sin, but there was one very difficult day that ended in great joy. It was the day when, for the first time ever, a baby was born into the world. There must have been great rejoicing in heaven and on earth, as myriads of angels, as well as one new father and one new mother, praised God. Hallelujah! Eve/Life had given birth to a little, living, human being! She had brought a beautiful baby boy into the world. A son had been given to her. Eve knew that God had been with her that day, helping her, as she laboured to bring forth this baby from her body. She said, "With the help of the LORD, I have brought forth a man." How Adam and Eve gazed with wonder at this gift from God! Their hearts were overflowing—with joy in his birth and love for this child and thanks to the LORD. And in their hearts also was hope! Had not God Himself promised them that "the seed of the woman," a child from Eve, would crush the head of the ser-pent? They must have thought that this beautiful baby boy was the child, the one who would destroy Satan; they must have thought that this perfect precious person was the son, who would save them from their sin. Eve named her firstborn son Cain.

For a while, Cain was the only child in the whole world. He must have been lonely, but later Eve gave birth to another baby boy, named Abel. He was a good gift, not only to his parents, but also to Cain, who now had a little brother. The two boys grew up together. They must have had many happy days together, running and playing and shouting—the way boys do everywhere. And as the days and the years passed, Adam and Eve must have wondered about their two sons. Which one was the promised seed? Was it Cain? Was it Abel? Neither of the boys was perfect; that they could see. But was there something about Abel, "righteous" Abel (Matthew 23:35), which made his parents hope in him, hope that he was the one whom God had promised? If Adam and Eve were relying on either of these sons to save them, then they would be greatly disappointed. If they were putting any trust in man, then they surely would be devastated—for God alone could save them from their sins. Only the LORD Almighty could deliver them from death.

Here is the awful account of what happened to the first two children born into the world. Here is the story of Cain and Abel: Time passed and the two little boys grew into men. Cain became a gardener, a man who worked the ground. Abel became a shepherd, a man who watched the sheep. Their parents had told them about God. Adam and Eve had also taught them how to worship the LORD. In the course of time, both men presented themselves to God. They did not come before the LORD empty-handed; they brought offerings to Him. Cain brought some of the fruits and vegetables from his garden. Abel brought the fat portions from some of the firstborn of his flock. Was God pleased with their offerings? Did Cain and Abel find favour with God? We read in the Bible that "the LORD had regard for Abel and his offering, but for Cain and his offering He had no regard." That was the judgement of God! Abel and his gift were accepted by God; Cain and his gift were rejected by God. Why? Why did God receive one gift, but not the other? Why did God receive one man, but not his brother? Was this right? Was this fair? Yes! God is always right. God is always fair. We should never question the justice or the goodness of God, but we can ask this question: WHY? And then we must search the Scriptures very carefully for the answers to our questions and we must ask God very humbly for the wisdom to understand His Word. "The LORD had regard for Abel and his offering, but for Cain and his offering He had no regard." Why? The answer is actually very simple: The LORD had no regard for Cain and his offering, because Cain had no regard for God and His offering!

Cain Had No Regard for God

Cain did not honour God. We see this in the offering that Cain brought, which was "some" of his produce—not the first of it and not the best of it, just "some" of it. It might even have been what was left over—the last of it and the worst of it! Abel, however, brought the best portions from the first-born of his flock. He did not kill a sick lamb or an old ewe, nor did he offer to God the lean portions or the useless parts. No, Abel offered to God the fat pieces of meat from the strongest lambs of his flock. Abel killed the best sheep for God, not caring what anyone else would think. Abel cared what God would think. Each man's gift showed what was in each man's heart. Abel feared God first and loved God best, but Cain didn't really care about God at all. He was not really worshipping God with his offering. It was just a perfunctory performance. He was just putting on a show, so that he would appear to be pious, so that he would seem to love God. Why? Why would he pretend to worship God? Why would he bother to offer anything? Perhaps he wanted to please his parents. Perhaps he wanted to impress his brothers and sisters. Perhaps he wanted the praise of people, which at that time would be all the people in the world. Cain brought some of his produce to show what he had done and to display the works of his hands. Cain was not interested in glorifying God. He was interested in glorifying himself. Perhaps he had been fooling his family for a long time, but God knows the secrets of the heart. God knew that Cain did not love the LORD with all his heart . . . or with any of his heart. God was not fooled. God knew what Cain was doing and why he was doing it. Cain may have been accepted and even applauded by the people around him, but he was not approved by God. The LORD had no regard for Cain and his offering—because Cain had no regard for God and His offering.

Cain had No Regard For God's Offering

Abel accepted the offering provided by God and commanded by God, but Cain did not. Cain picked fruits and vegetables from his garden, but

Abel sacrificed lambs from his flock. Had not God shown Adam and Eve that a lamb must be sacrificed to cover their sin? Had not God revealed to his fallen creatures from the very first day of sin, that without the shedding of blood there is no forgiveness? Had not the first two parents of all mankind taught this to the world's first two children? Yes! Of course they did! It was a matter of life and death! It was their only hope! Cain and Abel both knew this. They knew what was required. Abel listened to the teaching of his parents and obeyed the command of God. Abel acknowledged that he was a sinner and confessed this by what he offered. Abel sought forgiveness from God and acceptance with God in the only way that God had ordained—the sacrifice of a lamb. But Cain rejected this way. Cain had no regard for God's offering. Cain decided to come to God in a new way, in his own way. Cain decided to worship God in a way that was pleasing to Cain, in a way that was fulfilling to himself. Why should a gardener bring lambs? A gardener should bring the work of his own hands, an expression of himself. Surely God would be pleased with creativity and spontaneity in worship. Perhaps Cain reasoned thus: "Am I not good enough to come before God in my own way? Are my works not good enough to be offered to God?" The answer was clear; God's answer was clear: "NO!" No man can come to God in his own way. No man's works are good enough in God's sight, not even those of the first-born man in all the world.

From these early days then, from this first worship service recorded in the Bible, God made His message clear to all people: There is only one way to come to God and that is through the sacrifice of a lamb. We will not be accepted by God any other way. What God revealed that day with Cain and Abel was another piece in the puzzle for us. God was not only teaching them what was true and right; He was also teaching us. Abel was looking forward by faith to the Lamb of God, Who takes away the sin of the world. Although he saw only the faintest shadow of that Lamb, Abel was trusting in this Sacrifice to cover his sin. Abel was hoping in the One whom God would send in the fullness of time, according to His Promise. We know that God's Promise was fulfilled in God's Son, our Lord Jesus Christ. Long before His coming, Abel saw His day—and was glad. Abel rejoiced in this Saviour, who would come at the appointed time. Abel believed in Jesus. Abel had regard for God and for God's Offering for our sin. But Cain did not believe. The Bible warns: "Woe to those, who have taken the way of Cain!" They are godless men, who do not believe. They deny Jesus Christ. They boast about themselves and follow their own evil desires. How can they escape, if they neglect so great a salvation? How can they be saved, if they have no regard for God or for His Offering? Destruction awaits them. Blackest darkness is reserved for them forever. "Woe to them! They have taken the way of Cain" (Jude 11).

"But you, dear friends, build yourselves up in your most holy faith and pray . . . Keep yourselves in God's LOVE as you wait for the mercy of our Lord Jesus Christ to bring you to eternal life" (Jude 20, 21).

The teacher's guide for this lesson starts on page 460.

CAIN'S CHOICE: LIFE OR DEATH

- Genesis 4:1–16
- Hebrews 11:4
- I John 3:11–15
- Jude

God accepted Abel's offering, but God rejected Cain's offering. How did Cain respond to God's judgement? Cain could have repented. He could have rejoiced in the truth that was revealed to him and offered the sacrifice that was required of him. He could have acknowledged that something was wrong with him, since God rejected him — and changed! God was not fooled. There was something missing in Cain's heart. He had no love for God. He had no faith in God. This was the time to change, to repent, to turn around, to be born again! Cain was not at peace with God; he found no favour with God — and the LORD in His mercy had made that clear to Cain. But how did Cain respond to God's judgement? We read in the Bible that "Cain was very angry" and his face showed it. Anger! That was Cain's response to God! And now Cain's heart, which was empty of love, began to fill up with something else: Hatred! Cain hated God and he hated his brother Abel . . . more than ever. But the LORD of LOVE continued to reach out to Cain, "for God does not desire the death of the wicked, but rather that they should turn from their wickedness and live" (Ezekiel 18:23, 32; 33:11; II Peter 3:9). The LORD Almighty took notice of Cain's face—and his heart—and He spoke to Cain words of love and words of life. God said to Cain, "Why are you angry? Why is your face downcast? If you do what is right, will you not be accepted? But if you do not do what is right, sin is crouching at your door; it desires to have you, but you must master it." God saw what was in Cain's heart. There was sin; there was hatred; there was unbelief—and it was about to destroy him. Cain must do what was right, by believing God and obeying God. Cain had a choice. God was setting before him life or death. If Cain did what was right, by coming to God through faith in God's sacrifice for sin, would he not be forgiven? Would he not be accepted? Would he not have life? Yes, he would! But if Cain continued in his rebellion, if he continued in his own wicked way, the way of self and sin—then he would be devoured by his sin and he would die in his sin. Life or death—Cain had to choose. To conquer sin or to be conquered by it, to follow God's way or to follow his own way, to live or to die—it was Cain's choice.

What did Cain decide? We know by what Cain did. He went to his brother Abel and said, "Let's go out to the field." Many times Cain and Abel must have gone out together. From the time they were little boys, one or the other of them must have said, "Let's go here! Let's go there!" But this time Cain had an evil purpose in mind. While they were out in the field alone, away from the rest of their family, Cain attacked his brother Abel and killed him. Cain committed murder, which was a hideous new kind of wickedness in the world. It was the first time human blood had been shed on the earth. Man's first death on record was not a peaceful passing from this life, but a vicious crime and a violent assault. A detestable deed! An abominable act! Cain took the life of another human being. He murdered his own brother, whom he should have loved and honoured and protected. He murdered a righteous man of God, whom he should have blessed and esteemed and imitated. But Cain despised and destroyed Abel.

Why? Why did he hate him? Why did he kill him? Was it envy? Was Cain jealous that Abel had found favour with God? Yes, but that is only part of the answer. The Bible says that Cain belonged to the Evil One. Cain was like his father, the devil. Cain hated holiness, just as Satan did. Cain hated God's worship, just as Satan did. Cain was like his father, the devil, who was a murderer from the beginning. Why did Cain murder Abel? The Scriptures themselves ask this question and give this answer: "Why did he murder him?

Because his own actions were evil and his brother's were righteous" (I John 3:12). That was a sufficient motive for murder! Cain, because he was wicked, wanted to extinguish the light of holiness and the testimony of truth, which shone from his brother Abel.

Was Cain successful in silencing Abel by killing him? No! The Bible says that "by faith Abel still speaks, even though he is dead" (Hebrews 11:4). Thousands of years later, Abel still speaks! How? There are two ways:

1) He speaks to us here on earth. Don't we still learn from Abel? His faithful example, recorded in Scripture, proclaims to us that the only way to be accepted by God is through the Sacrifice of the Lamb.

2) Abel speaks to God in heaven. He was the first of the great multitude to cry out: "Salvation belongs to our God, who sits on the throne, and to the Lamb" (Revelation 7:10). Abel was the first martyr, the first man to be killed for his faith in Christ, the first soul beneath the altar in heaven "of those who had been slain because of the Word of God and the testimony they had maintained." His was the first voice that called out, "How long, Sovereign Lord, Holy and True, until you judge the inhabitants of the earth and avenge our blood" (Revelation 6:9, 10)?

No, Cain could not silence Abel, even though he killed him; nor could Satan stop the Word of God from being proclaimed and fulfilled upon the earth. Even death could not silence God's praises! The LORD is exalted forever!

But what happened to Cain? After he murdered his brother, he probably tried to hide his sin. Perhaps he buried his brother's body out in the field, so no one would see the evidence of his crime. Perhaps people began asking, "Where is Abel?" Perhaps Adam, the father of all mankind, asked his oldest son, "Where is your brother Abel?" Perhaps Eve, the mother of all the living, asked her first-born son, "Where is your brother Abel?" But Cain's answer was always the same: "I don't know." Cain had killed Abel in secret and he planned to keep it a secret. Lying did not bother him. He was like his father the devil, who was both a liar and a murderer from the beginning. Abel was missing—and no one seemed to know anything about it. But there was Someone who knew what was hidden, who knew what was secret. We read in the Bible that there was Someone who had seen what Cain had done. There surely was a witness to his crime, who came forward to question him. The LORD said to Cain, "Where is your brother Abel?" Cain answered the LORD with a lie, as if he could deceive God! Cain said, "I don't know. Am I my brother's keeper?" Then the LORD said, "What have you done? Listen! Your brother's blood cries out to me from the ground." God could see what no one else could see, and God could hear what no one else could hear, things which have no sound—blood! God could hear the innocent blood of Abel crying out to Him from the ground. God knew what Cain had done and God would punish him. The LORD said to Cain, "Now you are under a curse and driven from the ground, which opened its mouth to receive your brother's blood from your hand. When you work the ground, it will no longer yield its crops for you. You will be a restless wanderer on the earth." Cain was under a double curse, because of his crime. Once before the ground had been cursed, because of Adam's sin, but now Cain was under another curse. Life on earth was already hard for all men because of sin, but the way of the transgressor is very hard. Cain was a criminal, under a double curse.

Before Cain had committed murder, there had been many blessings in his life:

1) He had been part of the "church" and, although his heart had never been right with God, still he had the privilege of being part of the small assembly of people who worshipped God. The way of truth and life had been close to him, although he had not followed it, but now he was being driven far from the blessings of the church.

2) Cain had been part of a large and still-growing family, with a father and a mother, brothers and sisters, all who loved him. He was the oldest of the children, the first-born in all the world. Cain had a special place in that family. Since sin had entered the world, it was not a perfect family, but it was a good family. They worshipped together; they worked together; they wondered at the world together; and although life was hard, they still had times when they laughed and played and talked and sang together, because they loved one another. Now Cain had lost that blessing. God was driving him away and never again would he be with his family.

3) Cain would also have to leave the land which he loved. He had a farm there and he knew the land. He had walked through the fields; he had worked the soil; he had grown crops; he had fed his family. Farming was his life and gardening was his gift. This work was his joy! Cain loved growing

things from the ground, but now it was all gone. God said, "When you work the ground, it will no longer yield its crops for you." Now Cain was being driven from the land. He had lost his farm forever. That blessing in his life had vanished, never to return. Cain was no longer a gardener; he was a murderer. Cain was no longer a farmer; he was a wanderer. He was under a curse. He was condemned to roam over the earth—without work, without a home or land to call his own, without a family and without God.

"No!" pleaded Cain. "No! My punishment is more than I can bear." But Cain's response was still wrong. Cain should have said to God, "Thank you"—because God had permitted him to live. Cain had been excommunicated, but he had not been executed. That was the Mercy of God for Cain, but Cain had always refused to see God's Grace. Cain had always rejected the LOVE of God. Instead of thanking God, he complained: "My punishment is more than I can bear. Today you are driving me from the land and I will be hidden from Your presence; I will be a restless wanderer on the earth and whoever finds me will kill me." Then the LORD of LOVE, who had spared Cain's life, went one gracious step farther. God protected Cain's life as well. Cain knew all about murderers, (since he was one)—how they attacked when a person was alone. Cain was afraid that someone would murder him, since he would be all alone in the world. "Not so," said the LORD. If anyone kills Cain, he will suffer vengeance seven times over." Then the LORD put a mark on Cain, so that no one who found him would kill him. Then Cain had to leave. He had to leave all the blessings in his life. He had to leave the safety of the surroundings, with which he had been blessed since his birth. He was afraid. He was leaving a shelter of blessing and going out into the world . . . to wander . . . alone . . . without God.

The Bible says, "Cain went out from the LORD's presence." Cain had chosen death.

The teacher's guide for this lesson starts on page 462.

TWO KINDS OF PEOPLE, TWO RACES OF MEN

• Genesis 4:16–5:24
• Luke 3:23–37
• Hebrews 11:5, 6
• Jude 14, 15

D o I take any pleasure in the death of the wicked?" declares the Sovereign LORD. "Rather, am I not pleased when they turn from their wicked ways and live" (Ezekiel 18:23)? God was merciful to Cain, who did not receive capital punishment for his crime of murder. Cain was exiled, but he was not executed. God gave him time, the time to repent and a chance to live. "God is patient . . . not wanting anyone to perish, but everyone to come to repentance" (II Peter 3:9). God's patience in Cain's punishment was to give him another opportunity to do what was right. "I take no pleasure in the death of anyone," declares the LORD. "Repent and live!" (Ezekiel 18:32). Cain's punishment was for his good and it could have led to his life. As he wandered all alone in the world, perhaps he would long for God and turn to God. Perhaps he would grow weary of his self and his sin. Perhaps he would finally cry out to God to rescue him. Sadly, this never happened because Cain refused his punishment! He continued in his rebellion. As he had done all his life, even now Cain refused to obey God. The LORD had condemned

Cain to be a restless wanderer on the earth, but instead of wandering in the world, having to rely upon God for provision and protection, Cain built a city for himself. Cain refused to rely upon God; he would rely upon himself. Cain refused to seek shelter with God; he would build his own shelter—a city! As he had always done, Cain refused to entrust himself to God. Instead he would trust in himself and in his children after him. He and his children would glorify man. They would sing hymns of praise to themselves: "A mighty fortress is our city!"

We read in the Bible that Cain took a wife and she gave birth to a son, named Enoch. Cain named the city he built after this son, making Enoch the name of the first city in the world. Cain had other children and grandchildren and great-grandchildren and great-great-grandchildren, and so on . . . and on . . . and on. Soon there was a whole tribe of people, a whole race of men, who were the children of Cain. They were like their father in many ways. These people were strong, clever, arrogant, aggressive, industrious, innovative, etc. Some of Cain's descendants "invented" musical instruments, both string and reed instruments, like the harp and flute. (God's holy angels, of course, already were heavenly harpists, "holding harps given them by God" Revelation 15:2). Some of Cain's descendants were the first to forge tools and weapons from iron and bronze. Oh yes, they accomplished many great things for themselves! However, they did nothing for God, because they followed their father Cain in that way as well. The children of Cain did not do everything to the glory of God; they did not do anything to glorify God. Their concern was to glorify themselves. They ignored God and despised God, just as their father had done. The children of Cain boasted in themselves and in their wickedness. They boasted that they did not fear God or need God. Following in the footsteps of their father, they became liars and murders—men without mercy, men without truth, men without God. They began to marry more than one woman, which meant they had many, many children. They increased rapidly, becoming a large population of powerful, brilliant and extremely wicked people. They were like their father Cain. They were like their father, the devil. The seed of the serpent was quickly multiplying upon the earth.

What about the righteous? What happened to the people who loved God and feared God? Did they disappear from the earth when Abel was killed and buried and gone? Since Abel had no children to teach about God, did the knowledge of God and the worship of God die, when he died?

Did Satan win after-all? Had he silenced the praises of God in this world? Were only Satan's children left? What happened to the promise of God? Didn't God promise that the seed of the woman would crush the serpent? But it seemed that just the opposite had happened. The righteous son had been crushed by the wicked one. Look at Eve's children and grandchildren and great-grandchildren! They weren't crushing the serpent; they were joining him! Satan had grown powerful upon the earth. His seed had multiplied and "serpents" were everywhere. A brood of vipers was covering the earth! Had God's Word failed? Had God's promise ceased? Never! God's Word never fails! In spite of all appearances to the contrary, the promises of God always prevail. Even in that day, though the wicked flourished upon the earth, God preserved for Himself a righteous remnant. Adam and Eve must have been very discouraged, but they still had hope. They still trusted God and God's Promise to them. In time, Eve gave birth to another baby boy, whom she named Seth, saying, "God has granted me another child in place of Abel, since Cain killed him." Seth would not be the Child, the Saviour, who would crush Satan, but Seth was a child of promise, a child of faith, a child of God. Through him would be another race of men upon the earth—men who feared and loved God. Through Seth would come the Messiah, God's only Son, the Promised Seed, the Precious Saviour—even Jesus Christ our LORD—but His coming was in the distant future, thousands of years later.

Meanwhile, the righteous remnant had battles to face right then, in their own day. The ungodly were increasing at an alarming rate. They were taking over the earth. Seth was just one little baby . . . one small boy . . . one young man. What could he do? He could believe God! Faith is the victory that overcomes the world. Seth could have faith in God and teach his children that same faith. In time Seth married and had a son of his own, whom he named Enosh. Does that name sound familiar? Enosh. Do you remember someone else with a similar name? Cain's son was named Enoch and the first city was named after him. Enosh, the son of Seth, may have had a similar name, but he was a very different man! While Enoch (son of Cain) was a great man of the world, Enosh (son of Seth) was a great man of God. Cain's Enoch inherited his father's city and extended a great kingdom for himself on earth, but Seth's Enosh extended God's kingdom on earth with the hope of another inheritance, that is, a city in heaven, one whose architect and builder was God. Enosh made his name great upon the earth, for the world's first city was named after him, but Enosh made God's name great upon the earth. Enoch ruled many people in his great city, but Enosh was an evangelist, a man who brought people under God's rule. In the days of Enosh there was revival. We read in the Bible that, when Seth's son Enosh was alive, "at that time men began to call on the name of the LORD." God's worship had not been extinguished. There was yet a faithful remnant, a growing number of people, who worshipped the LORD with faith in God and His Word. Thus the people of God also began to fill the earth!

Now there were two kinds of people, two races of men, upon the earth. Both races were human beings, members of one family, with a common ancestry. All people were the descendants of the same father and mother, Adam and Eve. Every child born into the world was born dead in their sins—because sin was the nature and death the result that Adam and Eve passed on to all their children after them. However, some of their children turned to God. Some of them cried out to the LORD for help—to forgive their sin and to rescue them from death. Some of them came to God in the way that He commanded—through the sacrifice of the Lamb. God heard their cries for mercy. God counted them righteous, because of their faith. God caused them to be born a second time. These people were born again and this time they were born of the Spirit. The Holy Spirit of God gave them new life. They were a new race of people upon the earth, known as "the children of God." They looked the same as other people, but inside their hearts, where God alone could see, they were very different. What was in their hearts (God's Law, God's Grace, God's Word, God's LOVE, God's Spirit, God's Peace, God's Promise, God's Joy, God's Mercy, God's Truth, etc.) also made them behave differently than the other race of people. These "children of God" or "sons of God" had been born again to a living hope and they lived their life here on earth with the hope of heaven. The "sons of God" lived by faith, labouring for a LORD, Whom they could not see. The "sons of God" lived by faith, labouring for a life, which was just a hope.

Not so the other race of men. These people, known as "the sons of men," worked long and hard only for the benefits of this life. They made things to make life easier, such as metal tools, and they made things to make life happier, such as musical instruments. These people made great strides of progress in this life and they accomplished great things for themselves, but they were wicked! They trusted in themselves and boasted in their sin. The records of the "sons of men" are filled with the accounts of their wickedness.

The Bible also contains the record of the "sons of God." An entire chapter in the book of Genesis is devoted to "the written account of Adam's line." What do we find in the records of the righteous? Do we read of great accomplishments? No, we read simply that they lived; they had sons and daughters; then they died.

1. Adam became the father of Seth . . . He had other sons and daughters . . . He lived 930 years, and then he died.

2. Seth became the father of Enosh . . . He had other sons and daughters . . . He lived 912 years, and then he died.

3. Enosh became the father of Kenan . . . He had other sons and daughters . . . He lived 905 years, and then he died.

4. Kenan became the father of Mahalalel . . . He had other sons and daughters . . . He lived 910 years, and then he died.

5. Mahalalel became the father of Jared . . . He had other sons and daughters . . . He lived 895 years, and then he died.

6. Jared became the father of Enoch . . . He had other sons and daughters . . . He lived 962 years, and then he died.

In those days the "sons of God" lived very long lives, but their end was the same: They died. Death spread to all men, except to the seventh son of God:

7. Enoch became the father of Methuselah . . . He had other sons and daughters . . . He lived 365 years, and then . . .

And then . . . what do we read? "And then he was no more, because God took him away." We read extraordinary things about this seventh son of God. He was a man of faith. "By faith Enoch was taken from this life, so that he did not experience death; he could not be found, because God had taken him away . . ." This man Enoch was commended for his faith. "Before he was taken, he was commended as one who pleased God—and without faith it is impossible to please God . . ." But Enoch was a man of faith! He came to God, believing! "Anyone who comes to God must believe that He exists and that He rewards those who earnestly seek Him" (Hebrews 11:5, 6). What is remembered about Enoch is that he spent his life seeking after God! The Scriptures testify that Enoch "walked with God." That was what he did with his life here on earth. Oh yes, he was a husband and father, who had to work hard to provide for his family, but we don't even know what work he did—because his great work was his holy calling to a life of faith. His great work was that "he walked with God." Enoch is also remembered as a prophet of God, who spoke about the coming of our Lord and his judgement against the wicked. "Enoch, the seventh son from Adam, prophesied about these men: See, the Lord is coming with thousands upon thousands of his holy ones to judge everyone, and to convict all the ungodly of all the ungodly acts they have done in the ungodly way, and of all the harsh words ungodly sinners have spoken against Him" (Jude:14, 15). Enoch was a godly man, who was spared from the judgement of God, even the judgement of death in this life. What great hope he must have given the people of God, not in any man, but in their God. They could trust God to deliver them from death, just as He had delivered Enoch from death. They could trust, not in their own works, but in the works of God. In the records of the righteous you read, not of their great works but of the great works of God for them and through them. The LORD was their Saviour! Hallelujah!

The teacher's guide for this lesson starts on page 464.

ONLY EVIL,
ALL THE TIME

- Genesis 5:21–6:13
- Proverbs 31:10–31
- II Corinthians
  6:14–18

It was a long time since that blessed day, the sixth day of creation, when God saw all that He had made, and saw that it was very good. Over 1,500 years had passed and now God's judgement was very different: "Now the earth was corrupt in God's sight!" How extensive was this corruption? We read that the earth was "*full* of violence." The ground was drenched in blood. "God saw how corrupt the earth had become, for *all* the people on earth had corrupted their ways." No one was hidden from God; nothing was done in secret—and God could see even farther than the darkest regions of the earth. God could see into the hearts and minds of men. What did God find there? Was there even a glimmer of goodness? No, the Bible says: "The LORD saw how great man's wickedness on the earth had become, and that *every* inclination of the thoughts of his heart was *only evil, all the time.*" The entire earth was corrupt in the sight of God!

Had all the people on earth corrupted their ways? What about the people of God? Were there not two kinds of people, two races of men upon the earth—the righteous and the wicked? Where had the righteous remnant gone? What had happened to the sons of Seth, the "sons of God," the faithful followers and worshippers of the LORD? How had the godly line disappeared from the earth? Had they all been murdered? No doubt, many of them had been killed because of their faith, for there was enmity between the "seed of the serpent" and the children of God. However, that is not the reason the Bible gives us. It was not persecution that destroyed the people of God. It was pollution! It was not the kind of pollution from drinking dirty water or breathing filthy air that killed the righteous on earth. It was a different kind of pollution, one that defiled their holy race. Listen to what it was that polluted the people of God: "The sons of God saw that the daughters of men were beautiful, and they married any of them they chose." The righteous intermarried with the wicked! The sons of light married the daughters of darkness. They mixed the two races of people. The sons of God married the daughters of men, who were beautiful-looking women, but they were God-hating women. The sons of God judged by outward appearance, choosing a wife because of her pretty face, rather than choosing one because of her righteous heart. Their homes were then divided—and a house divided against itself cannot stand. When children were born into these divided families, the mothers did not teach them to love the LORD. Far from it! They ignored God's command; they laughed at God's promise; they despised God's worship; they scoffed at God's sacrifice. They did not believe in God. Slowly . . . no, very quickly, within two or three generations, the knowledge of God disappeared and the people of God vanished.

The children from these marriages were great in the eyes of the world. They were giants! They were heroes! In those days of old, they were men of renown—but God erased their memory from the earth. Not even one of their names is remembered. They may have been great in the eyes of men, but in the eyes of God they were nothing. What the LORD saw was how great their wickedness was! God had created man in His own image. God had made man to be holy. But man had made himself evil, completely and continually evil, *only evil, all the time!* The LORD Almighty who is HOLY, HOLY, HOLY, the God who is LOVE, grieved over mankind and wept over the earth. The Bible declares that "the LORD was grieved that He had made man on the earth, and His heart was filled with pain." So the LORD said, "I will wipe mankind, whom I have created, from the face of the earth, both men and animals . . . for I am grieved that I have made them." No longer would God's Spirit strive with men to bring about their repentance, for they were utterly corrupt. Their day of grace was over. God determined to destroy them—the creatures that He had made, the creatures whom He had loved. Their reason for existence was gone. They were not glorifying God; they were grieving Him. They did not bring God joy; they brought Him pain. God Himself would erase mankind from the face of the earth. "I am going to put an end to all people," declared the LORD. "I am surely going to destroy both them and the earth . . . I am going to bring floodwaters on the earth to destroy all life . . . every creature that has the breath of life in it. Everything on earth will perish!"

Satan, it seems, had won the war over this world. The praises of God had been silenced. The only sound that came from the earth, was man's great roar of rebellion. Nowhere flickered the light, which Lucifer hated—the light of God's holiness. All was dark on the earth, for it was covered in a thick blanket of wickedness. The worship of God in men's hearts and the praises of God on men's lips, had been completely blotted out . . . and now, finally, God was going to blot out man! The Evil One had conquered. Wickedness prevailed. In every human heart there was *only evil, all the time.*

There was but one exception, a man named Noah. Who was Noah? We all know this name, don't we? Who doesn't rejoice in the name of Noah? We all know this man, although he lived many thousands of years ago. The great men of his day, the giants and heroes—not one of their names is recorded or remembered—but the name of Noah is still revered. He is still commended as a man of faith. In his day he was the only man left who still loved God. Who could hear the voice of one man praising God, in the midst of all the cursing and laughing and screaming of the wicked? God could hear. God also could see. "Noah found favour in the eyes of the LORD!" What blessing for the world! Satan had not completely extinguished the light of holiness or the word of righteousness from the earth. One man still shone. One man still sang. It was Noah! Who was Noah? The Bible records: "He was a righteous man, blameless among the people of his time, and he walked with God." Who was Noah? He was the great-grandson of that other man, Enoch, who also walked with God. Noah never knew his great grandfather, because God took Enoch before Noah was born, but it was through Enoch that the godly line did continue:

1. Enoch became the father of Methuselah. Enoch walked with God 300 years and had other sons and daughters. He lived 365 years— a year of years, a perfect span of life! Enoch, the seventh "son of

God," whose life was a number of perfection and completion, was a type of Christ; that is, he was a picture of the Perfect Son of God, the One who was promised, the One who was coming. Enoch's life was a testimony to the coming of Messiah! Enoch walked with God; then he was no more, because God took him away. Enoch did not die.

2. Methuselah became the father of Lamech. He had other sons and daughters. He lived 969 years! Methuselah lived the longest life of any man on earth, but he also died.

3. Lamech became the father of Noah. In Hebrew the word "noah" means "rest" and his father named him Noah or Rest, because he hoped that this newborn baby boy would be the Child of God's Promise. Lamech knew that life was very hard and that the world was very bad. How he longed for God's Salvation! How he longed for the One, who would say in truth, "Come unto Me, all who are weary and burdened, and I will give you rest . . . You will find rest for your souls" (Matthew 11:28, 29). Rest! Noah! How his father longed for the One, who would rescue them from the curse of this life, which ended in death. Lamech named his son Noah or Rest saying, "He will give us rest in the grief and pain and toil of our hands caused by the ground the LORD has cursed." It seems that Lamech had hope in the promises of God—and even hoped that this baby boy was the Saviour, whom God had promised to Adam in the Garden of Eden so very long ago. Besides Noah, Lamech had other sons and daughters. He lived 777 years, and then he died.

4. Noah was the tenth "son of God"—which is another perfect number. Noah was not *the* SON OF GOD or *the* SAVIOUR, but he was used by God to save the human race and all the other creatures of the earth. In Noah there would be a rest, a brief rest from the curse. In Noah the whole world would be blessed. Noah was also a type of Christ, foreshadowing the Messiah, Who surely was coming to save the world.

Noah was in the line of the godly, a line which was growing weaker and fainter as the years passed. During Noah's time the righteous dwindled, while the wicked flourished. Nonetheless, there were still a few people alive, who had faith in God. Noah's great-great-great-great-great-grandfather Enosh, the evangelist, was still living when Noah was born. Perhaps when Noah was young he heard this old man preach and teach about God. Noah's great-grandfather, Enoch, was taken by God before Noah was born, so Noah never heard the voice of this great prophet. What about Noah's grandfather, Methuselah? Did he teach his grandson about the LORD? We don't know. Was Methuselah's long life a life of faith, a reward for a righteous man? We don't know. Methuselah died in the very same year as the flood, which could mean two things: Either Methuselah was a wicked man, who died by drowning when he was swept away in God's judgement or he was a righteous man, who, having lived longer than any other human being, died peacefully by God's grace, just a short time before the floodwaters covered the earth. And what about Noah's father, Lamech? Did he teach his son the things of God? Yes, he probably did. It seems that his father, Lamech, had hope and faith in the promises of God. Lamech lived 777 years, a perfect number, which could indicate a good life. Lamech died five years before the flood, which means he definitely was not swept away with the wicked in the waters of God's wrath. He was spared the horror of that devastation. The LORD does not sweep away the righteous with the wicked.

Noah had fathers before him, who taught him of God and Noah also became a father; after he was 500 years old, he had three sons: Shem, Ham and Japheth. Noah taught them the faith, which had been passed on to him by his forefathers. The knowledge of the LORD had not completely vanished from the earth. The way, the truth, and the life had been preserved in a remnant, a tiny remnant, which was now just one family, headed by one man—Noah.

The rest of the people in the world had corrupted their ways. They were *only evil, all the time*. God was about to destroy them.

The teacher's guide for this lesson starts on page 466.

BY FAITH, AN ARK!

• Genesis 6:9–7:5
• Matthew 24:37–39
• Hebrews 11:7
• I Peter 3:20
• II Peter 2:5

T his is the account of Noah:

The earth was corrupt in God's sight, but Noah found favour in the eyes of the LORD. So God spoke to Noah. How gracious is the LORD, that He still spoke to men, though all but one had corrupted their ways. The LORD told Noah that He was going to destroy the world! Imagine how Noah must have felt when he heard this terrifying news.

God told Noah *why* He was going to destroy the world: "I am going to put an end to all people," said the LORD, "for the earth is full of violence because of them. I am surely going to destroy both them and the earth." Praise be to the LORD of LOVE, that these were not His final Words to man! In his mercy God also said: "So make yourself an ark . . ." God told Noah exactly how to build this great boat and Noah soon realized why he would need such a boat, because . . .

God told Noah *how* He was going to destroy the world: "I am going to bring floodwaters on the earth to destroy all life under the heavens, every creature that has the breath of life in it. Everything on earth will perish." However, God had more to say and God's final word was not death, but life! God promised Noah: "But I will establish my covenant with you, and you will enter the ark—you and your sons and your wife and your sons' wives with you. You are to bring into the ark two of all living creatures, male and female, to keep them alive with you . . . You are to take every kind of food that is to be eaten and store it away as food for you and for them." God was going to destroy the whole world. Everything on earth would die . . . but life would continue. In the ark, every form of life would be preserved. That was God's plan! That was God's promise! Hallelujah!

How did Noah respond to God's Word? Noah believed God's Word and Noah obeyed God's Word! "By faith Noah, when warned about things not seen, in holy fear built an ark to save his family" (Hebrews 11:7). All Noah's work was summed up in just one small sentence: "Noah did everything, just as God commanded him." Noah did everything! Even with his family to help him, it must have taken Noah many years to finish everything. It was long hard work building such a boat. It involved making plans, cutting trees, hauling logs, sawing boards, pounding pegs, building rooms, mixing tar, sealing seams, etc. It was also long hard work finding all that food. It involved planting and harvesting, searching and gathering, threshing and sorting, drying and storing, etc. But the hardest work of all was not the work they did with their hands, but the work that went on in their hearts—the work of believing. Day after day, year after year, they had to believe God's Word. Sometimes, when the sun was shining and the birds were singing and the flowers were blooming, it must have been hard to believe that the world was coming to an end. Everything appeared to be fine. Everyone continued as always. People were living their lives; they were getting married, building homes, having babies, planting trees, making cities . . . as if life on earth would go on and on . . . forever. It was hard to believe that it was all going to end very soon. Was God really going to destroy the world? Were floodwaters really going to cover the earth? There was no sign at all that this was about to happen and no one else in the whole world knew anything about it. What was Noah doing? Noah was building an ark by faith, not by sight. He was building an ark in fear, believing God's warning about the destruction of the world. Noah was living by faith.

Noah had no sign that the flood was coming. He had God's Word; that was all, but that was enough. However, the rest of the world had a very great sign that the flood was coming. God had not left them in the world without a witness. Noah's life and Noah's work and Noah's word were three witnesses about the coming disaster. The people of Noah's day were without excuse because of:

1. *Noah's Life.* They had living among them a righteous man, who walked with God. Noah's holy life was a witness against them.

2. *Noah's Work.* God had not left the wicked without a warning to repent. They could see something quite remarkable in their day: An ark, an enormous ark, was being built before their eyes! Surely the ark was a sign to them that the flood was coming. Noah built the ark in the midst of a wicked generation, while God patiently waited. The banging of Noah's hammer was like the tolling of a bell, warning the world of the coming disaster. Every time it struck, it rang out the alarm: "Repent! Repent!" The banging of Noah's hammer was like the ticking of a clock, telling the people that the day of judgement drew closer, closer, closer. Time was running out! The banging of Noah's hammer was like the speaking of a prophet, urging anyone with ears . . . to hear, hear, hear. Listen to the sound of the hammer! Listen to the voice of the prophet! "Repent!"

3. *Noah's Word.* The LORD did not leave the ungodly without a witness. Noah was a prophet, who proclaimed God's Word to the ancient world. The Spirit of God spoke through Noah to the disobedient unbelievers of his day. Noah was "a preacher of righteousness" (II Peter 2:5), who spoke of the coming judgement.

We read in the Bible that "by his faith, Noah condemned the world" (Hebrews 11:7). By his faith—a faith demonstrated by his life and his work and his word—Noah condemned the world, in accordance with the judgement of God, for the earth was utterly corrupt in the sight of God. The LORD was grieved that He had made man, and Noah's righteous soul was also tormented by the filthy lives of the lawless men among whom he was living day after day. Their condemnation was just. Their destruction would be swift.

Noah's name meant "rest"—but his work must have been exhausting. He was involved not only in physical labour, but also in spiritual battle. His work was not only building; it was also believing—and the whole world was against him. As Noah worked, I'm sure people mocked. They thought Noah was a stupid fool. How they must have laughed and jeered, as he built an enormous boat in the middle of nowhere. "Where do you think you're going?" they shouted. "You won't get very far without any water! Ha-ha-ha!" People thought Noah was a crazy fanatic. "You say God spoke to you, but He hasn't told anyone else. The only voice you heard was the cuckoo bird calling." But Noah ignored their taunts. He went on building and he went on believing. At last the day came when his hammer stopped banging. The ark was finished! Noah had done everything, just as God commanded him.

Then the LORD spoke to Noah again and . . .

God told Noah *when* He was going to destroy the world: "Seven days from now I will send rain on the earth for forty days and forty nights, and I will wipe from the face of the earth every living creature I have made." The time had come. It was time to leave this corrupt world. God gave Noah his marching orders: "Go into the ark, you and your whole family . . ." Why? At this time God also told Noah why he and his family would be spared. "Go into the ark . . . because I have found you righteous in this generation," said the LORD. Holiness seemed worthless in the eyes of the world, and faith seemed foolishness to those who were perishing, but Noah and his family were saved because of that righteousness, which comes by faith.

As it was in the days of Noah, so it is now. "The righteous will live by his faith" (Habakkuk 2:4). Believe... and you will be saved! Believe in the Lord Jesus Christ!

The teacher's guide for this lesson starts on page 468.

THE FLOOD

- Genesis 7
- Psalm 46
- Isaiah 66:15, 16;
  Matthew 24
- II Thessalonians
  1:5–10
- II Peter 3

T he ark was finished. The last week had arrived. In just seven days God would destroy the world. The time had come for Noah and his family to enter the ark. The LORD said to Noah, "Go into the ark, you and your whole family . . . Take with you seven of every kind of clean animal, a male and its mate, and two of every kind of unclean animal, a male and its mate . . . to keep their various kinds alive throughout the earth. Seven days from now," said the LORD, "I will send rain on the earth for forty days and forty nights, and I will wipe from the face of the earth every living creature I have made." Again we read of Noah's faith. Again the Bible records that "Noah did all that the LORD commanded him." There was no sign of an approaching storm. Why should they leave their comfortable homes and move into a boat, when there was still not so much as a drop of water? But they moved, because they believed God's Word. They entered the ark in faith; they entered the ark to escape the waters of the flood—although those waters were yet unseen. Then pairs of every kind of animal, according to their kinds, came to Noah and entered the ark. The animals going into the ark were male and female of every living thing. There were pairs of all creatures that had the breath of life in them.

When every person and every creature was aboard, according to God's command, the LORD Himself closed the door in the side of the ark. It was a special act of grace and a final act of love before the flood. It was God's own hand that shut them safely inside the ark. (There was a terrible tragedy reported in the newspapers a few years ago. A large ferry-boat sank. The boat was filled with hundreds of people, who drowned. How did this accident happen? A man, whose work it was to close the big doors of the ferry-boat, was careless. He didn't close the doors properly, so the boat sank and many lives were lost.) But the Bible reports that God closed the door of Noah's ark. There would be no accidents! Not one life of the creatures inside the ark, not even that of a little ladybug, would be lost. Those who were shut inside by the hand of God were safely and securely in the ark—but those who were shut outside were truly without hope in the world, for the only door of escape had been closed, closed by the hand of God. The day of grace had passed. The offer of salvation had ended. The years of warning about God's judgement, the years of urging for man's repentance, were over. The door was closed. The whole wicked world was locked on the outside. They would hear Noah's voice no more. They would not see his face again. God had closed the door and "what He shuts no one can open" (Revelation 3:7).

What did the people think during those final seven days? Those who were outside the ark saw many things in that last week:

1) They saw Noah and his family leave their homes and move into the ark. Surely that was a sign to them that the flood was coming very soon.

2) They saw an extraordinary sight: Animals were coming to Noah in pairs—every kind of animal, from every part of the world! They saw ferocious wild beasts come to Noah and calmly enter the ark. They saw timid little creatures come out of hiding and bravely walk into the boat. There were pairs of beautiful birds—hundreds of them—flying and singing around the ark and then swooping through the window and disappearing from sight. What was this strange movement in the animal kingdom? What did it mean? Surely not what Noah said! Surely not a flood that would cover the earth! As the people watched the activity around the ark, perhaps they noticed something else. Noah allowed every kind of animal into his ark, even pairs of ordinary pests, like rats and mice! Was he crazy? Yes, of course, they all

knew that he was, but why was Noah doing this? They could understand why he made room for a pair of pretty peacocks, but why would he also allow two old crows to fly into his boat? It was all very strange to them. Did the people also notice that hundreds of these animals entered two by two, one pair of every kind of creature, except those used by Noah for sacrifices to his God? Did they notice that not two sheep, but seven sheep, entered the ark? Perhaps they thought that this was a wise choice, since sheep were so useful to man, providing meat and wool and milk, but did they remember that Noah also needed sheep for the worship of his God? Did they think? To make a sacrifice for sin was more important to Noah than food or clothes, and an offering to God meant more to Noah than a roast of lamb or a robe of wool for himself. Noah needed more than two sheep—and God commanded him to take seven sheep. Did the wicked notice that small flock of sheep, that perfect number of sheep, enter the ark? It was the last sign their eyes would see, showing them God's way of salvation. Those seven sheep were the last faint shadow, their final glimpse, of the Lamb of God. Their eyes may have seen the seven sheep, but their minds did not understand, nor did their hearts believe.

3) They saw the door of the ark close. That should have filled them with terror, but still they did not comprehend. Still they did not repent. They ignored all the signs, which showed them that the day of God's judgement was upon them. They continued mocking and laughing and shouting right to the end. "Look at Noah now! He's locked inside his ark with all the animals—and nothing to do, nowhere to go! There's not a puddle on the ground, not a cloud in the sky! What a fool!" Perhaps they came close to the ark and shouted to Noah: "You'll starve to death in there, before a flood ever comes. You didn't build a boat; you made yourself a coffin—and even nailed it shut! It's too bad you won't get a decent burial, because you made your coffin too big. We can't dig a hole deep enough to bury you. Perhaps we should burn it, maybe even now, before you start to stink!" Some people continued to torment Noah in their last moments. Most people continued to ignore him. No one repented. No one trusted in the LORD. They did not believe that the flood would come, until it swept them away.

The flood came—suddenly and horribly. God had waited patiently, while Noah built the ark, but now God came in anger to destroy the world. What God said, He did. The LORD was not slow in keeping His promise.

The Day of Destruction arrived! The LORD ripped apart the earth and the sky. God tore down the ancient barriers that held back the waters. He caused all the springs of the great deep to burst forth. All the water that is under the earth, all the underground rivers and lakes and seas, burst through the earth's surface. Everywhere giant geysers gushed water with tremendous force, flooding the whole world. Also, the restraints on the waters above the earth were removed. God opened the floodgates of heaven. Never before had such a thing happened in the world. It was not just a rainstorm or a cloud-burst or a downpour. It was not even a devastating storm, like a howling hur-ricane, that was unleashed upon the earth. This was a cataclysm! It was the destruction of the world! It was the fury of Almighty God!

For forty days and forty nights the floodwaters gushed up and poured down upon the earth. The water level increased steadily and rapidly. The waters rose so high, that even the tops of the mountains were covered. No man could measure the depth of those waters, but God has revealed to us in the Bible that "the waters rose and covered the mountains to a depth of more than twenty feet." Not even the tallest man in the world, standing on tiptoes on the tallest mountain in the world, could survive. The water would have been over his head, filling his nostrils, taking his breath, drowning his life. There was not one spot of ground or one speck of life left upon the sur-face of the earth. Everything died. Not one living creature survived. The fastest animal on earth, the cheetah, could not outrace the flood. The tallest animal on earth, the giraffe, could not stand above it. The strongest animal, the elephant, could not fight against the flood, nor could the fiercest ani-mal, the lion, frighten it. The tiniest creature could not hide from the flood, and the prettiest creature could not charm it away. They all perished! What happened to human beings? Did any of them survive? No, they were all swept away in the flood, every one of them. The greatest athletes—neither their strength nor their speed could save them. The greatest thinkers—they could devise no plan to rescue themselves, for they had not the wisdom to fear God or heed God's Word. The great artists of the day, the dancers and musicians, the painters and poets—their works were worthless. Their dances found no favour with God; their music did not please the LORD; their paint-ings had no power; their words could not calm the wind or the waves. The great warriors—they could not fight against the flood. The great beauties—they could not entice the waters to spare them. Every person perished! There were no survivors! They all died in the flood! The Bible states: "Every liv-ing thing that moved on the earth perished . . . all the creatures . . . all mankind. Everything on dry land, that had the breath of life in its nostrils, died. Every living thing on the face of the earth was wiped out; men and animals . . . were wiped from the earth."

Only Noah was left, and those with him in the ark. Why? Why did Noah survive, when every other living creature perished?

1. *The Grace of God.* The LORD is merciful. Although He destroyed mankind, He also preserved mankind—in Noah. The justice and holiness of God demanded that the wicked should perish, that the evil of man should be erased, but the LOVE of the LORD spared the human race, allowing it to continue. God preserved for Himself a remnant, a righteous remnant.

2. *The Faith of Noah.* Noah was spared because he was a righteous man. It was a righteousness that came by faith. By faith, Noah was saved. He believed God; he feared God; he obeyed God. By faith Noah lived a holy life, and by faith when warned by God, Noah built an ark to save his family. Again and again the Scriptures testify that "Noah did everything, just as God commanded him . . . Noah did all that the LORD commanded him." Truly, Noah was a man of faith.

God the Creator became God the Destroyer. In six days God created the world, but in forty days He destroyed it. For one hundred and fifty days water flooded the earth. Once again the world was empty, as it was in the beginning, when water and sky were all that could be seen. The only difference now was this: Besides the occasional spouting of a whale or leaping of a dolphin or flying of a fish, besides the sparkle of the sun in the waves and the ripple of the moon upon the waters and the twinkle of the stars in the sky, there was now something quite extraordinary floating on the surface of the world's vast ocean. On that endless horizon was an ark, carrying its precious cargo of life, every form of life that had ever existed upon the land. God the Destroyer, was also God the Deliverer!

"Long ago by God's Word the heavens existed and the earth was formed out of water and by water. By these waters also the world of that time was deluged and destroyed. By the same Word the present heavens and earth are reserved for fire, being kept for the day of judgement and destruction of ungodly men . . . That day of the Lord will come like a thief. The heavens will disappear with a roar; the elements will be destroyed by fire; the earth and everything in it will be laid bare. Since everything will be destroyed in this way, what kind of people ought you to be?" Like Noah, who was a righteous man, blameless among the people of his time, "you ought to live holy and godly lives, as you wait eagerly for the day of God to come. That day will bring about the destruction of the heavens by fire, and the elements will melt in the heat. But in keeping with God's promise, we are looking forward to a new heaven and a new earth, the home of righteousness. So then, dear friends, since you are looking forward to this, make every effort to be found spotless, blameless, and at peace with God. Bear in mind that our Lord's patience means salvation . . ." Just as in Noah's day there were mockers, so also in these last days, "scoffers will come, scoffing and following their own evil desires. They will say, 'Where is this coming He promised? Ever since our fathers died, everything goes on as it has since the beginning of creation . . .' But the Lord is not slow in keeping His promise . . . He is patient with you, not wanting anyone to perish, but everyone to come to repentance. But the day of the Lord will come" (II Peter 3:3–15). God's angel will announce: "There will be no more delay" (Revelation 10:6). The Day of Destruction will surely come! "No one knows about that day or hour, not even the angels in heaven, nor the Son, but only the Father. As it was in the days of Noah, so it will be at the coming of the Son of Man . . . Therefore keep watch, because you do not know on what day your Lord will come . . . You must be ready, because the Son of Man will come at an hour when you do not expect Him" (Matthew 24: 36–44). "See, the Lord is coming with fire! His chariots are like a whirlwind. He will bring down His anger with fury, and His rebuke with flames of fire. For with fire and with His Sword, the LORD will execute judgement upon all men, and many will be those slain by the LORD" (Isaiah 66:15, 16).

How can we be ready? Where is the ark that will float above the fury and the fire? What must we do to be saved? God's Word says: "Believe in the Lord Jesus, and you will be saved" (Acts 16:31). It is not to the ark of Noah, but to the cross of Jesus, that we must flee for shelter. It is there, at the foot of the cross, under the covering of His blood, that we will find refuge from the wrath of God. Jesus died on the cross to save us from sin and death and that dreadful Day of Destruction. How then shall we escape, if we ignore such a great salvation?

The teacher's guide for this lesson starts on page 470.

A JOURNAL OF PRAISE

• **Genesis 7:6–8:19**

When people go on a journey, they often keep a journal. Explorers are careful to keep a day by day record of everything that happens on their expedition. Noah (and all those with him in the ark) went on a most amazing journey. Did Noah keep an account of all that happened? Did he take scrolls with him into the ark on which to write everything? No, the writings of Noah do not exist, because Noah lived so long ago that people hadn't invented writing yet. We will have to wait until heaven to hear Noah himself tell the story of his voyage over the water-covered world. Of course Noah and his sons told their children and grandchildren and great-grandchildren about the flood, and the story was passed on from generation to generation. It is not surprising then that people in every part of the world have in their own language an ancient "legend" about a flood that covered the world and a boat that saved earth's creatures. However, the accurate account is found in the Bible. You would think there would be a whole book in the Bible, the "Book of Noah," telling all about that incredible journey, but there is only one small section in the Book of Genesis, (which was written by Moses as it was revealed to him by God.) It is there that the main events of the flood are recorded. As we read that account we can imagine what it was like for Noah. We can imagine what he experienced. Had he kept a journal, I think we would have found that it was "A Journal Of Praise." Let's pretend that we are reading some pages from Noah's journal:

17/02/600 A.N.[1] My family and I moved into the ark a week ago, as God commanded, but today is the seventh day. Early this morning we walked up the ramp of the ark for the very last time. All week animals have been coming to us, but today I was filled with a feeling of grief and awe and dread, as the last two tiny creatures climbed aboard, for I knew that the end was very near, that the Day of Destruction was upon us. Yes, today is the seventh day, the day God promised that He would destroy the earth and every living creature upon it. I believed God's Word. Outside the whole wonderful world was teeming with life of every kind. There was a whole world of people too, still refusing to believe that God, who has endured their wickedness for so long, would delay no longer. I was thankful that our God Himself shut the door of the ark. Would I have had the strength to do it? How thankful I am that the opening and shutting of doors in heaven and on earth are in the hands of my Mighty and Merciful Master! I am thankful that we cannot see the dreadful destruction that is taking place. God is doing all that He promised, but who could imagine how terrifying that would be? Even now, as I write, the ark shakes violently with the earthquakes. And the rain—it is not pattering or even pounding against the roof of the ark, as I imagined. No, there is a steady roaring noise. When it first began, it seemed as if the roof would collapse upon us. The noise of the deluge is deafening, terrifying. It is difficult, even in this place of safety, not to panic. I realize now, even here in the ark, even here in this shelter of God, that we must live by faith. We must entrust our lives to God and not be afraid. Sometimes, beyond the roar of the rain, I think I hear the bellowing of animals and the screaming of people.

Lord, I thank you for saving us.

18/02/600 A.N. We have survived the first day of the flood. We see nothing beyond the walls of the ark. We hear nothing beyond the roar of the rain. The ark continues to rattle as the LORD rips apart the earth. No one slept last night. We spent the hours of darkness on our knees, praying to the LORD to spare us. Daylight, which was also dark, brought no relief. I wonder: How long will it take God to destroy the world? How long will His anger pour down? He told me: "Forty days and forty nights." I cannot imagine the terror of this destruction continuing for so long, for even another day. How will we be able to endure it? We must live by faith. We must not be overwhelmed by fear.

Lord, I thank you for giving me, and all those with me in the ark, another day of life!

19/02/600 A.N.   An amazing thing happened today. The ark jolted violently and then began to float. For so many years the ark has stood still on dry ground. It always seemed more like a barn than a boat. But now it is floating! It seems strange that there is water here, deep water covering my home, my fields, the roads where I walked, the towns where I preached. It is all underwater. Where I once lived no longer exists. It has all vanished from the face of the earth. The ark is my only home now. God is my only refuge. I am drifting over the earth now, but I am firmly rooted in my God.

Lord, thank you for this new home, that floats safely above the waters of destruction.

24/02/600 A.N.   Floating on these wild waters has brought a new fear, the fear of being dashed to pieces on the rocks. We do not know where we are going. We cannot see where we are going. The waters are all uncharted. There are no harbours, no havens. We can neither anchor our ship nor steer it. The ark has neither sails nor oars. What can we do? The ark is completely out of our control. Perhaps for that we should be thankful, for we can only entrust our lives to God. We must do so daily, hourly. We must combat our fear with faith. As we float in the ark, we must rest in God.

Lord, we thank you that day after day in these raging waters you steer the ark safely away from the rocks, for these waters are not unknown to you.

17/03/600 A.N.   We have been shut in the ark for one full month. The roaring of the rain continues. We have not grown used to the noise. Even when we sleep, we hear it driving into our dreams. How strange it is that many of the animals have fallen into a deep sleep. They do not awake, even to eat, yet they are alive.

Lord, we give you thanks. The one who watches Noah and his ark never slumbers, nor sleeps. Your eyes are always upon us.

27/03/600 A.N.   Forty days have passed since the beginning of the flood. Today marked a definite change in the intensity of the rain. By evening the drops drumming on the roof of the ark sounded like a normal rainstorm. We could actually talk without having to shout. When we prayed to the LORD together, we could hear each other's prayers. When we sang praises to our God, we too could hear the music of our voices. Some of our pet song-birds joined in the chorus. How wonderful to our ears was that time of worship! We all rejoiced that the roar of the rain had subsided, that the sounds of life were no longer drowned in the deafening roar of destruction. Blessed be the name of our God!

Lord, we thank you for the sounds that we heard this night — the sounds of your praises. Your anger is ending. We give you thanks that your work of destroying the world is almost complete.

28/03/600 A.N.   The forty days and forty nights are finished! Just as God promised, the rain has ceased! There is peace on the earth. Not even a drop of rain ripples the water's surface. Outside the ark all is quiet. There is not one sound, not one whisper, not one breath . . . from any creature. They are all gone. God said, "Every creature that has the breath of life in it, every-thing on earth, will perish." It is finished, according to the Word of the LORD. The silence is overwhelming. The stillness in this new world is awesome. Inside the ark, I listen. I hear only a few sounds: a cricket chirping in the corner of my room, a dog barking somewhere on a lower deck, people talk-ing quietly in the loft above me. Except in this place, in the ark, the sounds of life have ceased upon the earth. In heaven the angels glorify God, but here on earth, there is only one place left, where one can hear the sounds of God's praises. It is here in the ark. We have a great responsibility to praise our God continually.

O Lord, I will exalt you, for you have lifted me . . . above death, above its silence, above the grave, which is now the whole world. May these lips ever praise your holy name.

07/04/600 A.N.   A new question plagues me. Since water now covers the entire earth, where will it go? How will God get rid of it? In a normal rainstorm, the water soaks into earth or it runs into streams and lakes and seas—but this time, there is nowhere for the water to go. The whole world is one enormous ocean! How can so much water ever disappear? Even the tops of the highest mountains are covered by it. Will the sun dry it up? That would take years . . . no, centuries! We would all starve to death in the ark. Will this ark become a huge floating coffin for the last creatures that live upon the earth?

Lord, forgive me for such questions. You have saved us from the waters of the flood—and you will continue to save us from them. I offer you my humble and fearful praise.

13/04/600 A.N.   Dreadful doubts continue to disturb me: Has God forgotten us? The whole world is silent—and so is God. He has not spoken to us since the day He said, "Go into the ark." I must have faith in my God. I must believe His Word, spoken to me so long ago. I must trust in His Promise; He said, "Everything on earth will perish, but I will establish My covenant with you."

Lord, I thank you that you are a covenant-keeping god. What you have promised, I know you will fulfill. Thank you for your Word, which gives me hope, when all appears hopeless. Confirm my faith. I believe you, Lord, but help my unbelief.

14/04/600 A.N.   We were awakened in the night by a new sound—a wind, one that was blowing hard! We wonder: Will it become a horrible, howling hurricane? The ark has been tossing terribly upon the waves, but what is worse is the turmoil in our hearts. We wonder: Is this another storm? Will there be more rain? Isn't the flood over yet? Is God angry again? How long will the LORD's wrath rage against this world? We fear that the flood will go on forever and ever.

Lord, we know not what you are doing. Your ways are not our ways. We can only trust you. We thank you that you are a merciful God, as well as the almighty God. We entrust ourselves to your love. You alone are our help and our saviour. O Lord, do not delay.

21/04/600 A.N.   All week the wind has continued, but there has been no rain. A realization has come to me: This is how the LORD is going to dry the earth—with a wind! God has not forgotten us! Let us shout this news over the waters of the whole world: "God has remembered Noah and all the wild animals that were with him in the ark! Hallelujah! God has sent a wind over the earth to take away the waters! Even the wind and the waves obey Him!" What was for us last week "a horrible, howling hurricane" has become a "wonderful, whistling wind." It is music for our ears and reassurance for our hearts because we know that the floodwaters are receding. We know that God has not forgotten us.

Lord, we thank you for the wind. We thank you for remembering us and loving us. We thank you for this ark, which rocks upon the waves like a giant cradle, giving your creatures peace. We thank you for your loving hands, which safely hold us and gently rock us to sleep.

29/06/600 A.N.　　The voyage is longer than any of us ever imagined possible. How vast is this world! We sail on and on and on . . . never sighting land, never coming to the edge, never reaching the end. We never arrive at that place where the water and the sky meet.

O Lord, creator of the heavens and the earth, how great you are! How awesome are your deeds! How mighty are your works!

17/07/600 A.N.　　Today is the seventeenth day of the seventh month. We have been locked in the ark for one hundred and fifty days. Most of that time we have been either gently rocking or wildly pitching. Since we have been upon the water there has been constant motion, but today it stopped. The ark is still. It is a strange sensation and we find it difficult to walk, having developed "sea legs" over these five months. Why have we stopped moving? I think the explanation is this: The ark has become stuck on a mountain, one that is beneath the water, because we still can see no land. We did not crash into the side of this underwater mountain; no, the ark just softly and safely came to rest upon it. It showed us—again—that God is in control of everything, both great and small. It was His mighty hand which destroyed the world completely; it was His gentle hand which landed our boat easily. Nothing is left to chance in this universe. There is no such thing as "chance." It is a figment of man's warped imagination.

Lord, we thank you for the safe landing of the ark. We thank you that the ark has come to rest after its long dangerous voyage. We thank you for stilling the ark . . . and us. Our hearts have also been turbulent, tossed upon waves of doubt. Forgive us. O Lord, who commands the universe, we thank you for noticing us, for seeing one small boat upon this vast ocean, and for causing it to obey you also. O Lord, we thank you for loving us!

17/09/600 A.N.   We have been at rest for two full months, but still there is no visible sign of land anywhere. However, we know that the water is being dried up by the wind, which has continued to blow steadily. We know this because the water-level mark on the side of the ark goes down. Since we have been stuck upon this mountain, we have been able to measure the receding waters in this way.

Lord, grant us patience. We thank you for the small encouragements you give us each day. We thank you for the great encouragement of your Word, in which we hope.

01/10/600 A.N.   Today is a day to remember, a day to celebrate, a day to praise our God! It is the first day of the tenth month—and on this date we sighted land! It is the first day we have seen the earth, since the LORD flooded the world. We can see the rocks of the mountains upon which the ark is resting. Hurrah! Hurrah! The tops of the mountains are visible! Never have rocks seemed so beautiful to me. I long to stand upon them, to feel the solid earth beneath my feet again.

Lord, I thank you that your anger lasts but a moment, your grace—a whole lifetime! I thank you that you did not destroy the earth forever in your wrath, but only for a season . . . and now you are creating it again! You are unveiling it before my eyes. Day by day I will gaze upon your wonderful work. Day by day I will praise you for your mercy, which endures forever.

21/10/600 A.N.   Daily God changes the shape of the earth. The "islands" of rock continually grow. I watch the little "shoreline" here changing, constantly changing, as new land emerges from out of the depths. I am watching with fascination a fragment of the recreation of the world. Daily, my eyes behold the wonders of God.

Lord, your mercies are new every morning. I thank you.

10/11/600 A.N.   Forty days have passed since we first sighted land. Today I opened the window and set free the first creature from the ark. To whom was this honour given? I did not give it to the prettiest of my pets. No,

I bestowed this honour upon a plain old raven, a scavenger! (I knew that he would survive, finding something to eat among the bits of flesh that must be floating outside the ark. A seed-eating bird might find no food. That was the reason I released a raven.) I set free my big black bird to be my spy. He was so happy to spread his wings again. He soared around and around the ark, cawing with delight and calling to his mate to join him. After some time he flew away over the waters, searching for a meal—glad to be hunting on his own, glad to be providing for himself. My family and I had great plea-sure watching the first of the birds fly away from the ark. I was surprised that a raven, a plain old raven, could bring tears of joy to my eyes. He was so magnificent as he soared through the air with his new-found freedom! Nor was he about to give up that freedom. He flew back and forth from the ark throughout the day, but he would not come to the window, where I could catch him and cage him again. No, he is enjoying his life out in the world. He perches proudly upon the ark, avoiding the window. He hops upon the nearby rocks to show us that he is the first to walk upon the land. Then he flies away again . . . just for the sheer joy of flying! I expect we will hear him cawing his praises around the ark all through the night.

Lord, we thank you for the lowliest of your creatures and for the joy they give us. We thank you that the exodus from the ark has begun today and for the hope which fills our hearts because of it. One day, we too will leave the ark and walk upon the earth again. Thank you, Lord.

17/11/600 A.N.   A week has passed since I set free the raven. He is do-ing well and continues to fly back and forth from the ark, impatient for the release of his mate. He will have to wait awhile. Today I set free a dove, a soft white dove. I wondered: Would such a bird be able to survive out in the world? Would she be able to find a nesting place? a feeding ground? My an-swer came this evening: She returned to the ark because the earth was not ready for her yet. She still needed the shelter and supplies of the ark. The earth could not yet provide these things for her. Gentle little creature—she flew to me by the window and alighted upon my outstretched arm, cooing softly, pleadingly, to be allowed back into the ark. I know now that it is not safe yet to leave our refuge. We must all remain in the ark awhile longer.

Lord, thank you for the information that we received today. Help us to be patient. Help us to wait until the right time to leave the ark. Thank you for this shelter you have provided for us all.

24/11/600 A.N.   Another week has passed. Again I sent the dove from the ark. Again she returned, but this time she brought me a present. In her beak she carried a freshly plucked olive leaf! We have all kinds of dried plants upon the ark to feed the animals—but nothing green, nothing fresh. To see a single fresh green leaf was a real gift for my water-weary eyes. The information my little spy brought me was good too: Although the earth is not ready yet for my little dove, trees are beginning to grow again. This is wonderful news! Now I know that the water is truly receding. There is now earth again, in which the plants can grow.

Lord, we thank you that you are causing the earth to be clothed with green and covered with plants once again.

01/12/600 A.N.   Another seven days has passed. I sent out my little dove one more time, but from this trip she did not return to me. She has found a place to build her nest. The earth, not the ark, is her home once again. Brave little bird—I wonder if she is lonely out there, since she is the only creature dwelling on the earth. (Even my scavenger friend, the crow, keeps the ark's roof as his headquarters.) It is an important day. The first of the ark's creatures has left "home" to settle in the new world. It will not be long, I pray, until we can all leave here, to live once more upon our beloved earth.

Lord, watch over the little dove, who is all alone in the world. We thank you for being a God who cares for even the smallest birds. Since you love them, Lord, we know that you love us too. We thank you for your great love. We ask, O Lord, that soon we too may return to the earth, which your hands have re-made for us. Lord, I have neglected to thank you for this, but I do so now: thank you for the flood, which has washed away the wicked, which has scoured the evil off the face of the earth. We long to live in this new, clean, unpolluted, undefiled world!

01/01/601 A.N.   Today is my birthday. I am six hundred and one years old. I have lived through the destruction of the world. My eyes have seen many things over these many centuries, but today I beheld a most wondrous sight. Today my sons and I removed the covering of the ark. The roof, which has sheltered us for so long, was lifted off today to celebrate my birthday. It was wonderful to see the sky again, the whole expanse of the heavens, and to stand in the sunshine and to breathe the fresh air. What could be a more wonderful gift on my birthday? But there was something more wonderful!

Wonder of wonders—today I gazed over the earth and I saw that the ground was dry! At times I had despaired that I would ever see land again, but there it was! I slowly turned and in all directions, for miles and miles and miles . . . there was land, dry land! The ark is resting high upon a mountain, so the view from here is magnificent. How beautiful is this new world that God has made for my eyes to see! My family was anxious to set out immediately, just to explore, but something (or Someone) restrains me. We will wait. To see the land is enough for today.

Lord, I thank you for giving me 601 years of life—and that you granted me life during a time when you destroyed all life. Lord, I thank you for allowing my old eyes to see the earth again. I thank you that the ark's roof, which has sheltered us for so long, was removed today, my birthday. Tonight, as I view the heavens, which you have adorned with countless twinkling gems, I know that truly you are the Lord of love!

17/02/601 A.N.   More than a month has passed since my birthday, but today is another special day, an anniversary. One year ago, on this very day, the flood began. We have been shut in the ark for one full year! Again my family wanted to go into the world. "Surely this is the day to leave the ark," they said. But I replied, "No. We entered at God's command; we will also leave at God's command." And so we wait for the Word of the LORD.

Lord, we thank you for this year of the flood, in which you have preserved our lives.

27/02/601 A.N.   Today was an exciting day, for the LORD spoke to me again. God has been silent for over a year, but today He spoke to me these blessed words: "Come out!" God said, "Come out of the ark, you and your wife, your sons and their wives. Bring out every kind of living creature that is with you . . . so they can multiply on the earth and be fruitful and increase in number upon it." It was a marvellous day! We watched the birds fly away in pairs, singing with joy because they were soaring into the sky again. We watched the wild animals descend, two by two, down the side of the mountain. Already some of them are just dots in the distance; many others are already out of sight. It is sad to think we may never see these magnificent creatures again. Other animals—such as the cows, sheep, goats, chickens, horses, rabbits, and maybe the monkeys—we are keeping with us as pets or stock. My family is outside, ready to go, ready to begin our climb down the mountain. This is the last time I will write in my journal of praise. Our life in the ark has come to an end. Now we will begin a new life in a new world. I want to conclude my journal with these words:

Praise the Lord!

Give thanks to the Lord, for he is good; his love endures forever. Who can proclaim the mighty acts of the Lord or fully declare his praise? No one can give God the glory due his name, yet he is pleased to accept our lowly offerings of praise.

Praise the Lord!

Notes

1. A.N. = Anno Noah (Age of Noah) because the dates are based on Noah's years!

The teacher's guide for this lesson starts on page 472.

A NEW BEGINNING

• Genesis 8:15–22

G od said, "Come out of the ark . . ." so Noah came out, together with his family and all the animals. They left the ark, just as God commanded. The ark had been their home for more than a year, but now it was time to find a new home and to begin a new life in a new world. As soon as Noah left the ark, he began to build. The first thing he did was to gather some large stones. What do you think Noah was building? A new house for himself? No! A house was not the first thing Noah had in his heart and mind to build. Noah knew what was most important for himself and his family. Their lives did not depend upon a house; their lives depended upon God. Noah had witnessed the terrifying anger of the LORD. Noah knew that a man's sin brought death to the world and that mankind's sin brought the destruction of the world! He knew, better than any man who had ever lived upon the earth, that a house could not shelter a person from death and destruction. Peace with God was the only way to have life! And so . . . the only living people upon the earth did not first build a house for themselves. No, the Scripture records that "Noah built an altar to the LORD." It was an altar to offer sacrifices for their sins. It was an altar to offer thanks for their lives. The very first thing that was built in this new world was an altar to worship God!

Adam had died before Noah was born; Abel had been killed before he was even a baby, but the truth of God had been preserved. It had passed from Adam to Seth and from Seth to Enosh. From father to son, from father to son, from father to son, the truth was told: *There must be a sacrifice for sin! Without the shedding of blood, there is no forgiveness.* Noah's father died before the flood, but Noah had been given 595 years to receive the truth from Lamech (and he had been given 74 years to receive the truth from Enosh.) That truth was not washed away with the flood. It was kept alive in the ark! That truth was not buried in the bottom of the ocean; it was buried safely and deeply in Noah's heart—to be brought forth as man's very first act in the new world. It was a good beginning!

At that time every creature upon the earth was an "endangered species" for their numbers had dwindled to just one male and one female of each kind of animal. From a human perspective, extinction threatened them all. Of the clean animals, (i.e., of the animals acceptable for sacrifice,) there were only seven left—three pairs of each kind, plus one extra. Noah, therefore, had just a small herd of cattle and just a small flock of sheep. He could not buy more livestock at the farmer's market. These were the only cows and sheep left in the whole world! With these few animals his family would somehow have to survive. Then we read of Noah's amazing faith! The Bible says that Noah took "some of all the clean animals and clean birds" and "sacrificed burnt offerings" to the LORD. If there had been any unbelievers left alive to witness this act of Noah's, they would have been outraged! They would have screamed: "How can Noah kill these animals? How can Noah waste these animals? Extinction threatens every species, yet here is this stupid idiot, this insane lunatic, this zealous fanatic, slaughtering one animal after another! What is he doing? He's pouring out those poor creatures' blood on the ground and burning their flesh on an altar . . . for what? for whom? It is an outrage!" That would have been man's response to Noah's sacrifice, but Noah was not concerned about pleasing men; he was concerned about pleasing God.

What was God's response? Was God pleased with Noah's offering? Yes! The Bible records that "the LORD smelled the pleasing aroma . . ." What Noah did was pleasing to God! Why?

1) The cost was great. Noah gave generously to God from the little that he had. Much later in human history there would be rich kings, who would offer many sacrifices to the LORD. We read in the Bible that wise King Solomon offered twenty-two thousand bulls and one hundred and twenty thousand sheep, but Noah offered just one of each, the seventh one, which was set apart for God. That one was more precious in the sight of man and God, than the thousands sacrificed later from the world's abundance.

2) The faith was great. Noah believed and obeyed God's Word, though it came to him from another world and another time. The flood did not cause Noah to forget. He continued to follow the ancient Law of God. Though the earth had been cleansed by water, Noah knew that still their hearts must be cleansed by blood. Noah trusted in God's way of dealing with man's sin—which was by sacrifice.

3) The sign was great. Noah's offering pointed to a greater offering—whom God would send for the world in the fullness of time. The pleasing aroma of Noah's sacrifice was a shadow, pointing to Christ's "fragrant offering and sacrifice to God" (Ephesians 5:2).

The importance of what Noah did on that first day in the new world, can never be properly appreciated. His sacrifice interceded for the whole world, for every living creature upon the face of the earth. When the LORD smelled the pleasing aroma of Noah's burnt offerings, He said in His heart: "Never again will I curse the ground because of man . . . And never again will I destroy all living creatures, as I have done." It was a double promise, spoken by God to Himself in His heart and revealed by God to us in His Word. Never again! Never again such a curse! Never again such a death! When man says "never again"—it happens again, for he is unable to keep his promise; but when God says "never again," His Word can be trusted. God made this promise, knowing that nothing had changed. The face of the earth had been renewed, but the depths of man's heart remained the same. Man's sinful nature had not been washed away with the flood. God said, "Never again . . . because of man . . . even though every inclination of his heart is evil from childhood." It was not because of man or a change in him that God made this promise! No, again man would fill the world with his wickedness; again God would be grieved that He had made man; again the world would deserve destruction—but God promised "never again" would He curse the ground or kill all life because of man. Never again would God stop everything because of man's sin. This great promise from God came from Himself, from God's own Mercy and Goodness, from God's own Grace and LOVE, not from anything in us! We are born as rebels and sinners. We are all condemned with the rest of mankind, when God says of the whole human race: "Every inclination of his heart is evil from childhood." But that day God promised that the world would continue until the end. The LORD promised:

> *As long as the earth endures,*
> *seedtime and harvest,*
> *cold and heat,*
> *summer and winter,*
> *day and night*
> *will never cease.*
>
> *Genesis 8:22*

Has God kept this promise? Yes! Century after century, season has followed season. From that day, until this very day, the world has continued . . . uninterrupted. Life has continued upon the earth, in spite of man's great and ever-increasing wickedness.

The teacher's guide for this lesson starts on page 474.

A SIGN IN
THE CLOUDS

• Genesis 9:1–17

Worshipping the LORD was the first thing Noah did in the new world. His first act was to build an altar and offer sacrifices to God. Did God accept Noah's worship? Was God pleased with it? Yes! We know this because:

1) The LORD promised that never again would He curse the ground or kill all life because of man. The LORD promised that until the end of the world, day would follow night and summer would follow winter . . . uninterrupted. Never again would God stop everything because of man's sin. That was a very great promise!

2) Then God blessed Noah and his sons, saying to them, "Be fruitful and increase in number and fill the earth." Do you remember another time when God said those same words? It was in the beginning, in the Garden of Eden, when the man and woman were perfect, that God blessed them with that same blessing. Now, after the flood, it was another beginning. These human beings were standing in a new world, a world

cleansed of wickedness—but the waters of the flood could not cleanse the human heart. These human beings were not like the first two who received God's blessing. Adam and Eve were perfect; Noah and his wife were not, nor were his sons and their wives. They were sinful human beings—yet how great was God's goodness to them! Still the LORD blessed them, saying, "Be fruitful and multiply and fill the earth." The LORD knew that they would be filling the earth with sinful creatures like themselves, but the LORD of LOVE, in His compassion, allowed man to continue. He commanded him to continue (in spite of his sin) because God had a plan that would cleanse man's heart and cover his sin, as surely as the floodwaters cleansed and covered the earth. The Mighty and Merciful God of heaven and earth had a plan of salvation for man! He had a Saviour for man, who would offer Himself as a Sacrifice for many! They would be the many sons and daughters of these survivors, whose descendants would one day fill the earth. God repeated the blessing. Once, yea twice, the LORD commanded, "Be fruitful and increase in number; multiply on the earth and increase upon it."

3) Although man was still a sinner after the flood, God affirmed man's rule over the creatures of the earth. He did not take man's kingship away from him, but gave it back to him in a different way. In the beginning God said to the man and woman, "Rule over the fish of the sea and the birds of the air and over every living creature that moves on the ground" (Genesis 1:28). Now, in this new beginning, God said, "The fear and dread of you will fall upon all the beasts of the earth and all the birds of the air, upon every creature that moves along the ground, and upon all the fish of the sea. They are given into your hands." Man still ruled the animals, but the harmony between them had been destroyed by sin, which the flood could not restore.

4) As in the beginning, when God gave man food saying, "I give every green plant for food" (Genesis 1:29, 30), so now in this new world, God gave man a new food. It was food that would strengthen him in the post-fall, post-flood world. Perhaps with all these catastrophic changes in man and in his world, the plants were no longer enough to sustain his life. Thus God gave man meat to eat. The LORD said, " Everything that lives and moves will be food for you. Just as I gave you the green plants, I now give you everything."

O thank the LORD for good is He;
His mercy lasts forever.
Thanks to the God of gods give ye;
His mercy lasts forever.
O praises give the King of kings;
His mercy lasts forever.
For He alone does wondrous things;
His mercy lasts forever . . .
He food bestows on all that live;
His mercy lasts forever;
Thanks to the God of heaven give;
His mercy lasts forever.

Psalm 136:1–4, 25, 26

Animals could now be killed for food, but they could not be eaten alive or raw, with the lifeblood still in it. Animals for food must be killed, drained and cooked.

5) God protected human life. Although the life of an animal could be taken for food, human life was sacred. God would surely demand an accounting from any beast or any man who shed the lifeblood of a human being. Man must also protect human life. The flood had not changed the human heart. Soon the world would be filled with violence again. Man must have laws, laws prohibiting and penalizing murder, laws for capital punishment. God declared, "Whoever sheds the blood of man, by man shall his blood be shed." A murderer must be executed, because human life was so sacred. Animals could be killed; there was no penalty for such an act, but people were precious and must be protected. Why was human life sacred? Why were human beings so precious? What elevated human life above animal life? God Himself gave the answer to these questions: "For in the image of God has God made man." Men and women were not just other flesh-and-blood creatures upon the earth; they were very special creatures; they had souls. The man and woman were created in the image of God and they had a special connection to God. Even though human beings had become sinful beings, God did not deny His special bond to these creatures or His special LOVE for them. No, God declared it again in this new beginning: "In the image of God has God made man." It was a blessed reminder!

6) Then God said to Noah and his sons: "I now establish My Covenant with you and with your descendants after you and with every living creature that was with you . . . every living creature on earth. I establish My covenant with you." What is a covenant? To explain it very simply, a covenant is a promise. A covenant is an agreement, by solemn promise, between two parties. (For example, when two people marry, they make a covenant with each other. They enter into an agreement, promising, in a solemn ceremony, never to leave each other until death separates them. So, what is the most important part of a wedding? Is it when the bride walks down the aisle in a beautiful white gown? Is it when the couple exchange rings? Is it when the man and woman kiss each other? Is it when the flower girls scatter petals or the guests throw confetti? Is it when the wedding cake is cut? Is it when the wedding gifts are opened? Is it when the bride and groom drive away in a limousine with streamers flying and car horns blowing? No, the most important part of the wedding is the marriage covenant, when the man and woman exchange their vows, when they make their promises to each other.) After the flood God made a promise to "never again" destroy all life. God also made more than a promise; He made a covenant! God entered into this covenant and established this covenant . . . with whom? To whom did God make His promise? God made it with Noah and all Noah's descendants, (which included us,) and with every living creature upon the earth. This was what God promised them and us: "Never again will all life be cut off by the waters of a flood; never again will there be a flood to destroy the earth." That was what God promised. How did Noah respond? What did Noah promise? Did he promise not to sin? No, he promised nothing! What did Noah's sons promise? Nothing! What did Noah's descendants after him promise? Nothing! What did you promise God? You promised nothing, for you were not even born! When God made this promise to all the animals, what did they promise to do in return? Nothing, for animals can't talk (usually) and they certainly can't make promises! So God entered into a covenant, in which He promised everything and we promised nothing. That was the LOVE of the LORD. That was the grace of God. He made a covenant that depended upon Him alone. If it depended upon us, the covenant would soon be broken—but the promises of God last forever.

7) God gave the world His Word—and that would have been enough. What God says, He does. What God promises, He performs. However, on

that day, God gave more than His Word, more than His promise, more than His covenant. God also gave Noah and us and every living creature a sign. It was a sign of the covenant, a reminder of the promise. God said, "This is the sign of the covenant I am making between Me and you and every living creature with you, a covenant for all generations to come: I have set my rainbow in the clouds, and it will be the sign of the covenant between Me and the earth. Whenever I bring clouds over the earth and the rainbow appears in the clouds, I will remember My covenant between Me and you and all living creatures of every kind. Never again will the waters become a flood to destroy all life. Whenever the rainbow appears in the clouds, I will see it and remember the everlasting covenant between God and all living creatures of every kind on the earth." Then a bright, beautiful rainbow must have appeared, like a bridge between heaven and earth, spanning the sky and touching the earth with its splendour. The rainbow must have appeared as rain began to fall on the earth again, but the few survivors need not fear another world-wide flood. Never again would God destroy the world with a deluge. There, as the sun burst through the storm clouds and shone through the raindrops, there was the sign of God's promise—a rainbow! The LORD said to Noah, "This is the sign of the covenant I have established between Me and all life on earth."

Was it really because of Noah's sacrifice that all these blessings flowed to mankind? No, it was what Noah's sacrifice represented, what Noah's sacrifice foreshadowed, which secured this peace with God. It was the perfect sacrifice for sins in the fullness of time by the eternal Son of God that allowed man to stand in this present grace. It was because of Jesus' death upon the cross that God could bless the sinful sons of men. The pleasing aroma from Noah's altar was but a fore-scent of Christ's "fragrant offering and sacrifice to God," with which the LORD was forever pleased.

God would preserve the earth and men until the end. The human race would not pass away until that final Day of the LORD, the day of God's anger, when the heavens and the earth would be destroyed, when God said, "I will punish the world for its evil and the wicked for their sins" (Isaiah 13:9, 11). When Noah stood that first day in the new world, a sign appeared in the clouds—a rainbow. On the last day in this same world there would be another sign in the clouds! All Noah's descendants, all the people in every part of the earth, would see that sign. Jesus Himself said, "At that time the sign of the Son of Man will appear in the sky, and all the nations of the earth will mourn" (Matthew 24:30). "At that time men will see the Son of Man coming on the clouds with great power and glory. And He will send His angels and gather the elect from the four winds, from the ends of the earth to the ends of the heavens . . . I tell you the truth, this race will certainly not pass away until all these things have happened. Heaven and earth will pass away, but My Words will never pass away" (Mark 13:26, 27, 30, 31). Because the day of God's vengeance is surely coming, Jesus said: "Be on guard! Be alert! Keep Watch!" He said, "Be careful or . . . that day will close on you unexpectedly like a trap. For it will come upon all those who live on the face of the whole earth. Be always on the watch, and pray! Pray that you may be able to escape all that is about to happen, and that you may be able to stand before the Son of Man" (Luke 21:34–36). Yes, on that final and terrible day there would be another sign in the clouds—the Son of Man! "Look, He is coming with the clouds, and every eye will see Him, even those who pierced Him; and all the peoples of the earth will mourn because of Him. So shall it be! Amen" (Revelation 1:7).

The teacher's guide for this lesson starts on page 476.

A DIVIDED FAMILY

• Genesis 9:18–11:32
• Acts 2; 17:26–28

The sons of Noah who came out of the ark were named Shem, Ham and Japheth. These were the three sons of Noah, and from them came all the people who were scattered over the earth. There was just one family, with Noah as the father of the entire human race. However, very quickly the family of man was divided.

The First Division

Just as Adam's sons had been divided and there arose two distinct peoples, known as the "sons of God" and the "sons of men," so also with Noah's own sons there was a division. One son and his descendants were "blessed." The other son and his descendants were "cursed." How did this happen? The Bible records the sad story:

Sometime after the flood, Noah returned to his work of being a farmer. He was "a man of the soil" and he planted many things for food. He also planted a vineyard, which in time produced grapes. From the harvest of grapes Noah made wine. Then we read how this good man, this great man, sinned. All have sinned and fallen short of the glory of God. Noah was not an exception. He was righteous, but he was not perfect. We read that Noah drank the wine and became drunk. He fell into a drunken sleep and lay naked in his tent. What a shameful picture of Noah, who was "righteous" and "blameless" and a man who "walked with God" (Genesis 6:9)—but what his youngest son did was more shameful! Ham came into his father's tent and saw him lying there drunk and naked. What should Ham do? What should Ham say? Ham should honour his father. Ham should honour the man who twice gave him life. He should gently cover his father with a blanket and say nothing to anyone about what he had seen. But Ham did not do this. He dishonoured his father. Ham thought it was funny and went outside to his two brothers to share the joke with them. Ham mocked his father. Ham urged his brothers to go into Noah's tent for a good look and a good laugh. Shem and Japheth refused. They loved their father and wanted to honour him. Love covers not only one sin, but a multitude of sins. How could they cover their father's sin? How could they cover his sin without seeing his shame? "I know what we can do," said one of the brothers. "We can put the end of a cloak over our shoulders, stretch it out by standing apart, walk into our father's tent backwards and drop it over his sleeping body." Shem and Japheth did that. They covered him with their faces turned the other way, so that they would not see their father's nakedness. Sometime later, when Noah awoke from his wine and his sleep, he found out what Ham had done to dishonour him. Noah was not only Ham's father; he was also a prophet of the LORD. Noah had the authority to bless his sons . . . or curse them. It was not only his word; it was God's Word. Noah said: "Cursed be Canaan!" Who was Canaan? Canaan was the son of Ham. Noah was cursing Ham and all his descendants after him. Cursed be Canaan, the son of Ham! Noah also said: "Blessed be the LORD, the God of Shem!" The LORD's blessing was upon Shem and his descendants. "Blessed are the people whose God is the LORD" (Psalm 144:15). Since the LORD would be the God of Shem, blessed indeed would be Shem! Japheth was included in Shem's blessing, but Canaan would be cursed and conquered, the lowest of slaves to both his brothers.

Thus the family of man was divided. What separated them was not something you could see or hear. Noah's three sons did not look or sound any different, but now God's blessing or God's cursing rested upon them. The effect of God's Word was immediate, but not apparent. As in every age, the wicked seemed to flourish. It was the cursed race, the sons of Ham, that grew in strength. Ham had sons, who became mighty men upon the earth. One of Ham's many grandsons was named Nimrod, which means "Rebel" — because the sons of Ham were proud of their rebellion against the LORD. Nimrod, or "Rebel," was a mighty hunter, a mighty warrior, a mighty ruler. Many were his conquests; many were his kingdoms. Just as the sons of Cain, the sons of Ham also formed armies and built cities. Babylon and Nineveh were two of the great centres of evil, constructed by Nimrod the Rebel. Not only wicked cities, but also wicked nations, came from the sons of Ham. Cursed be Canaan! From Canaan came the Canaanites, but from Shem came the Shemites or Semites, among whom were the Israelites.

Blessed be the LORD, the God of Shem! The descendants of Shem also grew in number, but we read not of mighty men or mighty cities or mighty nations. Instead we read a genealogy of fathers and sons, with their year of birth and death. Instead we find a simple list of names:

1. Shem
2. Arphaxad
3. Shelah
4. Eber
5. Peleg (whose name meant "Division," because in his time the people of earth were again divided)
6. Reu
7. Serug
8. Nahor
9. Terah
10. Abram

Although the number of generations counted may not have been literal numbers, they were perfect numbers: ten generations from Adam to Noah and ten generations from Noah to Abram. Who was Abram? He was the man who became Abraham, the "Father of many" and the father of faith! He was the man who believed God, and it was reckoned to him as righteousness. Abraham was the man with whom God spoke and made a covenant. Abraham became the father of God's chosen people, the Israelites. Through Abraham also came the Messiah, the Saviour from sin and death, whom God had promised to the world. The LORD said to Abram, "All peoples on earth will be blessed through you." Through Abram, son of Terah, son of Nahor . . . son of Shem, came Jesus Christ, the Son of God. Blessed be the LORD, the God of Shem!

Noah cursed Canaan, saying "May Canaan be the slave of Shem." It was almost a thousand years later that this curse was finally fulfilled, when the Israelites (descendants of Shem) conquered the Canaanites (descendants of Ham). Though the Word of God operates slowly, it operates surely. The LORD is not slow in keeping His Promise, as some understand slowness, for with God a thousand years are like a day. On that very day, Canaan was surely cursed . . . as surely as Shem was blessed.

We do not read of Noah again. As his fathers before him and his sons after him, Noah died. Altogether Noah lived 950 years. No man on earth would live that long again. Noah had seen two worlds and he had lived long enough to know that there is much evil and sorrow under the sun. Noah went to a far better world, one in which there was no sin or pain. Noah went to be with God.

The Second Division

In the beginning God created man with the gift of speech. The LORD enabled people to speak, so that with their tongues they could talk to one another and glorify God. It was a good gift, but the human race was divided in how that gift was used. Some people, the "sons of God," used their speech to worship the LORD; other people, the "sons of men," used their speech to blaspheme God's holy name. The human race was divided. Some used the gift of language for good; others used it for evil . . . but everyone used the same language, for the whole world had just one speech. The native tongue of every man was the same.

After the flood, the whole world still spoke a single common language, for the whole world was still one family. The sons of Noah, both the "blessed" ones and the "cursed" ones, increased in number upon the earth. As the population grew, people needed more room, so they moved to new areas for settlement. This was what God had intended; this was what God had commanded. "Increase in number and fill the earth" (Genesis 1:28). From the beginning it was God's purpose that people should cover the earth, building the Kingdom of God, extending His dominion from sea to sea. God's praises were to be sung from one end of the world to the other! The Name of the LORD was to be magnified in the entire earth! That was the plan of God.

But the "sons of men" had another plan. They said, "Come, let us build *ourselves* a city, with a tower that reaches to the heavens, so that we may make a name for *ourselves*, and *not* be scattered over the face of the whole earth." They refused to go forth in faith, obeying God's command. They refused to go forth in faith, relying upon God for provision and protection. They had found a fertile plain, which produced abundant food; they would go no farther. They would stay wherever they pleased. Who was God, that they should honour Him? Who was God that they should believe or obey Him? Who was God that they should rely upon Him? The LORD had shown the whole world who He was. Had the sons of men so soon forgotten the flood? Had they so soon forgotten Noah's God? Had they so soon turned into rebels, denying the LORD and defying His Word? Yes, to their own destruction they made this decision: They would trust in themselves; they would live for themselves; they would make a name for themselves. It was not the Word of God, but the words of men, that they would obey! They said to each other, "Come, let us build *ourselves* a city, with a tower that reaches to the heavens, so that we may make a name for *ourselves*, and *not* be scattered over the face of the whole earth." These were the words that the sons of men followed. Just as Cain had built a city to protect and exalt himself, so these men began to build a city for the same reasons. God was not their refuge and their strength; their city was. God was not their fortress and their tower; they were building their own, one that would reach the heavens. It was man's first skyscraper! This tower would rise above the plain. It would be a landmark for miles and miles, a focal point of power, to keep earth's people united in a single kingdom. In unity they sought safety and security. Themselves they sought to magnify:

> A mighty fortress we will be,
> Ourselves to glorify.
> A tower all mankind will see,
> That reaches to the sky.

Like the sons of Cain, the sons of Ham were inventive. They used new methods of construction, building with bricks (instead of stone) and tar (instead of mortar). These people were industrious. Their tower rose higher and higher and higher, because of their hard work. The Canaanites were co-operative and communicative. They discussed their plans and plotted their schemes, as if they had one heart and mind. They had a single purpose, clearly defined by a common language. *Together* they conspired against the LORD. *Together* they laboured and accomplished great things. They became famous in their day, for their tower was the single wonder of that ancient world. It must have attracted much attention. People must have come from the most remote edges of human settlement to see with awe what these men were making.

The LORD also came to see the city and the tower that the sons of men were building. Was God impressed with their work? Did He marvel at their monument to man? No, for the LORD sees into the human heart and what God saw was an ugly sight: Rebellion! Rebellion against the LORD! This tower was being built to disobey His command. It was a work of unbelief. It was an evil undertaking. This tower was built to the praise and glory and majesty of man. It was built to blaspheme God. The LORD would not allow such a wicked work to continue. God said, "If as one people, speaking the same language, they have begun to do this, then nothing they plan to do will be impossible for them." Man had spoken: "Come, let us build . . ." Now God spoke: "Come, let us go down and confuse their language, so they will not understand each other." What God says, He does.

Suddenly, there was chaos on the construction site. No one could understand anyone else. Each man was talking in a different language. There was confusion, suspicion, division. The builders could no longer work together, or even live together. God had brought their plans to nothing. Their project was abandoned. The city grew no larger; the tower rose no higher. The sons of men left their work unfinished and their dream unfulfilled. God had shattered the Kingdom of Man by dividing it into many kingdoms, according to their many languages. People of a common speech set off and settled together in their own region, apart from other peoples and languages. Thus God forced man to obey His command to populate the entire earth. (He is the LORD! He said, "I am God, and there is no other. I am God and there is none like Me . . . I say: My purpose will stand and I will do all that I please . . . What I have said, that will I bring about; what I have planned, that will I do" Isaiah 46:9–11.) From that tower, from that city, the LORD scattered man over all the earth. That infamous spot was called "Babel" (also Babylon), which means "Confusion"—because there the LORD confused the language of the whole world. From there the LORD scattered them over the face of the whole earth.

The "sons of men" wanted to make a great name for themselves by building this tower, but none of their names are remembered, not one. It is the LORD's work that is remembered and honoured: Babel! Confusion! It was not any mighty man, but the Mighty LORD, who was glorified. No plot against God can succeed. No plan against Him can prevail. The One enthroned in heaven laughs, for even the wrath of man will praise Him.

The "sons of men" united themselves in their rebellion against the LORD, but God, by confusing their one language, divided mankind, scattering him over the earth. Never again would all men be united in their evil. The Kingdom of Man was divided against itself. Nation would fight against nation, checking one another's power. Kings would arise, whose desires were to rule the world, but none of them would succeed, for their evil ambition would be stopped by other kings. God was merciful to man in this: He restrained man's evil. God was also merciful in this: God determined the times and places of nations and scattered mankind over the face of the earth, "so that men would seek Him and perhaps reach out for Him and find Him" (Acts 17:27).

Although this division of the Kingdom of Man into many languages has lasted thousands of years, even to this very day, there was a time when God reversed the curse of Babel/Confusion. In those days God poured out His Spirit upon His people. They were filled with the Holy Spirit and began to speak in other tongues or languages, as the Spirit enabled them. God's people, from every nation under heaven, heard them speaking in his own language. It was a miracle! Utterly amazed, they asked, "How is it that each of us hears them in his own native language? We hear them declaring the wonders of God in our own tongues" (Acts 2:8, 11)! That day, in Jerusalem, (around 33 A.D.) the gospel was preached and the good news concerning the Saviour was proclaimed—in many tongues, in every language! On that day people from every nation were being gathered into the Kingdom of God. On that day people from every nation were being united in Jesus Christ, the King of kings and Lord of lords. The Word of the LORD went forth from Jerusalem, to bring God's salvation to the ends of the earth.

In the end and forever, the Kingdom of Man would be destroyed. "Fallen! Fallen is Babylon the Great! Woe! Woe, O great city, O Babylon, city of power! In one hour your doom has come!" (Revelation 18:1, 10). However, the Kingdom of God would stand forever.

Hallelujah! For the LORD God Almighty reigns.
Let us rejoice and be glad and give Him glory.

Revelation 19:6

In the end and forever, there would be a great multitude that no one could count, from every nation, tribe, people and language, standing before the throne of God, in front of the Lamb of God, who is Jesus Christ our Lord. They would cry out:

Salvation belongs to our God, who sits on the throne,
and to the Lamb.

Revelation 7:10

In heaven there was new song of worship to the Lamb:

You are worthy . . . because You were slain,
and with Your blood You purchased men for God
from every tribe and language and people and nation.
You have made them to be a kingdom . . .
to serve our God, and they will reign on the earth.

Revelation 5:9, 10

The voice of many angels, numbering thousands upon thousands, and ten thousand times ten thousand, sang in a loud voice:

Worthy is the Lamb, who was slain, to receive power and wealth
and wisdom and strength and honour and glory and praise!

Revelation 5:12

Every creature in heaven and on earth sang:

To Him who sits on the throne and to the Lamb be praise and
honour and glory and power, for ever and ever! Amen!

Revelation 5:13, 14

The teacher's guide for this lesson starts on page 478.

THE CITY OF GOD

The "sons of men" had tried to make themselves into a great nation by staying together in one place, but the LORD divided them into many nations and scattered them over all the earth. The "sons of men" tried to make a great name for themselves by building a city and a tower, which would unite them. They said, "Come let us build ourselves a city, with a tower that reaches to the heavens, so that we may make a name for ourselves . . ." but the LORD erased their names from the memory of man. Were their names carved on the foundation stones as a memorial to themselves? If so, then it was vanity of vanities! Their names vanished! Not even the tower remained as a monument to these men. In time the tower, which was built to touch the sky, tumbled to the ground, becoming a heap of rubble; then even those ruins disappeared, as the bricks crumbled into dust. Yes, their dreams turned to dust in the wind. In the place where once stood the mighty tower of proud men, there was finally only green grass growing under the sun. Not a trace was left of these men or their work. Their bones and their bricks turned to dust and their names were buried with them in the earth. No one would honour them; no one would even remember their names.

Now begins the story of a man whose name is revered and whose faith is renowned throughout the world. Although this man lived thousands of years ago, his life has not been forgotten. The LORD promised this man: "I will make your name great," and God kept that promise. Even you children know this man's name, though he lived so long ago and so far away. Abraham! At birth he was named Abram and for many years, until he was a very old man, his name remained Abram. So we begin the story of Abram, the son of Terah, the son of Nahor . . . the son of Shem. Blessed be the LORD, the God of Shem!

When God confused the language of the whole world and divided the kingdom of man into many nations and scattered the human race over all the earth, He did so for a reason. God did this so that men would not trust in themselves. "God did this so that men would seek Him and reach out for Him and find Him" (Acts 17:27), but they continued to reject the Grace of God. Men continued in their rebellion against the LORD. People exchanged the truth of God for a lie. They worshipped and served created things rather than the Creator, who is blessed forever. They exchanged the glory of the immortal God for images and idols, which their own hands had made. Different nations and regions made for themselves different gods. Instead of filling the earth with the praises of the one true God, once again people filled the earth with every kind of evil, including now the evil of idolatry. Into such a world was Abram born, where strange gods were glorified. Into such a country was Abram born, where idols filled the land. Into such a family was Abram born, where his own father and grandfather worshipped false gods. The sin of idolatry had corrupted the world to such an extent, that even the godly line of Shem was infected by it. Once again it seemed as if Satan was winning the war on earth, for there was not one nation which worshipped the LORD, no not one. In every nation and every people and every language, the LORD's name was blasphemed on the earth. The world was again ripe for destruction, but God had made a covenant with earth's creatures. This time, God would allow life in the world to continue . . . until the end. This time, God would do something else. The wickedness of man flourished on the earth, but God had a plan, because God so loved the world. From the beginning God had a plan to save His people from their sins—and that plan involved the man named Abram! From this man, God would make for Himself a new nation. From this man, God would build His kingdom on earth. From this man, God would bless all peoples. From this man, God would send the Saviour of the world!

Abram was ten generations from Noah, who was now dead. God had spoken to Noah after the flood, but almost four hundred years had passed since then. God had not spoken again. He had been silent for a long time, but then we read that the God of glory appeared to Abram and said, "Leave your country, your people and your father's household and go to the land I will show you." God was calling Abram to leave everything and to go . . . where? Abram didn't know. God didn't say. The LORD was calling Abram to leave everything and to follow Him—by faith. It was not an easy assignment. How would you like to be sent away from your country and your city, your people and your family, to go to a strange land? How would you like to move, leaving everyone and everything behind you, without knowing what was in front of you? That was exactly what Abram had to do. God said, "Leave . . . and go to the land I will show you." Abram had to trust the Word of God. He had to believe that, when he set out on this journey, God would lead him to the right place. Abram had to go forth by faith. He had to do the very thing that the unbelieving men of Babel were unwilling to do. They united themselves in fear; Abram must separate himself by faith. They fortified themselves in fear; Abram must move forward by faith. Would he do it? Would he believe God? Would he obey God? We read that "Abram left, just as the LORD had told him." We read: "By faith Abraham, when called to go . . . obeyed and went, even though he did not know where he was going" (Hebrews 11:8).

When God called Abram, He made this promise to him:

> *I will make you into a great nation*
> *and I will bless you;*
> *I will make your name great,*
> *and you will be a blessing.*
> *I will bless those who bless you,*
> *and whoever curses you I will curse.*
> *All peoples on earth will be blessed through you.*
>
> *Genesis 12:2, 3*

It was a very great promise! This Word of God was the treasure that Abram kept in his heart as he set out for the place which he did not know.

His other possessions were packed on camels or donkeys, but this promise was worth more than all the gold in the world. Abram left with faith in God's Word: "I will bless you!" Abram obeyed because Abram believed. This blessing of God was more real to him, and more dear to him, than anything else he had. Abram was willing to leave everything, for the sake of this promise.

Abram did not leave all by himself. His wife Sarai went with him. How difficult it must have been for her to leave everything too. She had to leave her beautiful home in the city of Ur . . . for what? Her husband did not even know where they were going! She would have to live in a tent . . . for how long? Her husband didn't know. She would have to say good-bye to her family and friends . . . why? Her husband said that God told him to go, of that he was sure, but he knew nothing else! Many women would have refused to set forth on such an uncertain venture, but Sarai did not give way to fear. She too had faith—and faith is being certain of what we do not see. Sarai could not see what was ahead, but she too placed her hope and her trust in God. She was submissive to her husband, following him and obeying him wherever he went, even when he did not know where he was going! So it was that Sarai was also included in this great plan of God. Everything in this world is uncertain, except the LORD's promises, which are true and sure. God's Word endures forever. Sarai could go forth in full confidence, trusting that God's blessing was upon her too, for she and her husband were one.

So, Abram and Sarai set out on their strange journey by faith. They had no children of their own, but Lot, who was the orphaned nephew of Abram, went with them as well as many servants. Eventually they came to the land of Canaan. Cursed be Canaan! The land was filled with the wicked, God-hating, idol-worshipping Canaanites. Their fortified cities guarded the land. Their evil kings ruled the land. It all belonged to the Canaanites. They owned everything. Abram travelled through the land, pitching his tents wherever he could. He must have wondered how God would fulfill His Promise to him. How would God make him into a great nation? He was an old man of seventy-five years, and he had no children. His wife Sarai was barren. The years had passed and she had never had a baby. Now she was too old to have any children. How could God make him into a great nation? He had no children and he had no land. Without people and without land, there is nothing. Could God make a nation from nothing? Yes! God made the world from nothing, so God could certainly make a nation, a great nation, from this man. If Abram had doubted the Word of God, he could have turned back. He could have returned to his homeland, for there was opportunity to do so, but Abram did not waver through unbelief regarding the promises of God. He remained in Canaan, by faith. He penetrated deeper into Canaan, by faith. He travelled through the land as if it belonged to him—and indeed it did belong to him—by faith. Abram travelled as far as a place called Shechem and there, by a great oak tree, he made his camp site. It was there, in the heart of the land of Canaan, that the LORD appeared to Abram again. God said to him, "To your offspring I will give this land." Abram had no offspring, and he had no land, but he had God's Promise! The land of Canaan was "The Promised Land," promised to Abram and to Abram's offspring. It mattered not that it belonged to the Canaanites. This, then, was the land that God promised to show him. This was it, the land of Canaan. Abram believed God's Word. At that place Abram built an altar to the LORD, who had appeared to him. Already Abram was claiming this land for God! Already God's Promise (and Noah's prophesy) were being fulfilled. Now, among the many idols of Canaan, there stood an altar to the one true God! Abram continued to travel through the land, this time pitching his tent between the cities of Bethel and Ai. There he built another altar to the LORD. There Abram assembled his people for worship and they called on the name of the LORD. Yes, Canaan was being conquered for God! Already the praises of the LORD were rising from this spot on the earth. It was a small, but also a great, victory!

Altars were the only thing that Abram ever built in the Promised Land. For the rest of his life there he lived in tents. He never built a home. He never built a city. He never yearned for his old country or searched for a new country. He was waiting. He was longing for another country, a better country—a heavenly country! Abram knew he was but a stranger and a foreigner on earth; he knew that his citizenship was in heaven. Abram was not thinking of his old city or planning a new city; he was waiting and longing for the City of God. It was not here; it would never be here on this earth. Abram was looking forward to the city with unshakable foundations, the city that would last forever, the city whose architect and builder was God!

The LORD has given to us a "picture" of that city, a beautiful description of it in His Word. The apostle John was given a "vision" of the City of God and he wrote this revelation for us when he was in the Spirit:

> I saw a new heaven and a new earth . . . I saw the Holy City, the
> new Jerusalem, coming down out of heaven from God . . . It shone

with the glory of God, and its brilliance was like that of a very precious jewel, clear as crystal. It had a great high wall with twelve gates and with twelve angels at the gates. On the gates were written the names of the twelve tribes of Israel . . . The wall of the city had twelve foundations, and on them were the names of the twelve apostles of the Lamb . . . The wall was made of jasper, and the city of pure gold, as pure as glass. The foundation of the city walls were decorated with every kind of precious stone . . . sapphire . . . emerald . . . topaz . . . amethyst. The twelve gates were twelve pearls, each gate made of a single pearl. The great street of the city was of pure gold, like transparent glass. I did not see a temple in the city, because the LORD God Almighty and the Lamb are its temple. The city does not need the sun or the moon to shine on it, for the glory of God gives it light, and the Lamb is its lamp. The nations will walk by its light and the kings of the earth will bring their splendour into it. On no day will its gates ever be shut, for there will be no night there . . . Nothing impure will ever enter it, nor will anyone who does what is shameful or deceitful, but only those whose names are written in the Lamb's Book of Life. Then the angel showed me The River of the Water of Life, as clear as crystal, flowing from the throne of God and of the Lamb, down the middle of the great street of the city. On each side of the river stood The Tree of Life . . . No longer will there be any curse. The throne of God and of the Lamb will be in the city, and His servants will serve Him. They will see His face, and His Name will be on their foreheads. There will be no more night. They will not need the light of a lamp or the light of the sun, for the Lord God will give them light. And they will reign for ever and ever. (Revelation 21:1–22:6)

This is the city God has prepared for those who trust in Him. The City of God endures forever and the Kingdom of God is everlasting, but the towers and cities of men, their nations and their kingdoms and their empires—they will all collapse; they will all crumble and vanish. Death will be their end. Dust in the wind . . . all they are is dust in the wind.

The teacher's guide for this lesson starts on page 480.

THE GOD WHO GUIDES AND GUARDS AND GIVES

• **Genesis 12, 13**
• **Hebrews 11:8–16**

B y faith Abram left his home, even though he did not know where he was going. God said to him, "Go to the land I will show you." Abram believed God and obeyed God. By faith Abram left, *trusting that God would guide him.* Did the LORD guide Abram? Yes! God brought him to the land of Canaan. There God appeared to him and promised, "To your offspring I will give this land."

By faith Abram made his home in this promised land, like a stranger in a foreign country—and he lived in a tent. Was Abram safe there? He was one righteous man among a whole country of wicked people. Remember what happened to Abel, who was murdered by his own brother, simply because he was righteous and his brother was wicked. Abel was murdered because he worshipped the true God in the right way and his brother Cain did not. What then would happen to Abram, who was worshipping God and building altars to the LORD in a nation filled with idol-worshippers and ruled by God-haters? Surely they would despise him! What would become of Abram, a righteous man, who was wandering in a country and living in a land of wicked people? Surely they would murder him! Abram had only a tent for a home. He did not have a house with a strong wood door, which he could lock. He did not have a city with a high stone wall, where he could hide. No, Abram had only a tent, but he was not without protection. Abram believed that the LORD was his Strength and his Shield. By faith Abram lived in this land, in a tent, *trusting that God would guard him.* Did the LORD guard Abram? Yes! God guarded Abram all the days and years of his life, which were many.

By faith Abram traded the pleasures and the riches of this world to follow God. His greatest joy was in God's Word; his greatest treasure was in God's Promise. The LORD said, "I will bless you" and Abram believed in that blessing. Abram trusted God to provide for him. He was dwelling in a strange land among foreign people, but Abram believed that God would take care of him there, giving him all that he needed to live. Abram lived by faith, *trusting that God would give to him.* Did God give to Abram? Yes . . . but in a way that tested Abram's faith. This was what happened:

While Abram was living in the land of Canaan, there was a famine. The clouds vanished; the rain stopped; the grass shrivelled; the crops failed. The flocks and herds grew weak and sick with no pasture or water. Soon the animals began to die. The Bible records that "the famine was severe." People also were starving because there was no food. What little there was became extremely expensive. People were forced to sell all they had just to get enough food to stay alive. Famines often lasted many years and at their end, the people left alive in these disaster areas were impoverished—because all their wealth had been traded for food. So, this was where God led Abram! Not long after his arrival in Canaan, he found himself in a foreign land, which could produce no food! Abram found himself in a land of famine! Was this really where God had led him? Should he continue to believe God's Word? Should he continue to obey God's Word? Perhaps he should just turn around and go home. Perhaps he should return to his own country where there would be food to eat and wealth to gain. Would God really take care of him? In the midst of this famine, could Abram still trust God to guide him and guard him and give to him? Yes, Abram trusted the LORD, but still he had to ask these questions: What should he do? Where should he go? We read in the Bible that "Abram went down to Egypt to live there for a while because the famine was severe." For a while, only for a while, did Abram go to another country, but he did not plan to move there permanently. No,

Abram considered Canaan his "home." That was where he planned to live the rest of his life on this earth, because that was the land promised to him by God, and Abram believed God's Word!

So, Abram went down to Egypt to live there for a while because the famine in Canaan was severe. However, Egypt also had its dangers! Abram trusted God, but he was also afraid. Abram was afraid that the Egyptians would kill him in order to steal his beautiful wife. Abram should have trusted that God would be with him here, too, guarding him. He should have entered this new country by faith, not by fear—but he didn't. Before he crossed the border into Egypt, Abram told his wife Sarai, "I know what a beautiful woman you are. When the Egyptians see you . . . they will kill me, but they will let you live. Say you are my sister, so that I will be treated well for your sake and my life will be spared because of you." This was not exactly a lie. Sarai was Abram's half-sister, but that was only a half-truth, for she was also his wife! When Abram and Sarai were checked at the border, sure enough, the Egyptian officials noticed that Sarai was a very beautiful woman. They reported this to Pharaoh, King of Egypt, and they praised her beauty to him. So Sarai was taken into the king's palace to become one of the king's wives. What happened to Abram? Just as he thought, he was treated very well by the Egyptians, because they thought that he was Sarai's brother. They gave Abram gifts of sheep and cows, donkeys and camels, menservants and maidservants, silver and gold. Abram became very rich during this time. He gained much wealth, but do you think he was happy? No, he had lost his wife! What did all these riches mean, when the most precious person in the world to him was gone? His own wife now belonged to another man! And this man was no one less than Pharaoh himself, the King of Egypt! Oh, what could Abram do? Nothing! If he spoke the truth now, then surely the Egyptians would just laugh at his lie and then take his life. If he now said, "She is my wife!"—surely they would kill him! Oh, what could Abram do? Nothing! He could do nothing! (Oh what a tangled web we weave, from which we cannot escape.) Abram was trapped by his own lie, trapped in the land of Egypt—and he could do nothing. How would he ever get back his wife, whom he loved? How would he ever get back to the land which was promised? Abram couldn't do anything . . . but God could do something! Did Abram turn to the LORD for help? We don't know. The Bible doesn't say whether Abram cried out to God for help, but we do know that the LORD delivered him from all his troubles!

The LORD intervened! The Bible records: "The LORD inflicted serious diseases on Pharaoh and his household because of Abram's wife Sarai." It was also revealed to Pharaoh why he had been struck with these diseases. Somehow, he found out about Abram's lie. He found out that Sarai was really Abram's wife. So Pharaoh summoned Abram. Abram had to walk into the palace, into the court of the king, and stand before his throne. He must have been terrified! He must have thought: Now I am going to be judged. The King of Egypt said to him, "What have you done to me? Why didn't you tell me she was your wife? Why did you say, 'She is my sister,' so that I took her to be my wife?" Abram must have thought: Now I am going to be killed. But instead, Pharaoh said to him, "Here is your wife; take her—and go!" Abram could hardly believe his ears. Was he really allowed to just take his wife and go back to the promised land? Yes, and more! Pharaoh gave orders to his soldiers not to harm them. Abram was allowed, by the command of the King of Egypt, to leave the country safely . . . along with everything he had acquired there. Could this be possible? Yes, with God all things are possible! This was the LORD's doing! This was the LORD's blessing! Had not God promised Abram, "I will bless you." Nothing can stand in the way of God's promises. Nothing can stand in the way of God's purposes. No one can stop the plan of God, not even the King of Egypt, not even the sin of Abram! The LORD Almighty has sworn, "Surely as I have planned, so it will be" (Isaiah 14:24). The LORD had great plans for Abram and Sarai together in Canaan—and so He brought them back there.

Thus it was that Abram left the land of Egypt and returned to Canaan with large flocks of sheep and herds of cows, caravans of camels and donkeys carrying loads of silver and gold, and long lines of servants. Abram returned to Canaan a very rich man. At the end of the famine, Abram was not poor like everyone else; no, he was a very wealthy man. Now, when Abram set up camp, there were hundreds of tents to pitch and thousands of animals to pasture. Did God give to Abram? Yes, God gave to Abram abundantly, more than he could ask, more than he could even imagine! God gave to Abram during a famine in a hostile land; He gave in a time and place when Abram thought he would lose everything, even his life. How gracious was the LORD! Abram could surely trust God to guide him and guard him and give to him all the days of his life. We can trust God too. As surely as God kept His Promise to Abram, He will also keep His promises to us. "I will never leave you, nor forsake you," says the LORD to His people (Hebrews 13:5).

Abram continued to wander in the land of the Canaanites, going from place to place, until he came to a spot where he had built an altar to the LORD. It was still there. At that place (between Bethel and Ai) Abram and all his household called on the name of the LORD. They did not forget God in their prosperity. No, there they worshipped the LORD, who had so abundantly blessed them all. Not only had Abram prospered; his nephew Lot had also shared in that blessing. It had been good for Lot to be connected with Abram, for God's blessings over-flowed to him. Now Lot also had large flocks and herds to move and many tents to pitch. It was becoming extremely difficult for so many people and animals to travel together. There was not enough grass in one place to feed all the animals. It was obvious that the land could no longer support Abram and Lot together. Their combined possessions were too great! Unfortunately (but naturally) quarrelling over pasture and water arose between the herdsmen of Abram and the herdsmen of Lot. Also, there were all the Canaanite peoples, who were also living off that land. The situation could not continue that way much longer. So Abram spoke to Lot, "Let's not have any quarrelling between you and me . . . Is not the whole land before you? Let's part company. If you go to the left, I'll go to the right. If you go to the right, I'll go to the left." Abram very generously gave his nephew the first choice. Lot looked over the land and saw that the whole plain of the Jordan River was watered well, like the garden of the LORD, so he chose that lush green grassland for himself. It may have looked like the garden of the LORD, but alas, it was a place where sin flourished! The pasture was good, but the people were not. The cities of that plain were centres of evil, where the wicked people in them were sinning greatly against the LORD. Lot chose to live among these cities. Alas, he had chosen by sight, not by faith! He pitched his tents near Sodom and Gomorrah, two of the most wicked cities in the world. Alas! Alas! He chose the people of Sodom, rather than the people of Abram, to be his close neighbours.

Abram remained in the hill country of Canaan, where the grass was not so green. He had given his nephew the first and the best. What now was left for him? Sometime after Lot had left him, the LORD said to Abram, "Lift up your eyes from where you are. Look north and south, east and west. All the land that you see I will give to you and your offspring forever. I will make your offspring like the dust of the earth, so that if anyone could count the dust, then your offspring could be counted. Go; walk through the length and breadth of the land, for I am giving it to you!" What was left for Abram?

Everything! God Himself gave Abram "all the land . . . forever!" God's Promise—that was what Abram had—and that was everything! As far as Abram could see in every direction—that was what God gave to him! That promise was also to his children, children so numerous that they could not be counted. God gave Abram everything in that promise, everything to make Abram into a great nation. The land, he would one day own; the children, he would one day have. It was a sure promise; it was a certain hope—for the mouth of the LORD had spoken it! Although Abram owned not even a small lot of land, God said, "Go; walk through the land, for I am giving it to you." It all belonged to Abram now—by faith. He could go where he pleased without care, without fear, for God had given it all to him. So Abram did as God commanded. He went and walked through the land, pitching his tents and building God's altars, wherever he chose.

The teacher's guide for this lesson starts on page 482.

AN ACCOUNT OF KINGS

- **Genesis 14**
- **Psalm 110**
- **John 8:48–58**
- **Hebrews 7**

T he LORD led Abram to the land of Canaan. First, there was famine in that land, then there was war! WAR? Yes, war broke out within the borders of God's promised land! Nine wicked kings and their armies were embroiled in battle. It had nothing to do with Abram, who was a foreigner in the land—but war has a way of touching everyone. Abram, who was a man too old and too good for a wicked world war, would find himself involved in the fighting. Before Abram ever set foot upon this land, God had promised him, "I will bless you" (Genesis 12:2). Now, in the midst of all this terrible trouble, Abram must hold tightly to this promise, believing that at the end, the blessing of God awaited him. Abram must have faith, that in all things, even in this war, God works for the good of those who love Him, for those who have been called according to His purpose. Once again, Abram must entrust himself into the hands of his loving God.

This was what happened:

When Lot moved to the green grasslands along the Jordan River and pitched his tents near the city of Sodom, no doubt he was expecting a peaceful and plentiful life there. That region looked like a "garden of God," not a field of battle . . . and Lot did not hear the winds of war already whispering in the lush pastures. Lot settled there, among the cities of the plain, but the kings of those cities were already preparing for war. Five kings (including King Bera of Sodom) joined their forces to fight against four other kings. These four other kings were fierce warriors and harsh tyrants; they were kings who ruled, conquered and terrorized the whole region. One of them, King Kedorlaomer, had subjected them for more than twelve years, but now the five kings were rebelling against him; yes, now they were marching with their armies and lining up for battle against him. There were five kings against four. Altogether, there were nine wicked kings waging war in the land of Canaan!

Who won? Surely the five kings could easily beat the four kings. No, King Kedorlaomer was victorious . . . again! It was the king of Sodom and the king of Gomorrah, who fled for their lives and hid in the hills, along with some of their men. Many of their soldiers were wounded or slaughtered in battle. Others slipped into tar pits where they were trapped and killed. It was a disaster! What happened to the cities of the five defeated kings? Since they were left unprotected, the four triumphant kings marched into them with their soldiers and seized everything—food and clothes, gold and silver, money and jewels, animals and people. Abram's nephew Lot was also taken prisoner, because he was living in Sodom. All his wealth was carried away by the four kings and worse than that; he and his family were captured. If they were not killed, they would be used or sold as slaves.

What would happen now? The people of Sodom and Gomorrah were exceedingly wicked. Their sins were grievous in the LORD's sight. This was God's judgement on them, God's final warning to them. They were simply reaping the just reward for their evil deeds. However, among them there was one righteous man—Lot. The soldiers of the four kings, who were wicked men themselves, did not realize that they had touched someone, who belonged to God. You cannot steal from the LORD, and not get caught. Already the LORD's hand was reaching out to rescue Lot: Someone escaped from Sodom and travelled to Abram and reported to him all that had happened. When Abram heard the tragic news, that his relative had been captured, he immediately assembled a small army and followed the four kings. Abram had 318 of his own men, who were trained as soldiers. Three of his Amorite neighbours, with their fighting men, also joined him. Still, it was a very small band of men, who pursued the four triumphant kings with their vast invincible army. However, Abram's strength was not in his army; it was in his God. The LORD was Abram's strength! Abram would attack these mighty kings, trusting in the power of Almighty God. He decided to divide his forces and attack by night. It was a surprise attack! The four kings and their soldiers were startled from their sleep . . . and completely routed. The LORD was with Abram's small army and his campaign was a great success. Abram was able to rescue everyone and recover everything. How happy Lot must have been to see his Uncle Abram! They must have embraced each other with joy and together worshipped their God with thanks.

As Abram led the happy procession of brave soldiers and freed captives home, two kings came out to meet him in a place called "The Valley of Kings." One was the bad king of Sodom; the other was the good king of Salem. The king of Sodom came out to bargain with Abram, but the king of Salem came out to bless him. Bera was the name of Sodom's king. Melchizedek was the name of Salem's king.

Melchizedek! Who was he? Was he simply another Canaanite king? The name Melchizedek means "King of Righteousness." His city was Salem, which means "Peace" — so Melchizedek was the "Prince of Peace." The Bible says he was the priest of God Most High. This Melchizedek brought Abram a supper to celebrate the victory. He served him nothing less than bread and wine. Was this not the sacrament of the Lord's Supper? Was this priest of God not administering strength and grace to Abram's soul? Yes! Then Abram the patriarch, the Father of Faith, who was blessed of God, was blessed again. How great was this man Melchizedek, that he could bless Abram! It was through Abram that all peoples on earth would be blessed, yet this man blessed him. Melchizedek pronounced this benediction upon Abram: "Blessed be Abram by God Most High, Creator of heaven and earth. And blessed be God Most High, who delivered your enemies into your hand." Then Abram did an extraordinary thing. He took a tenth of everything and gave it to Melchizedek. Abram took one tenth of all the wealth that was taken from the four kings, which was taken from the five kings, and he gave it to this one king, Melchizedek, as if he were the King of kings! Yes, Abram gave the tithe, which belonged to God, to this man. Abram gave the first portion and the best portion to Melchizedek. What manner of man was he, that Abram should tithe to him? We know that he was the priest of

God Most High, but we know very little else about Melchizedek. When was he born? Who were his parents? When did he die? We don't know the answers to these questions. He is a mystery man in the Scriptures. For Melchizedek, there is no genealogy. The Bible says: "Without father or mother, without genealogy, without beginning of days or end of life, like the Son of God he remains a priest forever" (Hebrews 7:3). Yes, Melchizedek was like the Son of God. We will always wonder: Was he the Son of God? Was Melchizedek simply an earthly king, or was he a heavenly king? Was this Melchizedek the King of Righteousness Himself, appearing to Abram thousands of years before he was born into this world? Or was Melchizedek a type of Christ, a living and breathing shadow of the great Priest and King, who would one day come to bless the world with the bread of His Body and the wine of His Blood? Did Melchizedek appear to Abram to point him to the Saviour who was coming or was Melchizedek the Saviour Himself? We don't know. Melchizedek is a mystery, a man of mystery. However, we do know this: On that day in the Valley of Kings, Abram was blessed! He was blessed by the priest of God Most High; he was blessed by the King of Righteousness; he was blessed by the Prince of Peace. What manner of man stood before Abram with his hands raised in blessing remains a mystery, but in one way or another, Abram saw the Messiah more clearly—and Abram rejoiced at the promise of His coming and the day of His appearing. Abram's greatest hope was the Messiah. That Messiah was God's greatest promise to Abram and to the whole world.

More than two thousand years later, there was another King of Salem, Jesus, the Prince of Peace Himself, who was teaching in Jerusalem. The Jews challenged him, "Are you greater than our father Abraham?" Jesus answered, "Your father Abraham rejoiced to see my day; and he saw it, and was glad." Knowing that Abraham lived two thousand years earlier, the Jews then said to Jesus, "You are not yet fifty years old, and have you seen Abraham?" Then Jesus relied, "I tell you the truth, before Abraham was born, I AM" (John 8:58)! Jesus was the Melchizedek, the King of Righteousness, from all eternity. Jesus was the priest of God Most High from the beginning, from before the beginning. Hundreds of years before Jesus was born, the LORD spoke through another king of Salem, King David of Jerusalem, to announce to all the world what God the Father had sworn to God the Son: "You are a priest forever, in the order of Melchizedek" (Psalm 110:4).

Abram gave King Melchizedek of Salem one tenth of all the wealth.

When King Bera of Sodom saw this, he decided to begin bargaining quickly, before Abram gave everything away. After all, King Bera of Sodom had a claim on these things. He was the one involved in this war; the king of Salem had nothing to do with it. Why should Melchizedek be given a tenth of everything? Was not most of this wealth taken from Sodom, Bera's city? Still, Abram was the one who had rescued everyone and recovered everything; Abram also had a claim to them. Bera had to be reasonable, so he said to Abram, "Give me the people and keep the goods for yourself." But Abram wanted nothing for himself. He would not take so much as a shoe lace from this king of wickedness. Abram had just been blessed by the King of Right- eousness, and that was all he wanted. Abram believed in the blessing of God, and that was enough for him. Abram's heart was fixed on the treasures of heaven. He saw clearly what the wealth of this world was, especially the wealth of this wicked war-lord. It was a trap! Abram refused to be ensnared by the deceitfulness of riches. He said to the king of Sodom, "I have raised my hand to the LORD, God Most High, Creator of heaven and earth, and I have taken an oath that I will accept nothing belonging to you, not even a thread . . . so that you will never be able to say, 'I made Abram rich.' I will accept nothing . . ." That was Abram's answer to Bera's offer. Abram gave to God what belonged to God and he gave to man what belonged to man. One tenth was given to the priest of God Most High and Abram also made sure that the soldiers and his neighbours received their fair share, but for him- self he took nothing. Abram had God's blessing. What more did he need? In having that, he had everything!

The teacher's guide for this lesson starts on page 484.

A VERY GREAT REWARD

- Genesis 15:1–6
- Romans 4
- Galatians 3:6–14
- Hebrews 11:11

A bram refused the wealth of this world. His hope was in the treasures of heaven and his trust was in the promises of God. Abram was a man of faith; he was look-ing and longing and living for the things which could not be seen. The unbelieving peoples around Abram must have thought that he was an old fool. The king of Sodom had of-fered him all the wealth of his kingdom—and Abram re-fused it all, not taking even one thread from that wicked king. The Canaanites must have wondered: What made Abram do such a stupid thing? How could he refuse such a splendid offer? Who was he that he could afford to insult a mighty king and reject so great a reward? After all, Abram was just an old man living in a tent. He was not some great ruler, who governed some great empire, that he could allow himself such a response. He was a stranger in their land, who owned nothing, not even his campsite. What was he doing? Only a fool would close his eyes to all that gold and silver sparkling in the sun! Only a fool would answer the king's offer by declaring, "I will ac-cept nothing belonging to you!" Only a fool would turn his back on all those riches . . . and for what? Did he really believe that some invisible God had made some impossible promise to him, to make him into a great nation one day. What a fool! He should grab the gold in front of his nose, forget the nonsense filling his head, and go home. But Abram did no such thing. He stood firm in his faith. He kept his oath to God. He took nothing. Abram rejected the reward of the wicked.

After this, the Word of the LORD came to Abram in a vision: "Do not be afraid, Abram. I am your shield; your reward will be very great." What reward would God give to Abram? Gold and silver? Gems and jewels? There was only one thing Abram wanted; there was only one thing he lacked. It was a reward which God alone could give to him. Do you know what that was? A child! The Bible says, "Children are the LORD's good gift; the fruit of the womb is God's reward" (Psalm 127:3), but Abram had not been given that good gift; he had not received that reward. Time was running out and the years were passing quickly. Abram's hair grew whiter and his eyes grew dimmer and his steps grew slower. Long ago in another land, God had promised to make him into a great nation, but nothing had happened. What Abram saw all around him was this: The wicked flourished; their families grew larger and their cities grew stronger—while he was withering, without having even one small child. God had given Abram much wealth, but what benefit was it? When he died, he had no son or daughter to inherit it. One of his servants would get everything—so what did it matter if God had a great reward for him? Abram said to God, "O Sovereign LORD, what can you give me, since I remain childless . . . You have given me no children, so a servant in my household will be my heir." Then the Word of the LORD-LORD came to Abram: "No . . . a son coming from your own body will be your heir." Then God took Abram outside, where the night sky was filled with millions of twinkling stars. "Look at the heavens," said the LORD, "and count the stars—if indeed you can count them." (It was impossible. God alone can count the stars in the universe. He is the only One who can even see them all.) Abram gazed into the clear dark sky, which sparkled with stars, the jewels of the night. Their splendour and their number were over-whelming! Abram could not begin to count them all. Then the LORD said to him, "So shall your descendants be." That was God's reward for Abram: a promise. God promised Abram not earthly gems or heavenly jewels, but something much more precious. Children! First God promised Abram a son; then God promised him many sons, and daughters too, "a great multitude that no one could count" (Revelation 7:9). Like the stars in the sky would Abram's descendants be. This was God's promise—and Abram believed the LORD! He did not think in his heart: I'll believe it when I see it. On this earth his old eyes would never see that multitude—except by faith. Abram believed the LORD when there was not even one child, not even the sign of a child, not even the hope of a child. "In hope, against all hope, Abraham believed" (Romans 4:18). God's very great reward was the promise of a child and so many children that Abram could not count them all. There was also a hidden treasure in that promise, the greatest reward of all. Among the millions of Abram's children, who would shine like stars in the sky, would appear One who shone brighter than all the rest, One called "The "Bright Morning Star" (Revelation 22:16). One day a Child would be born, a Son would be given, to Abram and to all the world. He would be the Saviour from sin and death, whom God had promised from the beginning. He would be the One in whom all the peoples on earth would be blessed. The Messiah! Whoever owned Him possessed the greatest gift in heaven or on earth. There was no richer reward that God could give to anyone, for it was His own Son. "God so loved the world that He gave His one and only Son, that whoever believes in Him should not perish, but have everlasting life" (John 3:16). That night, when Abram stood beneath the starry sky, he believed!

"*Abram believed the LORD and He credited to him as righteousness*" (Genesis 15:6). This is one of the most amazing statements in the entire Bible, for it quickly and clearly declares how a person is made righteous in the eyes of God. It is not by our works or our words that we are made righteous. It is by faith! It is the only way that any person (then or now) can be made righteous. This righteousness from God comes through faith to all who believe. "In the gospel a righteousness from God is revealed, a righteousness that is from faith to faith / a righteousness that is by faith from first to last" (Romans 1:17). "The righteous will live by faith" (Habakkuk 2:4). "There is no one who is righteous, not even one . . . Therefore no one will be declared righteous in God's sight by observing the Law . . . But now a righteousness from God, apart from Law, has been made known . . . This righteousness from God comes through faith in Jesus Christ to all who believe . . . A man is justified by faith apart from observing the Law . . . To the man who does not work, but trusts God who justifies the wicked, his faith is credited as righteousness" (Romans 3:10, 20–22, 28 & 4:5). "Blessed are they whose transgressions are forgiven, whose sins are covered. Blessed is the man whose sin the LORD will never count against him" (Psalm 32:1, 2). Blessed is the man to whom God credits righteousness apart from works. Blessed was Abram! And blessed are we, "to whom God will credit righteousness—for us who believe, who believe in Him who raised Jesus our Lord from the dead" (Romans 4:24).

When Abram looked into the night sky and saw the stars twinkling above him and heard God say, "So shall your descendants be"—he believed. "Against all hope, Abraham in hope believed . . . Without weakening in his faith, he faced the fact that his body was as good as dead . . . and that Sarah's womb was also dead. Yet he did not waver through unbelief regarding the promise of God, but was strengthened in his faith and gave glory to God, being fully persuaded that God had power to do what He had promised" (Romans 4:18–21). That is what faith is—being fully persuaded. "Faith is being sure of what we hope for and certain of what we do not see" (Hebrews 11:1). Abram trusted God's Word. Abram believed God's promise. And the LORD credited that faith to him as righteousness. RIGHTEOUSNESS! Who can place a value on that? Without righteousness we cannot see God. Without righteousness we cannot enter heaven. It is worth more than life. RIGHTEOUSNESS! It is something we do not have and cannot earn. It is a gift from God, a pearl of priceless value. It is something which God credits to our account because we trust in Him. RIGHTEOUSNESS! It is a rich reward from God for our faith. Perhaps righteousness was that very great reward, which God promised to give to Abram. He did not have to wait long for it. The LORD gave it to him on that very night—and it was a reward that would last for ever and ever into eternity.

The teacher's guide for this lesson starts on page 486.

KNOW FOR CERTAIN

• Genesis 15:7–21
• Galatians 3:15–18

That same night, when Abram stood in the promised land under the twinkling stars with the hope of a child and the hope of many children and the hope of the One Child shining brightly in his heart, the LORD spoke to him again, concerning another matter: "I am the LORD, who brought you out of Ur of the Chaldeans to give you this land, to inherit it, to possess it, to own it!" Yes, the LORD had surely brought him out of Ur, the city where he had been born, the city where he had lived so many years . . . a lifetime ago . . . and yes, the LORD had surely brought him to this place where his feet were now standing and where his tent was now blowing gently in the cool night air. But how could he ever own this land? It already belonged to other people. Many wicked nations already possessed this land, nations with strong cities and large armies. Abram did not own even a small plot of this land. What God promised seemed impossible. Abram believed the LORD's Word, but . . . but . . . but what? "O Sovereign LORD," said Abram, "How can I *know* that I will gain possession of it?" It was hard for Abram to believe this. He was like the man who cried out, "I believe, but help me overcome my unbelief" (Mark 9:24). Abram needed God's help, for in this area his faith was weak. He was still living in a tent; he was still wandering from place to place; he was still residing as a stranger and a foreigner in this land. "How can I *know?*" asked Abram. "How can I *know* that I will gain possession of this land?"

This was God's answer:

1) The LORD said to Abram, "Bring me a cow, a goat and a ram, each three years old, along with a dove and a pigeon." What a strange answer! What did these animals have to do with Abram's question? They had everything to do with it. The first part of God's answer directed Abram to the holy ground of sacrifice. God commanded a sacrifice and Abram obeyed God. Although it was the middle of the night, Abram went out among the flocks and herds to find the right animals to bring to the LORD. Next he slaughtered them. Then he cut the large animals in two. Finally he arranged the halves opposite each other, and with one bird's body on each side. Then Abram waited. He waited for God's answer to his question: How could he know that he would gain possession of the land? It was now a new day, but still Abram waited. The sun baked down on the pieces of flesh and vultures circled overhead in the shimmering heat. Still the LORD was silent; still Abram waited. Then the birds of prey came down on the carcasses, but Abram was standing guard by the LORD's answer—and he drove the birds away. Abram, the man of faith, continued to watch . . . and to wait.

2) Finally, as the sun was setting, Abram fell into a deep sleep, and a thick and dreadful darkness came over him ("the thick darkness where God was" Exodus 20:21.) The LORD was approaching to answer Abram and to impress that answer into the very depths of Abram's soul.

3) Then the LORD spoke. "Know for certain . . ." God commanded. It was a call to faith! "Faith is being sure of what we hope for and *certain* of what we do not see" (Hebrews 11:1).

4) Now the LORD would tell Abram what he hoped for; He would also tell him things that he would never see, as well as some things he would not want to see. God would tell Abram what would happen hundreds of years in the future, long after Abram's death. The LORD said to him, *"Know for certain that your descendants will be strangers in a country not their own, and they will be enslaved and mistreated four hundred years. But I will pun-*

ish the nation they serve as slaves, and afterward they will come out with great possessions. You, however, will go to your fathers in peace and be buried at a good old age. In the fourth generation, *your descendants will come back here,* for the sin of the Amorites has not yet reached its full measure." This was God's answer to Abram, in which He told him how he would possess the land, when he would possess the land, and why he would possess the land. Abram would gain possession of the promised land through his descendants. He would not own it personally, but his many children would inherit it after his death . . . and after four hundred years of slavery in another land. The day of judgement was already set for the wicked inhabitants of Canaan, the land promised to Abram. God was waiting until their sin had reached its fullness, so that His Justice might also be complete. This time God would not use the waters of the earth nor the fires of heaven to judge the wicked. No, God would use the hands of men; He would use the children of Abram. That was God's plan. God's plans span centuries, for a thousand years are like a day in the sight of the LORD. God told Abram His plan for him and his children, so that Abram would understand how it would be accomplished, so that Abram would "know for certain" that God would give him the promised land. Understanding bolsters our believing. Just knowing these few things must have cleared up the doubt, the questions and the confusion, which had been troubling Abram. A few facts can fortify our faith. Also, this was important information for future generations (including ours) to "know for certain." As the years passed and the events happened, according to this Word of God, the children of Abram would also be encouraged to trust in the LORD. Have faith! What God says, He does. Know for certain! What God promises, He also fulfills.

5) While the thick and dreadful darkness covered Abram in that deep and awful sleep, another darkness descended. The sun set and night fell. Now the LORD appeared to Abram in a vision. Though he was "sleeping," Abram saw a smoking pot and a blazing torch pass between the pieces of the sacrificed animals. God was there—in the midst of the sacrifice! It was the first time He had given any man a visible sign of His Glorious Presence. Fire and smoke! Hundreds of years later God would reveal Himself in that same way to Abram's descendants. In fact, God would lead them back to the Promised Land, going before them as a cloud of smoke by day and a pillar of fire by night.

6) Before this night God had spoken to Abram and made promises to Abram, but now God made *a covenant* with Abram. How gracious was Almighty God to enter into a covenant with Abram! He could "know for certain" because it was a covenant and he could "know for certain" because it was God's covenant. It did not depend upon Abram (or any other man) to keep a vow or fulfill a promise. It depended upon God. It was God Himself and God Alone who entered into the covenant. God was the One who passed between the bloody pieces of flesh. God was the One who made the promise: "To your descendants I give this land." What did Abram do? What did Abram promise? Nothing! He was lying on the ground in a deep sleep. What did Abram's descendants do? What did they promise? Nothing! They had not even been born. The covenant depended upon God alone and therefore Abram could "know for certain" that he would inherit the land. If it depended upon him or his descendants, they would never gain what was promised. If it depended upon them, their inheritance surely would be lost. However, Abram could know for certain that the Promised Land belonged to him because it depended entirely upon the LOVE of the LORD—and that is the only certain thing in all the universe. "Oh give thanks to the LORD, for He is good. His LOVE endures forever . . . His LOVE endures forever . . . His LOVE endures forever" (Psalm 136).

Abram could rest assured about his inheritance because he now held the deed to his property. He held it not in his hands, but in his heart. This covenant was like any legal document in which the boundaries of the property were stated and the persons to be dispossessed were named. (God said, "To your descendants I give this land, from the river of Egypt to the great river, the Euphrates—the land of the Kenites, Kenizzites, Kadmonites, Hittites, Perizzites, Rephaites, Amorites, Canaanites, Girgashites and Jebusites.") It was like any legal document . . . except that it was more sure, because the LORD Almighty had declared it. Abram could know for certain that he would inherit the land.

7) God has promised us an inheritance too. He has promised eternal life to all who believe in Jesus Christ. How can we know for certain that we will inherit eternal life? God's answer to us is the same answer that He gave to Abram. First, He takes us to the place of sacrifice, where Jesus was crucified upon the cross. It is there that we must wait for God's answer. It is there that we will know for certain. God's answer and our assurance is the New

Covenant, sealed not with the blood of animals, but with the blood of God's own Son. We can surely trust such a covenant! It was not a vision of fire and smoke in the midst of the sacrifice, but it was the Son of God Himself who was the Sacrifice. "The Son is the radiance of God's glory and the exact representation of His being" (Hebrews 1:3). We did not enter into that covenant. It depended upon God alone. Jesus hung upon the cross alone and He alone secured our salvation for us. We can surely hope and trust in so great a salvation! How can we know for certain that we will possess eternal life? We must trust God's Word: "Whoever believes in the Son has eternal life" (John 3:33). We must trust God's LOVE: "Herein is LOVE, not that we loved God, but that He loved us and sent His Son as an atoning sacrifice for our sins" (I John 4:10). We must trust in God's COVENANT. It is through the blood of this eternal covenant that God brought back from the dead our LORD Jesus and it is through the blood of this eternal covenant that He also will raise us to everlasting life.

Abram was looking forward to this eternal life and eternal home with God in heaven. If Abram believed this, the greater promise, the heavenly promise—then he could "know for certain" that God could and would accomplish the lesser promise, the earthly promise. The God who was promising heaven, was the same God who was promising Canaan. Abram could trust that God!

When Abram awoke, he knew it was not a dream. He knew for certain that the land in which he was living, this very land on which he was lying, would one day belong to his descendants. God had given Abram a glimpse of the future, which must have filled his heart with joy . . . and grief. He would have children, as numerous as the stars in the sky, but his children would suffer in slavery for 400 years. The promised people would be a persecuted people. When Abram awoke from that deep sleep, when he emerged from that dreadful darkness, did he laugh with joy . . . or weep with grief . . . or both? We do not know how the Father of Faith responded, except that he believed the Word of the LORD. He believed that God would deliver his children from that land of slavery and bring them safely and surely to the Promised Land. Abram knew that for certain, for he had God's covenant promise! One day, when Abram was a very old man, he would leave this world in peace, with the certain hope that God would keep His covenant.

The teacher's guide for this lesson starts on page 488.

GOD HEARS!
GOD SEES!

• Genesis 16
• Galatians 4:21–31

A bram told his wife what God had promised him—a child, a son coming from his own body, but Sarai knew that she was far too old to have a baby. It must be that God's promise did not include her. The LORD said that Abram would have a son from *his* body, but He didn't promise that the son would come from *her* body too. No, that would be impossible. Sarai had been sterile all her life. Even when she was young and pretty, even when she was strong and healthy, she had borne Abram no children, for God had made her barren. Now her body was too old and weak to bring forth a child. How could life come from a womb that was dead? Sarai thought it must be that God planned to use another woman to give Abram a son . . . but who? Sarai had a servant girl, an Egyptian maid who was young and strong. Her name was Hagar. Sarai had the idea that Hagar's body could be used to make a baby for herself and Abram, since her own body was completely useless for such a task. What an idea! Where was Sarai's faith? She should have believed in God. Nothing is impossible with God! The LORD brings forth life from death and He could surely use her barren body, even now, as old as it was, to bring forth the promised child. But Sarai did not exercise her faith; instead, she implemented her plan. She said to her husband Abram, "The LORD has kept me from having children. Go, sleep with my maidservant. Perhaps I can build a family through her." The plan made sense to Abram, so he agreed to do what Sarai said, without first consulting the LORD. The Bible says: "Trust in the LORD with all your heart and lean not on your own understanding; in all your ways acknowledge Him, and He will make your paths straight" (Proverbs 3:5, 6). Because Abram and Sarai did not consult God, they were about to zigzag along a very crooked path. They had been living faithfully in the land of Canaan for ten years, but now they were about to do something, which was not faithful at all.

Sarai took her maidservant, Hagar, and gave her to Abram to be his wife. Abram was 85 years old when he took Hagar as his second wife. He slept with her and she conceived. A tiny baby began to grow inside her strong young body. Wasn't that wonderful? A baby was going to be born. Abram was going to be a father . . . at last! Everyone must have been so happy. There must have been great rejoicing in Abram's household—but there was not. How could there be? God had not commanded Abram to take another wife. God never intended a man to have more than one wife. In the beginning, it was not so; in the beginning God created one man and one woman for each other. That was the God-ordained family. Now that Abram had two wives there would be trouble. The love and peace and joy would vanish from Abram's home—and be replaced by a plague of problems.

First there was trouble between Hagar and Sarai. When Hagar discovered that she was pregnant, she began to despise Sarai. Hagar was still the servant of Sarai, but she no longer acted that way or reasoned that way. Instead Hagar thought: Why should I serve Sarai? Hasn't God blessed me, instead of her? I'm the one who is carrying the promised child. Doesn't Abram love me, more than her? I'm the one who is finally giving him a baby! Why should I serve Sarai? I'm young and strong, pretty and healthy—and I'm the one carrying a very special child inside me. I'm blessed of God and loved of Abram. Sarai isn't; she is old and frail, useless and childless, and utterly unable to bring forth a son for Abram. She's as good as dead! Can a living, breathing, moving child ever come from her? Never! Why should I serve her? Let Sarai serve me! And so Hagar, the Egyptian servant, no longer treated her mistress with respect—but with contempt.

Then there was trouble between Sarai and Abram. Although it had been Sarai's idea, she now blamed Abram for the miserable situation. "It's your fault," she said to Abram. "You are responsible for the wrong I am suffering. I put my servant in your arms, and now that she knows she is pregnant, she despises me." Sarai viewed her husband as an enemy and said to him, "May the LORD judge between you and me." Abram washed his hands of the whole situation. Hagar was Sarai's servant. "Do with her whatever you think best," he said.

So then there was trouble between Abram and Hagar. After all, Hagar was now his wife, who was carrying his child, but Abram was refusing to take any responsibility for her. Without Abram protecting her, Hagar was treated terribly by Sarai.

The whole situation grew worse and worse. Sarai treated her servant so badly, that Hagar finally ran away. Now Abram was angry at both his wives. Sarai had driven off the woman who was carrying his child, his only child, the child that God had promised to him and probably the only child he would ever have. Abram was also angry at Hagar, who had no right to run away with their child. The baby growing in Hagar's womb was not just her baby; the child belonged to both of them.

That was the family situation—a mess! Everyone was angry at everyone else. Instead of having a home of peace and love and joy, Abram's household had become a place of arguing and suffering—because of sin, because they had not acted in faith, because they had not believed the Word of the LORD, because they had not trusted God's promise. The difficulties had escalated and now culminated in this crisis: Abram's child, his unborn child, was gone! His mother had run away, carrying the baby within her—and no one knew where they had gone. One night they had disappeared into the vast darkness of the great wilderness and no one knew where to find them. What could Abram do now? Perhaps he did now what he should have done before this situation ever began. Perhaps now he prayed to the LORD for help. God alone could restore the broken hearts and lives in their family.

God hears and God sees—everything and everyone. Hagar was just a servant girl, but God took notice of her. He saw her tears; He heard her cries. God had compassion on her misery. Hagar had run away from home to escape the harsh hand of her mistress, but she had not escaped her misery. She had only exchanged one kind of suffering for another. Now she was alone in the world. She was a young pregnant woman wandering around in the remote desert regions with no one to protect her and no one to provide for her. Her life was in danger. No one knew where Hagar was or where to find her—except for one Person.

That Person was God. From God Hagar could not flee, nor hide. The angel of the LORD found her near a spring in the desert. She was travelling on the road, which led back to her homeland, Egypt. Was she really returning to Egypt? Was she really forsaking the blessing of Abram's home and Abram's God? That road would only lead to death, unless God's grace intervened in her life, unless God's Word turned her around. The angel of the LORD said to her, "Hagar, servant of Sarai, where have you come from and where are you going?" Think carefully Hagar. Think carefully about where you have come from—a home of blessing! Think carefully about where you are going—a land of cursing! Hagar answered truthfully. She said, "I am running away from my mistress, Sarai." Then the angel of the LORD told her what she must do: "Go back to your mistress and submit to her." This would not be an easy thing for Hagar to do, but afterall, it was Hagar's own sin which had caused all her suffering. She should go back to Sarai humbly and serve her mistress happily and respectfully. That was what God was commanding her to do. It would be best for everyone, especially Hagar and her unborn baby. If she obeyed, a measure of harmony could be restored to Abram's household. If she obeyed, once again she would be under the canopy of Abram's blessing. If she obeyed, there was a special promise for Hagar, a promise from God. The angel of the LORD said, "I will so increase your descendants that they will be too numerous to count." The angel also said to her: "You are now with child and you will have a son. You shall name him Ishmael (or God Hears) for the LORD has heard your misery." Hagar knew she was pregnant, but she did not know until now that she was carrying a baby boy inside her womb. God's Word is more sure than any modern ultra-sound projection. If God said that she would have a son, then it was true. God also told this expectant mother what kind of man her son would become—a piece of information which no eye of technology could ever see. God said about her little unborn son that he would be a wild man, hating and fighting everyone, even his brothers. God said, "His hand will be against everyone, and everyone's hand will be against him." Hagar probably liked this description of her son, for he would be a wild man, a free man, fighting people instead of serving them. Yes, Hagar could admire such a man!

Then the angel disappeared and Hagar was once again alone in the desert. She realized that it was not a mere angel whom she had seen. No, she had seen the One, who sees everyone. How amazed she must have been that God had spoken to her! She knew that God had spoken to her master Abram, but she was just a run-away slave in his household. How gracious was Abram's God that He had noticed her too! He sought for her; He came to her; He spoke with her. This God also made promises to her . . . and He revealed Himself as the Angel of the LORD to her. Hagar gave this name to the LORD: *Elroi* or *You-are-the-God-who-sees-me*, because she said, "I have now seen the One who sees me." Even that well by the side of the road became known by a new name. Thereafter it was called: *Beer Lahai Roi* or *Well-of-the-living-one-who-sees-me*. It was Hagar's memorial to the LORD.

It was time to leave that well in the desert. Hagar had a very important decision to make. Should she continue on her journey or should she return to Abram's household to serve her mistress Sarai? Hagar returned home, not to her first home, which was Egypt, but to the blessed home where God in His mercy had placed her. Hagar returned to Abram and Sarai. In time, as God had promised, she gave birth to a son, a son for Abram. He named the child *Ishmael/God hears*. God had heard Abram's misery also; He had heard the anguished cries from the heart of this childless old man. Now, at the age of eighty-six, God had given him a son! Abram was overjoyed. He loved Ishmael. Surely this was the son whom God had promised him. God had told him that his descendants would be too numerous to count . . . and hadn't God told the same thing to Hagar? It must be that their son, Ishmael, was the child of God's promise. But was he? Was he the promised child . . . or was there someone else?

The teacher's guide for this lesson starts on page 490.

THE COVENANT CONFIRMED

- **Genesis 17**
- **Jeremiah 4:4**
- **Acts 15:1, 6–11**
- **Romans 2:25–29; 4; 9:6–9**
- **Galatians 3:6–14; 5:1–6; 6:14–16**
- **Philippians 3:3**
- **Colossians 2:9–13**

T ime passed. It had been many years since God had spoken. Abram no longer held his infant son in his arms. Ishmael had grown to be a young man of thirteen and Abram had grown to be an old man, a very old man of ninety-nine, but Abram was not yet at the end of his years, for the LORD had not yet accomplished His plans and purposes in Abram's life. The LORD still had surprises for Abram . . . and promises. The LORD still had works for him to do and words for him to trust. The LORD was just beginning to use Abram!

So, after many years of silence, when Abram was ninety-nine years old, the LORD again appeared to him. God spoke to Abram about the covenant, which God had made with Abram fourteen years earlier. For each one of those fourteen years of silence, God now spoke of the covenant. Fourteen times on this occasion the word covenant comes from the mouth of LORD! How important this covenant must be! God said, "I am *El Shaddai*/I am God Almighty." This was a new name for the LORD, one which no man had ever heard. *El Shaddai*, God Almighty, had a message for

Abram; He said, "Walk before Me and be blameless. *I will confirm my covenant between me and you,* and I will greatly increase your numbers." What did God mean? When He said, "I will *confirm* my covenant," what did that mean? Long ago, twelve plus twelve years earlier, almost a quarter of a century ago, God had made a promise to Abram to make him into a great nation. The promises of God are sure, but ten years later, God made this promise more sure by making a covenant with Abram. On the night when the covenant was made with Abram, the LORD vowed, "To your descendants I give this land." By this covenant God again promised to make Abram into a great nation, by giving him both land and people. Then seven plus seven more years passed. Now, when Abram was ninety-nine years old, God said, "*I will confirm my covenant between me and you.*" Now God was going to establish that covenant between Himself and Abram. He was going to strengthen that covenant; He was going to fix it firmly forever. The promises of God are sure, but God had made His promises more sure by a covenant. The covenants of God are sure, but God would make his covenant more sure by . . . what? What could be more sure than the Word of God, the promise of God, and the covenant of God? How would God confirm His covenant?

1) First of all, the LORD appeared to Abram and revealed Himself by a new name. God said, "I am *El Shaddai.* I am God Almighty." Nothing in all the universe could stop or thwart the plan of God, for He alone was the Almighty God. Abram fell facedown upon the ground before *El Shaddai.*

2) God not only repeated his covenant promises to Abram; God extended them. God said to Abram, "As for Me, this is My covenant with you: You will be the father of *many* nations. You will be the father of a *multitude* of nations." To be the father of even one child was a wonderful word for Abram. That this one child would one day become a great nation was even more wonderful. But now God was promising the most wonderful thing of all—that Abram would be the father of many nations, a multitude of nations! How could this be true? *El Shaddai,* God Almighty, had declared it. One day far in the future, standing before God's throne in heaven, there would be "a great multitude that no one could count from every nation . . ." (Revelation 7:9) worshipping the LORD. Abram would be the father of this great multitude of nations, for all who believe are children of Abram. All peoples and nations, who have the faith of Abram, are blessed along with Abram, the man of faith, the father of faith.

3) God said, "No longer will you be called Abram, Exalted Father; your name will be Abraham, Father of Many or Father of a Multitude, for I have made you a father of many nations, a multitude of nations!" God changed Abram's name, the name by which he had been known for ninety-nine years! For eighty-five childless years, his name had been Abram, Exalted Father. During those years, when he had not even one child, how difficult that name must have been for him. It was not until his old age that this name, Abram, seemed to suit him. But now God gave him a new name, a covenant name, by which he was forever connected to the promises of God. Every time he heard his name, Abraham, he would remember God's covenant! However, this new name, Father-of-Many or Father-of-a-Multitude, was a little strange because he had only one son. Surely people would mock this new name and tease this old man, whispering behind his back or ridiculing to his face: "He has only one child, and he changes his name to Father-of-a-Multitude?" For Abram to accept such a name showed that he believed God's Word; it showed that he lived by faith and not by sight. What was seen was only one child. What was not seen was "the great multitude that no one could count from every nation."

4) God said, "I will make you very fruitful; I will make nations of you, and kings will come from you." Abraham was an old man, a foreigner, who lived in a tent and wandered from place to place. He did not have a country; he did not rule a city; he did not own so much as a foot of land. But God said, "Kings will come from you." What an amazing promise! Some of his children would be kings who owned and ruled empires! By faith, could Abraham see the long procession of kings that came from him? We can look back; we know who they were—King Saul, King David, King Solomon, etc. The names and the reigns of all the kings of Israel and Judah are recorded for us in the Bible. There were other kings too, mighty kings from foreign lands, who became believers in the one true God. They had the same faith as Abraham, and so they too were his sons. In this way, many kings came from Abraham, whose names we do not even know. However, there is a Name above all names, which every tongue will bless, and there is a King above all kings, to whom every knee shall bow. He also came from Abraham. Four books of the Bible are written about this one king alone. In fact, the entire Scriptures, from beginning to end, proclaim the greatness of this king. Jesus was the Son of Abraham, the Son of God, whose reign would

last forever and extend over all the earth. His coming was announced to Abraham on that day long long ago. Two thousand years before Jesus was even born, God promised Abram, "Kings will come from you."

5) Before Abram had even left his homeland, God had promised, "I will make you into a great nation" (Genesis 12:2). Later, when Abram was in the land of Canaan, God promised by covenant, "To your descendants I give this land" (Genesis 15:18). Now God was confirming that covenant. Again God repeated the promise of both the land and the people to make Abraham into the great nation, but this time God added, "I will establish my covenant as an *everlasting* covenant between Me and you and your descendants after you for the generations to come . . . The whole land of Canaan, where you are now an alien, I will give as an everlasting possession to you and your descendants after you . . ." The nation that came from Abraham would continue unbroken, uninterrupted, from generation to generation. It would endure forever! The kingdoms of this world rise and fall. Nations flourish for a time and then they vanish, but this nation would last for eternity.

6) What makes a nation great? Russia is the greatest country in the world, if you are considering the size of the land. China is the greatest country in the world, if you are considering the number of people. Perhaps the United States of America is the greatest country in the world, if you are considering how much wealth they possess. God said to Abram, "I will make you into a great nation." Would that nation have the greatest area of land or the greatest number of people or the greatest amount of wealth? No, as that promise was fulfilled here on earth, the nation coming from Abraham could not boast about any of those things. It was not a great nation if one looked at its size or counted its people or assessed its wealth. However, God gave this nation something, which would make them the greatest nation on earth. Do you know what that was? The LORD said, "I will establish My covenant as an everlasting covenant between Me and you and your descendants after you . . . to be your God and the God of your descendants after you . . . I will be their God!" The Lord, by an everlasting covenant, gave to Abraham and his descendants after him, the greatest treasure in all the world. What was it? God gave them Himself! *El Shaddai*, God Almighty, had united Himself to them forever. He had promised, by covenant, to be their God! The LORD Himself was their great national treasure! He was what made them a great nation!

7) God said to Abraham, "I will confirm My covenant between Me and you . . ." God would confirm His covenant with a sign. Do you remember the sign of the covenant that God made with Noah? It was the rainbow. This time the sign of the covenant would not be far away in the sky among the clouds. This time the sign of the covenant would be down to earth and very close, so close that it would be touching Abraham and all his sons after him. This time the sign of the covenant would be on their bodies, cut right into their flesh. This time the sign of the covenant would not be the beautiful, etherial, magical rainbow. No, the sign of this covenant would be personal and painful; it would be earthy and bloody. *Circumcision*—that was the sign of the covenant. *Circumcision*—that was how God would confirm His covenant to them. The LORD said to Abraham, "As for you, you must keep My covenant, you and your descendants after you for the generations to come. This is my covenant with you and your descendants after you, the covenant you are to keep: *Every male among you shall be circumcised. You are to undergo circumcision, and it will be the sign of the covenant between me and you.* For the generations to come every male among you who is eight days old must be circumcised, including those born in your household or bought with money from a foreigner—those who are not your own off-spring . . . They must be circumcised. *My covenant in your flesh is to be an everlasting covenant.* Any uncircumcised male, who has not been circumcised in the flesh, will be cut off from his people. He has broken my covenant."

Why did God command circumcision to be the sign of the covenant? Why did God choose a sign that would be painful for His people? What was the meaning of this sign? What was the reason for it? Circumcision was to represent cutting away a certain part of themselves—their sinful natures. (To cut away the sin from our lives is often a painful process, but God demands it.) Before the LORD said to Abraham, "You are to undergo circumcision . . ." He said, "I am *El Shaddai*, God Almighty. Walk before Me and be blameless." God commands His people to be holy, just as He is holy. In this covenant the LORD vows to Abraham, "I will establish my covenant as an everlasting covenant between Me and you and your descendants after you . . . to be your God and the God of your descendants after you." God promises to be their God and they must be His people—a circumcised people, who have cut away the sin from their lives, a people who are holy, blameless and undefiled. However, cutting the foreskin of their flesh would not purify them from sin. Circumcision was only a sign—an outward physical sign of what must be inward and spiritual. The cutting of the flesh by the hands of men was to represent the working in the heart by the Spirit of God. Circumcising themselves would not make them righteous. Circumcision was simply a sign, a seal of the righteousness that comes through faith. Abraham believed God and it was credited to him as righteousness. Righteousness is by faith, not by works, not by any works, not even by those covenant works commanded by God, such as circumcision. God declared Abraham righteous fourteen years before he was circumcised. Abraham believed God and it was because of his faith that he was counted as righteous. He received circumcision as the sign of God's covenant and as the seal of the righteousness that he already had by faith. Abraham loved the LORD his God with all his heart. Abraham's heart was already circumcised . . . by faith. His heart was yielded to God and his heart trusted in God.

Circumcision represented purification from sin, but it could not purify a person from sin. Circumcision was simply an outward physical sign of what must happen in a person's heart. It wasn't enough for a person to have the sign of God in his flesh, if he did not have the faith of God in his heart. What did it matter if he had the sign of the covenant, but not the God of the covenant? The Old Testament prophets declared: "Circumcise yourselves to the LORD. Circumcise your hearts" (Jeremiah 4:4). The New Testament apostles declared: "Neither circumcision, nor uncircumcision, has any value. The only thing that counts is *faith* expressing itself through *love* . . . Neither circumcision, nor uncircumcision, means anything. What counts is a new creation" (Galatians 5:6 & 6:15).

Circumcision was simply a sign. It was a sign of the covenant. It was a sign on the people of God that they must cut away or put to death their sinful natures. Circumcision was an important sign commanded by God, but it was just a sign; it could not save them from their sins. A greater circumcision was required, one which they could not perform. God alone could execute that circumcision—not only the one in their hearts, but also the one on the cross. Jesus Christ was crucified, that He might remove the sins of His people forever. The Bible says that in Christ "you were also circumcised, in the putting off of the sinful nature, not with a circumcision done by the hands of men, but with the circumcision done by Christ . . . When you were dead in your sins and in the uncircumcision of your sinful nature, God made you alive with Christ. He forgave us all our sins" (Colossians

2:11, 13). Christ's crucifixion was our circumcision. "Those who belong to Christ Jesus have crucified the sinful nature with its passions and desires" (Galatians 5:24). "We know that our old self was crucified with Him, so that the body of sin might be done away with, that we should no longer be slaves to sin" (Romans 6:6). Christ's crucifixion was the last time that blood must be shed for sin. The sign of the New Covenant was baptism, a painless and bloodless sign, which replaced the Old Covenant sign of circumcision. They both represented purification from sin. One was a washing away of sin; the other was a cutting away of sin—but both were simply signs. Neither baptism nor circumcision could purify a person from his/her sin. That can be accomplished only by the work of God in a person's heart. Our hearts are purified by faith in the sacrifice of Jesus, the only Son of God. The sign of circumcision confirmed God's covenant because ultimately it pointed to the crucifixion of Christ, which was the pinnacle of God's everlasting LOVE for His people. There was nothing, in heaven or on earth, that could confirm God's covenant LOVE more clearly or surely or gloriously, than the LOVE of God in Christ Jesus our Lord, when He died upon the cross to save us from our sins. All God's promises are "YEA" and "AMEN" in Christ Jesus!

When *El Shaddai*/God Almighty appeared to Abraham, He said, "As *for Me*, this is My covenant with you." God then repeated and extended His former covenant promises to Abraham, in which He confirmed His vow to make him into a great nation. God also promised, "I will establish My covenant as an everlasting covenant . . . *to be your God!*" Then God said to Abraham, "As *for you*, you must keep My covenant . . . Every male among you shall be circumcised." But what about the females in Abraham's family? Were they not part of the covenant? Yes, of course they were! God did not exclude them. *El Shaddai*/God Almighty also said, "As for your wife." God included the woman in the covenant promises. The head of the home, the man, would bear the sign of the covenant in his body, but the woman would bear the fruit of the covenant in hers. It was through her body that God would bring forth the promised children and the Promised Child. The LORD said, "As *for your wife*, Sarai, you are no longer to call her Sarai; her name will be Sarah/Princess. I will bless her and will surely give you a son by her, so that she will be the mother of nations. Kings of peoples will come from her." Abraham would be the father of nations; Sarah would be the mother of nations. Multitudes of nations and kings of peoples would come from them both. Sarah would be the great-great-great . . . grandmother of the greatest King of all, the King of kings and the Lord of lords, even Jesus Christ the Saviour! No, God did not leave the woman outside His blessing, outside His promise, outside His covenant. She was an integral part of God's glorious plan. All the blessings of the covenant belonged to her fully! She was a fellow-heir and equal-heir in the rich inheritance of the saints.

Now, when Abraham heard that Sarah, his ninety-year-old wife, would have a baby, he was so astounded that he fell facedown and laughed. He said to himself, "Will a son be born to a man one hundred years old? Will Sarah bear a child at the age of ninety?" It seemed impossible! He had a son, a son whom he loved dearly. He had not hoped for any other child. Wasn't Ishmael the one whom God had promised? Oh, if only this son would survive and increase, then all God's promises could be fulfilled in him. But now God had promised another son, a son through Sarah. What would happen to Ishmael? Was God going to take him away? Abraham said to God, "If only Ishmael might live under your blessing!" God answered, "Yes, but your wife Sarah will bear you a son, and you will call him Isaac/Laughter. I will establish my covenant with him as an everlasting covenant for his descendants after him. And as for Ishmael, I have heard you: I will surely bless him; I will make him fruitful and greatly increase his numbers. He will be the father of twelve rulers, and I will make him into a great nation. But *my covenant I will establish with Isaac*, whom Sarah will bear to you by this time next year." The LORD had spoken—and when He had finished speaking with Abraham, He went up from him. Abraham was left facedown on the ground . . . alone. What did he think? God had told him extraordinary things. Were they true? Did he believe them? Yes, he believed God's Word! The Scriptures record that "against all hope, Abraham in hope believed . . . Without weakening in his faith, he faced the fact that his body was as good as dead—since he was about one hundred years old—and that Sarah's womb was also dead. Yet he did not waver through unbelief regarding the promise of God, but was strengthened in his faith and gave glory to God, being fully persuaded that God had power to do what He had promised" (Romans 4:19, 20).

As Abraham lay facedown on the ground, he must have pondered for some time everything that God had revealed to him. Among the many things to consider, there were four new names:

1. *El Shaddai.* Nothing in heaven or on earth was impossible for God Almighty. Glory to God in the highest!

2. *Abraham.* His earthly father had named him as a baby, Abram. For all the days that are contained in almost one hundred years, He had been called by that name. Now he had a new name, for his heavenly Father had named him Abraham, Father of Many, Father of a Multitude. God had promised to make him the father of many nations, a multitude of nations.

3. *Sarah.* He had known her since the day she was born. For almost ninety years he had called her Sarai, but now her name was changed. God had given her a new name too, a covenant name, because she would be Sarah, the Princess, from whom would come kings and princes, nations and peoples. This was the covenant blessing promised to Sarah by God.

4. *Isaac.* Next year there would be a new person in the world named Isaac/Laughter. He would be Sarah's son, his son, their son together. Next year he would be holding Laughter in his arms—and he would be laughing, for God would surely bring this bundle of joy into their lives!

There were other things to consider too. God had given Abraham other promises, promises that were to him and to his descendants after him forever! God would give them the whole land as an everlasting possession and God would give them Himself. God had established an everlasting covenant with him and with his unborn child, his yet-to-be-conceived son, Isaac—and with the generations following them. *El Shaddai* promised to be their God. The LORD had given Himself to them by covenant. Now Abraham (and all his household with him) must give themselves to God. Were they not joined together by covenant? They must put on themselves, on their very bodies, the sign of the covenant. It was a permanent sign. Once it was on, it could not be removed; once the foreskin was cut off, it could not be replaced. God had commanded: "You are to undergo circumcision. It will be the sign of the covenant between Me and you."

Ninety-nine-year-old Abraham arose from the ground slowly. There was something that had to be done . . . immediately. God had commanded a difficult task, a painful procedure and an unnecessary operation for such an old man—but Abraham would obey his God. He lived not by what felt good or seemed right to him. No, Abraham lived by faith; he lived by every Word that proceeded from the mouth of God. So, on that very same day, Abraham took his son Ishmael and every other male in his household, and circumcised them. Abraham was ninety-nine years old when he was circumcised, and his son Ishmael was thirteen; Abraham and his son Ishmael were both circumcised on that same day. Abraham believed God and Abraham obeyed God.

This was the way *El Shaddai*, God Almighty, confirmed His covenant with Abraham on that day.

The teacher's guide for this lesson starts on page 492.

THREE VISITORS

Long long ago, in a dry and dusty land, on an extremely hot day when the sun was baking down at noon, a very old man sat in the shaded entrance of his tent. His head, which was covered with the white hairs of old age, was bowed. Perhaps he was sleeping or thinking or praying. Who was this very old man? It was Abraham. After awhile he lifted his aged head—and there before him, standing nearby, he saw three men. He had not heard them or seen them coming. Who were they? Abraham did not know, but he sensed that they were special visitors, so he hurried from his tent to greet them. Then Abraham bowed low to the ground and said to one of the men, "Oh Lord, if I have found favour in your eyes, do not pass by your servant." Who was this stranger that Abraham should bow before Him? What manner of man was He, that Abraham should call him "Lord"? Was it right what Abraham did and said? Was he standing in the presence of God? Yes, for the Bible records, "The LORD appeared to Abraham" (Genesis 18:1). This time God came to Abraham in the form of a man. Who then were the other two men? The Bible declares that they were "two angels" (Genesis 19:1), who also appeared on earth as ordinary men. Was Abraham aware that he was about to entertain angels? If he did sense that they were beings of another kind and creatures from another realm, he treated them nonetheless as earthly guests with earthly needs. They may have come from heaven, but there was dust on their feet! Abraham said, "Let a little water be brought to you, and then you may all wash your feet." Earth's sun was hot at mid-day in this part of the world. "Rest under this tree," said Abraham. Then he offered, "Let me get you something to eat . . ." The three visitors agreed to accept Abraham's hospitality and ministry to them. "Do as you say," they answered, so Abraham hurried away. First he went into the tent to Sarah and said, "Quick . . . bake some bread!" Then Abraham, at ninety-nine years old, ran out to the pastures where his herds of cattle were grazing. He himself selected one of his best calves, so that the meat would be tender and delicious. Abraham said to one of his servants, "Quick . . . prepare the meat!" When everything was ready, Abraham personally waited on his guests. He served them a fine meal of freshly-baked bread, savory veal cutlets, creamy sweet milk and his tastiest cheeses. While they ate, Abraham stood nearby them under a tree, like a faithful servant, ready to get for them whatever they wanted.

Now these three visitors from heaven had not come to earth just to have a picnic under a tree. No, they had come on a very important mission, a double mission: One was a mission of life; the other was a mission of death. They had come to build and to destroy. They had come to earth to build the kingdom of heaven and to destroy the kingdoms of this world. Their purpose was to populate the holy city of God and to annihilate the wicked cities of Satan. Their mission involved the creation of a righteous nation and a holy people; it also involved the destruction of evil nations and wicked peoples. These three "men" had not come from heaven for a picnic. No, they had come for battle, a battle in the war between the LORD God Almighty and "the Great Dragon . . . that Ancient Serpent called the Devil, or Satan" (Revelation 12:9).

A Mission of Life

Do you remember that in the beginning, just after sin and death entered the world, the LORD spoke to the man and woman for the last time in the Garden of Eden. At that time God promised to send a Saviour. God promised that the seed of the woman would crush the head of the serpent, that one day a child born of a woman would defeat that Ancient Serpent called the Devil. These three visitors from heaven had come to earth because of that promise. Sarah was one of the women chosen by God to be used in His plan of salvation. The woman's seed, Sarah's seed, would be used to fulfill God's Word and to crush Satan's head. It was Sarah's son, her grandson three-times-fourteen generations later, who would be the Saviour! But Sarah didn't know this. She was ninety years old, too old to even imagine having a child. God had promised her husband that she would bear a son in a year's time, but did she believe her husband's words? No, Sarah could not conceive such a thing. It was impossible! So God was paying a visit to Sarah, to deal with her old heart that was as frail and brittle as her old bones, a heart that was entangled with the sin of unbelief. God wanted Sarah to have faith in His Word; He wanted her to bring forth this promised child by faith! The LORD had come to Abraham's tent to strengthen Sarah's faith.

As the three "men" sat underneath the tree, they asked Abraham, "Where is your wife Sarah?" Abraham replied, "There, in the tent." Yes, Sarah was right there hidden in the tent . . . and she was listening. Then the LORD said, "I will surely return to you about this time next year, and Sarah your wife will have a son." The LORD was speaking . . . and Sarah was listening. With her own two ears she heard the LORD's promise from His own mouth, but did she believe God's Word? Or did she listen instead to her own thoughts, which argued that it was impossible for a ninety-year old woman and a hundred-year old man to have a child? How did Sarah respond? When she heard God's Word, she laughed. She laughed to herself and thought to herself, "After I am worn out and my husband is old, will I now have this pleasure?" But the LORD knows our inner thoughts and He hears our secret laughs. The LORD spoke indirectly to Sarah, through her husband Abraham, saying to her, through him, "Why did Sarah laugh? Why did she say, 'Will I really have a child, now that I am old?' Is anything too hard for the Lord?" Is anything impossible for God? Then the LORD repeated His promise: "I *will* return to you at the appointed time next year and Sarah *will* have a son."

Now Sarah was afraid. Who were these strangers? Who was this man that he could hear her laugh of unbelief, which had made no sound? How could he hear her thoughts and doubts, which she had not voiced, not even in a whisper? How did he know what was in her heart? Sarah was afraid. In her fear, she tried to hide her unbelief and cover her sin . . . by lying. She said right out loud, "I did not laugh." But the Lord answered her, directly this time, "Yes, you did laugh."

The LORD God Himself had dealt with Sarah's unbelief. He had uncovered it, and He had confronted it. God challenged her faith with these words: "Is anything too hard for the LORD?" Sarah had to answer that question. In her heart she had to ask herself, "Is anything impossible for God?" And she had to answer truthfully: "No, nothing is impossible with God!" She knew that *El Shaddai*, God Almighty, Creator of heaven and earth, could do anything, anything! If it was God's Will and God's Word, that she (a ninety-year-old woman) should give birth to a baby—then it would surely come to pass. Sarah believed God's Word. The Bible records, "By faith, even Sarah herself received the ability to conceive, even beyond the proper time of life, since she considered Him faithful who had promised" (Hebrews 11:11 NAS). Sarah could hardly believe that she would have what she hoped for all her life—a baby! But she did believe. She believed God's Promise that soon she would have a baby boy, named Isaac/Laughter. God in His mercy and for His glory, had come to Sarah, to change her laugh of doubt into a laugh of joy!

The three visitors from heaven had accomplished the first part of their mission. They had come on a mission of life to an old woman, who had lost hope in the power and promise of God. They had come to strengthen Sarah's faith, that by faith, she might conceive and nurture life within her womb. Their mission was life for Sarah—and it was life for the whole world. Long ago God had promised Abraham that all peoples on earth would be blessed through him. The promised Saviour from sin and death would come through Abraham and Sarah. Through their child, Laughter, would come the One who was joy to the world! Yes, this was indeed a mission of life to the whole world, which was imprisoned by sin and sorrow, death and the devil. This was the way God Almighty, in His eternal LOVE, was bringing salvation to the world.

Two thousand years later, the New Testament would open with a great cry of victory: "Jesus Christ . . . the son of Abraham!" In that cry of victory, one could hear the laugh of an old woman.

A Mission of Death

It was time for the three visitors from heaven to leave Abraham and Sarah, for their work with them was finished. However, they would not leave the earth, not yet. They had other work here; the second part of their mission was not yet accomplished. As the three visitors arose to leave, they stood in the shade of the trees by Abraham's tent. From this place, high in the hills, they looked across the lush green plain of the Jordan River, that beautiful valley which men called the "Garden of God," and in the distance they could see the city of Sodom. They had looked down upon Sodom before this day . . . many times . . . from heaven. They knew the city of Sodom; they knew what a wicked place it was! Nonetheless, it was towards Sodom that the three visitors from heaven began to walk. Why were they going there? What mission could they have there? Why would the holy angels of heaven, and the Most Holy One Himself, want to visit the evil citizens of Sodom? Perhaps Abraham himself wondered these things as he walked with them. Abraham would accompany these men on the start of their journey, but he would not go all the way to Sodom, even though he had rescued its people, even though he had a relative living there. No, he had no desire to visit that great city and centre of sin, Sodom.

Then the LORD said, "Shall I hide from Abraham what I am about to do? Abraham shall surely become a great and powerful nation, and all nations on earth will be blessed through him. For I have chosen him, so that he will direct his children and his household after him to keep the way of the LORD by doing what is right and just, so that the LORD will bring about for Abraham what He has promised him." From Abraham God would make a nation for Himself, a holy people who would keep the way of the LORD, a godly people who would do what was right and just. God would make a nation who delighted in Him, a nation created for the display of His splendour. This nation would inherit the earth forever. And the wicked nations, whose people delighted in evil—what would happen to them? God would destroy them. Should Abraham not know this? Should he not see with his own eyes what God had promised to do? "Lift up your eyes from where you are and look . . . All the land that you see I will give to you and your seed forever" (Genesis 13:14, 15). On that day, as they walked towards Sodom, the LORD told Abraham what He was about to do: "The outcry against Sodom and Gomorrah is so great and their sin is so grievous, that I will go down and . . ." and what? What would God do to those wicked cities? Abraham knew; God would destroy them. But God said He would go down "and see." God would see for Himself. The LORD would weigh the souls of men carefully and He would judge them righteously. God said, "I will go down and see if what they have done is as bad as the outcry that has reached Me. If not, I will know." Yes, God would know. They could not hide their sin from the LORD.

Then the two angels turned and went towards Sodom. The were on a mission of death. The LORD had sent them to that city of sin to destroy it. Abraham was dismayed, for there was someone he loved very much, who lived in Sodom. Do you remember who it was? It was his nephew, Lot, who had been like a son to him. Yes, Lot, who was a righteous man, still lived in Sodom. What would happen to Lot? What would happen to Lot's wife and children? Abraham was dismayed! The two angels had already set out for Sodom on their mission of death. Time was running out. With each step they took closer to Sodom, its destruction drew nearer. What could Abraham do? How could he rescue Lot this time? All he could do was appeal to God for mercy:

The LORD had not yet left him, so Abraham approached his God and pleaded: "Will You sweep away the righteous with the wicked? What if there are fifty righteous people in the city? Will You really sweep it away and not spare the place for the sake of the fifty righteous people in it? Far be it from You to do such a thing—to kill the righteous with the wicked, treating the righteous and the wicked alike. Far be it from You! Will not the Judge of all the earth do right?"

The LORD said, "If I find fifty righteous people in the city of Sodom, I will spare the whole place for their sake."

Then Abraham spoke up again: "Now that I have been so bold as to speak to the LORD, though I am nothing but dust and ashes, what if the number of the righteous is five less than fifty? Will you destroy the whole city because of five people?"

God said, "If I find forty-five there, I will not destroy it."

Once again Abraham spoke to the LORD: "What if only forty are found there?"

God said, "For the sake of forty, I will not destroy it."

Then Abraham said, "May the LORD not be angry, but let me speak. What if only thirty can be found there?"

God answered: "I will not do it if I find thirty there."

How far would Abraham go in this bargaining? How far would God go? Abraham spoke again: "Now that I have been so bold as to speak to the LORD, what if only twenty can be found there?"

God said, "For the sake of twenty, I will not destroy it."

Then Abraham said, "May the LORD not be angry, but let me speak just once more. What if only ten can be found there?" Would God spare such a wicked city, if only ten righteous people could be found among hundreds of thousands of evil-doers? What would God answer this last time?

The LORD is merciful. He answered, "For the sake of ten, I will not destroy it."

Abraham dared not ask for more. There must be ten righteous people in that great city. Surely in Lot's immediate circle of family and friends there would be found ten righteous people! When the LORD had finished speaking with Abraham, He left, and Abraham returned home.

All through that long dark night, Abraham must have wondered: "What was happening in Sodom? What was happening to his nephew? Would the angels find ten righteous people? Would Sodom be spared? Would that great city survive . . . or would it be destroyed? Would he awake to find that thousands of people had been swept away in the wrath of God?" That night, Abraham had to have faith in God, faith in the goodness and justice of God. Through that long dark night Abraham must find comfort in his own words: "Will not the Judge of all the earth do right?"

The teacher's guide for this lesson starts on page 496.

A DAY OF DESTRUCTION, A DAY OF SALVATION

Would ten righteous people be found in the city of Sodom? Would it survive or was it altogether corrupt? God said, "I will go down and see . . . I will know" (Genesis 18:21). The LORD sent two messengers, two angels disguised as men, to be His spies. This was Sodom's last chance, the night of their final exam. Would the citizens of Sodom pass God's test? Or would they be condemned and destroyed? This was what happened:

In the evening, as it began to grow dark, two travellers arrived in Sodom. They looked like ordinary men, who were dusty and hungry and tired from their journey, but really these "men" were the angels sent by God. As they entered through the city gates, they were warmly greeted by a good man. It was Lot! He treated these visitors the same way that Uncle Abraham did—respectfully and hospitably. When Lot saw them he arose to meet them and bowed down with his face to the ground before them. He addressed them as "my lords" and referred to himself as "your servant." He also invited them to his home to spend the night. At first the angels refused, saying that they would stay in the city square—but Lot insisted so strongly that they finally did go with him to his house. (Lot knew what would happen to strangers, who were left outside in the city of Sodom at night. Lot had lived in this city for many years and he was distressed by the wicked way these people lived. Day after day and night after night, his righteous soul had been tormented by all the lawless deeds he saw and heard around him. No, these travellers, whose noble faces almost shone with holiness, must not be left unprotected in Sodom's darkness. Lot insisted that his house be their shelter for the night.) There in Lot's home, the heavenly guests were treated kindly and generously. Water was brought for their refreshment, bread was baked for their supper, and beds were prepared for their night's rest. So far, only good things had happened to God's spies in Sodom.

One might come to the wrong conclusion; one might think: "Sodom is such a friendly place! Strangers are noticed and welcomed here. As soon as they walk through the city gates, they are invited to someone's home, where they are given food to eat and a place to sleep. Surely there is some mistake. This is not the city God intends to destroy, is it? Look how his messengers are treated! Surely Sodom has passed God's test!" Be careful. Don't judge too quickly. The night is just beginning. The plot is just unfolding. Keep watching. Many hours of darkness remain for the citizens of Sodom to do their evil deeds.

That night, Sodom was on trial. The judge of all the earth was watching from His heavenly throne, carefully weighing that city in the supreme balance of divine justice. "From heaven the LORD looks down and sees all mankind; He watches all who live on earth" (Psalm 33:13, 14). "God observes the sons of men; His eyes examine them" (Psalm 11:4). There were also invisible hosts of angels watching to see what would happen this night in this city on earth. There were other eyes too, watching and waiting in the shadows of doors and from the corners of streets in Sodom. These were human eyes, evil eyes, searching for an opportunity to sin. These eyes were burning with lust. They belonged to workers of wickedness, who were waiting for the hour of darkness, so that they might do the deeds of the devil. When night came, the men of Sodom— all of them, from every house, from every part of the city, both young men and old men, both rich men and poor men—they all were drawn together into the darkness by the degrading desires of their hearts. They came to Lot's house and surrounded it. Why? They too wanted to "welcome" the strangers to their city—and they had their own way of doing it!

Lot's guests had not yet gone to bed. Outside they heard the frightening sounds of sin, like a whirlwind of wickedness, growing louder and wilder . . . like a rising storm in the night, roaring with rage . . . like the crashing waves of the sea, foaming up their filth. Yes, something evil was brewing in the city of Sodom just outside Lot's house. What was happening? Why had the men of Sodom surrounded his house? Never before had such a thing happened to Lot. What did the Sodomites want? Lot did not have to wait long to find out, nor did he have to ask. The men of Sodom began to shout: "Where are the men who came to you tonight? Bring them out to us, so that we can have sex with them!" Lot's guests had not slipped into his house unnoticed. The eyes of the men of Sodom were always watching, always searching, always lusting . . . for more prey. What they wanted to do with these visitors was disgraceful, despicable! They wanted to use their bodies in wicked and perverted ways, in ways which God never intended and against which God clearly commanded. They wanted to do abominable things to Lot's guests, for their minds were filled with disgusting thoughts and their hearts were filled with degrading passions. "Bring them out to us," they shouted! The men of Sodom were all homosexuals. The city of Sodom was the "Gay Capital" of the ancient world. In Sodom, every week was "Gay Pride Week"—for they were proud of their perversion and rebellion. They did not try to hide their sin. They flaunted it and applauded it; they revelled in it and delighted in it. "Bring them out to us," they shouted! If Lot had known who his guests really were, that they were angels sent from heaven and not mere men of this earth, and if he had told this to the sinful citizens of Sodom, do you think they would have cared? Since they committed these degrading deeds against men, who were created in the image of God, they would not stop for angels. I think they would have laughed and mocked and yelled: "All the better! We will commit these crimes against the holy angels of the Most High God! What do we care? Bring them out to us!"

What was Lot going to do? He could not fight against the whole city. Perhaps he could reason with these people. Afterall, he knew these men. They were the town's people with whom he lived and worked every day. They knew him, too. He had settled in Sodom years ago and had always dealt fairly and honestly with these folk. Uncle Abraham had even rescued them. These people owed him, not only their wealth, but their lives. Surely they would remember all this. Also, his wife was friends with their wives and his daughters were married to their sons. Yes, these people were friends, neighbours and relatives. Surely it was just a matter of talking to them. So Lot went outside to meet with them, closing the door behind him. "My friends," he said. Yes, Lot knew many of the faces in the crowd and he considered these men his friends, although he could not always condone their behaviour. Tonight he would have to take a firm, but friendly, stand against them. "No, my friends. Don't do this wicked thing," said Lot. The crowd was enraged! Who did Lot think he was? How dare he say "no" to their fun! How dare he call their plan for tonight "wicked"! Who did he think he was, moving into their town and then judging them? Lot thought he could reason with these Sodomites, but they were given over to a dark and depraved mind. Reason would not work with brute beasts.

What could Lot do now? In desperation he tried to bargain with these wicked men. He tried to appeal to their animal instincts by offering these vile men his virgin daughters. However, these Sodomites were worse than animals. Lot could not even appeal to natural instincts, because these men had abandoned natural relations with women for unnatural ones with men. Even their instincts were warped, twisted, and perverted. These men were inflamed with lust for other men. Lot said, "Look, I have two daughters, who have never slept with a man. Let me bring them out to you, and you can do what you like with them. But don't do anything to these men, for they have come under the protection of my roof." To his utter disgrace, Lot actually made this evil proposal to appease their demands. Was there any worse way a father could betray a daughter? In attempting to bargain with the wicked, Lot himself was abandoning natural relations, (that of a father protecting his children, especially his daughters,) and was sinking into Sodom's cesspool of sin. Lot shamed himself for nothing. His wicked offer to degrade his daughters was in vain. The men of Sodom were not interested.

"Get out of our way," they shouted! "We'll treat you worse than them," they threatened! What could Lot say? What could he do? His very life was in danger. These men would rape and kill him . . . and then laugh about it. There was no justice in Sodom. The angry crowd surged forward, pressing in upon Lot. If he would not open his door to them, they would trample him to death . . . and then break down the door. Either way, whether Lot yielded to their demands or not, they would get what they wanted—and what they wanted was sex with those two handsome men inside the house.

Thankfully, those two men were not men, but angels. Thankfully, they were beings of great strength, power and authority. Thankfully, they were agents of God Almighty Himself and they had no fear of these creatures, who were but dust and ashes. As Lot stood his ground between the wicked mob and his godly guests, the angels reached out, pulled Lot back into the house, and shut the door. Then the angels struck the Sodomites with blindness, which stopped them in their tracks. They could do nothing now, for they could not see. It would take them the rest of the night just to grope along the streets of Sodom to find their way home. These Sodomites were twice blinded. They had been blinded by sin and Satan before this night, walking their whole lives in spiritual darkness, but now they would spend their last night on earth without even the faintest glimpse of light. Never again would they see God's grace in the lustre of the moon or the twinkle of the stars. Woe to the Sodomites! This second blindness was just a taste of what was soon to come. Soon, in just a few hours, these men would be cast into blackest darkness forever. Woe to the Sodomites! Their doom was sealed. They had failed the test. The city of Sodom was about to be destroyed!

God told Abraham that Sodom would be spared if even ten righteous people could be found there, but throughout that great city, only one good man was found—and that was Lot. All the others had clearly demonstrated that they were utterly corrupt. Sodom was doomed to destruction. Would God sweep away the righteous with the wicked? Would God treat the righteous and the wicked alike? Far be it from the LORD to do such a thing! "The Lord knows how to rescue godly men from trials and to hold the unrighteous for the day of judgement" (II Peter 2:9). God would surely rescue the one righteous man (and any people related to him.) The two angels asked Lot, "Do you have anyone else here . . . anyone else in this city who belongs to you?" Yes! Lot had a wife and two daughters at home. There were also other daughters, whose husbands were men from Sodom. "Get them out of here," warned the angels, "because we are going to destroy this place . . . God has sent us to destroy it!" Perhaps now Lot realized that he had been entertaining angels unawares. His house-guests were from heaven's host sent on a holy mission of destruction. Lot believed the word of the angels. He went outside again, fearing not for his own safety, and warned the men, who were married to his daughters. They were standing outside his house with the other Sodomites. Lot pleaded with them, "Hurry and get out of this place, because the LORD is about to destroy this city!" His sons-in-law laughed. They thought Lot was joking. The fools said in their hearts: "There is no

God." Lot tried to convince them, but the more he said, the more they laughed. They had always thought that their father-in-law was a religious fanatic, but now they thought he was a religious lunatic! He actually was urging them to run away from Sodom in the middle of the night—for no reason whatsoever. He probably wanted them to wake up their wives and children too. He said that some angels told him that God was about to destroy their city. It was ridiculous, hilarious! Lot left them laughing and returned to his house. There was not much time left. Lot had to get ready to leave the city. What should he take with him? He was a rich man and had so many beautiful and valuable things. As Lot tried to decide what to pack, the night was quickly slipping away. Already the sky was turning grey in the east with the coming of dawn. What was Lot doing? What was taking him so long? "Hurry!" urged the angels. They told Lot what to take with him. "Take your wife and your two daughters, who are here, or you will be swept away when the city is punished!" Still Lot hesitated. Why? What was he clinging to? What was he waiting for? He must run! He must run for his life! But Lot stood there, unable to move. His life was somehow rooted in Sodom. Finally the angels grasped Lot's hand and the hands of his wife and his two daughters. The angels then led them, pulled them, uprooted them, safely out of that city—for the LORD was merciful to them. When they were outside the city gates, one of the angels commanded them, "Flee for your lives! Don't look back, and don't stop anywhere in the plain! Flee to the mountains—or you will be swept away!" Lot looked towards the mountains in the distance, pink now in the light of dawn. The mountains looked so far away. I can't do it, he thought. His legs felt weak; his heart felt faint. I'll never make it, he thought to himself. I can't run that far. Didn't Lot know that God would wait for him? Didn't Lot know that God could strengthen him? No, Lot was filled with fear. "Please," he begged the angels, "You have shown great kindness to me in sparing my life, but I can't flee to the mountains. This disaster will overtake me and I will die! Look, there is a town near enough to run to, and it is small. Let me flee to it, for it is very small, isn't it? Then my life will be spared." "Alright," said the angel. "I will grant this request too. I will not overthrow the town you speak of. But flee there quickly, because I cannot do anything until you reach it!"

By the time Lot reached the little town called Bella, (the name of which was later changed to Zoar or Small, because Lot said, "It is small . . . very small") it was mid-morning. The sun had already risen over the land. It was a beautiful day. Sodom was humming with the day's work . . . and buzzing with the night's news. One could hear the sounds of life in the city: Birds were singing, dogs were barking, kids were playing, bells were ringing. People were in their homes eating and drinking, laughing and talking (and discussing the strange blindness that had come and gone so strangely in the night.) People were in the market place buying and selling, just as they did every work-day. It was such a lovely spring morning that the farmers were planting their fields and builders were making new houses. The sons-in-law of Lot must have laughed again to think how he had tried to scare them. It was a day like any other day in Sodom. The only thing that was out of the ordinary, was that Lot's house was quiet and empty. Someone had seen him running away with his wife and daughters at dawn, but since he had taken almost nothing with him, he would no doubt be back soon. It seemed as if everyday life was continuing in Sodom, just as it always had, just as it always would.

But that same day, "the day Lot left Sodom, fire and sulphur rained down from heaven and destroyed them all" (Luke 17:29). As soon as Lot reached the little town, the LORD rained down burning sulphur on Sodom and Gomorrah and the other cities of the plain. It was from the LORD! The fires of hell fell on them from out of heaven. In a moment God destroyed them in his fierce anger. He condemned those cities by burning them to ashes. It was not a natural disaster. It was a supernatural one! The people who had fanned the flames of wickedness in their hearts and lives and towns were now consumed by the fires of God's holiness. In an instant these people and their cities were gone. Nothing was left of them . . . but dust in the wind, black ashes blowing in a scorching wind. No rescuers rushed in; no survivors crawled out. Not so much as a green blade of grass was left. That lush valley, that fertile plain, which was so beautiful that it was called the "Garden of God," that whole area became a burning waste of salt pits and sulphur. Never again would a seed be planted there or a sprout be watered there. Nothing good or green would ever grow there again. Neither man, nor beast, could survive in that place. The entire plain had become a desolation forever!

Lot and two of his daughters were the only ones to escape, because God was the One who delivered him out of the catastrophe. Even Lot's wife perished in the destruction. She refused God's warning. She did not obey the Word of the LORD spoken to her by the angel: "Do not look back!" She did not believe the Word of the LORD: "You will be swept away!" Lot's wife looked back. That one final look was a fatal glance of unbelief. Lot's wife became a pillar of salt. It had happened before and it would happen again: "The LORD delivered His people . . . but later destroyed those who did not believe" (Jude 5).

Early the next morning, Abraham arose and returned to the place where he had stood before the LORD, pleading for God's Mercy. Once again Abraham looked down towards those great cities of the ancient world, Sodom and Gomorrah. Abraham gazed across the whole land of the plain. All Abraham saw was thick black smoke rising from the land. The smell of smoke and the odour of sulphur and the stench of death filled the air. There was nothing else. The cities were gone . . . and so was that beautiful and bountiful valley. What remained was one of the most ugly and barren blemishes on the face of the earth. All life had vanished, never to return. (Today, if you travelled to the land of Israel, you would not find those cities rebuilt or the valley resettled. That whole area has been covered by the Dead Sea or the Salt Sea, in which no form of life can survive. Surrounding the Dead Sea is a dead land—a salty, sandy, wasteland covered with scars and pits and pillars of salt. The judgement of God on that area is evident thousands of years later, lest mankind forget: The Holy God of heaven is a consuming fire!) But when Abraham stood there, viewing the destruction, the display of God's wrath was only a few hours old. The smoke was still rising from the land. What did Abraham think? What did Abraham say? Perhaps, as he stood in that same spot, he echoed the same words he had spoken two days earlier: "Shall not the Judge of all the earth do right?"

Yes, God's destruction of Sodom and Gomorrah was true and just and right. The people of Sodom and Gomorrah and all the surrounding towns were without excuse:

1) They lived in one of the most beautiful and bountiful valleys in all the world. All around them were the evidences of God's goodness and grace. What may be known about God was plain to them, because God had made it plain to them. The heavens and the earth declared God's glory, but these people exchanged the glory of the immortal God for the shameful gods of their own evil imaginations. Although they knew God, they neither glorified Him as God, nor gave thanks to Him. They exchanged the truth of God for a lie, and worshipped and served created things rather than the Creator, who is blessed forever.

2) These people were without excuse. They had suppressed the truth of God by their wickedness. They had God's Law, for "the requirements of the Law were written on their hearts, their consciences also bearing witness, and their thoughts now accusing them . . ." (Romans 2:15). But they ignored God's Law within them. Instead, they gave themselves over to sexual immorality and perversion. Therefore, God gave them over! He gave them over to their sinful desires and their shameful lusts—for the degrading of their bodies with one another. It was not just the men of Sodom and Gomorrah, who did these wicked things. It was not just the men, who committed indecent acts with one another. Even their women exchanged natural relations for unnatural ones. Thus God gave them over, all of them! He gave them over to a depraved mind, to do what ought not to be done. And although they knew God's righteous decree, for their own thoughts often accused them, they did not stop. They knew that those who did such things deserved death, but they not only continued in their sin, they approved it and they applauded it. Thus God gave them over—to sin and death and everlasting destruction.

3) These people were without excuse. They had contact with two righteous men. Abraham, the father of faith, lived in their time. He had even rescued these people. They knew of Abraham's faith and Abraham's God, and they themselves had received the benefits of Abraham's relationship with God. There was also Lot, who lived in their town. That very night, before they were all destroyed, Lot had preached to them: "No, my friends. Don't do this wicked thing!" That same night Lot had sounded the alarm: "Hurry and get out of this place, because the LORD is about to destroy the city!" But they refused to repent, although it was passionately and compassionately offered to them.

Shall not the Judge of all the earth do right? The people of Sodom and Gomorrah refused to believe in God. They refused to repent of sin. The destruction they received, they deserved. They were without excuse. Rejoice, for true and just and right are God's judgements!

As Abraham stood there, watching the dense smoke rising from the land, what did he think? What did he say? Abraham was a man of faith, the father of faith. No doubt, he gave thanks to God here on earth, just as he would in heaven. One day the voice of Abraham, Father of a Multitude, would be heard in the roar of the great multitude in heaven shouting:

Hallelujah!
Salvation and power and glory belong to our God,
    for true and just are His judgements.
He has condemned the great prostitute,
    who corrupted the earth by her adulteries . . .
Hallelujah!
The smoke from her goes up forever and ever.

Revelation 19:1–3

"Sodom and Gomorrah . . . serve as an example of those who suffer the punishment of eternal fire" (Jude 7). God made Sodom and Gomorrah "an example of what is going to happen to all the ungodly" (II Peter 2:6). Their destruction points to the great Day of the LORD, the day of God's wrath, when the whole earth will be laid waste, when "the heavens will disappear with a roar; the elements will be destroyed by fire, and the earth and everything in it will be burned up . . . That day will bring about the destruction of the heavens by fire, and the elements will melt in the heat" (II Peter 3:10, 12). "See, the Day of the LORD is coming—a cruel day with wrath and fierce anger—to make the land desolate and destroy the sinners within it . . . The earth will shake from its place at the wrath of the LORD Almighty, in the day of His burning anger" (Isaiah 13:9, 13). "See, the LORD is coming with fire! His chariots are like a whirlwind. He will bring down His anger with fury, and His rebuke with flames of fire. For with fire and with His Sword, the LORD will execute judgement upon all men, and many will be those slain by the LORD" (Isaiah 66:15, 16). "See, the LORD is going to lay waste the earth and devastate it. He will ruin its face and scatter its inhabitants . . . The earth will be completely laid waste and totally plundered . . . The earth is defiled by its people; they have disobeyed the laws, violated the statutes, broken the everlasting covenant. Therefore a curse consumes the earth; its people must bear their guilt. Therefore earth's inhabitants are burned up" (Isaiah 24:1, 3,5, 6). "Its inhabitants die like flies" (Isaiah 51:6). The LORD has spoken this word. God's day of judgement is coming.

Is there any hope? Is there any escape? Are there any survivors? Yes! We read in God's Word, that "before the coming of the great and dreadful Day of the LORD, *everyone who calls on the name of the LORD will be saved* . . . There will be deliverance, as the LORD has said, among the survivors whom the LORD calls" (Joel 2:31, 32). But, "unless the LORD Almighty had left us some survivors, we would have become like Sodom, we would have been like Gomorrah" (Isaiah 1:9). It is by God's grace that we are saved!

Shortly after this, Abraham left that smoking wasteland, and moved to another region. What became of Lot? The Scriptures record that he and his two daughters left the little town of Zoar, because he was afraid to stay there. Perhaps Lot discovered that this small town was as wicked as the big cities and he feared God's judgement on this place too. Perhaps, when he viewed the awful destruction all around him, he decided that the only safe place to live was where God told him to go, so Lot moved to the mountains and lived in a cave. But even there he was not safe from sin. His daughters, who had learned the wicked ways of Sodom, slept with their father because there was no other man for them to marry. They enticed their father to drink and seduced him when he was drunk. Through the sin of incest two sons, (who were also grandsons,) were born to Lot: Moab, who became the father of the Moabites, and Ben-Ammi, who became the father of the Ammonites. Both these nations became enemies of the people of God. That was how Lot ended his days—in sin and shame. He ended his days on an isolated mountain. He ended his days in poverty, subsisting like a beggar in a cave. Lot, who had once been so wealthy, had lost everything. Why didn't he return to his uncle, Abraham? I don't know. Perhaps he was ashamed . . . of many things. However, in spite of all his failings, Lot is recorded and remembered in the Scriptures as "a righteous man" (II Peter 2:7, 8). That is the final word about Lot.

The teacher's guide for this lesson starts on page 498.

THE SERPENT STRIKES, BUT FAILS

• **Genesis 20, 21:1–7, 22–34**

The LORD had struck the wicked kingdoms of this world, which belonged to Satan. In his righteous wrath God had destroyed those cities of sin, which were jewels in the crown of the Prince of Darkness. God rained down fire from heaven and in a moment they were gone, but this was not the work of God which defeated the devil. No, that ancient Serpent did not surrender, nor did he slither away. He struck back . . . immediately! The Serpent struck at God in the only way he could. He attacked the kingdom of God on earth. Where was this kingdom? It was only a promise to an old man and an old woman. The kingdom of God was only the promise of a child, who was not yet in the world or even in the womb—and Satan would try to keep it that way. He would try to keep the Promise of God unfulfilled . . . forever. The promised child must never be born! The kingdom of God must never begin!

Here is one of the stories of how Satan tried to stop the plan of God:

Abraham had not moved for many many years. Long ago he had

pitched his tent and made his home over-looking the beautiful green valley of the Jordan River, but God had destroyed that whole region. The "Garden of God" had become the "Valley of Death." Black soot blew in the wind and the smell of smoke lingered in the air. It was no longer pleasant to sit in the shade of the trees by his tent, for the stillness of death was in the shadows. It was everywhere. Staying there was like camping in a grave yard. Abraham decided it was time to move again . . . but where?

Abraham followed the setting sun. He moved westward, into the land of the Philistines. At least there were living people in this region. However, Abraham was afraid. The Philistines were a wicked people, ruled by a wicked king. Surely, there is no fear of God in this place, Abraham thought to himself. These people will do anything. They will steal my wife and kill me. Abraham began to live by fear, rather than by faith. He forgot to trust in God's protection. He forgot to trust in God's Promise, that a son would be born to him in a year's time and that God would make him into a great nation. Abraham stopped trusting fully in God's LOVE and God's Word—which was exactly what the Serpent wanted. The Tempter was ready to ensnare Abraham in one of his old sins—lying about his wife, because he was afraid. Once again Abraham said of his wife Sarah, "She is my sister." Then Abimelech, a powerful king of the Philistines in the city of Gerar, sent for Sarah and took her to be like one of his wives. What did Sarah say to King Abimelech? Did she protest, that she was already married to another man? No, as her husband had instructed her, Sarah simply said about Abraham, "He is my brother."

So Abraham and Sarah were separated. The king's soldiers and hell's demons stood between them, keeping them apart. How could the promised child ever be born to them? They no longer lived together as husband and wife. Sarah now belonged to someone else, who was no one less than the king himself. If a son was born to Sarah, the father would be Abimelech, not Abraham. What about God's plan? It seems that Satan, through Abraham's sin, had brought the purpose of God and the promise of God to a halt. If this situation continued much longer, no son would be born to Abraham and Sarah next year . . . and the Word of God would fail.

But there is no power in heaven or on earth that can stop the Word of God. All the armies of all the kings on earth combined with all the legions of hell could not stop the Word of God Almighty. Once again, the LORD intervened. God came to King Abimelech in a dream one night and said to him, "You are as good as dead because of the woman you have taken. She is a married woman!" Now the king had not slept with Sarah, not yet. For some reason, which he himself did not know, he had not gone near her. So Abimelech said, "LORD, will you destroy an innocent nation? Didn't he say to me, 'She is my sister,' and didn't she say, 'He is my brother?' I have done this with a clear conscience and clean hands." Then God answered Abimelech in the dream: "Yes, I know you did this with a clear conscience, and so I have kept you from sinning against Me. That is why I did not let you touch her. Now, return the man's wife, for he is a prophet, and he will pray for you, and you will live. But if you do not return her, you may be sure that you, and everyone belonging to you, will die." The LORD had spoken!

And this mighty king of the Philistines listened to the Word of the LORD spoken to him in his dream. Early the next morning Abimelech summoned all his officials. When he told them what had happened, they were very much afraid. Yes, they were afraid! Abraham was wrong; there was the fear of God in this place! Then Abimelech called Abraham to the king's court and said to him, "What have you done to us? How have I wronged you, that you have brought such great guilt upon me and my kingdom? You have done things to me that should not be done." It was a just rebuke. Abraham had sinned against Abimelech. "What was your reason for doing this?" he asked. Abraham tried to explain his thinking: "I said to myself, 'There is surely no fear of God in this place, and they will kill me because of my wife.' Besides, she really is my sister, the daughter of my father though not of my mother; and she became my wife. And when God had me wander from my father's household, I said to her, 'This is how you can show your love to me, by saying that I am your brother.' " That was it. Abraham had not tried to harm anyone. In his fear he had just tried to protect himself.

Then Abimelech obeyed God's Word. He returned Sarah to her husband, Abraham. He also gave Abraham gifts of sheep and cattle and slaves. The king of the Philistines then said to Abraham, "My land is before you. Live wherever you like." Abimelech also said to Sarah, "I am giving your 'brother' a thousand shekels of silver. This is to cover the offense against you before all who are with you. You are completely vindicated." Then Abraham prayed to God for King Abimelech—and the LORD allowed him to live. The LORD healed Abimelech and his wife and his slave girls, so that they could have children again. During that time, the LORD had closed up every womb in the king's household because of Sarah, Abraham's wife.

So, Abraham and Abimelech parted as friends. Once again Abraham could live at peace in a foreign land, not because of the king's protection, but because of God's protection. The LORD had intervened in a terrible situation to ensure the safety of his servant and the fulfillment of His Promise. But this is not the happy ending to the story. Great joy awaited Abraham and Sarah in the land of the Philistines. The end of this story is laughter, for the LORD was gracious to Sarah as He had said, and the LORD did for Sarah what He had promised. Sarah became pregnant and bore a son to Abraham in his old age, at the very time God had promised him. Abraham gave the name Laughter or Isaac to his new-born son and had him circumcised when he was eight days old, just as God commanded. Abraham was one hundred years old when Isaac was born to him. Sarah said, "God has brought me Laughter! Everyone who hears about this will laugh with me!" And she added, "Who would have said to Abraham that Sarah would nurse children? Yet I have born him a son in his old age."

This story ends with the defeat of the serpent. His scheme against the Word of God and his attack against the Promise of God failed. This story ends with a very great victory for God: Isaac! It ends with great joy for God's people: Laughter!

The teacher's guide for this lesson starts on page 500.

THE LORD GIVES AND THE LORD TAKES AWAY

- **Genesis 21:1–21; 25:12–18**
- **Isaiah 54**
- **Romans 9:6–9**
- **Galatians 4:21–31**

Now Abraham had two sons. Ishmael was Abraham's older son, born to him by the slave woman, Hagar. Ishmael was born in the ordinary way. There was nothing unnatural or unusual about his birth, for his mother was a strong, young woman. However, Isaac, Abraham's new-born son by his wife, Sarah, was not born in the ordinary way. Isaac was born as the result of God's promise. He was conceived by faith and born by the power of God's Spirit. Isaac's birth was not only unusual; it was unnatural. His mother was a very old woman, who had been barren all her life. At ninety years old, when she should have been preparing for her death, she was preparing to give birth. Isaac was a miracle! "Sing oh barren woman . . . burst into song . . . shout for joy!" And Sarah did rejoice. She praised God and she laughed as she held little Laughter in her arms. She said, "God has brought me laughter, and everyone who hears about this will laugh with me." It was a strange sight to see. That new mother, who sat nursing her first-born baby, was a very old woman, so old she could have been a great-great-grandmother. Just to look at them made one smile . . . and laugh . . . with pleasure at the goodness of God. All the angels in heaven and the godly on earth rejoiced at Isaac's birth.

However, not everyone rejoiced; not everyone laughed with love. There are two kinds of laughter in this world. There is a good kind of laughter, which God likes to hear, for it makes people happy. There is also a bad kind of laughter, which mocks people and hurts people. When Isaac was born, some people looked at the old woman's pride and joy—and laughed with scorn behind her back. Perhaps some people said nasty things, such as: "An old withered tree bears only rotten fruit." One of these people was within Abraham's own household. It was Abraham's own son—Ishmael! Ishmael was fourteen years old when Isaac was born. When he saw his new baby brother, he should have loved him; he should have praised God for him—but he didn't. Ishmael mocked him; he envied him; he hated him. Already Ishmael was living "in hostility" toward the only brother he had. Already the Word of the LORD regarding him was being fulfilled: "You shall name him Ishmael . . . and he will live in hostility toward all his brothers" (Genesis 16:11, 12).

For awhile Ishmael kept his hostility toward Isaac locked away secretly in his heart—but the sins of the heart, unless they are uprooted, always grow. Eventually they overflow the heart. They cannot remain hidden for long. Ishmael's envy and hatred, his jealousy and mockery, were going to come out of the darkness of his heart into the clear light of day. It was a very special day, when Ishmael's sins were revealed. Two or three years had passed. It was the day of Isaac's party. Abraham held a great feast to celebrate the fact that Isaac was no longer a baby, snuggling and nursing next to his mother. He was a big boy now, two or three years old, walking and talking, eating food from a plate and drinking milk from a cup. He must have been so cute, toddling around the tents. Abraham and Sarah must have been so happy just to watch him. They must have been so thankful to God for bringing Isaac safely through those early years. Many little babies don't survive infancy, but God was gracious to them, and their old eyes were watching their little boy enjoying his I-am-not-a-baby-anymore party. It was such a happy occasion! It was a party for Laughter, a party for everyone to enjoy themselves . . . and then something happened. Ishmael did something, which spoiled that special day, which ruined the party for everyone. Ishmael began to laugh at Laughter and mock Isaac in a very mean way. Ishmael, who was sixteen or seventeen years old, began to tease and taunt his little brother in a very cruel way. It says in the Bible that "the son born in the ordinary way persecuted the son born by the power of the Spirit" (Galatians 4:29). Persecuted! That is a very strong word, because what Ishmael did was a very serious sin. Isaac was a special boy, for he was a child of God's promise, and this was a special day. Ishmael should have honoured his younger brother, but instead he persecuted him.

On this day his sin did not go unnoticed. Sarah saw what he did and said to Abraham, "Get rid of that slave woman and her son, for that slave woman's son will never share in the inheritance with my son Isaac." Get rid of him? Ishmael was Abraham's own son, his oldest son, for many years his only son. Abraham loved Ishmael. What should he do? Should he listen to Sarah? Should he really send his son away? Abraham was greatly distressed! This day, which should have been a joyous celebration, an occasion for laughing and singing, feasting and dancing, had become a day of anger and sorrow and distress—because of Ishmael's sin.

Should Abraham get rid of Ishmael? Could Sarah be right? When Sarah said, "that slave woman's son will never share in the inheritance with my son"—she spoke the truth. Perhaps she was thinking only of an earthly inheritance, of the wealth Abraham would leave to his son, but there was a greater inheritance, a heavenly one, promised by God. It seems that Ishmael had no part in that inheritance. If he had, he would not have despised the child of God's promise. If Ishmael loved the Word of God, he would have loved Isaac, and honoured him, and delighted in him, because Isaac was the fulfillment of God's Word. Although Ishmael was a child of Abraham, "it is not the natural children who are God's children, but it is the children of the promise. They are the ones who are regarded as Abraham's offspring" (Romans 9:8). Ishmael was already cut off from the heavenly inheritance. But should Abraham actually get rid of him? Should he cut him off from an earthly inheritance? Surely that was too severe! Abraham was greatly distressed. He did not know what to do.

The LORD settled the matter. God said to Abraham, "Do not be so distressed about the boy and your maidservant. Listen to whatever Sarah tells you, because it is through Isaac that your offspring will be reckoned." It was through Isaac that Abraham's children would be counted! Earlier God had promised Abraham, "I will make you into a great nation" (Genesis 12:2). It was through Isaac that this great nation would come. God said, "I will establish my covenant with him as an everlasting covenant . . . My covenant

I will establish with Isaac" (Genesis 17:19, 21). But what would happen to Ishmael? Abraham loved this son too. God said, "I will make the son of the maidservant into a nation also, because he is your offspring." Because Ishmael was Abraham's child, God would bless him too. God had spoken. Abraham may not have listened to the voice of his wife, but he would listen to the voice of his God. Abraham may not have obeyed Sarah's demands, but the command of the LORD he would obey—even if it hurt him to do it. Abraham obeyed God. Early the next morning, Abraham took some food and a skin of water. That was all he gave to Hagar. There was no silver or gold for Ishmael, no earthly inheritance—just a few provisions for their journey, only what they could carry themselves. Then Abraham sent Hagar away with her son, with his son, Ishmael. Abraham never saw him again. He was gone. Abraham could no longer take care of him.

What happened to Ishmael? He and his mother wandered about in the desert for a few days. Then their water ran out and they became faint with thirst. Hagar had her son lie down in the shade of a bush, while she went off a short distance and sat down to cry. I cannot watch the boy die, she thought. Ishmael was also crying. Everyone had forsaken them and forgotten them. His own father had cast them out. He and his mother were going to die in the desert—and no one cared. But, had Ishmael forgotten his name? His name means: God hears! And God heard the boy crying. Once before, long ago, God had seen Hagar and Ishmael in the desert. God heard their misery then and had compassion on them—and God would have compassion now. The angel of God called to Hagar from heaven and said to her, "What is the matter, Hagar? Do not be afraid. God has heard the boy crying as he lies there. Lift the boy up and take him by the hand, for I will make him into a great nation." Then God opened her eyes and she saw a well of water. So she ran and filled the skin with water and gave the boy a drink. Ishmael survived.

Ishmael more than survived. God was with him as he grew up and he became a man, a wild kind of man, just as God had promised before Ishmael's birth. When he became a man, there was no party for Ishmael, but God blessed him. His mother got a wife for him from Egypt. In time, he had children—twelve sons, who became the rulers of twelve tribes, and many daughters as well. Ishmael lived in the desert, shooting wild animals with his bow and arrow. He was a wild man living a wild life in a wild place. His descendants became a whole nation of people, known as the Ishmaelites or the Midianites, who lived in the wilderness near the border of Egypt. These people were a wild bunch, just like their father. They lived in a wild desert region, always fighting amongst themselves and against their neighbours—fulfilling God's Word spoken long ago.

Ishmael lived a long life of one hundred and thirty-seven years. He never returned to his father's household, except to attend a funeral. Yes, after many years away, Ishmael came home to bury his father Abraham. But all those years that passed, from the day he said good-bye to his father until the day of that final farewell, Ishmael lived apart from the blessing of Abraham's household. Ishmael had been sent away, by the command of God.

It is a sad story, how Abraham lost his first son, through that son's sin, laughter, mockery . . . and ultimately, unbelief. One son arrives; the other departs. The LORD gives and the LORD takes away. Blessed be the name of the LORD!

The teacher's guide for this lesson starts on page 502.

THE LORD WILL PROVIDE

- Genesis 22
- II Chronicles 3:1
- John 1:29
- Romans 4:16–25
- Hebrews 6:13–19
- Hebrews 11:17–19
- James 2:14–24
- I Peter 1:6, 7

B y God's command, Ishmael had been sent away. Now Isaac was Abraham's only son. How Abraham loved him! Isaac/Laughter filled Abraham's heart. Abraham's attachment to this son was greater than to anything or anyone else in the whole world. He had waited one hundred years for this child and in him Abraham had great joy and hope. In him were bound all God's promises of blessing, not only for Abraham, but for the whole world. As the days and the years passed, Abraham's love for his son Isaac grew along with the boy. Such love! Such love this father had for his son! On earth, such love was unsurpassed.

Then one day God tested Abraham. It was a test of Abraham's faith. It was a test to prove that Abraham's faith was real and true. This test would show, forever, without any doubt, that Abraham believed God . . . because Abraham obeyed God. This test was designed to show what was in Abraham's heart. Did Abraham trust God? Did Abraham love God? Did Abraham fear God? These were the questions of the test, which had to be answered not with words on his lips, but with deeds in his life. Abraham was an old man, who had faced many trials in his life—but this was the worst! This was the greatest and hardest test of faith that he or any other man, except the Son of Man, would ever have to face. Would Abraham be able to pass this test? God said to him: "Abraham! Take your son, your only son, Isaac, whom you love, and go to the region of Moriah. There, on one of the mountains which I will tell you, sacrifice him as a burnt offering."

Sacrifice Isaac? Kill him? Burn him? What was God asking him to do . . . and why? God had already taken one son. Now was He going to take the other son too? Isaac was Abraham's only son! Isaac was Sarah's only son! Isaac was the child of promise! Isaac was the one with whom God had established His covenant forever. It was through Isaac that Abraham's children would be numbered. It was through Isaac that the whole world would be blessed. To kill Isaac would be to end all hope for life! The nation promised by God—it would die with Isaac. The children promised to him—they would die with Isaac. The Messiah Himself, the Saviour from sin and death—He too would die with Isaac. All God's promises, everything in which Abraham hoped, the promise of life itself—would come to nothing and end in ashes. Sacrifice Isaac? Yes, those were the words God had spoken. "Take your son, your only son, Isaac . . . and sacrifice him." Abraham did not argue with God. Abraham said nothing, not one word in response. This was the test: Did he trust God and love God and fear God—even when God said, "Take your son . . . and sacrifice him"? The Scripture records that Abraham simply and silently obeyed.

Early the next morning Abraham got up and saddled his donkey. He took with him two of his servants and his son Isaac. When he had cut enough wood for the burnt offering, he set out for the place God had told him— the mountains of Moriah. On the third day Abraham looked up and he saw the place in the distance, that dreaded place that God had chosen for the sacrifice of his son. Abraham and Isaac would go to that place alone. He told his servants, "Remain here with the donkey while I and the boy go over there. We will worship—and then we will come back to you." Why did Abraham say, "We will come back to you"? Wasn't he going to sacrifice Isaac there on that distant mountain? Wasn't he going there to kill him and burn him? Yes! Abraham was going there to obey this command of God, but Abraham had faith in the promises of God. Abraham knew that all God's promises must come through Isaac—so "Abraham reasoned that God could raise the dead," that he could "receive Isaac back from death" (Hebrews 11:19). Abraham had resurrection faith. Abraham believed in God—"the God who gives life to the dead." Is anything too hard for the LORD? No, the LORD could do anything, *anything*—even raise the dead to life! "Against all hope, Abraham in hope believed." This was not the first time he had had such faith. Years ago Abraham had "faced the fact that his body was as good as dead, since he was about one hundred years old, and that Sarah's womb was also dead," but he had believed God then, "being fully persuaded that God had power to do what He had promised" (Romans 4:17–21). And God did! God gave Abraham and Sarah a son. God gave Isaac life from death. God had accomplished the impossible then—and God could do it now. This was how Abraham reasoned: After he sacrificed Isaac, God would raise him from the dead—to the praise and honour and glory of God! That was why Abraham said to his servants, "The boy and I will go and we will worship and then we will come back to you." Abraham believed that Isaac would come back to them (and to everyone) from the dead!

So Abraham took the wood off the donkey's back and placed it on the shoulders of his son, Isaac. Abraham himself carried the fire and the knife. How awful it must have been for Abraham to carry that knife, the knife which he must use to kill his beloved Isaac! How awful it must have been for Abraham to carry that fire, the fire which he must use to burn his beloved Isaac! How could he do such a thing? This was his own son, his only son, his beloved son! Every step of that journey must have been agony for Abraham. How heavy his hands must have felt carrying that knife and that fire. Surely it was too great a burden for the old man to bear—but Abraham continued up the mountain for one reason only: The LORD had commanded him to do it. As the two of them went on together, something was puzzling to Isaac. He noticed that the most important thing for their worship was missing, so he spoke up and said, "Father?" "Yes, my son," replied Abraham. "Father, the fire and wood are here, but where is the lamb for the burnt offering?" How those words must have torn Abraham's heart! Isaac knew that a lamb was required for the sacrifice; he knew that without the shedding of blood there is no forgiveness, so he asked, "Where is the lamb?" What Isaac didn't know was that a son was required, a beloved son. Abraham did not tell him, not yet. However, Abraham did answer him, in faith and in truth, and perhaps not fully understanding his own answer. Abraham, the LORD's prophet, said these blessed words: "My son, *God Himself will provide the lamb for the burnt offering.*" And the two of them went up the mountain together.

When they reached the place appointed by God, Abraham built an altar there. Many times in his life and in many places Abraham had joyfully built altars to worship his God. But this altar, upon which he must sacrifice his own son, was built with unimaginable sorrow. Each stone the old man picked up and placed on the pile was itself a test—a test of his faith. How heavy were those stones! How painful was this task! Could his heart endure such agony? Could he continue? By God's grace, yes, Abraham went forward, step by step, in the test of faith. Too soon Abraham completed the altar. The next sad task was to arrange the wood on the altar. Then he had to bind with cords the sacrifice. As Abraham was tying rope around Isaac's arms and legs, he must have told him the awful truth, that God required his only son, his beloved son, to be the sacrifice. Isaac did not argue or struggle. He surely could have escaped from this very old man, but Isaac had the same faith as his father. He too would believe and obey, because the God of Abraham was also the God of Isaac. Thus the boy allowed himself to be bound as the sacrifice, for he trusted his father and he trusted his God. Then Abraham held his son one last time as he lifted him onto the altar of his death. There were only three steps left: Abraham stretched out his hand. Then he picked up the knife. With this hand, with this knife, he must kill his son . . . now!

But at that moment, at the very last instant, just before the final and fatal step was taken, the angel of the LORD called out to him from heaven. "Abraham! Abraham!" "Here I am," he replied. Yes, there he was, standing on Mount Moriah, with the knife in his hand above his son Isaac, who was lying on the altar. "Here I am," said Abraham. The LORD said, "Do not lay a hand on the boy. Do not do anything to him. Now I know that you fear God, because you have not withheld from Me your son, your only son." A blessed word from a gracious God! With exceedingly great joy, Abraham put down the knife and untied his son. God had given back his son, and Abraham received him as if God had raised him from the dead. How Abraham rejoiced in God, His Saviour! Abraham had passed the test. Forever, he would be commended for this act of faith—to the praise and honour and glory of God. He had "sacrificed" his only son, yet not one bruise was on his body; not one drop of blood was shed. It was not this son, it was not Isaac, who could pay for their sins. It was not the body of Isaac that would be broken. It was not the blood of Isaac that would be poured out. No, God had a substitute. God had a lamb . . . waiting.

1) On that day there was a lamb waiting for Abraham and Isaac on Mount Moriah. Abraham looked up and there in the bushes he saw a ram caught by its horns. Abraham went over to the bush, took the ram, bound it securely, then killed it and burned it on the altar instead of his son. It was an offering pleasing to God and it was an offering pleasing to them. How Abraham and Isaac rejoiced that day! It was with abundant joy that they worshipped the LORD, because they understood that the lamb was sacrificed as a substitute for Isaac. The lamb took Isaac's place. God had provided the lamb for the offering, just as Abraham had said. So Abraham called that place "Jehovah Jireh" which means "The LORD Will Provide." There is a saying: "On the mountain of the LORD it will be provided."

2) On that day God had another Lamb waiting, one who had been waiting from before the foundation of the world, one who was still waiting for the appointed time. Today was not the day for the sacrifice of that Lamb. The ram slain on Abraham's altar was only a shadow of the One who was to come. Two thousand years later in those same mountains, would stand a city, called Jerusalem and on Mount Moriah would stand the temple of the LORD. At that time and in that place another son of Abraham would be "led like a lamb to the slaughter" (Isaiah 53:7). He would carry a wooden cross upon his shoulders and this Promised Child, this Son of Abraham, would be sacrificed for sin. There would be no last-minute rescue for that Son. His body would be broken and his blood would be poured out . . . unto death! When Abraham said, "God Himself will provide the lamb . . ." he probably did not understand the fullness or the greatness of his prophesy. One day God would provide His own Son, His only begotten and beloved Son, to die on the cross to pay for our sins. Pointing to Jesus, a great prophet declared: "Look, the Lamb of God, who takes away the sin of the world!" For God so loved the world that He gave His one and only Son, that whoever believes in Him shall not perish, but have eternal life. We cannot save ourselves from sin and death. We need a Saviour. We need a Substitute. But we can rejoice because, as Abraham proclaimed that day on Mount Moriah: "Jehovah Jireh! The LORD will provide!" Jesus was God's provision. Jesus was the Promised Child, the Beloved Son, the Sacrificed Lamb. It was Jesus who would save His people from their sins. *On the mountain of the LORD it will be provided!* Yes, there, on that mountain, the LORD provided Jesus, to die in our place, to pay for our sins. In Jesus the promise of life is fulfilled!

In heaven Abraham, Isaac and all his descendants would worship the eternal Lamb of God. In a loud voice they would sing:

Worthy is the Lamb, who was slain,
to receive power and wealth and wisdom
and strength and honour and glory and praise!

Revelation 5:12

They would sing the Song of the Lamb:

Great and marvellous are your deeds,
Lord God Almighty.
Just and true are your ways, King of the ages.
Who will not fear You, O Lord,
and bring glory to your name?
For You alone are holy.
All nations will come and worship before You,
for your righteous acts have been revealed.

Revelation 15:3, 4

Before Abraham and Isaac left the mountains of Moriah and began their three-day journey home, the angel of the LORD called to Abraham from heaven a second time and said, "I swear by Myself, declares the LORD, that because you have done this and have not withheld your son, your only son, I will surely bless you and make your descendants as numerous as the stars in the sky and the sand on the seashore. Your descendants will take possession of the cities of their enemies, and through your offspring all nations on earth will be blessed—because you have obeyed Me."

That day, the LORD had a very great reward for Abraham's obedience. There was nothing greater God could give Abraham, than the treasure He had already given to him several times: The promise of God! The blessing of God! Once again the LORD promised, "I will surely bless you." Once again God promised numerous descendants to Abraham, "descendants as numerous as the stars in the sky and as the sand on the seashore." Again God promised Abraham that his descendants would take possession of the land; He said, "Your descendants will take possession of the cities of their enemies." God would surely make from Abraham a numerous people and a victorious people—a nation for Himself. Again the LORD gave Abraham the greatest promise of all—the promise of Messiah! The Saviour, Who was promised to the whole world and to every nation under heaven, would come through Abraham. "Through your offspring, through your seed, all nations on earth will be blessed."

It was not the first time God had made these promises to Abraham, but it was the first time that God had sworn by an oath. Now when men make an oath, they swear by someone greater than themselves to confirm what is said. They put their hand on a Bible and swear to God that they are telling the truth. They may swear by the king of their country; they may swear by heaven and earth; they may swear by everything sacred or they may swear by God Himself—that they are not lying. But "when God made His promise to Abraham, since there was no one greater for Him to swear by, He swore by Himself" (Hebrews 6:13). "I swear by Myself, declares the LORD, that . . . I will surely bless you."

Many years earlier, before Abraham had left his homeland, God made this promise for the first time to Abraham (Genesis 12:1–3). Later, God confirmed this promise with a covenant (Genesis 15). Then the promises were repeated and the covenant was confirmed with the seal and the sign of circumcision (Genesis 17). Now, on Mount Moriah, the promise was repeated on more time. God swore by Himself, confirming His promise with an oath. Why? Why did God repeat the same promise again and confirm it with an oath? The LORD wanted to impress upon Abraham and Isaac and all the heirs of what was promised, that they could surely trust the Word of God. It is impossible for God to lie, because of who He is. His Word is true. His oath is true. The LORD does not change His plans. The LORD does not change His promises. They are certain. They are forever sure. They are as unalterable and unchangeable as God Himself, who is the same yesterday, today and forever. God confirmed what was promised with an oath "because God wanted to make the unchanging nature of His purpose very clear" (Hebrews 6:17). The purpose of God, which was to save a people for Himself, was established before the foundation of the world. What God purposed and what God promised would never and could never be changed. The LORD swore His purposes and His promises on an oath, for the sake of His people, so that they could be greatly encouraged. God wanted their hope strengthened by His oath. This hope was an anchor for their souls, an anchor firm and secure, lest they drift away from God. All who put their hope in the promises of God could rest in Him, assured that they would never be disappointed—

for God had sworn on an oath and God had sworn by Himself. He would surely do it. God would surely save a people for Himself. There would surely be a great multitude, as numerous as the stars in the sky and as the sand on the seashore, descendants of Abraham from every nation, standing before the throne of God and in front of the Lamb, crying out forever: "Salvation belongs to our God, Who sits on the throne, and to the Lamb" (Revelation 7:9, 10)!

Abraham had a very important part in this plan of God. His obedience was not insignificant. The LORD said to Abraham, " . . . because you have done this and have not withheld your son, your only son, I will surely bless you . . . *because you have obeyed me.*" Consider the results of Abraham's obedience:

1. He was blessed by God.

2. He was commended for his faith. Four thousand years later we still read these words about Abraham: "Faith is what the ancients were commended for . . . By faith Abraham, when God tested him, offered Isaac as a sacrifice" (Hebrews 11:2, 17).

3. He was considered righteous. "He was called God's friend" (James 2:23). The Bible says: "Was not our ancestor Abraham considered righteous for what he did when he offered his son Isaac on the altar? You see that his faith and his actions were working together, and his faith was made complete by what he did" (James 2:21, 22).

4. Because Abraham obeyed God, God confirmed His promises with an oath—to the great encouragement of all believers.

5. Abraham was a prophet and by his obedience on Mount Moriah he displayed the clearest prophetic picture of the Saviour that is found in the entire Scriptures. By offering his only son as a sacrifice, Abraham was pointing to the only Son of God, who offered Himself as a sacrifice for many. To this very day people are brought to a saving knowledge of Christ by the faith and work of Abraham on that day so long ago. I am one of those people.

6. Abraham's obedience was to the praise, honour and glory of God!

The teacher's guide for this lesson starts on page 504.

A LOVED ONE LOST, A LOVED ONE GAINED

- Genesis 23, 24
- Hebrews 11:13–16
- Revelation 21:3–4

Many years passed since that dreadful and joyful day on Mount Moriah. Isaac was no longer a boy. He was a man now, thirty-seven years old. His mother Sarah, who had been an old woman from the day he was born, was now a very, very old woman of one hundred and twenty-seven years. God had been gracious to Isaac; God had allowed him to have his mother all those years, but at last the LORD took Sarah home to heaven. She died in the land of Canaan, where she had lived as a stranger in a tent for almost half her life. She was living by faith when she died, still trusting in the promises of God, still looking and longing for a permanent home—a heavenly one. Abraham and Isaac went to Sarah's tent, and wept over her dead body. They mourned because they had lost a loved one. They grieved because Sarah was gone, but Sarah herself had gone to her long-awaited home, to heaven, where there is no more weeping or mourning, because there is no more pain or death. Sarah had gone to be with the LORD, where He Himself wipes away every tear from the eyes of His people. In heaven there was singing, but here on earth there was weeping and mourning, as many tears were shed by the husband and son, who had lost their loved one—Sarah.

However, Abraham could not sit forever beside his dead wife. He must get up and bury her body . . . but where? Although God had promised him and his descendants the whole land of Canaan, Abraham owned no land at all here, not even a burial plot for his wife. Abraham went to the people, the Hittites, who owned all the land in the area of Canaan where he was then living and said to them, "I am an alien and stranger among you. Sell me some property for a burial site here, so I can bury my dead." The Hittites dealt with Abraham courteously and generously. They said, "You are a prince of God among us. Bury your dead in the choicest of our tombs. None of us will refuse you his tomb for burying your dead." So Abraham chose the place he wanted and he paid the fair and full price for it—400 shekels of silver. At last Abraham owned a piece of land in Canaan! He had bought a field with a few trees in it and a cave at the end of it for a tomb. This field was deeded to Abraham as his own property. It was a legal transaction, done in the presence of all the Hittites. Then Abraham buried Sarah's body in the cave at the back of his newly-purchased field. No longer would Sarah wander from place to place in the land of Canaan. She had found a final resting place, which belonged to her, in the Promised Land.

Abraham was also very old. God had blessed him in every way, but he too must die. Perhaps it would be soon that God would call him to join Sarah in heaven. Then Isaac would be all alone in the world, grieving the death of his parents. Isaac's name, Laughter, would no longer suit him, for he would be a lonely and unhappy man. Now what could be done for Isaac? A wife must be found for him! From the beginning the LORD God said, "It is not good for the man to be alone" (Genesis 2:18) and it was not good for Isaac to be alone. He needed a wife. He needed someone to help him and comfort him and love him in this life. He needed to begin a new family for himself. Isaac's mother was already dead—and who knew how much longer his old father would be alive? Yes, Isaac needed a wife . . . but "an excellent wife, who can find? She is worth far more than jewels" (Proverbs 31:10). Such jewels were exceedingly rare in the land of Canaan! To find one would be impossible. Oh, there were many beautiful women here, but where could a good woman, a God-fearing woman, be found? It was not a wife with a pretty face, but one with a faithful heart, that Abraham wanted for his son. Abraham knew that "beauty is vain, but a woman who fears the LORD—she shall be praised" (Proverbs 31:30). The Canaanites were a wicked people, a God-hating, idol-worshipping people, doomed by God for destruction. Their evil was clear; their ruin was sure. Abraham did not want to get a wife for his son from the Canaanites, lest his son be ensnared by their sin. Isaac was the son of promise and for Isaac must be a woman of praise. But where could he find such a woman here in Canaan? Abraham began to look somewhere else . . . somewhere beyond the borders of the land of Canaan.

Long-ago years in a far-away land Abraham had left behind a brother, whose name was Nahor. This brother had many children—twelve sons and probably many daughters too. These nephews and nieces of Abraham had grown up, married, and brought forth many children of their own. Then these grandnephews and grandnieces of Abraham had also grown up and were of an age to marry. Back in the land that Abraham had left sixty years ago, Isaac had a great many cousins, whom he had never met. Surely among all those cousins there was a young woman, who loved the LORD, a young woman who could be Isaac's wife! This was Abraham's plan.

Abraham was too old to return to his homeland, so he sent his most trusted servant on this most blessed mission. Abraham said to the chief servant in his household, the man in charge of everything, "I want you to swear by the LORD, the God of heaven and the God of earth, that you will not get a wife for my son from the daughters of the Canaanites, among whom I am living, but will go to my country and my own relatives and get a wife for my son Isaac." It was a good idea, but the servant saw immediately that there was a problem, a serious problem, with this plan. What woman would be willing to leave her family and her country to live in a land she had never seen and to marry a man she had never met? The servant said to Abraham, "What if the woman is unwilling to come back with me to this land? Shall I then take your son back to the country you came from?" Abraham answered, "No!" He knew there were difficulties with his plan, but he was a man of faith. All his life he had lived according to the promises of God, and he would do so now. All his life he had lived believing that nothing was impossible for God, and he had never been disappointed. Should Isaac leave this land, the land promised to him by God? No! Isaac must stay in the Promised Land! So Abraham answered his servant with these words of faith: "Make sure that you do not take my son back there. The LORD, the God of heaven, who brought me out of my father's household and my native land and who spoke to me and promised me on oath, saying, 'To your offspring

LESSON 49: A Loved One Lost, A Loved One Gained ———273

I will give this land'—this same LORD and God, He will send His Angel before you, so that you can get a wife for my son from there . . ." Abraham believed that God would proceed his servant, and protect him and provide for him. In all his wanderings and on all his journeys, God had always guided Abraham and guarded him and given to him. Would God not do so now? Abraham believed that his servant's journey would be a success, not because it was an easy task, but because God was with them. The servant was hesitant to swear an oath, but Abraham said, "If the woman is unwilling to come back with you, then you will be released from this oath of mine. Only do not take my son back there." So the servant swore an oath to his master Abraham concerning this matter. He promised not to get a Canaanite wife for Isaac, nor to take him away from the Promised Land—but to go to Abraham's own country and his own relatives, to get a wife for his only son Isaac.

Then Abraham's chief servant set out with a caravan of ten camels. These camels were loaded with provisions for the journey and possessions for the family from Abraham's store of earthly wealth. He also took with him some other men servants to help on the journey. The many days of travelling turned into many weeks, but at last their camel caravan came to the land and then to the town where Abraham's relatives lived. It was almost evening. They had been travelling all day in the hot sun and it was the end of a long journey through desert regions. Everyone was tired. They had to find a place to spend the night. They had to feed the camels and draw water for them. There were many things they had to do before they could rest for the night, but Abraham's man was truly a good and faithful servant. His main concern was the mission on which his master had sent him. Although it was almost evening, he wanted to have success before the day was ended. Now that he had reached the right place, he wasted no time before beginning the work for which he had been sent. So the servant had the camels kneel down outside the town, near the well of water. He knew that soon the women of the town would come there, one by one, to draw water from the well for their families. Had he not been sent to this town to find a woman? He had to start his search someplace, and this seemed like a good place to begin, for soon all the young women would be passing right by him. But how in the world would he be able to find the right woman to be Isaac's wife? How could he know who she was? He could choose a beautiful woman, but how could he choose a faithful woman? A man could see a woman's face, but God alone could see her heart. The servant knew what he must do. He must pray! God must be the One to choose the right woman to be Isaac's wife. What he had to do was find the woman whom God had chosen. So the servant prayed, "O LORD, God of my master Abraham, give me success today, and show kindness to my master Abraham. See, I am standing beside this spring, and the daughters of the townspeople are coming out to draw water. May it be that when I say to a girl, 'Please let down your jar that I may have a drink,' and she says, 'Drink, and I'll water your camels too'—let her be the one that *you have chosen* for your servant Isaac. By this I will know that you have shown kindness to my master." Abraham's servant was planning to ask this test question to every girl in the whole town who came by the well—until finally God gave one of them the right answer, the one whom He had chosen for Isaac's wife. But before the servant had even finished praying, while he was still talking to God in his heart, a very beautiful maiden with an empty jar on her shoulder, went down to the spring, filled her jar, and came up again ready to go home. Could this be the girl? The servant didn't know. He hurried to meet her, to ask her the test question. "Please give me a little water from your jar," he said. "Drink, my lord," she answered. She quickly lowered the jar to her hands and gave him a drink, but she said nothing about the camels. Such a shame! She was such a pretty girl. The servant drank, and when he was finished, the girl added, "I'll water your camels too, until they have finished drinking." The servant was astonished! Had his prayer been answered so quickly? Had success come so easily? Was this girl with the beautiful face, also the one with a faithful heart? Without saying another word, the servant waited and watched her closely, still wondering whether or not the LORD had made his journey successful. She had answered correctly, but who was she? Was she from Abraham's family? As the servant watched, the girl worked hard, drawing water for all his camels. Not many girls would have made such an offer. She emptied her jar into the trough and then ran back to draw more water. It was hard work. Back and forth she went to the well again and again, until she had hauled enough water for the whole caravan of thirsty camels. All this time, the servant had said not a word. But when the camels had finished drinking, he took out a gold ring and two gold bracelets and gave them to her. Now it was the girl's turn to be astonished! She had expected no reward for her work or payment for her kindness. These were very expensive pieces of jewelry. Then the servant asked her who she was. It turned out that she was the grand-daughter of Abraham's own brother, Nahor. She was a second cousin to Isaac. Her name was Rebekah. Once again it was the servant's turn to be astonished! The very first girl he spoke to in this town was Abraham's own niece! The servant bowed down right then and there to worship the LORD. He said aloud, "Praise be to the LORD, the God of my master Abraham, Who has not abandoned His kindness and faithfulness to my master. As for me, the LORD has led me on this journey—right to the house of my master's relatives!" And now it was Rebekah's turn to be astonished one more time! Uncle Abraham? This was the servant of her great uncle, Abraham, who lived so far away in the land of Canaan! Could it really be true? She had never met Uncle Abraham, but she had heard her grandfather speak of his brother many times. In her excitement, Rebekah ran home to tell her family the joyful news. Now it was her family's turn to be astonished! When Rebekah's brother, Laban, saw the gold jewelry and heard the whole story, he hurried out to the man at the well and found him standing by his camels. "Come, you who are blessed by the LORD," he said. "Why are you standing out here? I have prepared the house and a place for the camels." So the caravan from Abraham went with Laban to spend the night at the house of Rebekah's and Laban's father, who was Abraham's nephew, Bethuel.

First the camels were unloaded. Then straw and fodder were brought for the camels to eat. The servant and his men were brought into the house, where the tired travellers were refreshed with cool water for their hot feet. Then dinner was set before them, but Abraham's servant would not eat until he had told them the reason for his journey. His work was not over yet, and he would not rest until his mission was accomplished, until he knew whether it had ended in success or failure. Rebekah's father and brother may not allow her to return with him. All along he had feared that this would be the real problem with Abraham's plan. Would Rebekah come back with him? Would she be allowed to go far away to a land her family had never seen, to marry a man they had never met? Would the father and brother say "yes" or "no" to the proposed marriage between Isaac and Rebekah? Before he ate a single bite, Abraham's servant wanted to know their answer. He said, "I will not eat until I have told you what I have to say." So he told them the whole story, from beginning to end. He told them the reason for his journey and the amazing way he had met Rebekah. He did not withhold any information from them. It was an important decision they had to make concerning their daughter and sister. The servant wanted them to have all the facts:

1) First, he formally introduced himself. He said, "I am Abraham's servant."

2) Next he told them how God had blessed Abraham with abundant wealth and how all this wealth would one day belong to Isaac. This was a very important piece of information, so the family would know that Rebekah would be well cared for. He said, "The LORD has blessed my master abundantly, and he has become wealthy. God has given him sheep and cattle, silver and gold, men servants and maidservants, camels and donkeys." He told how God had also given him a son. "My master's wife Sarah has borne him a son in his old age, and he has given this son everything he owns."

3) Then the servant told the family that Abraham wanted this son to marry a woman from his own family. "My master made me swear an oath, and said . . . 'Go to my father's family, to my own clan, and get a wife for my son.'" He told of his concern, that the woman would not come back with him, and he told of Abraham's answer and Abraham's faith: "The LORD, before whom I have walked, will send His Angel with you and make your journey a success, so that you can get a wife for my son . . . from my father's family . . . You will be released from my oath, if they refuse to give her to you."

4) The servant told the family about his prayer to God by the well of water that very day; he had prayed, "O LORD, God of my master Abraham, if You will, please grant success to the journey on which I have come." He told about the test he devised to know the one the LORD had chosen and how Rebekah had appeared, before he had even finished praying in his heart. He told the family what had happened at the well, how Rebekah had answered exactly as he had prayed.

5) He told them his second prayer, when he discovered who she was. He said, "I bowed down and worshipped the LORD. I praised the LORD, the God of my master Abraham, who had led me on the right road to get the granddaughter of my master's brother for his son."

6) Then Abraham's servant asked the family to make a decision. They had all the information. Would they allow Rebekah to go back with him to become Isaac's wife? Would they say "yes" or "no" to the proposal? The servant said, "If you will show kindness to my master, tell me; and if not, tell me, so that I may know which way to turn."

Then Laban (Rebekah's brother) and Bethuel (Rebekah's father) answered that it was not for them to decide, since God had surely ordained it. They said, *"This is from the LORD!* We can say nothing to you one way or the other. Here is Rebekah. Take her and go, and let her become the wife of your master's son, as the LORD has directed."

When the servant heard this answer, he again bowed down to the ground before the LORD. God had answered his prayer. That very same day God had given him success, complete success! He was awed by God's goodness, and before he did anything else, he gave thanks to God. Then the servant expressed his thanks to Rebekah, by giving her gifts of expensive jewelry and clothing. He also thanked her family by giving them costly presents too. Then, and only then, when all his work was completed for his master, did Abraham's servant sit down to dinner. That night he ate with joy and he slept with peace, for he had found the wife of God's choice for Isaac.

When the servant awoke the next morning, he was eager to be on his way home. Although he must have been tired from all his travels, he wanted to start home immediately. He was anxious for Abraham's old eyes to see the faithful wife he had found. He was anxious for Isaac's sad eyes to see the beautiful wife he had found. He wanted his masters to see the gift God had provided—faithful, beautiful Rebekah! But Rebekah's family did not want to lose her so soon. They loved her too. "Oh, let the girl stay with us just ten days or so; then she may go." But the servant replied, "No, do not detain me, now that the LORD has granted success to my journey. Send me on my way, so I may go to my master." The servant wanted Rebekah to go; her family wanted her to stay—so they decided to let Rebekah choose. The family called Rebekah and asked, "Will you go with this man?" She replied in faith: "I will go."

So Rebekah set off for the Promised Land, as soon as she and her maids were ready to go. She went with her family's blessing: "Our sister, may you increase to thousands upon thousands; may your offspring possess the gates of their enemies." She also went with God's blessing, although she may not have known it yet. One day her husband, Isaac, would tell her of God's promise to Abraham, which now belonged to her. Isaac himself had been with his father on Mount Moriah when the angel of the LORD called from heaven and said, "I swear by Myself, declares the LORD, that . . . I will surely bless you and make your descendants as numerous as the stars in the sky and the sand on the seashore. Your descendants will take possession of the cities of their enemies, and through your offspring all nations on earth will be blessed . . ." Rebekah would be blessed, not because of her family's farewell words, but because of God's infallible Word! Rebekah would never see her family again. She would never see her country again. She was making the same journey, that Abraham had made by faith so long ago. She too was setting forth by faith—to a land she had never seen, to a man she had never met—but she trusted in God, the God of Abraham and the God of Isaac. The LORD would surely bless her! She was marrying a very rich man, for Isaac, as the servant had told her family, would inherit all the earthly wealth that God had given to Abraham. But those material riches were insignificant compared to the spiritual treasures that would be her portion, which were the promises of God! Isaac would inherit the promises of God—and Rebekah would become a partaker in those promises! The LORD would use her to bring about the fulfillment of His Word. The LORD would use her to bring forth the fulfillment of His great promise to the whole world. As Rebekah rode along on her camel toward the land of Canaan, she could not know what was at the end of her journey—that one day she would become the mother of the nation of Israel, that one day she would become the mother of the Messiah, the Saviour from sin and death, the Promised Child in whom the whole world would be blessed. How could she know, as she rode along on her camel, that she was going forward to become the great-great-great-great-great . . . grandmother of Jesus?

Back at home, in the land of Canaan, Isaac waited. Many weeks had passed since the chief servant had left on his journey. Isaac had no way of knowing whether the mission had been successful or not. Had God provided a wife for him? He did not know. One evening Isaac went out to a field, just to be with God, to think and to pray. After meditating awhile, he looked up—and there in the distance he saw a camel caravan approaching. Perhaps it was the chief servant, returning with his wife. Quickly he got up and began walking toward the caravan. Rebekah also looked up—and in the evening light she saw a man walking towards them through the fields. She climbed down from her camel and asked the chief servant, "Who is that man in the field coming to meet us?" The servant answered, "He is my master." When Rebekah heard that it was Isaac, the man she was to marry, she felt a shyness. She took a veil and covered herself. When they met, Rebekah could see Isaac, but, except for her eyes, Isaac could not see her. Isaac could not see her beauty, but he was told of her faith. The chief servant told Isaac the whole story, of how God had chosen this woman to be his wife. So Isaac married Rebekah. He brought her into the tent of his mother Sarah—and she became his wife. How Isaac loved her! Rebekah brought Isaac comfort after his mother's death. He was no longer sorrowful, but joyful. Once again his name was right for him—Laughter! Rebekah brought happiness into Isaac's life . . . and he loved her.

That is the beautiful love story of how Isaac and Rebekah met and married. It is a love story, not only of their love for one another, but of God's LOVE for His people. The LORD brought them together for their mutual joy and comfort and happiness. God also brought them together for a great purpose, for the fulfillment of His own plan and promise. Their life together was not only beautiful; it was meaningful. They were part of the greatest love story in all the world—the LOVE of God, in Christ Jesus our Saviour and Lord.

The teacher's guide for this lesson starts on page 506.

GOD BLESSES ISAAC

- Genesis 25:1–26; 26
- Romans 9:7, 8
- Hebrews 11:39, 40

Isaac had married Rebekah when he was forty years old. Father Abraham was 140 years old. Abraham thought that God would soon take him home to heaven, but God had other plans. God wanted Abraham to live another thirty-five years in the Promised Land. Now Abraham was not only a very old man; he was also a very lonely man. His wife Sarah was buried; his son Isaac was married. Isaac had left his mother's grave and his father's home, to cleave unto his own wife. Abraham was all alone—and it was not good for the man to be alone. So Abraham remarried. His new wife's name was Keturah and she bore to Abraham six more sons. Abraham was no longer lonely with his new wife and six children around him. However, we know nothing about these sons. Only their names are mentioned in the Bible. Long ago God declared, "It is through Isaac that your children will be counted" (Genesis 21:12). Although Abraham had Ishmael and six other sons, it was only the story of Isaac and his children that God preserved for us in His Word. We read in the Bible that God blessed Abraham's son . . . Isaac!

It was through Isaac and Isaac's children that the promises of God to Abraham would be fulfilled. Once again, Abraham's faith in God's Word was tested. Year after year passed—and no children were born to Isaac. The beautiful and faithful wife, that had been so carefully chosen for him, was barren. Yes, Rebekah was barren! Twenty years had passed. Abraham was now 160 years old and still his son Isaac had no children. Rebekah had not given birth to even one baby. Something was wrong and she was unable to have children. Would the promises of God fail now? No, both Abraham and Isaac hoped in the LORD and trusted in God's Word. Isaac loved his wife earnestly and he prayed for her constantly. Isaac prayed to the LORD on her behalf and at the right time, the LORD answered Isaac's prayer. To her great joy and relief and amazement, Rebekah became pregnant.

How thankful and joyful Rebekah was to feel the movement of life within her. Like most expectant mothers, she would sit happily with her hands on her growing belly, feeling the little kicks inside her. But soon her delight changed to alarm. The punching and pounding grew stronger and wilder, as if something awful was happening inside her. Why is this happening to me? she wondered; what is wrong? In those days there was no ultrasound to check what was happening in a mother's womb. No one could see inside her; no one could answer her questions—except God. So Rebekah went to inquire of the LORD. She prayed, presenting her concerns to God, who sees and knows everything. God answered her question. The LORD said to her: "Two nations are in your womb, and two peoples from within you will be separated; one people will be stronger than the other, and the older will serve the younger." Now Rebekah understood what was happening. There were two babies inside her, not one! She was carrying twins— and they were already fighting with each other!

When the time came for Rebekah to give birth, there were twin boys in her womb—just as God had said. It was not a surprise to Rebekah or Isaac that twins were born. The two tiny boys continued to fight each other, even during the birth. The first baby boy to be born was a funny-looking little thing. He was red and his whole body was covered with hair—so they named him Esau, which means "Hairy." (He was also called Edom, which means "Red.") The second baby boy was born holding on to the heel of his older brother. His little hand was actually grasping his brother's foot and he didn't let go, not even during the birth. He wanted to be the first one born—and he was not far behind! His parents named him Jacob, which means "Grasper," because he was grasping the heel of his brother. (The name Jacob meant literally "he grasps the heel." In Hebrew, this was also a way of saying, "he deceives." Thus Jacob's name also meant "Deceiver.")

Isaac was sixty years old when his two boys were born. Grandpa Abraham was 160 years old. God had blessed Isaac. God had given him the blessing of children and God had given Abraham the blessing of seeing his children's children. Abraham knew God's promise—that through Isaac his children would be counted. God, in His LOVE and grace, had allowed him to see the first two of these grandchildren, Esau and Jacob.

The LORD also allowed Abraham to see these grandsons grow into young men, but at last it was time for Abraham to depart. While he was still alive, Abraham gave gifts to all his sons and sent them away to the land of the east, away from his son Isaac. Abraham gave these sons gifts, but to Isaac he left everything he owned. Abraham's entire inheritance was left to Isaac, because Isaac was the son of God's promise. The LORD said, "I will establish my covenant with him" (Genesis 17:19) and Abraham had faith in that covenant. Abraham died at a good old age. He was 175 years old when he breathed his last. He was an old man, full of years and full of faith. He was gathered to his people, to the people of God who had gone before him. His two sons, Ishmael and Isaac, buried his body in the cave, beside the bones of his wife Sarah. His old body was laid to rest at last in the only plot of ground he ever owned in the Promised Land. He had lived there as a foreigner and a wanderer for 100 years, a perfect number of years. He owned no land there, but he owned God's promise! He died believing that one day, many generations later and hundreds of years later, his descendants and the descendants his son Isaac would possess the entire land, because God had promised it to them. Although Abraham himself never received the things promised, he died hoping and trusting in God's Word. Abraham had lived—by faith—in the Promised Land for 100 years and there he also died, commended by God for his faith.

We read in the Bible that "after Abraham's death, God blessed his son Isaac" (Genesis 25:11). God made promises to Isaac. God proceeded him and provided for him and protected him—just as He had done for his father Abraham. Once, when there was a famine, Isaac moved to the land of the Philistines, but the famine was there also. Isaac decided to leave the Promised Land for a time and move to Egypt, where he could provide food for his family. However, the LORD appeared to Isaac and said, "Do not go down to Egypt. Live in the land where I tell you to live. Stay in this land for awhile, and I will be with you and I will bless you . . ." So Isaac stayed right where he was! He obeyed the LORD. Although there was a famine, he stayed in the Promised Land by faith, trusting in the Word of the LORD, that God would be with him there and that God would bless him there. At that same time the LORD said to Isaac:

> *I will be with you and I will bless you.*
> *For to you and your descendants*
>   *I will give all these lands*
>   *and I will confirm the oath that I swore*
>   *to your father Abraham.*
> *I will make your descendants as*
>   *numerous as the stars in the sky,*
> *and I will give them all these lands,*
> *and through your offspring all nations*
>   *on earth will be blessed,*
> *because Abraham obeyed Me*
> *and kept My requirements, My commands,*
> *My decrees and My laws.*

> *Genesis 26:2–5*

Do these promises sound familiar? Yes, these were the same promises that God had made many times to his father. Now the LORD promised to make Isaac into a great nation. From him would come many people to whom God would give all this land. And the Messiah, the one in whom all nations on earth would be blessed, would come from him too. Isaac had believed the promises spoken to his father, but this was the first time that God had spoken these promises to him. It must have been amazing to Isaac that the LORD was now appearing to him and speaking to him, just as He had done with his father.

So Isaac stayed in the land of the Philistines, trusting in God's promises, hoping in God's Saviour. Although there were difficulties, God was with Isaac and God blessed Isaac. He planted crops in the land and that same year, the year of the famine, when the crops failed all around him, Isaac reaped a hundred-fold harvest, because the LORD blessed him. In that poor year Isaac became rich, and his wealth continued to grow until he became very rich. He had so many flocks and herds and servants that the Philistines envied him. Then there was trouble. The Philistines were so jealous of Isaac's success, that they stopped up the wells that his father's servants had dug. They filled Isaac's wells with earth, so there was no water for his flocks and herds. Then the king of the Philistines said, "Move away from us! You have become too powerful." Isaac did not own any land. Like his father before him, he was a foreigner here and a wanderer. Although God had prospered him here, the only land he had inherited from his father was a burial plot. Isaac had to obey the king—or else fight a war. So Isaac left. He moved away and settled somewhere else. His servants dug in the valley and found fresh water there, but again there were disputes with the people who owned the land. His servants dug another well, but again there was opposition. The Philistines claimed that well too. Isaac had to move even farther away. Finally Isaac found a place and dug a well . . . and this time, no one quarrelled with him. At last he had room to live! Isaac named that place Rehoboth, which means "Room." He said, "Now the LORD has given us room and we will flourish in the land."

Sometime later Isaac moved to Beersheba in the land of the Philistines. Isaac had lived there many years ago, when he was a boy. His father had planted a tree there and had worshipped the LORD there. At Beersheba, Abraham "called upon the name of the LORD, the Eternal God" (Genesis 21:33). Now Isaac returned to Beersheba. Perhaps he set up his tent by the tree that his father had planted. It would be a large tree now and offer him shade in the heat of the day. But it was at night, that first night in Beersheba, that something wonderful happened to Isaac. That night the LORD appeared to Isaac and spoke to him. The LORD said: "I am the God of your father Abraham. Do not be afraid, for I am with you. I will bless you and increase the number of your descendants for the sake of my servant Abraham." The next day, Isaac built an altar and worshipped God. He too called on the name of the LORD in that place, just as his father had done before him. Isaac decided he would stay here at Beersheba. He pitched his tents and dug a well. This seemed like a good place to live for a long time, because God had come to him here.

Someone else came to Isaac at Beersheba. It was the king of the Philistines, the same king who had sent him away. When Isaac saw him approach with his advisor and his army commander, Isaac must have thought: Oh no! More trouble! Isaac asked these Philistines what they wanted. "Why have you come to me, since you were hostile to me and sent me away?" Their answer must have astonished Isaac. They said, "We saw clearly that the LORD was with you . . . You are blessed by the LORD." Even these Philistines could see it! They wanted to make a peace treaty with Isaac. They wanted to be his friend. Isaac was very pleased with their offer. He did not want trouble. He did not want to be continually moving, chased from one place to another. He wanted to live at peace in the land. So Isaac made a feast for the king and his men. Then early the next morning they swore an oath to each other to live peacefully together. That same day Isaac's servants dug a well and discovered water. This time there would be no fight. This time there would be no move. Isaac would live at Beersheba for a long time in peace and prosperity — because God kept his promise: "I will be with you and I will bless you."

The teacher's guide for this lesson starts on page 508.

GOD CHOOSES JACOB; JACOB CHOOSES GOD

- **Genesis 25:19–34**
- **Malachi 1:1–5**
- **Matthew 13:44, 45**
- **Romans 9:10–16, 18, 23**
- **Ephesians 2:1–10**
- **Hebrews 12:14–17**

Isaac's two sons, Esau and Jacob, were twins; but they were not identical twins. From the day they were born it was obvious that they did not look alike. Even as a baby Esau's whole body was like a hairy garment, but Jacob's skin was smooth as silk. With these twin babies there was no difficulty in telling them apart, for Esau was a striking red colour, but Jacob was dark. As the twins grew up, they had very different interests too. Esau was rough and tough, an outdoor man, a hunter. Jacob was a quiet person, who liked to stay at home among the tents. It became quite clear that everything about these twin brothers was different—their looks, their lives and something which only God could see . . . their hearts. In Esau's heart no faith in God was found, but in Jacob's heart there was faith.

Now each of the parents had a favourite twin. The father favoured the older son, but the mother favoured the younger son. The Bible expresses it in much stronger terms, declaring: "Isaac loved Esau, but Rebekah loved Jacob." Why? Why were the twins not loved by each parent equally? People are strange. They have many reasons why they like or dislike other people—and often their reasons are wrong. Why did Isaac love Esau? Perhaps Isaac loved Esau from the day he was born, simply because he was the first-born son. Maybe it was because Isaac liked Esau's colour. Perhaps Isaac loved this son because he was an athletic boy. Perhaps he preferred Esau's personality. The Bible indicates that, when Esau was a man, his father loved him because he was such a good hunter and because Isaac had a taste for the wild game meat that Esau brought home from his hunting trips. What about Jacob? Why did Rebekah love Jacob? Perhaps Rebekah loved her younger son because she remembered God's Word to her before the boys were born: "The older will serve the younger." Maybe this new mother placed her hope in Jacob from the day he was born, because she believed God's Word. Perhaps Rebekah preferred Jacob because of his colour or his character. Perhaps Rebekah loved this son because he was a quiet boy, who liked to stay with her among the tents. Both parents had their reasons why they loved one son better than the other.

It was not just the parents who made a distinction between the two boys. God Himself made a separation between them—and that was the most important difference between the twin brothers. Even before they were born, God had chosen one, but not the other. The LORD said, "Jacob I loved, but Esau I hated" (Romans 9:13). Why? Why do you think God loved one twin, but hated the other? Was it because one was good and the other was bad? Was it because one had faith and the other did not? No, for the Bible says that before the boys were born, before they had done anything good or bad, God had already chosen Jacob. Before they were born means before they believed. Jacob was not chosen because he was good or because he had faith. God does not choose anyone because of his goodness, because "there is no one righteous, not even one; there is no one who understands, no one who seeks God" (Romans 3:10, 11). If God's choice depended on our goodness, no one would be loved and no one would be saved by Him. Thankfully, God's plan of salvation does not depend upon any person; it depends upon God's grace alone, which no one deserves. God's eternal salvation stands not by our works, but by God's grace. "It is by grace you have been saved, through faith—and even this is not from yourselves; it is the gift of God" (Ephesians 2:8). The LORD's purpose in election depends solely upon God, who loves us and calls us and saves us. God says, "I will have mercy on whom I have mercy, and I will have compassion on whom I have compassion" (Romans 9:15). The LORD, He is God, the Great King of all the earth. "He does whatever pleases Him" (Psalm 115:3). It pleased God to choose Jacob, before he was even born, before the world was even made. God loved Jacob from the beginning. God prepared Jacob in advance to be a vessel of His mercy and His glory. Why? We do not know why. Who can understand the mind of God? However, we do know this: Although people love or hate for unjust reasons, with God there is no injustice. "The LORD is good and just . . . All the ways of the LORD are loving and faithful" (Psalm 25:8, 10). We must entrust ourselves to Him, trusting in His mercy, for He is our only hope, our only Saviour. In His sovereign choice, we must re-joice: "Praise the LORD . . . Praise the LORD, for the LORD is good . . . for the LORD has chosen Jacob to be His own . . . The LORD is great . . . The LORD does whatever pleases Him . . . *Praise the LORD*" (Psalm 135:1, 3–6, 21)!

God made a distinction between Jacob and Esau before they ever en-tered this world. So, although the two boys were born with the same cor-rupt human nature and although they grew up together in the same family and were taught by their parents the same things, there was a very real dif-ference between the two men. The grace of God became evident in Jacob's life, but Esau remained a godless man. Esau's concerns were carnal, not spir-itual. He was a hunter and that was his only interest in life—getting what he could see, right here and right now. The things of God did not interest him. He did not live for the things which were unseen; he did not live by faith, hoping and trusting in the Word of God, looking and longing for the promises of God. These things meant nothing to Esau. The LORD Himself meant very little to him. Esau seldom even thought about God. Instead, he thought about himself and how best to take care of himself. He did not need God, for he was an excellent hunter. He could provide for himself and pro-tect himself without any help from the LORD. No, Esau did not live by faith in God. He placed his trust in himself, living by his own strength and skill and speed—by which he proved himself to be a mighty man indeed. Esau was like one of the enemies of God about whom it was written: "Their des-tiny is destruction, their god is their stomach, and their glory is their shame. Their mind is on earthly things" (Philippians 3:19).

By nature, Jacob was a child of wrath, even as the rest. By birth, his spir-itual condition was no different than that of his twin brother. But God, be-cause of His great LOVE, had mercy on Jacob. What made the difference between Jacob and Esau was God's grace! What made the difference between Jacob and Esau was God's choice! As time passed, it became apparent that there was something in Jacob's heart, which was missing in Esau's heart—*faith*—a living, growing, yearning, wrestling, saving faith in God! Jacob grew to be a man, who believed the Word of God and valued the promises of God. Although he was a quiet man, who stayed among the tents, perhaps it was there that he listened to the stories about the faith of his forefathers. Perhaps it was there that he learned of the promises of God to his family. The LORD had promised to make his grandfather and his father into a great nation of countless people and to give them all the land where they were now living. God had promised to bless them, and to bless the whole world through them. God had actually spoken to his father and his grandfather many times. Although Jacob had never heard the voice of the LORD, he believed those promises and he longed to have a portion in them . . . but how? Jacob must have wondered about those promises. They had passed from his grandfather Abraham to his father Isaac, although Abraham had many other sons. Why was his father Isaac the only one to receive those promises? Was it because Isaac was the only son of his grandmother Sarah? What would happen now? To whom would God's promises pass? He and his brother Esau both had the same father and the same mother. They were twins. Who would inherit what God had promised? Naturally, the birthright and the blessing belonged to the oldest son Esau and naturally, his father, who loved Esau, would give it to him. The promises would pass to Esau, because he had been born first. Jacob had missed the birthright by just a matter of moments. How this grieved Jacob! How he longed to receive the inheritance of the firstborn son in the family of faith. He wanted to have the double portion of what God had promised, because he believed those promises were real and true and of great value. Most of all, Jacob wanted to have a share in God. Would it be the God of Abraham, the God of Isaac, and the God of Esau? No! More than anything, Jacob desired that the God of his fathers would be his God too—the God of Abraham, the God of Isaac, and the God of Jacob! The birthright and the blessing of this family meant everything to Jacob, because in them he saw, by faith, the wealth of an entire future kingdom. Jacob caught a glimpse of that pearl of priceless value, the kingdom of heaven—*and he wanted it!* Jacob treasured what God promised . . . but Esau, to whom it all belonged by birth, was not excited, or even interested in the things of God. Those promises, which meant so much to Jacob, meant nothing to

Esau. He was interested in other things, worldly things. Esau's eyes were focused on present concerns and earthly matters, while Jacob was often gaz-
ing into the distance at the kingdom promised by God. How could he, the
younger son, secure a prominent place for himself in that kingdom? How
could he, Jacob the Grasper, get the birthright from his older brother Esau?

One day the opportunity came. It was just an ordinary day: Esau was
out hunting; Jacob was home cooking. Jacob had baked some bread and
boiled a beautiful-looking, delicious-smelling, red stew. He was just going
to sit down and eat this meal, when Esau arrived home from his hunting
trip . . . hungry! "Quick!" he said. "Let me have some of that red stew! I'm
famished!" Now was Jacob's chance. Esau wanted something from Jacob—
and Jacob wanted something from Esau. Of course, it wasn't a fair trade,
but this might be the right time, the only time, to strike a deal with his
brother. It was worth a try. "First sell me your birthright," replied Jacob.
Esau should have said, "Are you joking? What kind of fool do you think I
am? Would I sell my birthright for a stinking bowl of stew? There's no way,
little brother Grasper, that you will ever take my birthright away from me!"
But Esau did not say that. Esau did not really care about his birthright. In
fact, he despised it. He wasn't concerned about some distant inheritance
that was wrapped up in some vague promise by some invisible God. Not at
all! He was concerned about his growling stomach. His belly was his god.
He wanted something to satisfy his hunger, right then and there. What good
was some far-away promise, if he was starving now? Esau answered, "Look,
I am about to die. What good is the birthright to me?" Was his answer really "yes"? Could it be possible that Esau was willing to sell his birthright
for a pot of stew? Jacob could hardly believe his ears. Esau had agreed to his
bargain . . . but Jacob wondered if he would keep that bargain. In his present weakened condition, Esau assessed his birthright as worthless, but what
would he think after he had eaten and regained his strength? Jacob had to
make sure that the deal was firm, that the bargain was secure. Before Jacob
gave his brother any food, he said, "Swear to me, first." So Esau swore an
oath to him, selling his birthright to Jacob. Esau was bound by his oath. It
could not be changed. Then, and only then, Jacob served Esau his very
costly meal: some bread and some lentil stew. Esau ate and drank; then he
got up and left.

That quickly, that easily, that *foolishly*, Esau sold his birthright. For a
single meal, he sold his inheritance rights of the oldest son. Esau was the

firstborn, but he despised his birthright. Oh foolish son! Oh godless man! He traded the promises of God for a pot of stew. For the passing pleasure of a single meal, he gave away his place in God's eternal kingdom. He valued not the privilege he had as the firstborn son in the family of faith. It meant nothing to him—and so it was taken from him. Now Jacob the Grasper held the birthright and he would never let it go! Esau had lost his inheritance . . . forever.

The teacher's guide for this lesson starts on page 510.

FIRST THE BIRTHRIGHT, THEN THE BLESSING

- Genesis 26:34–27:40
- Jeremiah 49:7–22
- Ezekiel 25:12–14
- Joel 3:17–21
- Amos 1:11, 12
- Obadiah
- Malachi 1:1–5
- Hebrews 11:20; 12:14–17
- Revelation 1:4–6

Jacob had bought his brother's birthright, but it made little difference in the day-to-day life of the brothers. Many years passed . . . and it seemed as if Jacob had gained nothing. Isaac remained the head of the family of faith and he continued to love his firstborn son, Esau. He loved him, in spite of all the things he had done which displeased his father. Did Isaac know what the brothers had done with the birthright? How distressed he must have been when he found out that Esau sold his birthright to Jacob for a single meal! How could he have done such a thing? Did Esau care so little about their family and his position in it? Did he care so little about God? Then Esau did something else, which troubled and angered both his parents. He knew how careful his grandfather Abraham had been to choose a godly wife for Isaac. Grandpa Abraham had said, "Swear by the LORD, the God of heaven and the God of earth, that you will not get a wife for my son from the daughters of the Canaanites, among whom I am living . . ." (Genesis 24:3)—but Esau married two Canaanite women! Double trouble! Esau was the same age as his father when he married, but he had not the same wisdom. At forty years old Esau took for himself two wives from the God-hating Hittites, a people doomed to destruction by the Word of the LORD. (See Genesis 15:20, 21.) Once again Esau showed how little he cared for his father, his family or his faith. By choosing such wives he again showed how little he cared for God or God's Word. Esau did not believe what God had promised in the future, nor was he concerned that his children be raised in the knowledge and the nurture of the LORD. Loving and trusting God, worshipping Him and obeying Him, were not given priority; it was not even a part of Esau's life. No, he cared about one thing only—serving himself. His mind was on earthly things. His eyes were fixed on meeting his own needs here and now. Just as he would not wait for a meal, so he would not wait for a wife. Esau married two unbelieving women from a godless race of men, because these women pleased him—but they were a source of grief to his godly parents, Isaac and Rebekah.

Nonetheless, Isaac still loved Esau. He loved to watch his firstborn son set out on a hunting trip. He looked so strong as he strode along with his bow and arrow, so handsome as the sun shone on his red hair. In spite of all his faults, just the sight of Esau made Isaac smile with pride and pleasure. But the sad day came when Isaac could no longer see Esau or anyone else. His eyes had grown dim with old age and he was blind. He feared that he would soon be dead. Isaac wanted to take care of something very important, before he was on his deathbed. He decided to give Esau his blessing now. Why wait? Jacob had grasped the birthright, but Isaac would make sure that his beloved firstborn, Esau, would receive the blessing. So Isaac called for his oldest son. When they were alone together in Isaac's tent, he said to Esau, "I am now an old man and don't know the day of my death . . . Go out to the open country to hunt some wild game for me. Prepare for me the kind of tasty food I like and bring it to me to eat, so that I may give you my blessing before I die."

Isaac thought that this discussion between himself and his firstborn son was private, but someone was listening. Isaac thought that his intention to give Esau the blessing now was a secret, but someone else knew. Rebekah! And she did not want her firstborn son to receive his father's blessing. Why?

1. God had not decreed it. Before the twins were born, He had chosen the younger one (Genesis 25:23).

2. Esau did not deserve it. He despised his birthright and grieved his parents (Genesis 25:34 and 26:34, 35).

3. Rebekah did not approve it. She loved Jacob (Genesis 25:28).

But what could she do? Isaac was determined to give God's blessing to Esau, the son he loved. Rebekah was desperate. She must stop this from happening, but how? Then she thought of a plan to help her younger son Jacob grasp the blessing for himself. Since Isaac was blind, perhaps he could be tricked into giving the blessing to Jacob. Since Isaac couldn't see, perhaps he could be deceived into thinking Jacob was Esau.

It wouldn't be easy and they didn't have much time. Esau wanted the blessing and he had left immediately for the open country to hunt for the game meat his father had requested. As soon as he was gone, Rebekah spoke to Jacob. "I overheard your father say to your brother Esau, 'Bring me some game and prepare me some tasty food to eat, so that I may give you my blessing in the presence of the LORD before I die.' Now my son, listen carefully," said Rebekah, "and do what I tell you: Go out to the flock and bring me two choice young goats, so I can prepare some tasty food for your father, just the way he likes it. Then you take it to your father to eat, so that he may give you his blessing before he dies."

There were problems with Rebekah's plan. Although blind people cannot see, they use their other senses very well:

1) There was nothing wrong with Isaac's ears. Even if the brothers sounded similar, wouldn't he be able to detect the difference in their voices? Blind people develop a very keen sense of hearing.

2) There was nothing wrong with Isaac's tongue. Wouldn't he be able to detect the difference in taste between goat meat and game meat? Wild animals have a very distinct flavour and blind people must rely more heavily on their sense of taste to distinguish different foods, since they cannot see them.

3) There was nothing wrong with Isaac's nose. Every person has their own distinct scent. Would Isaac be able to distinguish between his sons by their scent? We usually don't use our sense of smell to identify people, but animals do. Have you ever had a dog come over to you and sniff you? That's how the dog knows who you are. Blind people also develop a very keen sense of smelling.

4) Finally, there was nothing wrong with Isaac's hands. Blind people use their hands the way we use our eyes. That is how they examine things. That is how they read. That is how they "see" — by touching. Wouldn't Isaac know the difference between Jacob and Esau simply by touching them? Jacob himself knew that this was a problem in his mother's plan and he objected to it, saying, "But my brother Esau is a hairy man, and I'm a man with smooth skin. What if my father touches me? I would appear to be tricking him and would bring down a curse on myself, rather than a blessing!" But his mother said to him, "My son, let the curse fall on me. Just do what I say . . ."

So Jacob brought the two young goats to his mother. Rebekah was a clever woman. While she could do nothing to change Jacob's voice, she did think of ways to deal with the other problems: First of all, she disguised the taste of the meat. Because the goats were young ones, they did not have a strong flavour of their own. Rebekah seasoned the stew, with the same things that she would use in cooking game meat. She prepared some tasty food, just the way Isaac liked it. Then Rebekah took the best clothes of Esau her older son, and put them on her younger son Jacob. Why did she do that? Blind old Isaac couldn't see what he was wearing. No, but he could smell. Esau's smell would be in Esau's clothes and Rebekah did this to disguise Jacob's scent. Finally, Rebekah covered the two places were Jacob's smooth skin was bare. She covered his hands and his neck with the hairy goat skins. Jacob's disguise was complete!

There was one other very serious problem with Rebekah's plan to trick Isaac, which neither she nor her son considered very carefully. Do you know what it was? What they were planning to do was wrong! It was wrong to deceive a blind person, who must trust other people's honesty. It was also wrong to deceive the head of their family. God commands wives to obey their husbands and sons to honour their fathers. It was wrong for Rebekah to trick her husband and it was wrong for Jacob to lie to his father. If they trusted the Word of God, they could rest assured that what the LORD had said, He would certainly do. The blessing would surely go to Jacob, because of God's plan! What Rebekah and Jacob were doing was not by faith; it was motivated by fear and executed by sin. That was the big problem with their plan! It was wrong! Did their consciences bother them? Jacob was certainly fearful of bringing a curse upon himself instead of a blessing, but nonetheless, he proceeded with the plan.

As soon as everything was ready, Rebekah handed Jacob the tasty meal she had made for Isaac. Jacob entered his father's tent with the wonderful aroma of freshly baked bread and savory stew wafting all around him. Jacob went to his father and spoke. "My father," he said. (Those were the only true words that Jacob spoke in his father's tent that day!) "Yes, my son," answered Isaac. He could smell the food that Esau was supposed to bring to him, but already Isaac was suspicious. "Who is it?" he asked. Jacob answered, "I am Esau, your firstborn." Jacob lied. He lied to his own father, saying, "I am Esau, your firstborn. I have done as you told me. Please sit up and eat some of my game so that you may give me your blessing." This was exactly what Isaac had discussed with his son Esau, but Isaac was not so sure that this was Esau. "How did you find it so quickly, my son?" Isaac asked. Jacob lied again. He even used the LORD's Name, to make his answer appear good and true. How did he find the game so quickly? Jacob replied, "The LORD your God gave me success." Isaac was not convinced. When did Esau ever speak of God? This answer was something that Jacob would say. It was also Jacob's voice! Isaac was not so easily fooled. "Come near, my son, so I can touch you, to know whether you really are my son Esau or not." This was what Jacob had feared would happen! Would the hairy goatskins trick his father? Or would he now bring a curse down upon himself, rather than a blessing? Jacob's heart must have been pounding with fear as he went close to his father. Isaac touched him and said, "The voice is the voice of Jacob, but the hands are the hands of Esau." Isaac was confused. Who was this standing before him? Jacob or Esau? His eyes could not see. His ears told him it was Jacob, but his hands told him it was Esau. Like all blind people, Isaac was forced to rely on the honesty of the person speaking to him, so he asked again, "Are you really my son Esau?" Again Jacob lied, "I am." Then Isaac said, "My son, bring me some of your game to eat, so that I may give you my blessing." Again Jacob must have been nervous. Would his father detect the taste of the goatmeat? Would he be able to tell the difference between goatmeat and gamemeat? But Isaac ate and drank—and noticed nothing. It was a delicious meal. Now his tasting, as well as his touching, told him that this was Esau. Isaac had one final test. "Come here, my son, and kiss me," said Isaac. Jacob did so and Isaac took a deep breath, when his son was so near him. It was the smell of Esau. Now old Isaac was convinced. When he caught the smell of his clothes, he blessed his son, saying, "Ah-h-h-h-h-h, the smell of my son is like the smell of a field that the LORD has blessed."

Then Isaac blessed Jacob with the riches of heaven and earth, saying, "May God give you . . . an abundance!" He blessed Jacob with dominion over nations and peoples, saying, "May nations serve you and peoples bow down to you. Be lord over your brothers . . ." He blessed Jacob with God's protection, saying, "May those who curse you be cursed and those who bless you be blessed." As surely as Isaac's hand rested on Jacob's head, so God's blessing rested upon him.

That was what Jacob wanted—the blessing! *God's blessing!* Jacob had been blessed with God's provision and God's protection and the promise that he would prevail. He and his descendants would not vanish from the earth. No, because of this blessing, they would inherit the earth. Jacob would become that great nation, promised first to Abraham, then to Isaac, and now to Jacob. He would rule the world. Nations and peoples would bow down and serve him. All the promises of God belonged to him! Yes, Jacob the Grasper had succeeded in grasping the blessing of God.

Jacob did not have much time to glory in his victory. After receiving the blessing, Jacob had scarcely left his father's tent, when his brother Esau returned home from the hunt. Esau prepared a meal for his father and brought it to his tent. Isaac was lying on his bed, resting after the dinner he had just eaten. Isaac said, "My father, sit up and eat some of my game, so that you may give me your blessing." Isaac was alarmed. He thought he had just given Esau his blessing. Who was this then, asking for the blessing? "Who are you?" Isaac asked. Now Esau was confused. He knew his father was getting old, but didn't he remember what they had just discussed? Isaac was, of course, old and blind, but his hearing had always been fine. What was wrong? Didn't his father recognize his voice? Esau answered, "I am your son," he answered, "your firstborn, Esau!" Isaac was shaken. When he heard this voice and this answer, Isaac began to tremble violently, he was so upset. "Who was it then that hunted game and brought it to me?" he asked. "I ate it just before you came and I blessed him—and indeed he will be blessed!" Who was it? They both knew. Jacob! Jacob the Grasper! Jacob the Deceiver!

When Esau heard his father's words, when he learned that his brother had taken his blessing, he burst out with a loud and bitter cry. Then he pleaded with his father, who loved him, "Bless me—me too, my father!" But Isaac couldn't do that. The blessing was gone. He had given it to Jacob. Isaac said, "Your brother came deceitfully and took your blessing." Then Esau said, "Isn't he rightly named Jacob/Grasper/Deceiver? He has deceived me these two times: He took my birthright—and now he's taken my blessing!" Then Esau asked his father, "Haven't you reserved any blessing for me?" No, Isaac had given everything to Jacob. He answered Esau, "I have made him lord over you. I have made all his relatives his servants . . . so what can I possibly do for you, my son?" Esau beseeched his father to bless him also. He said, "Do you have only one blessing, my father? Bless me too, my father!" But Isaac would not do it. Although Esau begged for the blessing, Isaac would not change what he had done. Esau had missed the grace of God. It was gone forever. Then Esau began to cry. Esau—that big man, that mighty hunter—wept aloud like a little boy. Now he wanted God's blessing, but it was too late. Although he sought for this blessing with a torrent of tears, he could bring about no change. He was rejected. Although each sob must have been like a wound in his father's heart, Isaac would not change his mind or recall his blessing. The words he had spoken would remain, just as the Word of the LORD endures forever. Isaac understood now that this was the will and the work of God. It did not matter what Isaac wanted; it did not matter how Esau pleaded. The Sovereign LORD had made His choice before the foundation of the world. God's plan would prevail. "It does not, therefore, depend on man's desire or effort, but on God's mercy" (Romans 9:16). It was the LORD, who had blessed Jacob. Before the boys were even born, God declared, "The older will serve the younger"—and now Isaac had echoed God's Word. Without knowing it, he had blessed Jacob, making the older brother Esau his servant. It was God's will—and Isaac would not change that blessing. Blind though he was, Isaac now saw clearly that God had chosen his younger son, not his older son. At last Isaac believed the Word of God—that the LORD had chosen Jacob. So, by faith, he would not, he could not, bless his beloved son Esau, who knelt before him weeping and pleading for a blessing. No, by faith, Isaac remained firm. Instead he said to this son that he would be separated from the riches of heaven and earth. God would not provide for him an abundance. "Your dwelling will be away from the earth's richness, away from the dew of heaven . . ." Esau would not have the protection of God. "You will live by the sword . . ." declared Isaac. Esau would not prevail. Instead, he would be a slave. "You will serve your brother . . ." said Isaac. There was nothing for Esau, no blessing at all. It was not by mistake, but on purpose—by God's purpose—and in the end by Isaac submitting to God's plan, that his two sons were blessed by him. The Bible says, "By faith, Isaac blessed Jacob and Esau in regard to their future" (Hebrews 11:20).

What Isaac said that day was prophetic, foretelling what would happen to all Jacob's and Esau's descendants after them. Isaac's words had the authority of God's Word. Esau's descendants became a nation, known as Edom. The Edomites were not blessed with a fertile land, but lived in a mountainous, wilderness country, "away from earth's richness." Neither were the Edomites blessed with peace. They "lived by the sword" and were ruled by many nations. The descendants of Esau were a people forever under the wrath of the LORD. Again and again the prophets of God spoke against them. This is what the LORD said concerning Edom: "All its towns will be in ruins forever" (Jeremiah 49:13). "Esau I have hated, and I have turned his mountains into a wasteland . . . Edom may say, 'Though we have been crushed, we will rebuild the ruins.' But this is what the LORD Almighty says, 'They may build, but I will demolish. They will be called the Wicked Land, a people always under the wrath of the LORD' " (Malachi 1:2–4). "This is what the Sovereign LORD says: I will stretch out my hand against Edom . . . I will lay it waste . . . I will take vengeance on Edom by the hand of my people Israel, and they will deal with Edom in accordance with My anger and My wrath; they will know My vengeance, declares the Sovereign LORD" (Ezekiel 25:13, 14). "Edom will be a desert waste . . . but Judah will be inhabited forever" (Joel 3:19–21). "This is what the Sovereign LORD says about Edom . . . Everyone in Esau's mountains will be cut down in the slaughter . . . and destroyed forever . . . But on Mount Zion will be deliverance; it will be holy, and the house of Jacob will possess its inheritance. The house of Jacob will be a fire and the house of Joseph a flame; the house of Esau will be stubble, and they will set it on fire and consume it. There will be no survivors from the house of Esau. The LORD has spoken . . . Deliverers will go up on Mount Zion to rule the mountains of Esau. And the kingdom will be the LORD's" (Obadiah 9, 10, 17, 18, 21).

The Kingdom of God, the pearl of priceless value—that was what Jacob wanted and that was what Jacob had risked everything to get. He believed in that kingdom and he believed in God. It was by faith that Jacob saw this kingdom, not by sight, for at that time on earth there was nothing. There was only one person—Jacob, the Grasper, the Deceiver, who had cheated his brother out of his birthright and his blessing. Was he the man on whom the Kingdom of God depended? No! The LORD Himself would build His Kingdom. It would not be built by the goodness of any man; nor could it be stopped by the wickedness of any man. Jacob would rule, not because of anything he had done, but because God had ordained it. How would he rule? In this life and on this earth a crown would never be placed on Jacob's head, but one day a son would come from Jacob, on whose head a crown of thorns would be placed. This son of Jacob would secure the Kingdom of God forever by the sacrifice of Himself for sin. This son of Jacob would be exalted to the throne of God, where He would reign forever and ever, as the King of kings and Lord of lords. This son of Jacob would be the ruler and conqueror of all the earth. In Him all the prophesies and blessings and promises to Jacob would be perfectly fulfilled. Who was this son of Jacob? It was Jesus Christ, the Son of God, who loved us and freed us from our sins by His blood, and made us to be a kingdom. To Him be glory, honour, majesty and dominion forever and ever. Amen.

The teacher's guide for this lesson starts on page 512.

JACOB BLESSED AND BLESSED AGAIN!

- **Genesis 27:41–28:22**
- **Hebrews 11:20; 12:14–17**
- **I John 3:11–15**

E sau sought the blessing with tears, but he was rejected. However, don't feel sorry for Esau! His desire to have the blessing was not because he had regard for God or faith in God. He wept because there was no blessing for himself, but he did not seek to make himself right with God. No, Esau hardened his heart . . . and he poisoned his heart. "Godly sorrow brings repentance that leads to salvation and leaves no regret, but worldly sorrow brings death" (II Corinthians 7:10). Esau did not have a godly sorrow that led him to salvation. This incident could have been a warning sign and a turning point in Esau's life, causing him to seek the LORD with his whole heart, lest he miss the grace of God forever. But Esau's sorrow was a worldly sorrow, a carnal kind of sorrow, which he turned to his own destruction. His sorrow turned to anger. A root of bitterness began to grow in Esau's heart, which surely would cause trouble. Esau held a grudge against his brother and it turned into a hatred. *hatred*! It spread through Esau like poison, like the venom of a snake. He hated Jacob! He hated him because of the blessing his father had given him.

Esau said to himself, "I will kill him! Yes, I will kill my own brother! I will kill Jacob!" That was what Esau decided to do. He would murder his younger brother, just as Cain had done before him, and for the same reason—because his brother had found favour in the eyes of God. How would he kill him? Perhaps Esau dreamed of stalking Jacob like an animal, shooting him with his bow and arrow, then watching his blood soak into the ground. Esau, the mighty hunter, took pleasure in the thought of catching his prey. When would he kill him? He would wait; he would wait until his father Isaac had died, which would not be long. "The days of mourning for my father are near," said Esau. "Then I will kill my brother Jacob." Esau, like many evil men before him and after him, thought that he could stop the plan of God. Esau thought that he could kill Jacob and so bring God's promises to nothing. Did God say that Jacob would prevail? No, thought Esau; he would prevail! He would conquer Jacob by his own strength. He would surely live—and "live by the sword"—just as it was said concerning him. It was a simple solution: Kill Jacob soon, while he had no children to inherit the birthright and the blessing. Then everything would have to go to Esau, the older son and rightful heir, for there was no one else. Thus mighty Esau thought he could reverse the blessing by himself, by the works of his own hands, by his own bloody deeds. Esau was like his father, the devil, who thought he could war against God and win. God's Word protected Jacob and Esau would have done well to listen: "May those who curse you be cursed and those who bless you be blessed." By plotting Jacob's destruction, Esau was bringing upon himself the cursing of Almighty God.

Now Esau was proud of his sin and boasted in his rebellion. He didn't just *think* about what he would do to Jacob; he *spoke* about it too. That was his mistake, for word came to Rebekah, perhaps through some servants, about Esau's wicked plan to kill Jacob as soon as Isaac died. It was alarming news! In one day Rebekah would lose the two men she loved most in this world—her husband and her son, Isaac and Jacob. Oh, it was a terrifying thought, and she doubted not that Esau would do it. Rebekah began to think: What could she do to stop that day of death from ever dawning? Rebekah always seemed to have an idea of what to do. She had a plan: Jacob must run away! He must flee from his family! He must leave the country! Where could he go? Jacob could stay with her own family, far away in another land. When it was safe, he could return. That was Rebekah's plan, but no one would like it. Rebekah herself did not like the idea of Jacob leaving on a long journey, perhaps for a long time. Rebekah loved Jacob. She might never see him again. Would she be willing to send her son, her beloved son, so far away? Yes, for it was the only solution she could see to save his life. And quiet Jacob, who preferred to stay at home among the tents—he certainly would not like this plan. It was clear that Jacob was in real danger if he stayed at home, but would he be willing to leave? And what about Isaac? Isaac would not like the plan for his own reasons. Isaac had been born here and had lived here his whole life. He had never left this Promised Land, not once, not even for a short time. In fact, his father Abraham had not allowed him to leave, not even to find a wife, and the LORD had not allowed him to leave, not even to find food during a famine. Would Isaac be willing to allow his son, his blessed son, to leave the Promised Land? Rebekah must convince them both to agree to her plan. First she sent for Jacob and told him the truth. "Your brother Esau is consoling himself with the thought of killing you," she said. "Now then, my son, do what I say: Flee at once to my brother Laban in Haran. Stay with him for awhile, until your brother's fury subsides. When your brother is no longer angry with you and forgets what you did to him, I'll send word for you to come back here. Why should I lose both of you in one day?" Then Rebekah spoke to Isaac. She did not want to alarm the weak old man, lest it hasten his death, so she did not tell him the truth. Instead she complained about Esau's wives, who were making her life miserable. She said, "I'm disgusted with living because of these Hittite women. If Jacob takes a wife from among the women of this land, from Hittite women like these, my life will not be worth living."

That was all she said, but it worked. Isaac not only allowed Jacob to leave; he commanded him to leave! "Do not marry a Canaanite woman," commanded Isaac. He told Jacob to "go at once" to his mother's country and to her family. "Take a wife for yourself there, from among the daughters of Laban, your mother's brother." Then Isaac blessed Jacob, *blessed him again*—this time knowing who he was! By faith Isaac blessed Jacob and said:

> *May God Almighty bless you.*
> *May God make you fruitful and increase your numbers*
> *until you become a multitude of peoples.*

May he give you and your descendants the blessing,
    the blessing given to Abraham
    father of a Multitude,
so that you may take possession of the land
    where you now live as an alien,
the land God gave to Abraham.

Genesis 28:3, 4

That was how Jacob left home—with the blessing of his father freely and fully upon him. Yes, that was how Isaac sent Jacob on his way—with the blessing of Almighty God! "By faith, Isaac blessed Jacob . . ." (Hebrews 11:20).

Jacob did not want to leave his home, but now he had no choice. Both his mother and his father had commanded him, "Flee at once! Go at once!" Jacob knew that his brother wanted to hunt him and kill him. Jacob knew he must leave immediately. He must run for his life! Early the next morning, before the sun had risen, Jacob slipped away in the darkness. He travelled many miles that first day, putting as much distance as he could between himself and his killer. Would Esau come after him? Jacob feared that he would, so he must flee far and fast. He pushed himself that first day until he was too weary to take another step. Finally, after the sun had set, Jacob stopped for the night. He did not spend the first night of his journey in a hotel or in a house or even in a tent. He did not sleep in a bed, nor did he have a sleeping bag. Jacob did not even have a pillow. He just lay down on the cold ground and put a hard stone under his head. He was exhausted, but could he sleep? He was all alone in the darkness and the wilderness. He heard strange noises, saw black shadows. No doubt his brother, a skillful hunter, was already on his trail. A murderer was tracking him to find him and kill him in the night. Jacob must have been afraid. Perhaps he prayed to the LORD as he lay on the ground in the dark, the kind of prayer which God's persecuted people would pray for thousands of years after him: "Listen to my prayer, O God . . . My thoughts trouble me and I am distraught . . . My heart is in anguish within me. The terrors of death assail me. Fear and trembling have beset me; horror has overwhelmed me . . . Oh, that I had the wings of a dove! I would fly away and be at rest" (Psalm 55:1–6). But Jacob did not have wings; he had only tired legs and a fearful heart. He was lying on the ground now, but was he at rest? Could he sleep? Did he trust in God? Perhaps Jacob wondered, as he lay with his head on a stone, if God's blessing really was upon him. Look what had happened in his life! He had received the blessing, and immediately there was trouble. It seemed that it was Jacob, not Esau, who had been cut off. He was the one who had become a fugitive, a "wanderer on the earth" like Cain, a man without a home, without so much as a pillow for his head. The very things Jacob had wanted so desperately, the blessings which he had grasped so earnestly—to be part of the promises of God—these were the very things he seemed to be leaving and losing. Would God bring him back home? Would he again dwell in the Promised Land? Would he again be part of the family of faith? Jacob had gained the blessing, but that night, when the ground was his bed and a stone was his pillow, when only darkness and loneliness surrounded him, Jacob must have grieved over his losses. The blessing of God was not what he had expected it to be. Could Jacob sleep that night? Yes, he was exhausted. In spite of his fear, perhaps because of his faith, Jacob slept.

We do not know what Jacob was thinking before he fell asleep, but we do know what Jacob was dreaming in the middle of that night. In the darkness, in his sleep, God gave something wonderful to Jacob. He did not have a soft pillow for his head, but God gave him something so much better, so much greater—a dream, a dream which would strengthen Jacob's faith and gladden Jacob's heart for the rest of his days (and nights) upon this earth! Jacob would never ever forget what he saw and heard that night. In his dream Jacob saw a stairway resting on the earth, with its top reaching to heaven, and the angels of God were ascending and descending on it. Above it stood the LORD Himself, and He spoke to Jacob, saying:

> *I am the LORD, the God of your fathers,*
> *the God of Abraham and the God of Isaac.*
> *I will give you and your descendants the land*
> *on which you are lying.*
> *Your descendants will be like the dust of the earth*
> *and you will spread out to the west and to the east,*
> *to the north and to the south.*
> *All peoples on earth will be blessed*
> *through you and your offspring.*
> *I am with you and will watch over you*
> *wherever you go,*
> *and I will bring you back to this land.*

I will not leave you until
I have done what I have promised you.

Genesis 28:13–15

That was what Jacob had wanted all his life! He had always wanted to be part of God's promises. He had always wanted to hear what his grandfather and his father had heard—and now God had spoken to him too! God Himself had blessed Jacob! The same promise of God had been extended to him, to Jacob and to Jacob's children. The heavenly inheritance had passed to him:

1) Although he owned nothing, not even a campsite to pitch his tent or a pillow to place his head, Jacob owned God's promise. God promised to him and to his descendants this land on which he was lying, this whole land which stretched farther than his eyes could see in any direction. God said, "I will give you the land . . ."

2) Although Jacob had not even one child (and had not even found a wife yet) God promised him that his descendants would be like the dust of the earth. God had made the same promise to Abraham and Isaac, promising them countless numbers of children, "like the stars of the sky and the sand on a seashore." Now Jacob was part of that great promise. God said his children would be "like the dust of the earth."

3) The greatest promise of all was that God would use Jacob to bless the whole world. Through one of Jacob's children God said "all peoples on earth will be blessed." The Saviour promised from the beginning, the Seed who would crush the serpent's head, the Child who would defeat the devil, the Messiah who would rescue man from sin and death—he would be the son of Abraham, the son of Isaac, *and the son of Jacob!* Yes, the LORD would use Jacob to bring forth His One and Only Son, Jesus Christ. Jacob would be part of the greatest promise of all. Wonder of wonders! The Holy One who was coming, was coming from Jacob! God said to Jacob, "All peoples on earth will be blessed through you and through your offspring."

But all these great promises were for the future. Some of them would not be fulfilled for hundreds of years. It would be thousands of years before the greatest promise came to pass. Right now, Jacob was on a dangerous journey. Someone was trying to kill him. He was fleeing for his life. He did not know what would happen to him or how he would live. He did not know if he would ever return to his family or his country. He was all alone in the dark, lying on the bare ground without even a pillow for his head. Jacob had very real needs and fears. So that night in his dream God spoke to Jacob about his present situation as well. The LORD promised: "I am with you. I will watch over you wherever you go. And I will bring you back to this land. I will not leave you until I have done what I have promised you."

Then Jacob awoke from his sleep and his dream. It was still dark, but his earlier fears had melted away. Now another fear gripped him—the fear of the LORD! Jacob thought, "Surely the LORD is in this place, and I was not aware of it." He ought to have fallen on the ground to worship, rather than to sleep. Jacob was afraid. "How awesome is this place!" he said. "This is none other than the house of God! This is the gate of heaven!" That night Jacob's closed eyes had been opened to see where he was. He was in the presence of Almighty God. Jacob saw what is usually invisible to our eyes— the holy angels of heaven going to and from the earth, as faithful servants working for the LORD. Just as people go in and out of a city's gates, so the angels go back and forth through heaven's gate—and Jacob saw this holy traffic going up and down that stairway. How peacefully Jacob must have slept after that dream, for he knew now that the LORD and His angels were watching over him. Jacob had found his resting place, his shelter in the storm of life. It was God!

Early the next morning when Jacob awoke, he wanted to make sure he would remember the exact spot where the heavenly stairway had touched the earth. He wanted to remember the place where God had revealed Him- self to him. So Jacob took the stone he had placed under his head and set it upright as a marker. His pillow became a pillar! Jacob poured oil on top of the rock, to anoint it as a special stone and a sacred rock. He named that place Bethel, which means "House of God." Like his father and grandfa- ther before him, Jacob was already claiming this land for God. He did not build an altar there to worship the LORD . . . not at that time. But many years later, Jacob would return to Bethel and there in Canaan, in the land filled with idols, he would build an altar to worship the only true God.

Before Jacob left Bethel in the land of Canaan, to flee to a far-away land, Jacob made a vow: "If God will be with me and will watch over me on this journey . . . and will give me food to eat and clothes to wear so that I return safely to my father's house, *then the LORD will be my God* and this stone I have set up as a pillar will be Bethel, God's House, and of all that You give me I will give You a tenth." Then Jacob continued on his way. He left the land of Canaan, the land God promised to Abraham, Isaac and Jacob. Would he ever return? Yes, because God had promised He would. God said, "I am with you and I will watch over you wherever you go, and I will bring you back to this land."

The teacher's guide for this lesson starts on page 514.

DECEIVER IS DECEIVED

• Genesis 29:1–30

Jacob left Bethel/House of God, where he had seen the angels of heaven, where he had heard the voice of God. Jacob didn't want to leave, but he must continue on his journey. He crossed the Jordan River with only a shepherd's staff in his hand. He left the Promised Land alone and, except for his staff, empty-handed. However, God went with him and in his heart Jacob carried the greatest treasures of all. He took with him not the riches of this world, but the dreams and the words, the promises and the blessings, of Almighty God. Jacob left the Promised Land by faith, believing the Word of the LORD, that God would surely bring him back to his country and his family some day. Jacob journeyed to a strange land by faith, believing that God was with him and that God would watch over him wherever he went, just as He had promised.

After a long time of travelling over deserts and mountains and rivers, Jacob came to the land of the eastern peoples. There he found a well in a field, where some shepherds were waiting to water their three flocks of sheep. "My brothers, where are you from?" asked Jacob. "We're from Haran," they replied. Haran! Long ago, that was where his mother Rebekah had lived . . . and even longer ago, that was where his grandfather Abraham had lived. Jacob wondered if he could find any of his relatives. Were any of them still alive? Would he be able to find Uncle Laban, his mother's brother? Jacob asked the shepherds, "Do you know Laban, Nahor's grandson?" The shepherds answered, "Yes, we know him." "Is he well?" asked Jacob. "Yes, he is," they answered. Then they pointed to a shepherd-girl approaching the well and they said, "Here comes his daughter Rachel with the sheep." When Jacob saw his beautiful cousin Rachel and his uncle Laban's flock of sheep, he knew what to do. He went over to the well and rolled away the enormous stone which covered it and watered his uncle's sheep, while the lovely shepherdess stood watching, surprised. Who was this man? Why was this stranger helping her? Then Jacob told Rachel who he was. He was her cousin, whom she had never met; he was the son of her father's sister, Rebekah, who had left this land long ago. Then Jacob kissed Rachel and began to weep aloud, he was so overjoyed at finding his relatives. The LORD had led him to his family in this foreign land. Imagine Rachel's amazement! She had heard of her father's beautiful sister, her Aunt Rebekah, but she had never seen her. How amazing it was that she was looking into the tear-filled eyes of Aunt Rebekah's own son! This kind man, who was weeping aloud before her, was her own cousin, whom she had never met! So Rachel ran home to tell her father. Then Laban hurried to the well to meet Jacob. There stood the son of his beloved Rebekah, the sister whom he had not seen since she left home so long ago. Laban hugged Jacob and kissed him and brought him to his home — and there they talked and talked and talked, probably late into the night, because they had so many years of family stories to tell each other. Laban treated Jacob like a son and said to him, "You are my own flesh and blood."

That was how Jacob found a new home in a strange land. I am sure he still missed his father and mother, but Jacob had found a very special person, whom he loved even more than his parents. It was the beautiful shepherd-girl, whom he had kissed when he first arrived. Jacob had found the woman he wanted for his wife. It was his cousin Rachel. Yes, Jacob was in love with Rachel! He wanted to marry her, but he had nothing to offer her. He was a refugee, who had fled to this land with nothing. Oh yes, he had dreams and visions and promises from God, but he had nothing in his hand to offer for her hand in marriage. He had come to Laban with a shepherd's staff — that was all — and that was not enough to offer Laban for his daughter Rachel. What could Jacob do? He was in love with Rachel, but he dare not ask to marry her.

Jacob stayed with Laban's family as a guest and he worked hard to help them with their flocks of sheep and goats. Jacob proved himself better than any hired man that had ever worked for Laban. After a month Laban realized that he didn't want Jacob to leave, because he was such a hard worker and such a good shepherd. Laban said to Jacob, "Just because you are a relative of mine, should you work for me for nothing? Tell me what your wages should be. What should I pay you?" Jacob knew exactly what he wanted from Laban—his daughter! Once again the Grasper was ready to grasp what he wanted. What did Jacob want as payment for his work? Jacob answered, "I'll work for you seven years in return for your daughter Rachel." It was a fair deal, unlike the bargain he had made with his brother, Esau. Because it was a generous offer, Laban accepted it. He agreed to the wages that Jacob wanted, saying, "It's better that I give Rachel to you than to some other man. Stay here with me." So Jacob stayed with Uncle Laban, working hard for seven long years to get Rachel, but they seemed like only a few days to him, because of his love for her. It was enough just to be near her during those years, just to catch a glimpse of her or speak a word with her as they tended the sheep. Rachel was so beautiful and Jacob loved her so much.

Then, more quickly than Jacob could have imagined, the seven years were gone. He had served his time. Now he could marry the woman he loved. Now he could hold her and kiss her; he could lie down next to her and make love to her. He could sleep with her all through the night and talk with her all through the day. Jacob had laboured seven years for this. Now they could live their lives together, as one, as husband and wife. Jacob did not want to wait another day. He had been engaged to Rachel for seven years. Jacob had kept his part of the bargain, and now it was time for Laban to keep his part. "Give me my wife," Jacob said to his uncle. "My time is completed . . ." So the wedding feast was prepared and the people were invited. As was the custom, the bride was presented to Jacob beautifully adorned, but heavily veiled. Jacob could not see his lovely lady . . . not yet. After the ceremony, when Jacob and his bride made their marriage vows to each other, and after the celebration, when all the people were singing and dancing and feasting, after the sun had set and the stars twinkled in the sky, Jacob finally took his new wife into his tent. It was dark when he lifted the veil from her face and he could not see her . . . not yet. However, he could hold her and kiss her and make love to her all through the night. He would see her beautiful face in the morning, in the light of a new day, their first day together.

When Jacob awoke the next day and looked at his new wife, he was shocked! The woman lying next to him was not the woman he loved! It was not Rachel! He had married the wrong person. Laban had given him Rachel's older, weaker, uglier sister—and he had married Leah. His uncle Laban had tricked him! His uncle Laban had cheated him! What Jacob had done seven years earlier to his blind old father, had now been done to him—and with his eyes wide open. He had been deceived! Jacob rushed out of his tent to find Laban. "What is this you have done to me?" Jacob cried. "I served you for Rachel, didn't I? Why have you deceived me?" Laban replied, quite simply, "It is not our custom here to give the younger daughter in marriage before the older one." That was Laban's explanation. He had seven years to explain that to Jacob, but he never said a word. Why? Laban had a plan to get seven more years of free work out of Jacob. Laban was benefiting from God's blessing on Jacob and he did not want Jacob to leave. Laban had an offer ready for Jacob, as well as an excuse. He said, "Finish this daughter's bridal week; then we will give you the younger one also—in return for another seven years of work." It was a hard bargain that Laban was driving; it was double the previously-agreed price. Jacob would have to work a total of fourteen years for Rachel, although Laban had originally agreed to seven. Laban was offering Rachel to him the following week. He could live with her, while he worked to pay off the next seven years. How could Jacob refuse? He loved Rachel. He had already waited for her and laboured for her seven years. Should he give up now? No, Jacob loved Rachel and longed for her, so Jacob agreed to the terms of Laban's bargain. Jacob would wait one more week and then marry Rachel—in exchange for another seven years of hard work.

Thus it happened that Jacob the Grasper was grasped by someone else. Jacob the Deceiver was deceived by someone else. What Jacob had done to his own brother and then to his own father, had now been done to him by his own uncle. Jacob would have seven long years to think about that. Meanwhile, in all these sinful dealings of men, God was bringing to pass His plan for the world. What men meant for evil, God meant for good. In all these unrighteous and apparently unimportant affairs of men, the LORD was fulfilling His great promises to Abraham, Isaac and Jacob. Through them, the LORD was accomplishing His plan for whole world.

The teacher's guide for this lesson starts on page 516.

THE STARS BEGIN TO SHINE

Genesis 29:31–30:24

Jacob now had two wives, which was not right. He had married two sisters, Leah and Rachel, but he did not love them equally. No, he had loved Rachel for many years, and although he had married Leah first, it was Rachel whom he still loved. Poor Leah! She found herself married to a man who did not love her. How unhappy her life was! However, when the LORD saw that Leah was not loved by her husband, He opened her womb so that she could have children. The LORD of LOVE filled Leah's life with the joy of many children. They were the ones who would love her and need her and want her.

The first child born to Leah was a baby boy, whom she named Reuben. His name meant "Behold! A son!" Leah had presented Jacob with a son! "The LORD has seen my misery," said Leah. "Surely my husband will love me now." But Jacob still loved Rachel. Even his firstborn son, whom Leah had given to him, did not change his lack of affection for her.

Leah became pregnant again. She gave birth to another baby boy, whom she named Simeon. His name meant "Heard!" Leah said, "Because the LORD heard that I am not loved, He gave me this one too." But even two sons did not change Jacob's heart. He still loved Rachel.

Leah became pregnant a third time and gave birth to another baby boy, whom she named Levi. His name meant "Attached." She said, "Now at last my husband will become attached to me, because I have borne him three sons." But Jacob did not become attached to Leah. He still loved Rachel.

Then the LORD gave Leah a fourth baby boy. She named him Judah, which is the Hebrew word for "Praise!" His joyful mother said, "This time I will praise the LORD!" Whether her husband loved her or not, she would praise the LORD, because she knew that God loved her. God had given her four children. God had given her Judah; God had given her praise! Not only would God's praises be on Leah's lips, but forever, Leah would be remembered, honoured and praised because she had brought forth this child. Judah was a very special boy. At that time Leah herself did not know how very special he was. It was through Judah that God would demonstrate His perfect LOVE to the whole world. It was through Judah that the Messiah would come, to the everlasting praise of Almighty God. "O praise the LORD for He is good. His LOVE endures forever" (Psalm 118:1).

After Judah was born, Leah stopped having children—but she was very busy and very happy with her four little boys. However, Rachel was very unhappy. Although her husband loved her, Rachel was miserable because she had no children. She was barren. Her life was full of her husband's love, but her womb was empty and her tent was lonely. It seemed unfair. Although she was younger and stronger and prettier than her sister, Leah was the one who had four little boys, while she had none. Rachel became jealous of her sister and angry at her husband. She said to Jacob, "Give me children, or I'll die!" Then Jacob was angry with her. Why was he being blamed? It wasn't his fault! Children are the LORD's good gift. God is the one who opens the womb or closes the womb. Jacob answered Rachel, "Am I in the place of God, who has kept you from having children?" Rachel should have been humbly pleading with God, rather than angrily complaining to her husband. She should have been waiting upon the LORD, waiting for Him to open her womb in His good time. However, Rachel was desperate for a child and she thought of a way to get one quickly. She gave her maidservant, Bilhah, to Jacob as a wife. Rachel said, "Sleep with her, so that she can bear children for me and so that through her I too can build a family." So Jacob slept with Bilhah and she did become pregnant and she did give birth to a baby . . . another boy. Rachel immediately claimed him and named him. She called him Dan, which means "Judge," because God had judged her favourably. "God has vindicated me!" she said. "He has listened to my plea and given me a son." Now there was a baby crying in Rachel's tent too . . . but it was Bilhah who nursed the baby to sleep.

Then Rachel's servant Bilhah conceived again and bore Jacob another son. Rachel said, "I have had a great struggle with my sister, and I have won!" She named this little boy Naphtali, which means "My Struggle."

Leah must have wondered about this strange name that her sister gave to Jacob's new son. And what in the world did Rachel mean, "I have had a great struggle with my sister, and I have won!"? Those weren't really her children, but if Rachel could cheat in this way, so could Leah. Since she had stopped having children, Leah gave her maidservant, Zilpah, to Jacob as another wife. Zilpah also became pregnant and gave birth to a son. Leah named him Gad, which means "Fortune," saying, "What good fortune! A troop is coming!" Leah's sons were growing into an army and Rachel would never be able to win in this little war between the two sisters.

Then Leah's servant Zilpah gave birth to another son. Leah said "How happy I am!" and she named the new baby boy Asher, which means "Happy."

Then Leah herself became pregnant again. God listened to her prayers and gave her another son, whom she named Issachar, which means "Reward." The Bible says, "Sons are a heritage from the LORD, children a reward from Him" (Psalm 127:3).

Again Leah conceived and bore Jacob a sixth son. Then Leah said, "God has presented me with a precious gift. This time my husband will treat me with honour, because I have borne him six sons!" She named her new baby boy Zebulun, which means "Honour." But it was still Rachel whom Jacob loved.

God had one more gift for Leah, a very special gift. It was a daughter. Sometime later Leah gave birth to a little baby girl, whom she named Dinah. Dinah means "Avenged," because God had avenged her suffering with this little baby girl. Leah now had seven children of her own, but Rachel still had not even one. Jacob had ten sons: six from Leah and four from the maidservants—but none from Rachel. Not one of all those children born in Jacob's household belonged to her.

Year after year passed. Rachel pleaded with the LORD to open her womb; she beseeched God to give her a tiny baby too—but her womb remained barren, her arms empty. Then finally God remembered Rachel. He listened to her and opened her womb. A baby began to grow inside Rachel. She too had the joy of feeling a little baby inside her. She too had the joy of bringing a new person into the world. She too had the joy of giving a small son to Jacob. Yes, it was another baby boy—but this time Rachel was the mother! God had taken away her disgrace. Rachel was a mother too. She named her little baby Joseph, and because she was so pleased and so proud, she could hardly wait until God gave her another child. The name Joseph means "Increase" for Rachel said, "May the LORD increase to me another son!" One day God would do that for Rachel, but for now Jacob's family was full!

Jacob had come to this land all alone. When he left his father had blessed him saying, "May God Almighty bless you and make you fruitful and increase your numbers . . ." God had surely done that. Now he had twelve children: one daughter, named Dinah, and eleven sons, whose names were Reuben, Simeon, Levi, Judah, Dan, Naphtali, Gad, Asher, Issachar, Zebulun and finally Joseph, Rachel's own little baby, Joseph. Jacob loved Joseph more than all his other sons, because he loved his mother Rachel and because Joseph was the last one of all these sons, born to him in his old age.

Long ago God promised Great-grandpa Abraham that his children would be like the stars in the sky. As each child was born it was like watching the stars appear, one by one, in the dark sky on a winter's night. Isaac was the first pinpoint of light to appear. Then Jacob twinkled next to him. Then one star after another began to shine—Reuben, Simeon, Levi, Judah, Dan, Naphtali, Gad, Asher, Issachar, Zebulun . . . and Dinah. Then a very bright star burst into the night sky with amazing brilliance. That star was Joseph. Was this not what God had promised? Yes, and more! When God took Abraham outside into the night and said, "Look up at the heavens and count the stars . . ." there were so many millions of stars that they could not be counted. The LORD had promised him: "So shall your children be" (Genesis 15:5). Now the stars were beginning to shine. Many more would come, millions more, so many that they could not be counted. In time, as hundreds and even thousands of years passed, stars as bright as Joseph would appear . . . with names such as Moses and Joshua, Deborah, Hannah and Ruth, David and Daniel, Ester and Elijah, Mary and Joseph. Then finally would come the bright Morning Star, eclipsing all the others in its beauty and its brilliance. Jesus said, "I am . . . the bright Morning Star" (Revelation 22:16). Amen. Come, Lord Jesus!

The teacher's guide for this lesson starts on page 518.

TIME TO GO HOME

• Genesis 30:25–31:55

When Jacob arrived as a refugee in the foreign land where Uncle Laban lived, he brought nothing with him, except the staff in his hand. Now, after working for fourteen years, Jacob still had nothing. He was as poor as the day he had arrived. He had worked very hard, both day and night, just to pay for his wives—and now he wanted to go home. He was tired. He had finished his fourteen years, as he had agreed to do, and, although he would leave with nothing, he *did* want to leave. He said to Laban, "Send me on my way, so I can go back to my own homeland. Give me my wives and children, for whom I have served you, and I will be on my way. You know how much work I've done for you!" Yes, Laban knew. Jacob had worked for him from the very first day, when he had just arrived and watered all the sheep at the well in the field . . . until now. Jacob had laboured for Laban with all his strength, day and night with very little sleep, for fourteen long years. Laban would be sad to see Jacob go, not because he loved him, but because he had become quite rich through Jacob's hard work. "Please stay," he said. "The LORD has blessed me because of you." Laban knew that Jacob would no longer work for nothing, so he finally offered to pay him. "Name your wages, and I will pay them," he said. Jacob had to be very careful. Laban was as tricky as he was stingy. His uncle had already cheated him once and it had cost him seven years of work. Again Jacob said to Laban, "You know how I have worked for you and how your livestock has fared under my care." Laban could have no complaints about that. Jacob continued, "The little you had before I came has increased greatly, and the LORD has blessed you wherever I have been." Laban couldn't deny it. Jacob then asked, "So now, when may I do something for my own household?" Jacob had a family too; he had twelve children, yet he had earned nothing in these fourteen years to provide for them. Yes, Laban had prospered, but Jacob had not. Jacob still had nothing! Was that fair? Laban knew it wasn't, so he replied, "What shall I give you?" "Don't give me anything," said Jacob. "But if you will do this one thing for me, I will go on tending your flocks and watching over them: Let me go through all your flocks today and remove from them every speckled or spotted sheep, every dark-coloured lamb and every spotted or speckled goat. They will be my wages." It seemed like a good idea to Laban. Jacob would have some share in the profits, (which Laban planned to make a small share,) and it would be impossible for Jacob to steal from him. You could tell at a glance which sheep or goat belonged to which person. Jacob even said, "My honesty will testify for me in the future, whenever you check on the wages you have paid me. Any goat in my possession that is not speckled or spotted, or any lamb that is not dark-coloured, will be considered stolen." Laban was sure he could still prosper at Jacob's expense, so he said, "Agreed! Let it be as you have said."

Immediately, Laban tried to cheat Jacob. That very same day he removed all the spotted-speckled goats and all the dark-coloured lambs — and he placed them in the care of his own sons, who were not such hard workers or good shepherds. Jacob would not be allowed to care for his own sheep and goats. He had agreed to care for Laban's flocks, not his own, and Laban would make sure that Jacob kept his part of the bargain. Laban sent his sons with Jacob's animals far away, so that a three-day journey separated the two flocks. In this way Laban hoped to prosper. Laban thought that he could trick God. He thought he could keep God's blessing for himself. Since the LORD blessed Laban wherever Jacob was and since Jacob was there tending his flocks, then wouldn't God's blessing be on Laban's animals? Also, all the plain goats and white sheep that belonged to Laban should give birth to young ones the same. They could not mate with the speckled-spotted goats or dark-coloured sheep, that belonged to Jacob. Thus Laban expected his flocks to increase greatly.

Jacob did what he could to encourage Laban's sheep to produce dark lambs and his goats to produce speckled or spotted kids—and God blessed Jacob's efforts. Laban's white sheep gave birth to dark lambs and his plain-coloured goats gave birth to spotted and speckled kids—all of which belonged to Jacob. Several times Laban tried to cheat Jacob, by changing the agreement, but the LORD was with Jacob. Although Laban tried to harm Jacob, God blessed him. God is the one in control of all things. He decides the colour of the sheep; He determines even the spots and the streaks on the goats. So whatever change Laban made, whatever he said would be Jacob's wages, that is exactly what all the flocks would bring forth. In this way Jacob grew exceedingly rich. He came to own large flocks of sheep and goats, as well as maidservants and menservants, camels and donkeys. Jacob no longer had nothing. He was now a wealthy man.

As Jacob grew rich, Laban and his sons grew angry and envious. There was trouble—and Jacob knew it. He heard what his cousins were saying: "Jacob has taken everything our father owned and has gained all this wealth from what belonged to our father." Jacob also noticed that his uncle's attitude toward him had changed—and not for the better. The situation with Uncle Laban had never been good and now it was becoming very bad. Was it time to go home? Yes! The LORD Himself commanded Jacob to leave. God said, "Go back to the land of your fathers and to your relatives, and I will be with you."

God said it was time to go home. Jacob was ready to leave. But what about Rachel and Leah? Would they be willing to leave their home? Would they be willing to leave their family and their country? Jacob sent word to Rachel and Leah to come out to the fields where his flocks were. There, in the midst of all his wealth, where the flocks of dark woolly sheep and fine speckled goats were grazing on the green hillsides, Jacob spoke to them and told them about the trouble between himself and their father. However, he also told them about the LORD's blessing on his life. He said, "But the God of my father has been with me. You know that I've worked for your father with all my strength, yet your father has cheated me by changing my wages ten times. However, God has not allowed him to harm me. If he said, 'The speckled ones will be your wages,' then all the flocks gave birth to speckled young. If he said, 'The streaked ones will be your wages,' then all the flocks gave birth to streaked young. So God has taken away your father's livestock and has given them to me." Rachel and Leah could see that this was true. The evidence was baaing and bleating in the pastures all around them.

Then Jacob told his wives a dream he had: In the dream he looked up and saw that the male goats mating with the flock were streaked, speckled or spotted. This meant that the young ones born would also be streaked, speckled or spotted—and so belong to Jacob. In the dream the Angel of God then said to him, "Jacob . . . look up and see that all the male goats mating with the flock are streaked, speckled or spotted." Why? Why was it happening that way? God told Jacob the answer: "Because I have seen all that Laban has been doing to you." Laban was trying to cheat Jacob, but Jacob was protected by God. Long ago in the Promised Land at Bethel, God promised Jacob, "I am with you and will watch over you wherever you go, and I will bring you back to this land"—and God was keeping His promise. God was watching over Jacob, so that no harm would come to him. In the dream, the LORD reminded Jacob of Bethel, saying, "I am the God of Bethel, where you anointed a pillar and where you made a vow to me." Did Jacob remember Bethel? Did he remember the dream he had there? Did he remember the stone, which first was his pillow and then a pillar? Did he remember his vow? Twenty years ago at Bethel in the Promised Land, Jacob made this vow: "If God will be with me and will watch over me on this journey and will give me food to eat and clothes to wear, so that I return safely to my father's house, then the LORD will be my God . . ."(Genesis 28:20). It was now time to go home. The LORD had promised to bring him back one day . . . and that day had arrived. God gave the marching orders to Jacob. He said in the dream, "Now! Leave this land at once and go back to the land where you were born."

Would Rachel and Leah go with him? Yes, when they heard what their husband said and what God had said, they were willing to go. Besides, Laban also had not dealt with them fairly. Their own father had sold them for a very high price (fourteen years of Jacob's work) but had given them nothing. Laban had not given his daughters any part in his estate, nor did he regard them as part of his family anymore. He viewed them as foreigners. Rachel and Leah concluded, "Surely all the wealth that God took away from our father belongs to us and our children." Their answer to Jacob was: "So do whatever God has told you." They were ready to leave.

So . . . Jacob left. He just put his wives and his children on camels, loaded all his treasures on donkeys, and drove all his flocks and herds ahead of him. Onward to the Promised Land! Onward to the family of faith! Yes, Jacob left that country and finally, after twenty long years, headed for home! He did not tell Laban he was leaving. Laban was away shearing his sheep, and while he was gone, Jacob fled with everyone and everything that he had acquired during his years there.

Three days later someone told Laban that Jacob had fled the country. Immediately Laban recruited a small army of men and followed him. Poor Jacob! He had left the promised land twenty years ago, fleeing for his life because his brother wanted to kill him . . . and now his uncle was after him. His life was in danger again. Laban chased Jacob for seven days, until he finally caught up with him. Jacob had not yet crossed into the land of Canaan. He was camped in the hill country of Gilead on the eastern side of the Jordan River. There Laban set up his camp too. What was he planning to do? Laban had the power to harm Jacob, to kill him and steal from him everything and everyone that Laban thought Jacob had stolen from him. As the sun set and night fell, it looked as if there would be fighting the following day. War was in the wind that night, blowing fear into the hearts of Jacob and his family. All night they must have huddled in their tents and trembled in the darkness, as they wondered what would happen in the morning.

But that night, God came to Laban in a dream, warning him to be very careful not to harm Jacob in any way. God warned him not to do anything (or even say anything) bad to Jacob. "Be careful!" God warned. So Laban's anger at Jacob was restrained by his fear of God. Laban decided to settle things peacefully. The following day he met with Jacob, not to fight with him, but just to talk to him. He said, "What have you done? You've deceived me! You've carried off my daughters like captives in war. Why did you run off secretly and deceive me? Why didn't you tell me, so I could send you away with joy?" Laban said he would have given them a good-bye party, but "you didn't even let me kiss my grandchildren and my daughters good-bye!" Laban threatened Jacob and said, "You have done a foolish thing. I have the power to harm you." Yes, it certainly looked that way. Jacob could see Laban's armed men in the camp opposite him, but did Laban really have the power to harm Jacob? No, for Jacob had protection from Almighty God. Laban himself admitted this, saying that the God of Jacob's father had spoken to him in the night. But why had Jacob fled like that? Laban understood

how Jacob longed to go home, how he longed to return to his own father's
house, but he also knew why Jacob had run away quickly and secretly. Something very valuable was missing from Laban's home. His gold and silver idols
had been stolen, and Laban was sure that Jacob was the thief. "Why did you
steal my gods?" accused Laban.

Why had Jacob run away like that? He answered honestly that he was
afraid. He said, "I was afraid, because I thought you would take your daughters away from me by force." Jacob had run away secretly, because he was
afraid of losing his wives—but he had not touched Laban's idols! The LORD
was Jacob's God. He despised those worthless gods of silver and gold. He
had not taken them. Jacob had not taken anything that did not belong to
him. He was not a thief. He had stolen nothing! "If you find anyone who
has your gods," said Jacob, "that person shall not live." What Jacob didn't
know, was that Rachel had stolen her father's idols. Jacob told Laban to
make a search through his camp. "See for yourself whether there is anything of yours here with me; and if so, take it." So Laban began the search.
First he went into Jacob's tent. He looked everywhere, but his gold and silver gods were not there. Next he went into Leah's tent. He searched all
through her things, but his valuable idols were not there either. Laban also
searched through Bilhah's and Zilpah's tent, but he found nothing. Then
he entered Rachel's tent. Rachel was sitting there, looking quite pale and
sick. She apologized to her father for not standing up in his presence, but
she explained that she was not feeling well. Laban searched through everything in Rachel's tent but he found nothing. He did not think to look under Rachel. That was where his idols were hidden. Rachel was sitting on
her father's gold and silver gods. Laban continued his search through Jacob's
camp, but he could not find his household gods—or anything else that belonged to him.

Now Jacob was angry. Laban had accused him of stealing. "What is my
crime?" he asked Laban. "What sin have I committed that you come after
me and hunt me like a common criminal? Now that you have searched
through all my things, what have you found that belongs to your household?
Put it here in front of your relatives and mine, and let them judge between
the two of us." Laban had nothing. He had accused Jacob falsely and now
Jacob was furious. He had not stolen anything from Laban. In fact, he had
served Laban faithfully and honestly for twenty years. Laban had prospered
because of him. Jacob had not taken, not once, even a little ram from La-

ban's flock to roast over the fire to eat on a cold night. And if the wolves ate any of Laban's lambs, Jacob was the one who paid for them. Jacob said, "I have been with you for twenty years now. Your sheep and goats have not miscarried, nor have I eaten the rams from your flock. I did not bring you animals torn by wild beats; I bore the loss myself. And you demanded payment from me for whatever was stolen by day or night. This was my situation: The heat consumed me in the daytime and the cold at night, and sleep fled from my eyes. It was like this for the twenty years I was in your household. I worked for you fourteen years for your two daughters and six years for your flocks—and you changed my wages ten times! If the God of my father, the God of Abraham and the fear of Isaac, had not been with me, you would surely have sent me away empty-handed." Who was dishonest? Who was the thief? After twenty years of work, Laban would have sent Jacob away with nothing! "But God has seen my hardship," said Jacob. "God has seen the toil of my hands—and last night, He rebuked you."

Laban answered Jacob, "The women are my daughters, the children are my children, and the flocks are my flocks. All you see is mine!" What did Jacob have before he came to Laban? Nothing! Everything Jacob owned came from him. "But what can I do about it?" said Laban. They could either go to war or make peace. Laban was afraid of Jacob's God, so he suggested that they make a covenant with each other. Jacob set up a stone as a pillar and Laban's men gathered stones and piled them in a great heap. Each man in his own language called the place "Witness Heap." Laban said, "This heap is a witness between you and me today." The place was also called Mizpah, which means "Watchtower" because Laban said, "May the LORD keep watch between you and me when we are away from each other." Both men promised that they would not go beyond the witness heap to the other man's side to harm him. Laban said, "May the God of Abraham, Jacob's grandfather, and the God of Nahor, Laban's grandfather, and the God of their father, Terah, (who was their common ancestor, the great-grandfather of both Jacob and Laban) judge between us." Then Jacob offered a sacrifice to the LORD. He invited his relatives to a meal. After they had eaten, they went to bed in their own tents. The day was over. It had ended in peace.

Early the next morning Laban got ready to leave for home. He kissed his grandchildren and his daughters good-bye and blessed them. Laban then went on his way, to his side, which was north-east of the witness heap, and Jacob went his way, to his side, which was south-west of the witness heap.

Jacob was finally going home. Twenty years ago he had left his family and his country, fleeing for his life. He had left with nothing and all alone. Now he was returning to his home, as the head of a large family and the owner of much wealth. He was returning laden with riches, surrounded by flocks and herds, cared for by servants, and accompanied by wives and children who loved him. Twenty years ago Jacob had said, "If God will be with me and will watch over me on this journey, and if He will give me food to eat and clothes to wear, so that I return safely to my father's house, then the LORD will be my God . . ." Jacob had been given so much more than just food and clothes to keep him alive. Jacob had received more than he asked or even imagined. He had received more than a subsistence. God had given him an abundance of every good thing. God had protected Jacob and prospered Jacob. God had been with Jacob and blessed him, just as He had promised.

The teacher's guide for this lesson starts on page 520.

JACOB RETURNS TO THE PROMISED LAND

• Genesis 32, 33
• Hosea 12:3–5

Jacob's return to the Promised Land was an important event. It was so significant that the angels of God met him on the way. Once again Jacob's eyes beheld the host of heaven. Long ago, when Jacob was leaving the Promised Land, he had seen the angels of God in a dream—and now he saw them again, for they appeared to him on the way to welcome him home. How encouraging it was for Jacob to know that his journeys, both his departures and his arrivals, were noticed by heaven. How comforting it was to know (and to see) that wherever he went, whether he was going from the land or coming to it, he had an invisible escort guarding him and guiding him along the way. What a blessing it was to know that the LORD was surely watching over him in all his wanderings upon the earth. When Jacob saw this army of angels he said, "This is the camp of God!" So he named the place where he was camping that night—Mahanaim, which means "Two Camps." Why did Jacob name that place Two Camps? Except for Jacob, other people could see only one camp, but there were two camps of God in that place. There were the tents of Jacob, where the people of God on earth were camped—and surrounding them were the hosts of heaven, where the angels of God were gathered. It surely was the camp of God! The Bible says, "The Angel of the LORD encamps around those who fear Him, and He delivers them" (Psalm 34:7). The Angel of the LORD and all the angels of the LORD were camped around Jacob's tents that night. There were indeed two camps! Jacob could sleep in peace, for he was in a very safe place; he was in the very centre of the camp of God. "Be still! Know I am God, exalted o'er all men, exalted o'er all earth. The LORD of hosts with us! Our fortress strong is Jacob's God" (Psalm 46:10, 11).

The LORD in His great LOVE gave Jacob a glimpse of the unseen realms, where an army of angels surrounded him to protect him. When the angels of God vanished, Jacob must remember what his eyes had seen and believe what God had said, "I will be with you"—for very soon his faith would be tested. Soon Jacob would be tempted to disobey the LORD and not return to the Promised Land. His entry into that land would not be easy! The angels of heaven might rejoice at the sight of his return, but the hordes of hell would stand in his way. Satan would try to block his entry and stop God's promise. And the devil had human servants here on earth to do his will. One of them was Jacob's own brother, his twin brother, Esau.

As Jacob continued on his journey, he came closer and closer to the border of the land promised by God. Then the messengers he had sent to his brother Esau returned with very bad news: Esau was coming to meet Jacob, and he was coming with an army of four hundred men! Esau had not forgotten or forgiven anything that Jacob had done. After twenty years Esau still wanted to kill Jacob! Now he had gathered a whole army of men to attack and destroy Jacob. When Jacob heard this alarming news he was greatly afraid and distressed. What could he do? He could never wait long enough or run fast enough or flee far enough or fight hard enough to escape the anger and murder that raged in his brother's heart. At last he would be caught and killed. Twenty years ago when he left the land and ran for his life, only one man was after him. How much worse was the situation now! Four hundred men had joined the chase to murder Jacob and slaughter all the people with him. How could he escape?

The first thing Jacob did was to divide all his people and animals into two groups. He thought, "If Esau comes and attacks one group, the group that is left may escape." The next thing Jacob did was to pray. In his fear, he sought the LORD. He cried to God for help. "Save me!" he prayed, and God heard Jacob's prayer. Jacob said, "O God of my father Abraham, God of my father Isaac, O LORD, who said to me, 'Go back to your country and your relatives, and I will make you prosper,' I am unworthy of all the kindness and faithfulness you have shown your servant. I had only my staff when I crossed this Jordan River, but now I have become two groups. Save me, I pray, from the hand of my brother Esau, for I am afraid he will come and attack me, and also the mothers with their children. But You have said, 'I will surely make you prosper and will make your descendants like the sand of the sea, which cannot be counted.'" In his prayer, Jacob reminded himself and God that he was obeying the LORD's command to return to his country and his family. This journey, which now seemed so dangerous and perilous, was not something which Jacob had done on his own. In his prayer, Jacob remembered all God's "kindness and faithfulness" to him in the past. God had prospered him greatly, since he left the Promised Land, according to God's Word. In his prayer, Jacob also reminded himself and God of all the promises to him for the future. If Esau was allowed to kill him and his children, how could God's promise be fulfilled? This prayer must have been a great comfort to Jacob, because of all the things he recalled: God's command to return to this country, God's kindness and faithfulness to him in the past, and God's Word, which never fails. What God promises, He performs! What God says, He does! The Word of the LORD is sure, and Jacob could rest assured that he was safe. "May Your unfailing LOVE come to me, O LORD, Your salvation according to Your promise . . . Remember Your word to Your servant, for You have given me hope. My comfort in my suffering is this: *Your promise preserves my life*" (Psalm 119:41, 49, 50).

That night Jacob did not flee for his life. No, this time he stayed where he was, trusting God's Word that the LORD would be with him, obeying God's command to go forward into the Promised Land. That night Jacob did not turn around and run away; he prayed and he slept—and then he had another idea. That is often the way God works: He gives us a plan after we have prayed. The LORD accomplishes His purposes as we enact our plans. Waiting upon the LORD and trusting in God does not mean doing nothing. Jacob had a plan, through which he hoped that God would save him. What Jacob did, he did by faith, believing that God would deliver him.

This was Jacob's plan: Before he met his brother, he would send a series of gifts to him, with special gift tags that said: "To Esau, with love from Jacob!" The gifts would go before Jacob. What should he send his brother?

Jacob, who was a shepherd, would select the finest animals from his flocks and herds. These would be the gifts and his servants would be the tags, which spoke the message to his brother.

1. First he would send a flock of 220 speckled and spotted goats, (200 female goats and 20 male goats.) When Esau met them and he asked about them, a servant was instructed to give this message: "These animals belong to your servant Jacob. They are a gift sent to my lord Esau. And your servant Jacob is coming behind us."

2. After awhile a second gift would be sent to Esau—220 dark sheep (200 ewes and 20 rams). When Esau met them another servant would give the same message: "These animals belong to your servant Jacob. They are a gift sent to my lord Esau. And your servant Jacob is coming behind us."

3. Then, a little while later, a third gift would go out—30 female camels along with their young ones. Again the message would be repeated: "To my lord Esau, with love from your servant Jacob, who is following along behind us."

4. Some distance after them, Esau would be greeted by another gift—a small herd of cattle (40 cows and 10 bulls), with a servant bearing the same message: "These are a gift for my lord Esau from your servant Jacob, who is coming behind us."

5. A fifth and final gift would then be presented to Esau—30 donkeys (20 females and 10 males). Again Esau would hear those words: "These animals belong to your servant Jacob. They are a gift sent to my lord Esau. And your servant Jacob is coming."

Yes, Jacob was on the way home. He was not turning back; he was not running away. He was returning to his country and his family. By the grace of God, he would stand before his brother Esau . . . and then continue on his way. He was returning to the Promised Land! Would his plan work? Jacob hoped for peace; he hoped that his gifts would pacify Esau, so that when the two brothers finally met, Esau's anger would have melted away. Esau had spent twenty years hating Jacob. Would it now vanish in a day? Would a few animals be enough to buy peace? Jacob knew his brother. A pot of stew had been enough to buy the birthright, so these fine flocks and herds might be enough to buy him entry into the land of his promised inheritance. Jacob knew his brother—and he trusted his God. Jacob trusted the LORD to give him success. So Jacob sent off his gifts one after another, but he himself spent that night in the camp. What would happen the next day, whether he would live or die, was in the hands of the almighty and merciful God!

In the middle of the night, Jacob got up and moved his family. In the darkness he had his wives and children cross the Jabboc River. When they were safely across the stream, he then sent all his flocks and herds through the water to the other side. So Jacob was left all alone that night . . . to be with his God . . . and to face death. It was a very strange night, the strangest night in Jacob's whole life. In the darkness, while he was praying, Someone came to Jacob—and they began struggling with each other. This Man wrestled with Jacob all through the dark hours of night until daybreak . . . but Jacob, the Grasper, would not let go. When the Man saw that he could not overpower Jacob, he simply touched the socket of Jacob's hip—and it was wrenched out of place. A dislocated hip is a very painful thing, but still Jacob would not let go. He was "The Grasper"—and only death would make him loosen his grip. The Man said, "Let me go! Let me go, for it is daybreak!" But Jacob replied, "I will not let you go unless you bless me." All his life Jacob had grasped after blessings and somehow he knew that this Man, who had so mysteriously appeared, was able to bless him. It was the beginning of a new day, a day in which he would live or die. Jacob wanted a blessing for this day . . . and for the rest of his life. Jacob would not let the Man go, until he had blessed him! So the Man said, "What is your name?" "Jacob/Grasper," he answered. Then the Man said, "Your name will no longer be Jacob, but Israel, because you have struggled with God and with men—and have overcome." Israel means: "He wrestles or struggles with God." His name would no longer be Grasper, but Wrestler with God! Who was this who had changed Jacob's name? "Please tell me your name," said Jacob. But the Man would not reveal His name to Jacob. His only reply to Jacob was: "Why do you ask my name?" Although he wouldn't tell him his name, the Man did bless Jacob. And then he left.

But who was it? What manner of Man was he? Where did he come from? What was his name? How could he just touch Jacob—and dislocate his leg? If he had such power, could he just touch Jacob—and kill him? Who was he, that he could give Jacob a new name? Who was this person, that he was able to bless the one who already had God's blessing? After that night, Jacob understood who this Man was. He named that place Peniel, which means "Face of God" saying, "I saw God face to face, yet my life was spared." The Man who had come to him that night was the LORD!

The new day had dawned and Jacob had been blessed. The sun rose and shone upon him as he left that place . . . limping. It was painful for him to walk, but he had wrestled with God—and won! He had seen God face to face—and lived! Now he had to face his brother, but he was ready. God had prepared him for this day. He would face Esau as a new man. It would not be Jacob the Grasper, who confronted Esau; it would be Israel, the Wrestler-with-God, who faced his old enemy.

As Jacob looked over the land that morning, he could see Esau approaching with his army. After twenty years, the time of their meeting had arrived. Would his brother do what he had sworn to do? Would his brother kill him? Jacob did not really know what would happen. This day could end in a blood bath. Jacob was concerned for the safety of his wives and children, so he divided them into three groups. He put the maidservants and their children first; then came Leah and her children; Rachel and his youngest child, Joseph, he put in the safest place, right at the back. Then Jacob went ahead of them all, to face his brother alone. If Esau murdered him, perhaps his family would be spared.

As Jacob limped towards his brother, he bowed down to the ground seven times. It would have been so easy for Esau to kill Jacob. Jacob was alone, unarmed, and crippled. Jacob could not fight him or flee from him. He had no army coming behind him, only a group of mothers with their children. Jacob would have been an easy target. When Esau ran up to him, it would have been so simple to drive a spear or shoot an arrow through Jacob's heart, but Esau did not do that. Instead he ran up to Jacob—and hugged him! He threw his massive hairy arms around Jacob's neck, not to strangle him, but to hug him and kiss him. Then Esau—the warrior, the hunter, the murderer, the wild man who was so tough and strong—began to cry . . . and so did Jacob. The twin sons of Isaac just held each other and cried. They had not seen each other for twenty years. Esau had been filled with hate towards his brother all that time, and Jacob had been filled with fear. Now the two brothers stood hugging each other and weeping and loving each other. What had happened? Had something or someone changed Esau's heart? Yes, the LORD had worked some sort of miracle in Esau's heart. The same God who can touch a hip joint and wrench it out of place, can also reach inside a person's heart and turn it completely around. God may have used Jacob's gifts to change Esau's mind and turn his heart. God may have used Jacob himself, as he went limping and bowing towards his brother, to draw compassion out of Esau. How amazing it was that the man, who had been breathing hatred and plotting murder for twenty years, who had so recently assembled an army prepared to attack, suddenly stood before his enemy hugging him and kissing him, with tears streaming down his cheeks and love pouring from his heart. How was this possible? Nothing is impossible for the LORD! It was a wonderful work of God! It was an amazing answer to Jacob's prayer! "O LORD . . . save me, I pray, from the hand of my brother Esau . . ."

After awhile, Esau looked up and saw the women and children. "Who are these with you?" he asked and Jacob answered, "They are the children God has graciously given your servant." Then one after the other the groups came forward and bowed before Esau: first the maidservants and their children, then Leah and her children, and last of all came Rachel and little Joseph. They all bowed down humbly before Jacob's brother. Then Esau asked Jacob why he had sent all those droves of animals ahead of him. "To find favour in your eyes, my lord," was Jacob's humble and honest answer. Esau said it wasn't necessary for Jacob to give him those gifts. "I already have plenty, my brother. Keep what you have for yourself," said Esau. But Jacob insisted that Esau accept his gift. "Please!" said Jacob. "Please accept the present that was brought to you, for God has been gracious to me and I have all I need." Because Jacob insisted, Esau accepted the gifts. Then Esau offered to accompany Jacob. His army could protect Jacob on the way home, but Jacob didn't need Esau's army to protect him. He was already escorted and guarded by an invisible army of angels. What need had he of Esau's mere men? (Besides, it was Esau whom Jacob had feared.) Jacob declined Esau's offer. He explained that he moved very slowly because of the children and the animals. "Let my lord go on ahead of his servant . . ." said Jacob. He said he would visit him sometime later.

So Jacob and Esau parted with each other in peace. Jacob was free at last. He was no longer running and hiding for his life. His enemy, Esau, had vanished. The way to the Promised Land lay open before him. Jacob went to a place called Succoth, which means "Shelters," because there Jacob built some shelters for his livestock. Eventually he crossed the Jordan River and arrived safely in the land of Canaan. Jacob had returned home. He had returned to the Promised Land!

The teacher's guide for this lesson starts on page 522.

JACOB'S REFUGE

- Genesis 34, 35, 36; 49:5–7
- Psalm 46
- Hebrews 11:9, 10, 13–16

At last Jacob arrived safely back in Canaan. Many years earlier God had promised, "I will bring you back to this land"—and now Jacob had returned. He set up his tents near the city of Shechem in the land of Canaan. Jacob even bought land there. Although all of Canaan was promised to him by God, Jacob bought a small piece of property for one hundred pieces of silver. At last he owned a plot of ground, where he could pitch his tent and call his home in the Promised Land. On his property he built an altar to the LORD, just as his father and grandfather had done before him. Jacob named that place of worship El Elohe Israel, which means "God, the God of Israel." Jacob had not forgotten his new name, nor had he forgotten the God who had given it to him. The LORD was his God, the God of Israel!

Jacob bought that land near Shechem, because he wanted to settle there, perhaps for the rest of his life. He was tired of running and hiding. He wanted to live at peace there, shepherding his sheep and worshipping his God. He did not want to bother the people of Shechem, or be bothered by them—but alas, the city of

Shechem proved to be a place of terrible trouble for Jacob! There was no place on this earth where God's people could find peace and rest; they must wait for heaven. Shechem was not Jacob's city and the plot of land he bought there was not his home. Jacob would always be a stranger and a foreigner there. He would never be a citizen of that city or a subject of that king, for Jacob belonged to another kingdom and another King, that were not of this world. Although Jacob longed for peace and rest, his refuge was not his tent on his land near the city of Shechem. No, the only refuge Jacob had was his God.

This was the tragic story of what happened in Shechem:

Dinah, Jacob's only daughter, grew to be a beautiful young woman. One day, when she was visiting her girlfriends in Shechem, the king's son saw her and took her. This young man was the king's most honoured prince and he could have whatever he wanted. What he wanted was Dinah, Jacob's daughter! The prince's heart was drawn to Dinah. He loved her. He was delighted with her. So he said to his father, King Hamor, the king of Shechem, "Get me this girl as my wife." So King Hamor went to speak with Jacob and said, "My son has his heart set on your daughter. Please give her to him as his wife. Intermarry with us. Give us your daughters and take our daughters for yourselves. You can settle among us; the land is open to you. Live in it; trade in it; acquire property in it."

This offer came from the devil himself, though the king of Shechem spoke it. It was Satan's assault upon the people of God, designed to ensnare them and destroy them. It was a bomb, ignited by the fires of hell, to demolish God's kingdom on earth. Intermarry with the Canaanites? God forbid such a thing, though his daughter would be a princess among them and kings would come from her. No, it was better that his daughter be a shepherd girl in the tents of God's people, than be a queen in the palaces of the wicked. Intermarry with the Canaanites? Jacob had not done so; nor had his father Isaac; nor had his grandfather Abraham. Intermarry with the Canaanites? Become one people with them? Jacob could never approve such a thing! If they united in marriage, what would happen to God's promise? The people of God and the worship of God would vanish from the earth! If they became one people, what would happen to God's plan? There would not be a distinct people or a chosen race, if they were absorbed by the people around them. Intermarriage would result in the assimilation and annihilation of God's people! And it was a real temptation, for the Canaanite king said to Jacob, "The land is open to you." But had not Israel's

King said, "The land is promised to you"? Whose word would Jacob trust? One king was offering Jacob the land now, during his own lifetime, when he could enjoy the benefits of it. The other King, who was the LORD, promised Jacob the land hundreds of years later. He would never live to see the day when he would own the land. He would be a foreigner here and a wanderer for the rest of his life on earth. It was a real temptation, to enter into an agreement with this Canaanite king, for his daughter to become a queen and for himself to possess the land—but Jacob did not do it, did not even consider it. His trust was in the LORD. Jacob's hope was in God's Word in God's time. Jacob the Grasper would hold onto the promises of God and never let go. God's promises were the real treasure and Jacob would never trade them for anything else in the whole world.

Jacob knew he could not join with this Canaanite king, but what should he do? If he just said "no," would that mean war? Another complicating factor was this: The king's son had already taken Dinah and had already slept with her, although she was not his wife. It was a disgraceful thing that this prince of Shechem had done to a daughter of Israel—and Jacob's sons were furious. They were grieved and shamed at what had happened to their sister. She had been violated by this ruler of Shechem—and in their anger, they planned to take revenge. Their father may be wondering what to do, but they were already planning what to do. The prince came to them and said, "Let me find favour in your eyes, and I will give you whatever you ask. Make the price for the bride and the gift I am to bring as great as you like, and I'll pay whatever you ask me. Only give me the girl as my wife." The sons of Jacob answered deceitfully because their sister had been defiled; they said, "We can't do such a thing. We can't give our sister to a man who is uncircumcised. That would be a disgrace to us. We will give our consent to you on one condition only: that you become like us by circumcising all your males. Then we will give you our daughters and take your daughters for ourselves. Then we will settle among you and become one people with you. But, if you will not agree to be circumcised, we will take our sister and go." Jacob's sons had no intention of becoming "one people" with them, but the king and the prince of Shechem believed their words. The king and prince went to the men of their city and convinced them all that they should be circumcised. They suspected no harm; rather, they expected great wealth. They said, "These men are friendly toward us . . . Let them live in our land . . . We can marry their daughters and they can marry ours . . . Won't their livestock, their property and all their other animals become ours?" All they had to do was be circumcised! Then all the wealth of Israel would be theirs . . . including the beautiful daughters, like Dinah! So, all the men in the city of Shechem were circumcised—the king in his palace, the prince in his house, the soldiers on the wall, the elders by the gate, every male in the whole city!

Circumcision was a painful operation. Three days later, while the men of Shechem were still in bed recovering, two of Jacob's sons, Simeon and Levi, took their swords and attacked the unsuspecting city, killing every man there. They put to death the king and his son. Then they took their sister Dinah from the prince's house and left. Later the other sons of Jacob looted the city and seized all its wealth for themselves. Jacob was appalled at what his sons had done—and once again his life was in terrible danger. What would the Canaanites in the other cities do to him now? Jacob said to Simeon and Levi, "You have brought trouble on me!" They had made Jacob a stench to all the people living in that land. "We are few in number," said Jacob, "and if they join forces against me and attack me, I and my household will be destroyed." To his dying day Jacob would remember this dreadful deed that Levi and Simeon had done. His last words to them would be: "Levi and Simeon are brothers; their swords are weapons of violence. Let me not enter their counsel; let me not join their assembly, for they have killed men in their anger . . ." Jacob was not a man of war. He had never killed anyone. He was a gentle man, a quiet man. On his deathbed Jacob said of Levi and Simeon, "Cursed be their anger, so fierce, and their fury, so cruel" (Genesis 49:5–7)! Jacob had nothing to do with their murder in that city, but what should he do now? Where should he go? He was in a desperate situation. His whole family was in danger. Would he again have to leave the Promised Land, fleeing for his life?

God spoke to Jacob and told him what to do: "Go up to Bethel and settle there. Build an altar there to God, who appeared to you when you were fleeing from your brother Esau." What should he do? God said he should go back to the place where he had been blessed. What should he do in this danger and distress? He should go to Bethel, House of God, and worship the LORD! How could they worship God now? How could they go to such a holy and awesome place? His family was in total disgrace. Their hearts were far from God. His sons' hands and clothes were covered with the blood of the innocent people they had massacred. His daughter was defiled. His camp was filled with Shechem's idols, and all the other gold looted from that city. How could this family go to Bethel, House of God, and stand before the gates of heaven, before the angels and before the LORD, who is *holy, holy, holy*? But God said, "Go to Bethel . . . build an altar." So Jacob said to his family and all the people who were with him, "Get rid of the foreign gods you have with you, and purify yourselves and change your clothes. Then come, let us go up to Bethel, where I will build an altar to God, who answered me in the day of my distress and who has been with me wherever I have gone." This was another day of distress, but surely God would be with Jacob on this journey too.

So the people did as Jacob said. They purified themselves and removed from their tents all the foreign gods they had acquired. Jacob took the idols and buried them in the ground. That was where they belonged. The God of Truth and Life should be exalted, but gods that are false and dead should be dumped in a grave! Then Jacob and his people left Shechem; they left that city of death, disgrace, defilement — and they travelled to Bethel, House of God. On the way the LORD protected them. None of the Canaanites pursued them or attacked them, for the terror of God had fallen on the towns all around them.

At last Jacob returned to Bethel, the place where he had dreamed of the angels, the place where God had revealed Himself to him. Long ago, when Jacob had been fleeing from his brother, he took his stone pillow and set it upright as a pillar to mark the place — but now Jacob built a stone altar to worship God. He called that place El Bethel, the God of Bethel — a name to honour and remember the LORD.

Then God appeared to Jacob again and blessed him. God said to him, "Your name is Jacob, but you will no longer be called Jacob; your name will be Israel." God also repeated the promise to him, the same promise that He had given Jacob many years earlier at Bethel, the promise of the nation that would come from him. The LORD said:

> *I am El Shaddai, God Almighty.*
> *Be fruitful and increase in numbers.*
> *A nation and a multitude of nations will come from you,*
>   *and kings will come from your body.*
> *The land I gave to Abraham and Isaac,*
>   *I also give to you,*
> *and I will give this land to your descendants after you.*

> *Genesis 35:11, 12*

One day a nation would come from Jacob, a nation that would be called by his own name—Israel. The land would be called Israel; the people would be called Israelites; and there would be a long line of kings who ruled in Israel. God promised it would all come to pass. Thus Jacob need not fear. He must not fear the Canaanites. They and their kings would vanish from the earth, but from Jacob there would be a King to rule in Israel forever and ever. From Jacob would come the great King of all the earth, the King of kings and the Lord of lords, before whom every knee would bow. From the ends of the earth kings would come, asking, "Where is the one who has been born King of the Jews?" All nations would come to Israel because of the glory of the LORD and the splendour of her King. "Oh shout for joy before the LORD, the King . . . because He comes; He surely comes" (Psalm 98:6, 9). How encouraged Jacob must have been to hear God's promise again!

When the LORD finished speaking to Jacob at Bethel, He went up from him at the place where He had talked with him. Jacob must not forget. Even in the midst of difficulties, he must never forget the goodness and the greatness of God's promises. As a reminder, Jacob set up another stone pillar at the place where God had spoken to him. He must remember the Word of the LORD. Jacob poured out a drink offering on the stone. He also anointed it with oil. It was no longer an ordinary stone. It was a memorial of God's visit to Jacob. Again Jacob named that place Bethel, House of God.

Then Jacob . . . or rather, Israel . . . moved on from Bethel. God's Word would strengthen him and comfort him on this journey, which would be filled with grief and pain. On the way to Bethlehem, Rachel, who was pregnant, went into labour, but something was wrong. It was a very difficult birth. The midwife said to Rachel, "Don't be afraid, for you have another son." But Rachel was dying. With her last breath she named her son Ben-Oni, which means "Son Of My Sorrow." But Jacob changed his name to Ben-Jamin, which means "Son Of My Right Hand." Poor baby Benjamin had no mother and Jacob had lost his wife, his beautiful and beloved Rachel. Her body was buried in a tomb along the road to Bethlehem. Jacob set up another pillar, this one to mark the place where Rachel's body was buried. (Many hundreds of years later, a wicked king in Israel would slaughter all the baby boys around Bethlehem and it was said, "A voice is heard in Ramah, weeping and great mourning, Rachel weeping for her children and refusing to be comforted, because they are no more"— because Rachel's grave was in that area near Bethlehem.) But on the day she died, there was weeping and great mourning for her, as her family wept and refused to be comforted, because she was no more.

Jacob . . . Israel . . . continued on his journey, not alone, but without the woman he loved. He pitched his tents in a new region, but while he was there, he faced more trouble. Reuben, his oldest son, his firstborn son, who excelled in honour and power, who was the first sign of Israel's strength, who was the first shining star from Jacob—this same Reuben committed a terrible sin, which would not even be mentioned among the pagans. Reuben slept with his father's wife. How could such a thing happen in Israel? How could such a sin be found in the hearts and the tents of God's people? Jacob was grieved again, as sorrow upon sorrow assaulted his life. Were these the sons who would become the great nation promised by God? Would they really become that holy nation, from whom would come the Messiah and through whom all peoples on earth would be blessed? Was it possible? Yes, with God alone all things are possible, but this hideous sin was surely a test of faith for Jacob. He never recovered from this blow. He remembered what Reuben had done for the rest of his life. On his deathbed his last words to Reuben were: "You will no longer excel, for you went up onto your father's bed . . . and defiled it" (Genesis 49:4).

Jacob continued on his journey and at last returned to his father's home. Isaac was a very old man. He never saw Jacob's twelve sons, for he had been blind for many years. Isaac did not see his children's children, but he met them. Perhaps he touched each one of them, before he breathed his last. Isaac had lived 180 years when he died and was gathered to his people. He was an old man, full of years and full of faith. He died believing in God's promises, but never receiving them. Isaac saw the things promised only from a distance, but he rejoiced in them and believed in them. All his life he lived by faith in the Promised Land, living in tents and making his home like a stranger in a foreign country. He never owned any land in Canaan, although the whole country was promised to him by God. Isaac lived and died longing for a better country—a heavenly one. Therefore God was not ashamed to be called his God, the God of Isaac! The LORD Himself had a home prepared for him in heaven, but on earth, his body must be buried. Isaac's body was placed in the tomb beside his father and mother, Abraham and Sarah, and beside his wife Rebekah, in the cave in the field which Abraham had bought so long ago. Isaac's only children, his twin sons, Jacob and Esau,[1] buried him.

Jacob's life was filled with sorrow. He faced sin and death again and again, for that is what is in this world, but God was with Jacob through it all. Jacob's life was blessed, not because it was peace and bliss; Jacob's life was blessed because he had God. Oh happy are the people, who can say they have the LORD to be their God! Yes, "blessed are the people whose God is the LORD" (Psalm 144:15). Through all the difficulties, even through sin and death, God was guarding Jacob and guiding him. In this life of sorrow, Jacob's refuge was Jacob's God.

Notes

1. After Isaac's burial, we never hear of Esau again, but we do hear of his descendants, the Edomites. Very quickly they gained and owned the land of their inheritance. Mighty kings and great rulers came from Esau. How discouraging it must have been for the sons of Jacob. Was it not their father, Jacob, who had received the blessing? But for hundreds of years the children of Israel possessed no land of their own. While the Edomites were kings, the Israelites were slaves! In spite of appearances, did they trust God's Word? No, they had all but forgotten it. But God is faithful. His Word is true. "The LORD is not slow in keeping His promise . . . for with the LORD . . . a thousand years are like a day" (II Peter 3:8, 9). According to God's plan, at the right time and in the right way, God fulfilled all His promises to the descendants of Abraham, Isaac and Jacob. How God kept His Word is the story of the rest of the Bible! "For no matter how many promises God has made, they are YES in Christ! And so through Him the AMEN is spoken by us—to the glory of God" (II Corinthians 1:20).

The teacher's guide for this lesson starts on page 524.

JOSEPH LOVED AND HATED

- **Genesis 37; 49:5–7**
- **Psalm 88**
- **Romans 8:28–39**

Jacob and his twelve sons continued to live in the land of Canaan, the land promised by God, but they were not one big happy family. Why? There was a set of twin sins in Jacob's family, which continually caused trouble and sorrow. These twins were named Envy and Hatred, and they were sins which lived comfortably in the hearts of at least nine of Jacob's sons. With the possible exception of the oldest son Reuben and the youngest son Benjamin, all the other sons of Jacob envied and hated their brother Joseph, their own little brother Joseph.

Three main things provoked their envy and hatred:

1) Like most little brothers, Joseph was a "tattle-tale." When the older boys did something wrong, Joseph would tell their father. Even after they were full-grown men this happened. Once, when Joseph was a young man of seventeen, he was tending the family's flocks with his brothers. Although they were adults, the brothers were not doing what was right—so Joseph brought a bad report about them to their father. The sons of Jacob were not upset about their bad behaviour; no, they were upset about Joseph

exposing them. Thus they envied and hated Joseph, because he was righteous, because he found favour in the eyes of their father.

2) Because Israel loved Joseph more than any of his other sons, he made
him a special robe. It was a many coloured, richly ornamented, finely em-
broidered robe—a gift of love. Joseph must have looked like a prince in his
royal robe, as he stood among the other shepherds in their plain clothes. How
proud and pleased Joseph must have been about that coat. When he was
sitting all alone in the fields watching the flocks, sadly remembering his
mother who had died or his brothers who were mean, Joseph must have
looked at his coat-of-many-colours, so bright and beautiful in the sunlight . . .
and he must have smiled. That coat made Joseph happy because it reminded
him how much his father loved him. However, it reminded his brothers of
the same thing. Whenever they saw that coat, (which was whenever they
saw Joseph,) they saw that their father loved him more than any of them—
and they felt jealous and angry! They didn't smile when they saw Joseph's
special robe; they frowned and said cruel things to him. Soon the brothers
could not give a nice look or speak a kind word to him at all. Every time
they saw that coat, envy and hatred grew in their hearts, spilling out in drips
and in drops, with a nasty word here and an angry look there. A worse time
was coming. One day those sins of the heart would pour out in a great flood
of wickedness. One day the twin sins, Envy and Hatred, would be restrained
no longer. One day the brothers, controlled by those sins, would commit a
terrible crime.

3) The sons of Jacob also despised Joseph because of his dreams. Yes,
even his dreams stirred up their envy and hatred! One time Joseph said to
his brothers, "Listen to this dream I had: We were binding sheaves of grain
out in the field when suddenly my sheaf stood upright, while your sheaves
gathered around mine and bowed down to it." What did this dream mean?
Joseph's brothers knew exactly what it meant. They said, "Do you intend to
reign over us? Will you actually rule us?" And they hated him all the more
because of his dream and what he had said. Another time Joseph told his
brothers, "Listen; I had another dream, and this time the sun and moon and
eleven stars were bowing down to me." What was the meaning of this dream?
Who was the sun? Who was the moon? Who were the eleven stars? When
Joseph told his father, Jacob understood its meaning and rebuked his son.
Jacob said, "What is this dream you had? Will your mother and I and your
brothers actually come and bow down to the ground before you?" Who did

Joseph think he was? He may have been robed like a king in his coat-of-many-colours, but he was just a shepherd boy, who must serve his father and his older brothers. However, Jacob kept this matter in his mind. He wondered about Joseph's dreams. Were they more than just dreams? Were they from God? Would they ever come true, sometime in the future? In the meantime, Joseph's brothers were even more jealous of him. The little prince in his fine clothes now had grand dreams of being a king—with their whole family bowing down to him! Who did he think he was? So they envied him and hated him all the more because of these dreams.

Here is the story of how the jealous brothers of Joseph tried to make sure his dreams never came true:

One day Israel called his son Joseph to him and said, "As you know your brothers are grazing the flocks near Shechem. Come, I am going to send you to them. Go and see if all is well with your brothers and with the flocks, and bring word back to me." Israel was concerned about them, that they were safe from harm and sin. Shechem was a dangerous place for his sons to be. Do you remember what happened at Shechem? That was the town where the sons of Jacob murdered every man and plundered everything. Yes, Jacob was concerned about his sons. ("Cursed be their anger, so fierce, and their fury, so cruel!" Genesis 49:7) What were they doing now? Israel did not trust them. Joseph, he knew, would tell him the truth. Joseph would bring an accurate report about his brothers, whether good or bad. It was a long way from Hebron to Shechem, but Israel trusted his son Joseph and Israel trusted God.

So Joseph began his long journey north to Shechem, but when he arrived there he could not find his brothers. He searched the hills all around the city, but there was no trace of them. A man found him wandering around in the fields there looking for his brothers. Joseph asked the man, "Can you tell me where they are grazing their flocks?" The man knew. They had gone even farther north to a place called Dothan. So Joseph faithfully continued his journey in search of his brothers, as his father had asked him to do. At last he saw them and their flocks in the distance. Joseph must have been happy to see that all was well. However, his brothers also saw him in the distance—and they were not happy to see him. Here was Joseph, coming to bring another bad report to their father. Here was Joseph, coming to show them his coat-of-many-colours. Here was Joseph, coming to tell them his latest dreams of grandeur. Even from a distance they knew it was Joseph, for his rich robe with its bright colours shone in the sunlight. That coat was like a red flag waving in front of a herd of angry bulls, who were ready to rip him to pieces. "Cursed be their anger, so fierce, and their fury, so cruel!" Before poor Joseph had even reached them, they had plotted to kill him. "Here comes that dreamer!" they said to each other. "Come now, let's kill him and throw his body into one of these old wells. We can say that a ferocious animal devoured him. Then we'll see what comes of his dreams!" They must have laughed to think of themselves bowing down to Joseph now, for soon he would be lying dead at the bottom of a deep dark hole. The blood of many innocent men was already on their hands; one more murder would not matter. They had no kind thought toward their younger brother. They envied Joseph! They hated Joseph! And they plotted his death with pleasure!

However, Reuben, the firstborn son of Jacob, the oldest of the brothers, was horrified at the bloody plans and wicked plots of the others. Reuben tried to rescue Joseph from their cruel hands. He said, "Let's not take his life. Don't shed any blood. Throw him into this old well here in the desert, but don't lay a hand on him." He would die anyway after a few days—and that was what they wanted. So the brothers listened to Reuben. When Joseph arrived they did not kill him. They did not shed his blood with their knives and swords, their "weapons of violence." However, they did grab him and they tore off his rich robe, that beautiful coat-of-many-colours, which they envied and hated so much. Then they threw Joseph into a deep dark pit, an old dry well, where he wouldn't drown, but where he would slowly die of thirst in the desert. Joseph cried and pleaded with his brothers to spare his life, but his brothers ignored him. They just laughed and sat down to eat their meal. They would never set Joseph free. He could starve down there. He could rot down there. That old well would become his grave. His bones would lie there forgotten in the dirt. Why should they let him go? Should they set him free, so he could bring another bad report about them to their father? Should they set him free, so he could parade around them like a prince in his royal robe? Should they set him free, so he could dream his nasty dreams about them bowing down to him? Never! They would never have to deal with Joseph again. He would die in a hole in the desert—and no one would ever know about it.

That was what the brothers planned to do. Reuben, the oldest brother, had his own plan. Reuben planned to rescue Joseph later, when the other brothers had left, and take Joseph back to their father. But God had other plans—and it is what God plans to do that comes to pass! "Many are the plans in men's hearts, but it is the LORD's purpose that prevails" (Proverbs 19:21). Joseph was not going to die in the desert; nor was he going to go home to his father. No, God had other plans. God wanted Joseph to go on a long journey. He wanted Joseph to leave the Promised Land, the land of Canaan, and go to Egypt. The LORD also had His own strange way of getting Joseph there. God had a great plan for Joseph's life; He was sending him on an important mission. One of the world's most incredible stories was unfolding, and Joseph had the leading role in it. It was a story that would encourage the saints and glorify God forever! What God had planned was for the good of His people. "We know that in all things God works for the good of those who love Him, who have been called according to His purpose" (Romans 8:28). Yes, we know that God causes all things to work together for the good of His people, but did Joseph know this?

When Joseph lay bruised at the bottom of that deep dark pit, pleading for his life, did he know that God was causing everything, even this, to work for good—for his good, for his family's good, and for the whole world's good? When he cried out to God for help, to deliver him from this dreadful pit, he did not know what would happen to him or if God would rescue him. God alone knew the story of his life from beginning to end. How long was Joseph crying and pleading and praying in that awful pit? Perhaps many long dark hours passed. Then suddenly his brothers were lowering a rope into the well and pulling him out. God had answered his prayers! His life had been spared! Yes, but when Joseph stood in the sunlight again, it was not as a free man. No, his hands were tied and he was sold as a slave and he was led away, far away to a strange land.

That was how God, the God of LOVE, rescued Joseph from the pit. That was exactly what God had planned for Joseph's life. When his brothers sat down to eat their meal, at that precise time God caused a camel caravan to approach them in the distance. When they looked up and saw it coming, Judah had an idea for making some money. He said to the others, "What will we gain if we kill our brother and cover up his blood? Come, let's sell him to these Ishmaelites and not lay our hands on him; afterall, he is our brother, our own flesh and blood." The brothers all agreed to this plan. They sold Joseph to these merchants for twenty pieces of silver. For two pieces of silver each, they sold their own brother as a slave. What a wicked deed they had done. With their own hands they took the money. With their own eyes they watched their little brother being led away as a prisoner to Egypt. With their own ears they heard him pleading and crying to them for mercy. But his brothers were filled with envy and hatred—and they wanted Joseph to be gone forever.

Reuben, the oldest brother, was not there when all this happened. He returned later, after his brothers had left, and planned to rescue Joseph from the pit; he planned to return Joseph safely to his father—but Joseph was gone; the old well was empty and silent. Reuben was so upset that he tore his clothes. Hadn't he told his brothers not to sin against the boy, but what could he do now? What could he tell their father? Reuben spoke to his brothers and together they decided what to do. First they killed a goat, not to atone for their sin, but to conceal their sin. Next they took their little brother's richly ornamented robe, his beautiful coat-of-many-colours that their father had made for him, and they dipped it in the goat's blood. Then they went back to their father, handed him the robe covered with blood, and said, "We found this. Examine it to see whether it is your son's robe." They let their father draw his own dreadful conclusions.

Jacob recognized the coat at once. He cried out, "It is my son's robe! Some ferocious animal has devoured him! Joseph has surely been torn to pieces!" Then Jacob wept, for he loved Joseph so much. Jacob's heart was broken. He tore his clothes, put on sackcloth and mourned for many days. Jacob's other sons and daughters came to comfort him, but he refused to be comforted. Joseph was the son he loved and he would grieve for him the rest of his life. He would never be happy again. His other children could not comfort him. "No," he said, "I will go down to my grave, mourning for my son." He would weep for the rest of his life. He would be buried with tears on his face, tears for his dead son Joseph.

Thus Joseph was loved and hated. He was envied and hated by his brothers, but he was honoured and loved by his father. His earthly father loved him more than anything or anyone in the whole world. His heavenly Father loved him perfectly. God is LOVE—and through this family tragedy God would bring great blessing to his people and to the whole world. One day the tears of pain would become tears of joy and the sound of sorrow would become the sound of laughter. It was all part of God's great plan. What man meant for evil, God meant for good. One day, many many years later, Joseph himself would say to his brothers, "It was not you who sent me here, but God! It was to save lives that God sent me . . . God sent me to save your lives by a great deliverance" (Genesis 45:5, 7,8).

The teacher's guide for this lesson starts on page 526.

THE LORD WAS WITH JOSEPH

- Genesis 39
- Psalm 105:16–22
- Proverbs 5;
  6:20–7:27; 23:26–28
- Ecclesiastes 7:26
- Romans 8:28–39
- I Peter 1:3–9;
  4:12–19

Joseph was filled with sorrow as he was led away to be sold as a slave in the land of Egypt. Joseph had lost everything in this world — his family, his home, his country, his work, his freedom, and even the beautiful coat that his father had made for him. Never again would that coat comfort him; it was gone . . . and so was every other good thing in his life. He had been like an honoured prince in his father's house, but now he was a slave among strangers, despised by all. His brothers had robbed him of everything, hadn't they? No! He still had his life and he still had his faith! In the loneliness of those sorrowful nights, Joseph was no longer warmed by his father's rich robe, but his eyes could still see the beauty of the moon shining on the desert sands. He was still alive! And he could still believe in God! He could trust that God was with him and that God loved him — even now, in this terrible situation. Could any trouble or danger ever separate him from the LOVE of God? Was there any person or power in all creation that could separate him from the LOVE of God? No! His brothers could separate him from everyone else, but they could not separate him from God! The Bible records: *"The LORD was with Joseph.*" The grace of God and the LOVE of the LORD, which were more precious even than life, could never be stolen from him.

> *O God . . . because Your LOVE is better than life,*
>> *my lips will glorify You.*
> *I will praise You as long as I live . . .*
>> *with singing lips my mouth will praise You.*
> *On my bed I remember You;*
>> *I think of You through the watches of the night.*
> *Because You are my help,*
>> *I sing in the shadow of Your wings.*
> *My soul clings to You;*
>> *Your right hand upholds me.*

> *Psalm 63:3–8*

Joseph was brought to a land far away from his family, the land of Egypt. Everything in this land was foreign to Joseph—the way the people looked and lived, the way they talked. The Egyptians spoke a foreign language, which Joseph did not understand. He would have to learn their language quickly, if he was going to survive in this country. Egypt was also a strange land in that it worshipped strange gods. It was a land filled with false gods and idol worship. People bowed down to all kinds of images. Joseph must not learn these things. He must never bow down to another god. He must never forget his god, the god of his fathers, the God of Abraham, Isaac and Jacob. He must always remember the LORD. Joseph would live in this land, the land of Egypt, for the rest of his life. As time passed, he would forget all his trouble and sorrow; in time he even would forget all his father's household (Genesis 41:51), but Joseph would never forget the LORD—and the LORD would never forget Joseph. Again and again we read in the account of Joseph's life: *"The LORD was with Joseph"* and the LORD blessed Joseph.

When Joseph arrived in Egypt, probably the first place he was taken was to a big slave market in the capital city, where he would be sold like an animal for money. The slave market would have been a frightening place. There would have been crowds of people, all pushing and shouting, with chains rattling, whips cracking and slaves screaming. What would happen to Joseph here? Who would buy him? A slave could be bought by a very cruel man, who would abuse him and torture him in many ways. Where would Joseph find himself at the end of the day? Who would be his master? As it turned out, (according to the plan of the Sovereign God,) a rich Egyptian named Potiphar bought Joseph. He was a very important man in Egypt. Potiphar was one of Pharaoh's own officials, no less than the captain of the king's guard. Thus Joseph, the shepherd boy who had lived all his life in tents, eventually found himself living and working in a luxurious Egyptian house. As a slave, he could have found himself forced to do the hard outside labour, such as ploughing fields or digging ditches or building pyramids, but the LORD was with Joseph and He placed him right in the house of his Egyptian master. Joseph not only survived there; the LORD prospered him there. Every task Joseph was assigned to do, he did exceedingly well. Even his master saw that God was with him and that God gave him success in everything he did. Potiphar took notice of Joseph. Soon he made Joseph his personal attendant. Then he put Joseph in charge of his entire household, entrusting to his care everything he owned. From the moment that Joseph was put in charge, the LORD's blessing was on Potiphar's home and on everything else he had. Potiphar could not help but see that he was prospering because of Joseph. The LORD's blessing was on everything in his house and in his fields because of Joseph. Potiphar was not a good man, who feared God. No, he and his wife were wicked people. Their home was filled with idols; their hearts and lives were filled with sin. But God's blessing rested on their home because of the one good man within it, because of the faithful slave who managed it—Joseph.

With Joseph in charge, Potiphar no longer concerned himself with anything, except the food he ate. Yes, eating was his only concern now. Perhaps Potiphar was becoming a fat old man. Joseph, however, was a very handsome young man with a well-built body, lean and strong. Now it was not only his master who took notice of Joseph. The mistress of the house also noticed him. Potiphar's wife noticed how attractive this Hebrew slave was, who lived and worked in her house. One time, when her husband was gone, Potiphar's wife commanded her slave to do a very wicked thing. "Come to bed with me!" she said. She wanted to commit adultery with Joseph. But Joseph was a righteous man. He refused. He said, "With me in charge, my master does not concern himself with anything in the house; everything he owns he has entrusted to my care. No one is greater in this house than I am. My master has withheld nothing from me—except you, because you are his wife. How then could I do such a wicked thing and sin against God?" How righteous was Joseph's response! He remained loyal to his master, who had been good to him, and he remained loyal to his God, who had blessed him. He also remained loyal to his mistress. The words he spoke to her were good words,

words that would bless her life. Although he refused her desire, he spoke to this woman about her sin and about his God. He opened the door for Potiphar's wife, not to her bedroom to join her in sin, but he opened the door to repentance, to faith in God, to forgiveness for sin, to everlasting life. This could have been the beginning of a new life for Potiphar's wife. From Joseph she could have learned about the one true God. Instead of longing to embrace Joseph's body, she could have longed to embrace Joseph's faith and Joseph's God.

But Potiphar's wife did not listen to Joseph. She did not take to heart Joseph's wise words or his righteous rebuke. She was not interested in knowing God or being good. Potiphar's wife was interested in getting what she wanted, which was Joseph in bed with her. Day after day she enticed Joseph to sin. She must have been a very beautiful woman and the words she spoke to him must have been smooth and sweet. The Bible says, "The lips of an adulteress drip honey and her speech is smoother than oil" (Proverbs 5:3). Joseph had to be extremely careful, lest he be caught and trapped by her alluring looks and charming words. The temptation was real. The Evil One wanted to destroy Joseph and had chosen an extremely tempting woman to entice him to sin—and to death. Although Joseph was now in a foreign land, he must not forget or forsake the commands of his father or the teaching of his mother from long ago and far away. No, he must bind them on his heart forever, to guide him when he walked and to guard him when he slept. Joseph must be careful to listen to the Law of God, speaking softly to him in his heart: "You shall not commit adultery." That still small voice in his heart must speak louder than the sweet smooth voice of this attractive woman with her seductive words. Yes, Joseph must be careful to obey the command of God and not the demand of sin. What does the Bible say? "My son . . . these commands . . . are the way to life, keeping you from the immoral woman . . . Do not lust in your heart after her beauty or let her captivate you with her eyes, for . . . the adulteress preys upon your very life . . . Do not let your heart turn to her ways or stray into her paths. Many are the victims she has brought down; her slain are a mighty throng. Her house is a highway to the grave, leading down to the chambers of death" (Proverbs 6:20–7:27). But this house was where Joseph must work. He was a slave; he had no choice. Day after day he must face this temptation. How could he escape? He had said "no" to his beautiful mistress once, but could he say it again and again and again? In a moment of weakness, might he yield to the temptation? Yes, Joseph feared that he might not continue to stand. After refusing to go to bed with her many times, Joseph finally began to avoid her entirely. He refused to even be with her, lest he fall into sin.

However, he still had to go into her house to attend to his duties. He was a slave—and he must do his work. One day Joseph found himself alone in the house with his mistress. (Perhaps she had planned it that way.) She caught Joseph by his cloak and said, "Come to bed with me!" But Joseph escaped. He slipped out of his cloak and left it in her hand, while he ran out of the house. Now Potiphar's wife was furious. Joseph had ignored her and insulted her, refused her and rejected her, one too many times. She would now force Joseph to yield to her, if not to the power of her love, then to the power of her hate. He would soon see what she could do to him. She would soon make Joseph wish he had feared her more than his God.

Potiphar's wife kept Joseph's cloak. First she lied to the other servants about Joseph. Then she repeated the story to her husband when he came home, saying, "That Hebrew slave you brought us came to mock me. He came in here to sleep with me, but I screamed. As soon as I screamed for help, he left his cloak beside me and ran out of the house." She showed her husband Joseph's cloak to prove that her story was true. Potiphar believed his wife. When he heard how his slave had treated his beautiful wife, he burned with anger. Joseph's master, the captain of the king's guard, took Joseph and threw him in prison, the place where the king's own prisoners were locked away, the place where innocent men were often beheaded.

But *the* LORD *was with Joseph* even in prison. This too was part of God's plan and part of God's LOVE. This was the way the LORD rescued Joseph from a much worse pit than the one in which his brothers had thrown him. The Bible says that an adulterous woman is "a deep pit " (Proverbs 23:26) and "her house is a highway to the grave, leading down to the chambers of death." Praise God! Joseph had escaped with his life! Joseph had escaped from a woman, who was "a trap more bitter than death" (Ecclesiastes 7:26). The Bible says that the adulterous woman "multiplies the unfaithful among men" (Proverbs 23:28). Praise God! Joseph had escaped with his faith! It was unjust that Joseph had been thrown into prison, but God was with Joseph there and God had great plans for him there. Joseph must not despair. These many trials had come upon him to test his faith and to prove his faith, which would result in the goal of his faith—the salvation of his soul. Joseph was suffering, but he was blessed, for the Spirit of glory and of God rested upon him.

The teacher's guide for this lesson starts on page 528.

DREAMS COME TRUE

- **Genesis 39:20–40:23**
- **Psalm 105:16–22;**
  146
- **Lamentations 3**
- **Daniel 2:27, 28**

J oseph was thrown into prison, although he had done nothing wrong. Now his life was worse than that of a slave. A slave at least could see the light of day, but Joseph was a prisoner in a dark dungeon. A slave at least was free to walk and work, but Joseph's neck was clamped in an iron ring and his feet were shackled in chains. His body was bruised and broken. He sat in the ash heap, in the dust of death; he slept with his face in the dirt, stained with his own blood. Like the weeping prophet, Joseph must have thought: "I am a man who has seen affliction . . . God has driven me away and made me walk in darkness . . . God has besieged me and surrounded me with bitterness and hardship. He has made me dwell in darkness, like those long dead. He has walled me in so I cannot escape; He has weighed me down with chains . . . He has trampled me in the dust. I have been deprived of peace; I have forgotten what prosperity is, so that I say, 'My splendour is gone and all that I had hoped from the LORD.' I remember my affliction and my wandering, the bitterness and the gall. I well remember them, and my soul is downcast within me" (Lamentations 3).

Poor Joseph! How far away his homeland was, where once he had walked as a free man among the lush green pastures of God's promises. How long ago that time of happiness was, when he had been clothed in the rich robe of his father's love and had dreamed of being a prince among his people. Yes, all that Joseph had hoped from the LORD was gone. He was a prisoner, dying in the filth and gloom of a dungeon, forgotten in a foreign land. Was there any help for Joseph? Was there any hope for him? Yes, Joseph must trust God, even here in this terrible place. Joseph must speak to himself in his despair. He must call to his mind the reason he still had hope: God! Joseph must remind himself that God's LOVE never fails! Joseph must believe in the LOVE of his LORD, even in this place, especially in this place. He must remember: "Because of the LORD's great LOVE we are not consumed, for his compassions never fail. They are new every morning. Great is God's faithfulness!" (Lamentations 3:22, 23). Although Joseph had lost everything, he must say to himself: "The LORD is my portion; therefore I will wait for Him. The LORD is good to those whose hope is in Him, to the one who seeks Him; it is good to wait quietly for the salvation of the LORD." How should Joseph wait quietly for the LORD's deliverance? How should he behave in this dreadful dungeon? Let him bear patiently his affliction, knowing that ultimately it was for his good and God's glory. "Let him sit alone in silence, for the LORD has laid it on him. Let him bury his face in the dust, for there may yet be hope. Let him offer his cheek to the one who would strike him, and let him be filled with disgrace," knowing that it was only for a season, for the time appointed by God because "men are not cast off by the LORD forever. Though He brings grief, He will show compassion, so great is His unfailing LOVE. For God does not willingly bring affliction or grief to the children of men." Did God not know what had happened to Joseph, how he was falsely accused and how he was unfairly treated? "To crush underfoot all prisoners in the land, to deny a man his rights before the Most High, to deprive a man of justice—would not the LORD see such things?" Yes! Joseph could make his appeal for justice and release to God, all the while knowing that it was part of God's plan for him to be here in prison. "Who can speak and have it happen, if the LORD has not decreed it? Is it not from the mouth of the Most High that both calamities and good things come?" It was God's will that he should be in this place. Knowing this, Joseph must not lose heart or give up hope. He must speak to himself, exhort himself to trust in the LORD and His unfailing LOVE. He must also speak to God and cry out to him in his distress. Like the weeping prophet he must say: "I called on your name, O LORD, from the depths of the pit. You heard my plea . . . You came near when I called You and You said: 'Do not fear.' O LORD, You took up my case; You redeemed my life. You have seen, O LORD, the wrong done to me. Uphold my cause!" (Lamentations 3:1, 2,5–7, 16–38, 55–59).

The LORD knew that Joseph was innocent of any wrong. He did take up Joseph's case; He did uphold his cause. While Joseph was there in prison, the LORD was with him. God not only protected him in that dangerous place; God also prospered him there. The LORD showed Joseph kindness and granted him favour in the eyes of the warden. Perhaps the warden had noticed something in the eyes of Joseph — hope, (instead of fear) and courage, (instead of despair). Perhaps the warden had noticed that even in that dark dungeon, there was a light which shone from Joseph, a light of holiness and righteousness. The warden noticed that this Hebrew slave was not like the other prisoners. Soon the warden began to trust Joseph. He put him in charge of all the other prisoners and made him responsible for everything that was done in the prison. Finally, the warden trusted Joseph entirely and paid no attention to anything under his care, because the LORD was with Joseph and gave him success in whatever he did!

Some time later two very important officials of the king of Egypt were thrown into prison. One was Pharaoh's chief cup-bearer, the man who served the king his wine. The other was Pharaoh's chief baker, the man who served him his bread. The king's welfare depended upon the faithful service of both these men. Not only must Pharaoh's food and drink be good; it must be safe. The king's cup-bearer and baker must ensure that what came to their master was delicious — and not poisonous! But somehow these men had offended their master. Perhaps there had been a plot against Pharaoh's life. Perhaps it was nothing more than a fly in his cup or an ant in his bread. Whatever it was, the king was very angry with them and had them thrown into the same prison where Joseph was confined. The captain of the guard, Potiphar, assigned them to the care of his slave, Joseph. Thus it happened that Joseph, as he daily attended them, came to know well these two important officials of Pharaoh's court.

One night, after they had been in prison for some time, these two men each had a dream — and each dream had a meaning of its own. When they awoke, they remembered their dreams and they were troubled by them, but they didn't know their meaning. In the morning, when Joseph came to the cup-bearer and baker, he saw that they were dejected, so he asked them, "Why are your faces so sad today?" "We both had dreams," they answered, "but there is no one to interpret them." In the king's court there had been all sorts of wise men—sorcerers, diviners and magicians—who could interpret dreams, but here in the prison, who could tell them the meaning of their dreams? Joseph knew that it is "God in heaven who reveals mysteries" (Daniel 2:28), so he said, "Do not interpretations belong to God? Tell me your dreams."

The chief cup-bearer spoke. He trusted Joseph with his dream and said to him: "In my dream I saw a vine in front of me, and on the vine were three branches. As soon as it budded, it blossomed, and its clusters ripened into grapes. Pharaoh's cup was in my hand, and I took the grapes, squeezed them into Pharaoh's cup and put the cup in his hand." The LORD revealed to Joseph what the dream meant and what He was going to do. "This is what it means," Joseph said to him: "The three branches are three days. Within three days Pharaoh will lift up your head and restore you to your position, and you will put Pharaoh's cup in his hand, just as you used to do when you were his cup-bearer."

Joseph knew that this dream would come true, that God would surely cause it to happen, so he said something else to the cup-bearer. Joseph said, "Please, when all goes well with you, remember me and show me kindness; mention me to Pharaoh and get me out of this prison. For I was forcibly carried off from the land of the Hebrews, and even here I have done nothing to deserve being put in a dungeon." When the cup-bearer stood beside Pharaoh again, (as Joseph knew he would,) he could speak to the king on Joseph's behalf. Pharaoh could set Joseph free and soon he could be heading home.

When the chief baker saw that Joseph had given a favourable interpretation, he decided to take the risk in recounting his dream too. He said to Joseph: "I too had a dream. On my head were three baskets of bread. In the top basket were all kinds of baked goods for Pharaoh, but the birds were eating them out of the basket on my head." That was all. It was a strange dream, but Joseph knew what it meant, for God revealed to him its secret. How sad Joseph must have been to tell this man the truth. "This is what it means," said Joseph: "The three baskets are three days. Within three days Pharaoh will lift off your head and hang you on a tree. And the birds will eat away your flesh."

Did Pharaoh's officials believe Joseph's interpretations? The wise men in the king's court were often wrong in what they said, but Joseph claimed these interpretations came from God and could not be wrong. Within three days they would see for themselves if what Joseph said proved true or false. Three days later the cup-bearer and the baker were summoned from the prison. It was Pharaoh's birthday and he was having a great party for all his officials. The chief cup-bearer and the chief baker were invited. At the birthday party Pharaoh lifted up their heads in the presence of all his other officials. A hush must have fallen upon the crowd. These were the two men who had been thrown into prison. What would the king do to them now? The cup-bearer and the baker knew what they had dreamt and what Joseph had said. Would their dreams come true according to his word? Pharaoh held their heads and their lives in his hands. What would he decide? What would be their fate? Pharaoh took the chief cup-bearer and restored him to his former position, so that he once again put the king's cup into his hand. But Pharaoh took the chief baker and had his head cut off. He ordered his body to be hung outside for all to see, outside where the birds would peck away the flesh. Pharaoh would do as he pleased. The crowd must have clapped and cheered at the king's pleasure. Happy Birthday, Pharaoh! Yes, the king could do as he pleased—but God was in control, for it all happened exactly as Joseph had said to them three days earlier.

Back in prison, Joseph must have heard what had happened. He must have thought that very soon his friend would speak to Pharaoh about his case, about the injustice that had been done to him. Day after day Joseph must have awaited for Pharaoh to summon him and release him, so he could begin his long journey home. But the chief cup-bearer did not remember Joseph. He forgot him. And Joseph remained in prison.

Joseph's only hope for help was in his God:

> It is better to take refuge in the LORD, than to trust in man.
> It is better to take refuge in the LORD than to trust in princes."
>
> Psalm 118:8, 9

> Do not depend on man for help . . .
> Blessed is he whose help is in the God of Jacob
> whose hope is in the LORD his God . . .
> The LORD who remains faithful forever . . .

He is the One who upholds the cause of the oppressed . . .
It is the LORD who sets the prisoners free . . .
The LORD reigns forever . . .
Praise the LORD!

  Psalm 146:3, 5–8, 10

The teacher's guide for this lesson starts on page 530.

FROM THE PRISON TO THE PALACE

- **Genesis 41:1–52**
- **Psalm 113**
- **II Corinthians 4**

Joseph remained in prison. His friend, who now stood beside the king of Egypt and had the chance to help Joseph, forgot all about him—but the LORD did not forget Joseph. One night, after two full years had passed, the LORD sent a message to Pharaoh in two dreams. After each dream, Pharaoh awoke troubled. The LORD not only disturbed the peace of Pharaoh's sleep in the night; God also disturbed his peace of mind the next day. Even in the light of morning, the two strange dreams continued to trouble the king. What was their meaning? Was there a warning? Pharaoh sent for all the wise men of Egypt—the sorcerers, the diviners, the magicians. Surely one of these men could reveal to the king the mystery of his dreams. Pharaoh told them the visions he had seen in the night, but not one of Egypt's wise men could interpret the king's dreams.

However, there was someone in Egypt who could interpret the king's dreams—and the chief cup-bearer knew who it was! Yes, suddenly the man remembered Joseph. He told Pharaoh the whole story from two years ago. The chief cup-bearer said, "Pharaoh was once angry with his servants, and he imprisoned me and the chief baker . . . Each of us had a dream the same night, and each dream had a meaning of its own. Now a young Hebrew was there with us, a servant of the captain of the guard. We told him our dreams, and he interpreted them for us, giving each man the interpretation of his dream." Then the cup-bearer told Pharaoh something quite remarkable; he said: "And things turned out exactly as he interpreted them to us! I was restored to my position, and the other man was hanged." Could a slave speak about a king's dreams? Could a Hebrew tell an Egyptian the mysteries of his mind? Could a prisoner, who was chained in a dungeon, teach Pharaoh, who ruled in his palace? Would such a man really have more wisdom than all the wise men in Egypt, more wisdom than the king himself? Pharaoh must have been greatly impressed with this story, for he immediately sent for Joseph.

Thus it happened, that by the command of the king (and by the command of the King of kings) Joseph was brought from the prison to the palace. One minute Joseph was in the company of criminals, dressed in filthy rags, locked in a dark dungeon. The next minute he found himself being led away to be washed and shaved and dressed in clean clothes; then he found himself standing before the king in the splendour of his palace. No, God had not forgotten Joseph . . . nor had Joseph, during those long years in prison, forgotten God! When Pharaoh said to Joseph, "I had a dream and no one can interpret it, but I have heard it said of you, that when you hear a dream, you can interpret it," Joseph replied, "I cannot do it, but God will give Pharaoh the answer he desires." In the very first sentence that Joseph spoke to Pharaoh, he testified to the goodness and the greatness of his God! Joseph had such faith in the power and mercy of God. Joseph also had such courage before men, even great men, like Pharaoh. Joseph was willing to show his faith and speak of God — even to the King of Egypt! "God will give Pharaoh the answer," said Joseph.

Pharaoh lost no time in telling Joseph his dreams; he said, "In my dream I was standing on the bank of the Nile, when out of the river there came up seven cows, fat and sleek, and they grazed among the reeds. After them, seven other cows came up — scrawny and very ugly and lean. I had never seen such ugly cows in all the land of Egypt. The lean, ugly cows ate up the seven fat cows, which came up first. But even after they ate them, no one could tell that they had done so; they looked just as ugly as before." Then Pharaoh said he woke up, although it was the middle of the night. After awhile, he fell asleep again and had a second dream. Pharaoh said, "In my dreams I also saw seven heads of grain, full and good, growing on a single stalk. After them, seven other heads sprouted—withered and thin and scorched by the east wind. The thin heads of grain swallowed up the seven good heads." Then Pharaoh woke up. It had only been a dream, but it troubled him deeply. Pharaoh told Joseph that he did not understand these dreams, nor could any of his sorcerers or magicians explain them.

Joseph could. He understood the dreams. He said to the king, "The two dreams of Pharaoh are one and the same. God has revealed to Pharaoh what He is about to do. The seven good cows are seven years, and the seven good heads of grain are seven years; it is one and the same dream. They both represent the same seven years—good years of plenty. The seven lean ugly cows that came up afterwards are also seven years, and so are the seven worthless heads of grain scorched by the east wind; they both represent the same seven years—bad years of famine. It is just as I said to Pharaoh: God has shown Pharaoh what He is about to do. Seven years of great abundance are coming throughout the land of Egypt, but seven years of famine will follow them. Then all the abundance in Egypt will be forgotten, and the famine will ravage the land. The abundance in the land will not be remembered, because the famine that follows it will be so severe. The reason the dream was given to Pharaoh in two forms is that the matter has been firmly decided by God, and God will do it soon."

So, that was the meaning of those two strange dreams, but Joseph did not stop speaking. He did not leave Pharaoh with just the meaning or just the warning. What should Pharaoh do with this vital information? What should Pharaoh do with this precious knowledge, which God in His Mercy had revealed to him so strangely in the night, when he lay upon his bed, and then proclaimed to him so clearly in the day, when he sat upon his throne? Joseph knew what he should do, so he presented Pharaoh with a plan. He said, "And now let Pharaoh look for a discerning and wise man and put him in charge of the land of Egypt. Let Pharaoh appoint commissioners over the land to take a fifth of the harvest of Egypt during the seven years of abundance. Under the authority of Pharaoh, they should collect all the food of these good years that are coming and store up the grain to be kept in the cities for food. This food should be held in reserve for the country, to be used during the seven years of famine that will come upon Egypt, so that the country may not be ruined by the famine."

The plan was brilliant, like a burst of light from heaven upon the dark future of Egypt. Pharaoh was no longer troubled. God had graciously given him a message to rescue his country, and a plan to save his realm. Joseph's idea seemed good to Pharaoh and to all his officials. Which of these wise men should be selected? Who should be put in charge of this project—and all of Egypt? Pharaoh knew the man he wanted. He asked his officials, "Can we find anyone like this man, one in whom is the spirit of God?" Then Pharaoh said to Joseph, "Since God has made all this known to you, there is no one so discerning and wise as you! You shall be in charge of my palace, and all my people are to submit to your orders. Only with respect to the throne, will I be greater than you."

God honours those who honour Him. Through those long hard years of bondage, Joseph did not forget or forsake his God. The very first words Joseph spoke to Pharaoh were words glorifying his God—and now God was glorifying his humble servant and prisoner, Joseph. Listen to all the honour and power and glory that were bestowed upon Joseph that day. Surely it was the hand of God, exalting His faithful friend and loyal son:

1. Pharaoh said to Joseph, "I hereby put you in charge of the whole land of Egypt."

2. Pharaoh took his signet ring from his own finger and put it on Joseph's finger. The sign and the seal of that ring gave Joseph the authority of Pharaoh himself.

3. Pharaoh dressed Joseph in robes of fine linen and put a gold chain around his neck.

4. Pharaoh had Joseph ride in the second finest and fastest chariot in all the land of Egypt, second only to Pharaoh's.

5. Joseph was also given horsemen to ride before him, shouting "Make way! Make way!" No one in all the land could stand in Joseph's way; no one could block his path. Joseph could go where he pleased and do as he pleased in all the land.

6. Pharaoh said to Joseph, "I am Pharaoh, but without your word no one will lift hand or foot in all Egypt." Joseph was more powerful than a modern monarch, president or prime minister. Pharaoh

made Joseph's word all-powerful in Egypt. Except for Pharaoh, everyone in the whole land must obey Joseph.

7. Pharaoh gave Joseph a new name, an Egyptian name: Zaphenath-Paneah, which meant "Revealer of Secrets." It was a name of honour and power. All who came before Revealer-of-Secrets would bow before him in fear and awe.

8. Pharaoh also gave Joseph a special friend, so he would not be lonely in his high position. Pharaoh gave Joseph a beautiful woman, named Asenath, to be his wife. She was the daughter of a very important man in Egypt—the priest of On, the sun god, whom all Egypt worshipped. Marrying Asenath, daughter of the priest of On, added to Joseph's honour and power.

All this must have been astounding to Joseph! On the same day he was raised from the lowest person in the lowest place in all Egypt to the highest position in the land. On this day he awoke as a lowly slave and a forgotten prisoner; that night he went to bed as a powerful prince. He had begun that day wearing the iron chains and filthy rags of a prisoner; by the end of that same day he was wearing the gold chains and royal robes of a prince. How had this happened? How had this extraordinary day come to pass? It was the LORD! God had caused it to happen! He had heard Joseph's prayers and blessed Joseph's faith. God had caused all things to work together for the good of this man who loved Him.

> Praise the LORD.
> He the lowly makes to rise
>   from the dust in which he lies,
> that exalted he may stand
>   with the princes of the land.
> Praise the LORD.
>
> Psalm 113:1, 7-8, 9b

Joseph was thirty years old when he entered the service of Pharaoh, king of Egypt. During the seven good years, the years of abundance, Joseph travelled throughout the land collecting all the excess grain and storing it in the cities. In every city in the whole land Joseph stored up the food grown in the fields surrounding it. He stored up huge quantities of grain, like the sand of the sea. There was so much grain, that he stopped keeping records, because it was beyond measure! During those years, Joseph's wife was also fruitful. Asenath bore Joseph two sons. He named his firstborn son, Manasseh, which means "Forgetful," because he said, "God has caused me to be forgetful of all my trouble." Joseph named his second-born son, Ephraim, which means "Fruitful," because he said, "God has caused me to be fruitful in the land of my suffering."

For many years Joseph had faced trouble and suffering in the land of Egypt. All through those long, hard years Joseph remained faithful to the LORD. Joseph did not forget God in his trouble; he did not forsake God in his suffering. Even as a slave, Joseph obeyed the commands of God, rather than the demands of men or sin. Even in prison, his faithfulness and righteousness shone forth. When at last Joseph stood before the king, in the very first sentence that he spoke to Pharaoh, Joseph glorified his God. No, Joseph had not forgotten his God—and God had not forgotten Joseph! At the right time, the LORD honours those who honour Him. God makes his servants forgetful of all their years of trouble and God makes them fruitful in the land of their suffering. "Our present sufferings are not worth comparing to the glory that will be revealed in us" (Romans 8:18). "Therefore we do not lose heart . . . For our light and momentary troubles are achieving for us an eternal glory that far outweighs them all" (II Corinthians 4:16, 17).

The teacher's guide for this lesson starts on page 532.

THE FIRST JOURNEY TO EGYPT

• Genesis 42

For seven years Joseph worked to store away the food produced in Egypt. Then the seven years of plenty ended and the seven years of famine began, just as Joseph had said, just as Pharaoh had dreamed. Joseph's words and Pharaoh's dreams had come true. The famine was severe and the people cried to Pharaoh for food. "Go to Joseph," said Pharaoh, "and do what he tells you." Joseph waited until the famine had spread over the whole country. Then he opened up the storehouses of grain and sold food to the Egyptians. There was famine in all the surrounding countries too, but their kings had not been warned about it by God. They had not saved a fifth of their crops during the good years and now they had nothing; now they were starving. There was only one place where food could be found—Egypt! So people from all the countries came to Egypt to buy grain from Joseph, because the famine was severe in all the world.

The land of Canaan, where Jacob lived, was no exception. The land of promise, the land flowing with milk and honey, was also bare and dry. The people living there also needed food. Abraham had faced a famine in Canaan. Isaac had faced a famine there also. Now it was Jacob's turn. He too must place his trust in God, and not the land, to provide his daily bread. He too must place his hope in the Promised Land, that was a heavenly one, not an earthly one. Jacob was living in the land of promise, the land promised to him by God, but there he faced famine. When Jacob learned that there was grain in Egypt, he said to his sons, "Why do you just keep looking at each other? I have heard there is grain in Egypt. Go down there and buy some for us, so that we may live and not die!"

So Jacob sent ten of his sons to Egypt to buy grain for their family, but Benjamin he kept at home, because he was afraid that harm might come to him. Jacob did not trust his sons. He had already lost Joseph. He did not want to lose Benjamin too, the only other child of his beloved Rachel. No, Benjamin was very dear to Jacob and he would not risk his life by letting him go. So it was that ten of Israel's sons joined the stream of people flowing from Canaan to Egypt to buy grain during the famine.

Now when the sons of Jacob arrived in Egypt, they had to go to the governor of the land, the one who sold the grain to all the people, Governor Zaphenath-Paneah. Do you know who he was? Yes, you know it was Joseph! But his brothers did not know who he was, nor did they recognize him. Twenty years had passed since they had sold their little brother as a slave. They now assumed he was dead. Joseph was gone. He was no more. The last time they had seen Joseph, he was a Hebrew shepherd boy, pleading for his life. Their memory of Joseph bore no resemblance to the mighty man before them. This great lord, who was ruling the land, was surely an Egyptian prince. He had an Egyptian name; he spoke the Egyptian language; he wore Egyptian robes. There was nothing about this man that would give them the slightest hint about who he really was. Not one of the brothers recognized Joseph.

However, Joseph recognized them . . . immediately. As soon as Joseph saw the ten Hebrew shepherds, he knew they were his brothers. When they came before the great governor to buy grain, they bowed down to him with their faces to the ground—and Joseph remembered his dreams from long ago, the dreams where his brothers bowed down to him. So . . . these dreams had also come true! There were his brothers, with their faces on the ground before him. Joseph also remembered how his brothers hated him because of those dreams. They had plotted to kill him and had actually sold him, so that those dreams would never come true. "Do you intend to reign over us?

Will you actually rule us?" That was what they had said so long ago. They had done everything possible to keep it from happening, but Joseph was not dead, nor was he a slave. He was the lord of the land and his brothers were bowing down before him, their very lives depending upon him—yet they did not know it. When Joseph saw that they did not recognize him, he pretended to be a stranger and spoke harshly to them. Joseph was not ready to tell them who he was . . . not yet. Joseph wanted to know what had happened to his father and his little brother. Joseph also wanted to know if the brothers had repented of their sins. Were they still the same men? Were they still that brood of vipers, filled with the poison of envy and hatred? Were their hearts still filled with greed and lust, deceit and murder? Joseph would find out what kind of men they were now. They must reveal themselves, before he revealed himself.

Although he knew the answer, Joseph asked the brothers, "Where do you come from?"

They replied, "We have come from the land of Canaan, to buy food."

"No," said Joseph, "You are spies! You have come to see where our land is unprotected."

"No, my lord," they answered. "Your servants have come to buy food. We are all the sons of one man. Your servants are honest men, not spies."

Joseph must have laughed to hear them protest that they were honest men. Do such men sell their brother and lie to their father? Joseph knew what kind of men they were, so he continued to accuse them. "No!" said Joseph. "You have come to see where our land is unprotected."

Again the brothers protested their innocence of this crime. They told him about their family. They said, "Your servants were twelve brothers, the sons of one man, who lives in the land of Canaan. The youngest is now with our father, and one is no more."

But Joseph insisted, saying, "You are spies! And this is how you will be tested: As surely as Pharaoh lives, you will not leave this place unless your youngest brother comes here. Send one of your number to get your brother; the rest of you will be kept in prison, so that your words may be tested to see if you are telling the truth. If you are not, then as surely as Pharaoh lives, you are spies!" Then Joseph threw them all into prison.

The ten brothers of Joseph must have been terrified! How had this happened . . . and why? They had simply come here to buy grain, like everyone else. For some reason Egypt's great governor suspected them; he had accused them of being spies and had thrown them in prison. How long would he keep them in this dungeon? What if Benjamin did not return? Who could rescue them in this foreign land? They were strangers here. Who would intercede for them? Who would testify for them? No one knew them here. No one could verify their claims. Would the brothers ever see their families again? Would they ever be allowed to go home? Perhaps the great governor of the land would forget all about them—or perhaps he would decide to execute them! Yes, spies were put to death and this man had total authority in the land of Egypt. He could do as he pleased. At the command of Governor Zaphenath—Paneah, their heads could be chopped off without another word. Yes, the brothers must have been terrified! Their minds must have been filled with fears and doubts. To whom would they turn in their distress? Would they trust in God?

Perhaps that was why Joseph threw his brothers in prison, so that they would turn to God and turn from sin. Joseph was not repaying evil for evil. Prison might be very good for these brothers, who had never paid the penalty for their crimes. Joseph himself had spent many long years in prison. A few short days would not harm his brothers, and it very well might help them. Joseph was a wise and discerning ruler, in whom was the Spirit of God. What he did to his brothers was both good and just.

Joseph was also merciful to them. He did not leave his brothers in prison for a time equal to his own bondage. He did not exact restitution—an eye for an eye, a tooth for a tooth, thirteen years for thirteen years. No, after three days Joseph released them from the dungeon and said, "Do this and you will live, for I fear God: If you are honest men, let one of your brothers stay here in prison, while the rest of you go and take grain back to your starving households. But you must bring your youngest brother to me, so that your words may be verified—and that you may not die."

The lord of the land had not listened to their pleas of innocence. Nine of them had been set free, but the death penalty hung over them all—and one of them would be held as a hostage. It was a terrible situation. The brothers began talking to one another in Hebrew, thinking that the Egyptian governor could not understand them. They said, "Surely we are being punished because of our brother. We saw how distressed he was when he pleaded with us for his life, but we would not listen; that's why this distress has come upon us." You see . . . the memory of that dreadful day had never left them. At the time, when they threw their little brother into the pit and then sold him as a slave, they had shrugged their shoulders and even laughed, but they had not had peace ever since that day. Twenty years had passed, but their consciences still bothered them; their sin still haunted them. The passing of time had not washed away the guilt of their crime. The burden of their sin had only become heavier as the years had passed. They had not confessed it, not to their earthly father and not to their heavenly Father. No, they had spent twenty years hiding their sin and living in the fearful expectation of God's judgement. It had finally come. "We are being punished," they said. "That's why this distress has come upon us." Reuben agreed, saying, "Didn't I tell you not to sin against the boy? But you wouldn't listen! Now we must give an accounting for his blood." As they talked, Joseph listened. He had not forgotten his native language, though he had not used it in twenty years. He understood every word they spoke—and it broke his heart. Tears welled up in his eyes, and Joseph had to turn from his brothers, so they would not see him weeping.

But Joseph could not tell them who he was . . . not yet. He dried his tears and turned back to his brothers. Again he spoke harshly to them. Then he chose the one who would remain in prison. He took Simeon. Why did he choose Simeon? Joseph now knew that his oldest brother, Reuben, was not responsible for the crime. He had taken no part in it. He had even argued against it. Simeon then, who was the second oldest, bore the greatest responsibility. He had been the one in charge of the brothers that day. Simeon was also a murderous man, who carried a weapon of violence. Perhaps he was the one who most viciously threatened Joseph's life. Simeon! Cursed be his anger, so fierce, and his fury, so cruel! Joseph remembered that dreadful day. He knew which brother had treated him the worst. No doubt, that was why he chose Simeon. Joseph ordered his soldiers to take Simeon from the brothers and to tie him up before their eyes. The brothers watched Simeon being dragged away to be a prisoner in Egypt, just as they had watched Joseph being dragged away twenty years earlier. Was this not justice? Again they must have thought, "Surely we are being punished . . ."

Then the remaining sons of Jacob loaded up their donkeys with the grain they had bought and began their long journey home. What else could they do? They could not rescue Simeon, unless they went home to get Benjamin. It was not a joyful journey home—and new terrors awaited them. At the place where they stopped for the night, one of the brothers opened his sack to get feed for his donkey—and there was the silver he had paid the

Egyptians for his grain. "My silver has been returned!" he gasped to his brothers. "Here it is in my sack!" You would think such a gift would be a cause for rejoicing, but the brothers had guilty consciences and the sight of this silver made their hearts sink. Now they would be accused of stealing, as well as spying. They turned to each other, trembling, and said, "What is this that God has done to us?" They must have remembered the silver, the twenty shekels of silver, that they received when they sold their little brother Joseph as a slave. Again they must have thought, "Surely we are being punished."

When they arrived back home in the land of Canaan, they went to their father Jacob. Although they had brought back good grain, they had also brought back bad news—and Jacob could see for himself that Simeon was missing. Where was he? What had happened to him? The brothers explained what had happened in Egypt, how the lord of the land had accused them of being spies and how he had said, "Bring your youngest brother to me so that I will know that you are not spies . . . Then I will give your brother back to you." This was terrible news for Jacob. What should he do? Should he send Benjamin to Egypt in order to save Simeon?

Then something happened, which shocked Jacob into a decision. As his sons were emptying their sacks of grain, there in each man's sack was his pouch of silver! When Jacob saw this, he was frightened. They all were frightened. What did this mean? Again Jacob suspected his sons of some sort of foul play. He said to them, "You have deprived me of my children. Joseph is no more and Simeon is no more, and now you want to take Benjamin. Everything is against me!" Reuben protested. He said to his father, "You may put both my sons to death, if I do not bring Benjamin back to you. Entrust him to my care, and I will bring him back." But Jacob had made up his mind. Should he trust Reuben? "No," Jacob said, "my son will not go down there with you. His brother is dead and he is the only one left. If harm comes to him on the journey you are taking, you will bring my grey head down to the grave in sorrow." That was Jacob's answer. Simeon would not be rescued at the risk of losing Benjamin. Simeon would remain a prisoner in Egypt . . . perhaps for the rest of his life.

Jacob said, "Everything is against me!" But Jacob was wrong. Everything was *for* Jacob, because *God was for Jacob*—and if God is for us, who (or what) can be against us? And we know that in all things God works for the good of those who love Him. Jacob must not despair. He must place his hope and trust in God. He must remember God's promises. The LORD was working out the amazing story of Jacob's life and the amazing story of God's salvation. It was all part of God's good plan and great purpose. Jacob did not know it then, nor could he see it then, but he had not lost Simeon, nor had he lost Joseph. One day all his sons would be restored to him . . . far beyond what he could even imagine . . . not just twelve sons, but sons more numerous than the stars in the sky or sand on a seashore.

The teacher's guide for this lesson starts on page 534.

THE SECOND JOURNEY TO EGYPT

• **Genesis 43**

The sons of Jacob had brought grain from Egypt to feed their starving households, but the famine continued to be severe in the land. Again the crops failed. Soon their food was gone and there was only one place where food could be found—Egypt. Jacob said to his sons, "Go back and buy us a little more food." Judah answered his father, "If you will send our brother [Benjamin] along with us, we will go down and buy food for you. But if you will not send him, we will not go." They could not return without Benjamin. The great governor of Egypt had warned them not to even try. He would not see them; he would not sell them grain; and worse . . . he would view them as spies! They would all be thrown into prison, not just Simeon. Perhaps they would be executed. The man had warned them solemnly, "You must bring your younger brother to me, so that your words may be verified and that you may not die!" But Jacob had declared, "My son [Benjamin] will not go down there with you." What were they going to do?

Jacob blamed his sons. "Why did you bring this trouble on me?"

he asked. "Why did you tell the man you had another brother." The sons of Jacob replied that it wasn't their fault. They said, "The man questioned us closely about ourselves and our family: 'Is your father still living? Do you have another brother?' We simply answered his questions. How were we to know he would say, 'Bring your brother down here'?" Anyway, it didn't really matter whose fault it was. What mattered right now was getting food before they all starved to death! They did not have any choice. There was only one way to get food. They must return to Egypt—with Benjamin! Judah promised that he would take care of Benjamin. He said to Israel his father, "Send the boy along with me and we will go at once, so that we and you and our children may live and not die. I myself will guarantee his safety; you can hold me personally responsible for him. If I do not bring him back to you and set him here before you, I will bear the blame before you all my life. As it is, if we had not delayed, we could have gone and returned twice."

They must not wait any longer. All their food was gone. There was nothing else they could do. Benjamin must go with them. At last Jacob relented. He saw that it must be so, that he must release Benjamin. So Israel said to his sons, "If it must be, then do this: Put some of the best products of the land in your bags and take them down to the man as a gift . . . Take double the amount of silver with you, for you must return the silver . . . Perhaps it was a mistake. And take your brother also." Jacob would do what he could to appease the man, (as he had done with his brother Esau earlier,) because he saw that he must let his sons, all of his sons, go to Egypt. What else could he do? "Go back to the man at once," said Jacob, "and may God Almighty grant you mercy before the man, so that he will let your other brother and Benjamin come back with you." Jacob must entrust his sons to the mercy of God Almighty. Yes, he must place them in the hands of the LORD of LOVE and let them go. He had no choice. What else could he do? If he lost his sons, he lost his sons. "As for me," said Jacob, "if I am bereaved, I am bereaved."

And so these ten sons of Jacob packed up their donkeys for the second journey to Egypt. They took with them gifts for the governor, the best products of their country. Canaan was famous for its honey; it was known as a land "flowing with honey." So the brothers brought some honey, as well as some other specialty items—spices and perfumes, balm and nuts. They also took with them double the amount of silver. And most precious of all, they took with them their youngest brother, Benjamin. As Jacob watched all his sons leave home, he knew he might never see them again. They might never return from Egypt, but Jacob had done all he could do to help them. He had sent them to a foreign land with his wisdom and he had sent them there with his blessing. He had sent them off with presents and with prayer: "May God Almighty grant you mercy . . ." Jacob's hope and help was in the LORD. His trust was in God that he would see his sons again. Jacob's faith was in the Almighty—and he would not be disappointed!

Meanwhile, the sons of Israel hurried down to Egypt. Their food was gone and there was no time to spare. They presented themselves before the great governor, but he said not a word to them. Instead, he said something in Egyptian, (which the brothers did not understand,) and they were led away. When they realized they were being taken to the governor's house, they were terrified. What did this mean? Their minds imagined all kinds of awful answers: Somehow the governor knew about the mystery of the silver in their sacks and now he would punish them as thieves. He was planning to attack them! He was going to overpower them! He was going to seize them as slaves! He was going to steal their donkeys! Again their guilty consciences tortured them with the fearful expectation of judgement. They thought it would be done to them as they had done to their brother. They would be made slaves in Egypt, just as they had made Joseph a slave in Egypt. For a pouch of silver they had sold their own brother and now, because of a pouch of silver found in each man's sack, they would all be seized as slaves. Was this not the justice they deserved? Was this not God's punishment for their sin? The brothers were terrified, but what could they do? To try and run was useless. How could they escape in Egypt? There were soldiers and chariots everywhere. Besides, where could they flee from the famine to find food for their families? They were trapped here. Perhaps they should speak to someone. They decided to speak to the man, who had led them to the governor's house. Perhaps he could help them. Before they even entered the house, they explained to the man the whole story about finding the silver in their sacks. "Please sir," they said, "we have brought it back with us. We have also brought additional silver with us to buy food. We don't know who put our silver in our sacks." The Egyptian told them not to worry. "It's alright," he said. "Don't be afraid. Your God, the God of your father, has given you treasure in your sacks." Then he told them that he was the one who had received their money—and returned it to them.

What a relief it was for the brothers to hear that! They had worried about those pouches of silver for many months! They didn't know why their silver had been returned, but right now, they didn't really care. It was just a relief to know that everything was alright. Then the man brought Simeon to join them. Another relief! Simeon was alive . . . and well! He had not been tortured or starved or beaten during his months in prison. What a joy it was to see him again! Then all the brothers were taken into the governor's house and they learned the reason why: The governor had invited them to eat dinner there. Water was brought to wash their feet and fodder was brought to feed their donkeys. All this must have been confusing to the brothers. First they were treated as spies; now they were treated as guests. All they wanted to do was to buy grain. Why was this governor paying so much attention to them? It was all very strange, but everything seemed to be working out on this second journey to Egypt. It seemed that God was indeed answering their father's prayer for them, granting them mercy with the governor. Perhaps their father's presents would also gain them mercy with the man. The brothers began to prepare their gifts to present to the governor when he arrived home for his noon meal with them.

At last Governor Zaphenath-Paneah arrived. The brothers presented to them their gifts and bowed down before him. Again Joseph must have remembered his dreams, as he saw his brothers with their faces on the ground before him. This time Joseph spoke kindly to his brothers. He asked how they were faring and if their father was still living. They answered, "Your servant, our father, is alive and well." Again they bowed low to pay him honour and to give him their father's respect. Joseph must have been startled to hear his own father called his servant and again he must have recalled the dream, in which even his father had bowed down to him. Then Joseph looked around and saw his brother Benjamin, his own mother's son. He asked, "Is this your youngest brother, the one you told me about?" Yes, it was Benjamin! The great governor said, "God be gracious to you, my son." Then Joseph, deeply moved at the sight of his brother, hurried out of the room to look for a place to weep. He went to his own room and wept there in private. But he did not want to tell his brothers who he really was . . . not yet. So he wiped his eyes and washed his face, took a deep breath—and walked back into the room with his brothers. Controlling himself he said in a steady voice, "Serve the food." There were three separate tables. The governor ate by himself, the brothers ate by themselves, and the Egyptians ate by themselves, (because it was detestable for Egyptians to eat at the same table with Hebrews.) There was nothing unusual about this. What was re-markable was the way the governor had arranged the brothers! They were seated before him in the order of their ages, from the firstborn to the youngest. How was it possible that this Egyptian governor could know the order of their births? Yet he had arranged them with Reuben, the oldest, at one end of the table; then he had seated Simeon, Levi and Judah; next came Dan and Naphtali; then came Gad and Asher; next to them Issachar and Zebulun were seated; and finally, at the other end, sat Benjamin, the youngest. It was amazing—and the brothers looked at one another in astonishment! The whole situation was very strange, but the governor was kind to them and sent delicious food from his table to theirs. However, it did not escape the no-tice of anyone, that Benjamin was given five times as much food as anyone else. Why had this governor chosen Benjamin as his favourite, just as their father had done? The brothers must have wondered about these things, but it was a delicious meal. They had probably never eaten such a feast in all their lives, and certainly not since the famine began. It was the first good meal they had eaten in many months. They could not help but enjoy it. In spite of the strangeness of the situation, they were soon having a good time, eating and drinking freely and gladly with the great governor of Egypt.

The next day the brothers left at dawn, with their sacks filled with grain, to return home. Their second journey to Egypt had been a great success! The brothers were all together again and no disaster had befallen them. God had indeed granted them mercy in the eyes of the governor, more than they had even hoped. Imagine dining with the lord of the land in his own house! It was really quite incredible. How thankful their old father would be to see them home safely again! How joyful they were to be heading home! But the brothers did not get very far that day because . . .

Joseph had one more trial for them to endure. Joseph wanted to test his brothers. He wanted to test their characters to see whether they would deal with their younger brother, in the same way that they had dealt with him. Did they envy Benjamin also? Was there hatred towards him too? Would they get rid of him at the first opportunity? Would they break their old fa-ther's heart again? Joseph would find out! Joseph had a plan, that would force his brothers to reveal themselves, before he revealed himself.

The teacher's guide for this lesson starts on page 536.

HIDDEN THINGS REVEALED

Genesis 44:1–45:15

The Governor's Goblet

The sons of Jacob were happily on their way home with their sacks filled with grain to feed their starving households. Simeon had been released from prison and Benjamin was safely with them. Everything had gone incredibly well on this journey to Egypt and now they were heading home. However, the eleven sons of Israel did not get very far that day. They had barely passed through the city gates, barely begun their journey through the countryside, when the governor's chief servant caught up to them and accused them of stealing the governor's goblet from the governor's table. "Why have you repaid good with evil?" he demanded. Why had they stolen the governor's own goblet, the very one which he used every day? "This is a wicked thing you have done!" he declared. The eleven brothers were utterly astonished by this charge. "Why does my lord say such things?" they asked. "Far be it from your servants to do anything like that! We even brought back to you from the land of Canaan the silver we found inside the mouths of our sacks. So why would we steal silver or gold from your master's house? If any of your servants is found to have it, he will die—and the rest of us will become my lord's slaves." The Egyptian replied, "Only the one who is found to have it will become my slave; the rest of you will be free from blame."

Quickly each of the brothers lowered his sack to the ground and opened it. Then the governor's servant began the inspection. One by one he checked their bags, beginning with the oldest and ending with the youngest. First he went to Reuben and searched his sack. The governor's goblet was not there. Then the Egyptian went to Simeon and searched him. They all breathed a sigh of relief, when nothing was found in Simeon's sack. Next it was Levi's turn. Then it was Judah's turn. Their sacks were searched, but they too were free from blame; they had not stolen the governor's goblet. Then came Dan and Naphtali; nothing was found with them. Gad and Asher were also free; the governor's goblet was not hidden in their grain either. Then the Egyptian checked Issachar's sack. Nothing was found with him. There were only two more sacks to search. Would it be found with Zebulun? No, he cleared the inspection. Now there was only one more sack to search. The Egyptian walked over to the youngest brother, Benjamin. He looked inside his sack—and there was the governor's goblet!

No one was more astonished than Benjamin! How did that cup get there? He did not steal it or hide it, but how could he prove his innocence? Who would believe him? The evidence clearly pointed to the fact that he was the thief. The blame would rest on him; he would be made a slave and kept a prisoner in Egypt for the rest of his life. The other brothers could go home to their father and their families, but he would be kept here forever. What could he do? Benjamin tore his clothes in utter dismay—and so did all the other brothers. They were all filled with shock and grief and fear.

How did the governor's goblet get in Benjamin's sack? The governor himself ordered his chief servant to put it there. Why? This was Joseph's test to see what his brothers would do. Would they abandon Benjamin? Would they take their freedom and go home, leaving their little brother all alone as a slave in Egypt? Benjamin was their father's favourite son. Would they use this as an opportunity to get rid of Benjamin? Many years ago, out of envy and hatred, they had sold their father's other favourite son. Would they do it again? Or had they repented of their sin? Joseph would find out what was really in their hearts, for now they had a choice: They could now forsake Benjamin and continue on their journey home or they could support

Benjamin and endeavour to help him and free him. What would the brothers choose? Would they do what was right? The sons of Israel did not abandon their brother, Benjamin. They all loaded up their donkeys and returned
to the city with him to face the governor's wrath together.

When the brothers came into the governor's house, they threw themselves on the ground before him. "What is this you have done?" asked the
lord of the land. The brothers trembled before the mighty Zaphenath-
Paneah, the great Revealer of Secrets. "Don't you know that a man like me
can find things out by divination?" The Egyptians used their black magic
and secret sorcery to uncover all kinds of crimes. Did these foolish Hebrews
think they could escape from the power of Egypt's wisest ruler? No,
Zaphenath-Paneah, Revealer of Secrets, had seen the wicked things that
they had done! What did they have to say for themselves? Judah dared to
answer the great governor and even spoke to him about the LORD, the God
of Israel. Judah said, "What can we say to my lord? How can we prove our
innocence? God has uncovered your servants' guilt, (their guilt from long
ago!) We are now my lord's slaves, (as their past sin deserved)—we ourselves,
(who are the truly guilty ones,) and the one who was found to have the cup."
Thus Judah spoke to the great governor. It was a confession of sin—and a
confession of the true God, the One who really is the Revealer of Secrets,
the One who had uncovered their sin. The governor answered Judah, "Far
be it from me to do such a thing! Only the man who was found to have the
cup will become my slave. The rest of you, go back to your father in peace."
Again Joseph was testing his brothers by offering them their freedom. Would
they take it? They could leave Benjamin as a slave in Egypt and go back to
their father in peace. Would they go? They had a perfect excuse for leaving
him now: The lord of the land had ordered them to go back home and they
must obey him. They should leave immediately.

Judah slowly stood up and bravely went to the great governor. "Please,
my lord, let your servant speak a word . . . do not be angry with your servant,
though you are equal to Pharaoh himself." Judah wanted to carefully explain
the whole situation to this man. They could not leave Benjamin there as a
slave. If they did, their old father would die. Judah told the governor about
their other brother and what their father had said to them: "You know that
my wife bore me two sons. One of them went away from me . . . He surely
has been torn to pieces—and I have not seen him since. If you take this one
from me too and harm comes to him, you will bring my grey head down to

the grave in misery." The governor must understand: Their father would die! Judah said, "If the boy is not with us . . . and if my father, whose life is closely bound up with the boy's life, sees that the boy isn't there—he will die! Your servants will bring the grey head of our father down to the grave in sorrow." Judah also explained that he was the one personally responsible for his youngest brother, that he had guaranteed the boy's safety to his father. Judah had a plan to propose to the governor. Judah offered himself as a substitute for Benjamin. He said, "Please, let your servant remain here as my lord's slave in place of the boy, and let the boy return with his brothers. How can I go back to my father, if the boy is not with me? No! Do not let me see the misery that would come upon my father."

The Governor's Secret

What would the great governor of Egypt decide? What would he say to this plea and this plan? Judah and all his brothers were utterly astonished at the governor's response. First, he shouted to all the Egyptians in the room: "Everyone, leave my presence!" Immediately the room emptied, so the brothers were left alone with the governor. Then, to their amazement, the great governor began to weep. He cried so loud and so long that the Egyptians heard him and it was reported to the household of Pharaoh. Joseph could not hold back his tears; he could no longer control himself. He just cried and cried—and then the great Revealer of Secrets revealed the greatest secret of all. "I am Joseph!" he said. The brothers were too stunned and too scared to speak. "Is my father still living?" asked Joseph, but his brothers could not answer, because they were terrified at his presence. They were in a state of shock. For many years they had thought that Joseph was dead, but here he was—alive! They had sold Joseph as a slave, but here he was—lord of all the land! Could it really be true? They knew it was and they were terrified! What would Joseph do to them now? Would he punish them for their sins? When Joseph was a helpless boy, they had treated him without mercy, without pity. Now that Joseph was a powerful man and they were the helpless ones, should they expect mercy or pity from him? Surely he would punish them for their crimes, as they deserved! The brothers stood looking at Joseph in total distress and dismay. They could not say a word to him. Their earlier fear of Egypt's governor was nothing but a nervous tremor, in comparison to the earth-shaking, soul-shattering *terror* they now experienced before Joseph. They had come forward to Governor Zaphenath-Paneah and had found the words to speak to him, but before their brother Joseph, they could not move a muscle or utter a sound. They were paralysed with fear.

Finally Joseph said, "Come close to me." The brothers obeyed, but said not a word. Joseph wondered if they believed what he had said, so he repeated it. "I am your brother Joseph, the one you sold into Egypt!" Still his brothers did not speak. Then Joseph realized what the problem was. They were terrified, because of their sin. "Do not be distressed," said Joseph, "and do not be angry with yourselves for selling me here, because *it was to save lives that God sent me ahead of you.* For two years now there has been famine in the land, and for the next five years there will not be ploughing and reaping. *But God sent me ahead of you to preserve for you a remnant on earth and to save your lives by a great deliverance!*" They must not focus on what *they* had done, but on what *God* had done. They must understand that God ruled everything and could over-rule anything, even their sin. What they had meant for evil, God had meant for good. They must believe that "God causes all things to work together for the good of those who love God, to those who are called according to His purpose" (Romans 8:28). The sons of Jacob were called of God; the sons of Israel were God's chosen people—and everything, even the selling of Joseph into slavery, was part of the LORD's good plan and great purpose for them. They must know that God had caused all these things to happen for their own good and for God's own glory. What was the LORD doing? He was building the Kingdom of God on earth! It was not to prosper the nation of Egypt, but to preserve the family of faith, that God had done these things. God had directed the events of the world and the history of nations to accomplish His purposes and to fulfill His promises. They all must trust in those promises, the promises given to their forefathers, to Abraham, Isaac and Jacob. One day God would make Israel into a great nation. This was the way God had chosen to preserve and promote His people, the people of promise. "So then," said Joseph, "it was not *you* who sent me here, but *God!* He made me father to Pharaoh, lord of his entire household, and ruler of all Egypt!" Was it not amazing what God had done for them? God had sent Joseph ahead of them and made him lord of all the land in order to save their lives by a great deliverance! There was not a loud shout: Praise the LORD! Joseph's eloquent testimony of God's goodness and greatness was met with silence.

Then Joseph told his brothers that they must waste no time in coming to Egypt, for the famine had just begun. They must hurry back to their father and bring him a message. "This is what your son Joseph says: God has made me lord of all Egypt. Come down to me. Don't delay. You shall live in the region of Goshen and be near me—you, your children, and your grandchildren, your flocks and herds, and all you have. I will provide for you there, because five years of famine are still to come. Otherwise you and your household and all who belong to you will become destitute."

Joseph had assured his brothers of God's plan and his own plans, but still they said nothing, not even thank-you. What was wrong with them? Perhaps they still didn't believe him. "Look," said Joseph, "You can see for yourselves, and so can my brother Benjamin, that it is really I who am speaking to you. Tell my father about all the honour accorded me in Egypt and about everything you have seen. And bring my father down here quickly." The brothers did not move quickly; they did not move at all . . . and still they said not a word. What was Joseph going to do with them? Finally he threw his arms around his brother Benjamin and wept. Then Benjamin embraced his long lost brother and wept also. One by one Joseph kissed his brothers and wept over them. At last they were assured of his love and forgiveness. Finally the brothers were able to speak and they talked a long time with Joseph. There were twenty years of family news to share with one another. What a joyous reunion they had at last! Praise be to the LORD, the God of Israel!

The teacher's guide for this lesson starts on page 538.

ISRAEL GOES TO EGYPT

• **Genesis 45:16–46:27**

Joseph urged his brothers to bring their father and their families down to Egypt quickly, where he could provide for them during the next five years of famine. When the news reached Pharaoh's palace about Joseph's brothers, he was pleased. Pharaoh also invited them to live in his country, where there was food. "Bring your father and your families back to me," said Pharaoh, "and I will give you the best of the land of Egypt and you can enjoy the fat of the land." There were lean years and hard times ahead. It was a gracious offer. Pharaoh also said, "Take some carts from Egypt for your children and your wives, get your father and come! Never mind about your belongings, because the best of all Egypt will be yours." So Joseph did as Pharaoh commanded. He gave his brothers carts for the journey. It would be too long for his old father or the young children to travel by foot. Joseph also gave his brothers provisions for the journey—and some presents. To each of his brothers he gave a new set of clothes. Yes, to the brothers who long ago had robbed him of his beautiful robe, his treasured coat-of-many-colours, Joseph now gave a beautiful robe to each of those brothers. That was how Joseph repaid their evil—with kindness and goodness. He returned love for hate. To his full brother, Benjamin, Joseph gave three hundred shekels of silver and five new sets of clothes. To his father, who had sent him gifts of the best products from the land of Canaan, Joseph sent the best products from the land of Egypt—ten male donkeys loaded with such gifts! Joseph also sent his beloved father ten female donkeys loaded with grain and bread and other provisions for his journey. When everything was ready at last, Joseph sent his brothers home, not only with gifts of blessing, but with words of warning: "Don't quarrel on the way!" Joseph knew his brothers, how quick they were to fight, how apt they were to blame. Joseph did not want them thinking about the past or blaming each other for their sin. Let them head home with joy and thanks, praising God for sending Joseph ahead of them to preserve for them a remnant on earth and to save their lives by a great deliverance. Let them rejoice in the LORD every step of the way home!

So the sons of Jacob went up out of Egypt and came to their father in the land of Canaan. They not only restored to Jacob his beloved Benjamin, but they also relayed to him the blessed news: "Joseph is alive! In fact, he is ruler of all Egypt!" Jacob was stunned. He did not believe them. This could not be true. Joseph was dead. He had been dead for years. With his own eyes Jacob had seen the blood on his son's coat. No, Joseph was gone and Jacob had been grieving his loss for over twenty years. How could he be alive? How could he be the ruler of all Egypt? Jacob was an old man; he did not understand. What was this nonsense his sons were telling him? Joseph is alive? Jacob could not believe his ears . . . but with his old eyes, as dim as they were, he saw the carts that had been sent to carry him back. He heard Joseph's message to him, "Come down to me; don't delay. You shall live near me . . . and I will provide for you there." At last Jacob believed the good news. At the thought of seeing Joseph again, his spirit revived. Israel said, "I am convinced. My son Joseph is still alive! I will go and see him before I die."

So Israel, although he was a very old man, set forth on the long journey from his native land to a foreign land. He set out with all that belonged to him—his children and grandchildren, his flocks and herds, and all his other possessions. It was a major move, especially for such an elderly man. Jacob was 130 years old, too old to be travelling again. Long ago, as a young man, he had fled from his homeland on foot, but now such a journey seemed too difficult, even by cart. Jacob began to have many doubts and fears about this journey: Would he make it to Egypt alive? Should he be going to Egypt at all? When his father Isaac had faced famine in the land, God had said to him, "Don't go down to Egypt" (Genesis 26:1–6). Should Jacob be leaving the land of Canaan? This was the land God had promised to his forefathers and to himself and to his descendants forever. Should he be leaving the land of God's promise? All his life Jacob had striven for the blessing of God. Now, at the end of his life, was he turning his back on those blessings? Was it right for him to leave the Promised Land? Would he ever see it again? Would his end be a violent death in a foreign land? Jacob was suddenly afraid. What should he do? Should he go to Egypt or should he stay in Canaan? What was God's will for him now, at the end of his life? What he decided affected not only himself, but all his children who were leaving the Promised Land with him and all his descendants in future generations. It was an important decision. What should Jacob do?

Jacob decided to stop along the way, at Beersheba, before he left the Promised Land. Beersheba was where his grandfather Abraham had lived for a long time. Abraham had pitched his tents there and planted some trees there. At Beersheba Abraham had also called upon the name of the LORD, the Eternal God. (See Genesis 21:33, 34.) Jacob remembered Beersheba because he had lived there when he was a child. His father Isaac had pitched their tents at Beersheba also and he had dug a well there. On the first night in Beersheba the LORD had appeared to his father Isaac and had said to him, "I am the God of your father Abraham. Do not be afraid, for I am with you. I will bless you and increase the number of your descendants." (See Genesis 26:23–25.) Then Isaac had built an altar there and called on the name of the LORD. Over one hundred years had passed, but Jacob remembered their family worshipping God at that altar. Was it still there? Were the stones still heaped up one upon another, or had they long ago tumbled to the earth? Jacob would go to Beersheba and see if Isaac's altar to the LORD was still standing. If not, he would build a new one. So Jacob stopped at Beersheba and he offered sacrifices to the God of his father Isaac. Just as his grandfather and father had done before him, so Jacob did; he called upon the name of the LORD and he cried out to God for help. Should he leave this land, the land of his fathers? His history was here in this land; his God was here in this land. Should he be going to Egypt, to a land where there was no Word of God, no altars to God, no promises from God? The LORD had promised Jacob, "A nation will come from you . . . and I will give this land to your descendants after you." (See Genesis 35:11, 12 & 28:13–15.) What would happen to that great nation promised by God, if they left the Promised Land? Would his descendants ever return to receive their inheritance from God? Or would they vanish from the face of the earth down in Egypt? Would they be assimilated there? Or annihilated there? What would happen to God's promise? What would happen to God's people? What would happen to him? Jacob was filled with all kinds of fears and doubts about this journey to Egypt, but he cast all his cares upon his God . . . and he worshipped. Perhaps the LORD would speak to him in this place, just as He had spoken to his father long ago.

That night God spoke to Israel in a vision. "Jacob! Jacob!" called the LORD. "Here I am," he replied. "I am God, the God of your father," He said. "Do not be afraid to go down to Egypt, for I will make you into a great nation there. I will go down to Egypt with you, and I will surely bring you back again. And Joseph's own hand will close your eyes." That was what Jacob needed to know. That was what Jacob wanted to hear. What a comforting, reassuring word from a loving, forgiving, understanding God to a frail, old man! Jacob's doubts and fears were put to rest. He could leave the Promised Land in peace, knowing that God was with him on this journey. God would fulfill His promise by making him into a great nation—there, in Egypt! This was all part of God's plan! The LORD promised, "I will surely bring you back again." Jacob need not be afraid of this journey to Egypt. God was with him. Jacob could make this trip! Yes, he could do it! Not only was God with him, but Joseph was there, waiting for him. He would see his beloved son again, before Joseph's own dear hands would close his weak old eyes for the last time. That was what Jacob said he wanted, to see Joseph before he died—and God Himself had granted this one last wish.

Did Jacob believe God's Word to him that night? Yes! We read that Jacob left Beersheba. He left the land of Canaan and went to Egypt. By faith, Jacob went forward, not letting his fears stand in the way. He left in the cart that Pharaoh had sent to transport him there. The sons of Jacob also brought their wives and children down to Egypt in carts. They did not leave behind their belongings, as Pharaoh had suggested, but took with them everything they had acquired in Canaan, all their animals and all their possessions.

Thus it happened that Jacob and all his offspring went to Egypt. He left no one behind in Canaan. He took with him to Egypt his sons and grandsons, his daughters and granddaughters—all his offspring. Jacob's direct descendants, who journeyed with him to Egypt, numbered sixty-six persons. (This was not counting his sons' wives.) In Egypt there was a total of seventy people in Jacob's family. Over one hundred years ago at Beersheba, God promised Isaac, "I will increase the number of your descendants." From Isaac's son Jacob, there were now seventy people. Yet that was a small number. Had not God promised Abraham, "I will make you into a great nation" (Genesis 12:2)? Two hundred and fifteen years had passed since God gave that promise, and the population of that great nation was now only seventy. Most great nations count their people by the millions! But God's promises are sure, even if they seem slow to us. The Bible says, (however it may appear to us,) that "the Lord is not slow in keeping His promise" (II Peter 3:9). God says, "The least of you will become a thousand, the smallest—a mighty nation! I am the LORD. In its time, I will do this swiftly" (Isaiah 60:22). "With the Lord a day is like a thousand years, and a thousand years are like a day" (II Peter 3:8). In its time, God surely would make Israel into that great and mighty nation.

So Israel went to Egypt with all his descendants and all his livestock and all his possessions—and, more precious than anything else, all God's promises. Israel went to Egypt believing God's Word: "I will make you into a great nation there." Israel also went down to Egypt with the LORD by his side, with the LORD going before him and coming after him. God was with Jacob. God promised, "I will go down to Egypt with you."

The teacher's guide for this lesson starts on page 540.

JACOB'S LAST YEARS

• **Genesis 46:28–49:33**
• **Hebrews 11:13–16, 21**

W hen Jacob arrived in Egypt, Joseph had his chariot made ready and he went to meet his father Israel. As soon as the great governor of Egypt appeared before the old man, he threw his arms around his father and wept for a very long time. Israel said to his son Joseph, "Now I am ready to die, since I have seen for myself that you are still alive."

Jacob was ready to die now—and in truth, he was a very old man, (older than any person you or I will ever see.) When Joseph brought his father to the king's palace, Jacob did something quite remarkable. As he stood before the majesty of the great king of Egypt, Jacob lifted his frail old hand above Pharaoh—and blessed him. It was a very strange thing for him to do. How could a withered old man, who was just a poor shepherd by trade, bless the king, who was one of the wealthiest and mightiest men on the face of the earth? But Jacob knew who he was and what he was doing. Jacob was a prince of God, a prophet of the Most High, a patriarch of the promised nation, an ambassador of a heavenly dominion. Pharaoh was simply an earthly king, whose wealth and might were of this world, but Jacob had a rich store of heavenly treasures and spiritual blessings. There was much that Jacob could give to Pharaoh! That word of blessing was a very great gift indeed! Pharaoh was amazed at the old man who stood before him. "How old are you?" asked Pharaoh. Jacob answered, "The years of my pilgrimage are 130. My years have been few and difficult, and they do not equal the years of the pilgrimage of my fathers." (That was true. His father Isaac had lived 180 years and his grandfather Abraham had lived 175 years.) Jacob confessed before this great king, that he was just a pilgrim here on earth. Life was short and hard. He was a stranger in this world, a stranger who longed for a better homeland, a heavenly one. Then Jacob blessed Pharaoh again and went out from his presence.

Jacob said he was ready to die, since he had seen for himself that his son Joseph was still alive. He had lived 130 years, but still he was a stranger on earth. Now, in his old age, he was a stranger in Egypt too. Life must have been hard for the old man, as he struggled to adjust to another foreign land. Jacob was ready to die; he was longing to go home to heaven — but God had other plans. Jacob would live seventeen more years! God doubled the time that he had on earth to spend with Joseph. After seventeen years Joseph had been taken from him, but now another seventeen years were given to Jacob to be with his favourite son.

After meeting with Pharaoh, Joseph settled his father and his brothers, giving them property in the best part of Egypt, the district of Rameses in the land of Goshen, just as Pharaoh had directed. There his father and brothers, who were all shepherds, found pasture for their flocks, but the rest of Egypt wasted away because the famine was so severe. During those seven, long, hard, lean years Joseph provided his father and brothers with free food, but the Egyptians had to buy their food. They sold everything they had to keep from starving. First, the Egyptians spent all their money on food. Then, after their money was gone, Joseph sold them food in exchange for their livestock. They traded their horses, sheep, goats, cattle and donkeys for grain to keep themselves alive — but when that year ended, the famine continued. Again they faced death. The Egyptians came to Joseph and said, "We cannot hide from our lord the fact that since our money is gone and our livestock belongs to you, there is nothing left for our lord except our bodies and our land. Why should we perish before your eyes, we and our land as well? Buy us and our land in exchange for food, and we with our land will be in bondage to Pharaoh. Give us seed, so that we may live and not die, and that the land may not become desolate." So, the Egyptians, one and all, sold their fields, because the famine was too severe for them. The people were reduced to servitude from one end of Egypt to the other. They lost everything—even their land, even their freedom. Yet they were grateful to be alive. They said to Joseph, "You have saved our lives!" Thus, from the beginning the LORD made a distinction between the Egyptians and the Israelites. The Egyptians were completely impoverished by the famine, but the Israelites prospered. They lost neither money, nor livestock. The Israelites even acquired some property in Egypt, when everyone else relinquished theirs. Just as Abraham and Isaac had prospered during the famines in their day, so Jacob did in his day. The Egyptians, living in their own country, lost everything they owned, but the Israelites, living in a foreign country, gained much wealth. We read that "the Israelites acquired property there and were fruitful and increased greatly in number." God's blessing was surely upon His people. The LORD had promised Jacob, "I will make you into a great nation there,"—in Egypt! God was fulfilling that promise, even while Jacob lived.

Jacob lived for seventeen more years. He saw how greatly God blessed his family in Egypt, but he had a concern, an old man's concern. When he died, where would he be buried? So when the time drew near for Israel to die, he called for his son Joseph and said to him, "Promise that you will show me kindness and faithfulness. Do not bury me in Egypt, but when I rest with my fathers, carry me out of Egypt and bury me where they are buried." Jacob did not want to be buried as a stranger in a foreign land. Like many old people, he wanted to be buried with his fathers in his native land. However, Jacob had another reason too. He wanted to be buried in the land promised to him by God. It was Jacob's faith in God's promises that prompted this request. Joseph said he would do as he requested. "Swear to me," said Jacob. So Joseph promised on an oath to bury his father in the Promised Land. Then Israel worshipped as he leaned on the top of his staff. Jacob was near the end of his days on earth. He had lived 147 years and was a very old man—but he had not forgotten God. Even though he no longer had the strength to stand on his own, "by faith Jacob, when he was dying . . . worshipped as he leaned on the top of his staff" (Hebrews 11:21). Although he was not standing firm on his feet, Jacob was standing firm in his faith right until the end!

Sometime later Joseph was told that his father was very ill. He would not live much longer. So Joseph went to him and took his two sons, Manasseh and Ephraim, with him. When Jacob was told that his son Joseph had come to him, Israel rallied his remaining strength and sat up on the bed. Before he died, there were a few last words that Jacob must say, a few last works that Jacob must do. Jacob told his son Joseph what had been most important to him all his life: God's promises! Jacob told Joseph what he had probably told him many times before this day—what God had spoken to him the night he dreamed of God's angels ascending and descending on the stairway to heaven and what God had said to him at that same place many years later. (See Genesis 28:10–19 & 35:6–13.) Jacob said, "God Almighty, *El Shaddai*, appeared to me . . . in the land of Canaan, and there He blessed me and said to me, 'I am going to make you fruitful and will increase your numbers. I will make you a nation, a multitude of peoples, and I will give this land as an everlasting possession to your descendants after you.' Now then, your two sons born to you in Egypt . . . will be reckoned as mine. Ephraim and Manasseh will be mine, just as Reuben and Simeon are mine." Why was Jacob saying this? He was giving Joseph a double portion of the inheritance. Although Joseph was his eleventh son, Jacob was giving him the firstborn's double portion. When Jacob's inheritance, (which was the whole land of Canaan,) was divided among his sons, Ephraim and Manasseh would each inherit a son's portion, although they were only grandsons. There would not be a tribe in Israel called Joseph; instead there would be two tribes for him—one called Ephraim and one called Manasseh. What faith Jacob had! As he lay on his deathbed, he was dividing up property—which he did not yet possess! He was bequeathing an inheritance—which he owned only by faith! What presently belonged to Jacob was only a ridge of land and a small graveyard in Canaan, but he believed in God's promise: One day he would own the whole land of Canaan! One day his descendants would be like the dust of the earth, spreading out over the land to the west and to the east, to the north and to the south. Jacob believed God's Word! By faith he divided up the territory that God had promised, giving Joseph a double portion in that inheritance.

Then Israel noticed two young men standing behind Joseph. "Who are these?" he asked. "They are the sons God has given me here," answered Joseph. Then Israel said, "Bring them to me, so I may bless them." Now Israel's eyes were failing because of his old age. He could hardly see. So Joseph brought his sons close to his old father. Then Grandpa Israel hugged them and kissed them. He said to Joseph, "I never expected to see your face again, and now God has allowed me to see your children too." Joseph bowed down with his face to the ground. Then he presented his sons to receive their blessing. Manasseh, the older son, he put by Israel's right hand; Ephraim, the younger son, he put by Israel's left hand. But Israel, who had himself grasped his older brother's blessing, did something tricky again. Although he was such an old old man, Jacob had one last trick at the very end of his life: He crossed his hands. He crossed his hands, so that his right hand rested on the younger boy's head. His first and best blessing would not go to Manasseh, the firstborn, but to Ephraim, who was born second. Before anyone could stop him, Israel spoke his blessing. He blessed Joseph by blessing his sons. He said:

> May the God, before whom my fathers
>> Abraham and Isaac walked,
> the God, who has been my Shepherd
>> all my life to this day,
> the Angel, who has delivered me from all harm—
> may He bless these boys.
> May they be called by my name,
>> and the names of my fathers,
> Abraham and Isaac,
> and may they increase greatly upon the earth.

Genesis 48:15, 16

Joseph was pleased with what he heard, but not with what he saw. He was not pleased that his father had crossed his hands. Joseph took hold of his father's right hand to move it from Ephraim's head to Manasseh's head and said, "No, my father, this one is the firstborn. Put your right hand on his head." But Israel refused. As he had known all his life, so he knew near his death, to whom the blessings must go. It was not a mistake. Israel knew exactly what he was doing. "I know, my son, I know," said Israel. He knew it was a disappointment for Joseph, who loved his firstborn son, (just as his father Isaac had loved his firstborn son, Esau.) But God was no respecter of persons. It was the LORD's choice that would prevail, not man's choice. The right-hand blessing would remain on Ephraim's head. Israel knew that this would be hard for Joseph to accept, so he assured him that Manasseh, the firstborn, would also be blessed. "He too will become a people, and he too will become great. Nevertheless, his younger brother will be greater than he, and his descendants will become a multitude of nations." Then Israel blessed them both that day and said:

> *In your name will Israel pronounce this blessing:*
> *"May God make you like Ephraim and Manasseh."*

> *Genesis 48:20*

So Israel put the younger ahead of the older; he put Ephraim ahead of Manasseh. However, Jacob blessed both of Joseph's sons and the Scriptures testify that this was an act of faith, for which Jacob was commended. The Bible says, "By faith Jacob, when he was dying, blessed each of Joseph's sons" (Hebrews 11:21).

Besides giving Joseph a double portion of the inheritance and these blessings to his sons, Israel also passed on to Joseph God's promise. He was about to die, but the LORD had promised to be with them and to bring them back to the land of their fathers. Israel said to Joseph, "I am about to die, but *God will be with you* and He will take you back to the land of your fathers." It was a word of comfort, not only from Israel, but from God. Israel was leaving a most important gift to his most beloved son—the Word of God!

Israel had one last little gift to give to his son Joseph. With his sword and his bow Israel had taken a small piece of God's promise beforehand, a ridge of land in Canaan that he had conquered himself. It was the one piece of property that he already actually owned. This he gave to Joseph, saying, "And to you, I give one portion more than to your brothers—the portion I took from the Amorites with my sword and my bow."

Jacob had given Joseph a double blessing, but Jacob had eleven other sons. Would he bless only one of them? His father Isaac had only one blessing for only one of his sons. His older brother Esau had cried loudly and wept bitterly with Isaac, asking and pleading, "Do you have only one blessing, my father? Bless me too, my father!"—but Jacob had taken the one blessing from their father Isaac. Many years had passed. Now Jacob lay dying. He had something to say to each of his twelve sons, a blessing appropriate for each one of them. Although there had been much sin in Jacob's household, still not one of his sons would be cut off from the family of Jacob or the inheritance of Israel. They would all receive a portion of God's promised Land. So Jacob called for all his sons and said, "Gather around, that I may tell you what will happen to you in days to come. Assemble and listen, sons of Jacob; listen to your father Israel:

Jacob began with his oldest son, Reuben. "Reuben, you are my first-born . . . the first sign of my strength, excelling in honour, excelling in power . . . You will no longer excel!" Was this a blessing? Why did Jacob say such a thing to his firstborn son? Reuben did not receive the double por-tion of the oldest brother, because of the hideous sin, which he had com-mitted against his father many years earlier. (See Genesis 35:22.) Jacob was still displeased with Reuben, but he did not disown him.

Jacob then spoke to the next two brothers, Simeon and Levi. He also had not forgotten their sin, how they had "killed men in their anger." Jacob cursed their anger, so fierce; he cursed their fury, so cruel—but he did not curse them. Simeon and Levi were not cut off from their inheritance in Israel.

Judah, Jacob's fourth son, must have wondered what would be said to him, since he had not been much better than his older brothers. (See Gen-esis 38.) What Jacob said was most astonishing: "Judah, (or Praise,) your brothers will praise you . . . Your father's sons will bow down to you!" Had Jacob made a mistake? Didn't he mean to say this to Joseph? No, there was not a mistake. Jacob was speaking as a prophet; he was speaking the Word of God. The LORD had chosen Judah. The Bible says: "The LORD . . . re-jected the tents of Joseph; He did not choose the tribe of Ephraim, but He chose the tribe of Judah . . . which He loved" (Psalm 78:67, 68). Yes, in spite of Judah's sins, the LORD chose him to bring forth His greatest promise! Something amazing was going to happen in the days to come. Jacob pro-claimed, *"The sceptre will not depart from Judah . . . until he comes to whom it belongs."* Jacob prophesied that from Judah would come a king; from Ju-dah would come a line of kings, until One came who was the King of kings! Jacob said that all nations would obey this king. He would be like a lion, conquering all his enemies. Thus, as Jacob lay dying, he saw in the distant future the One whom God had promised from the beginning; yes, Jacob saw His day and was glad. On his deathbed, Jacob spoke of the coming Mes-siah—and revealed to his sons and to the whole world from whence the Messiah would come—the tribe of Judah! In Jacob's dying words was his greatest testimony of faith. Jacob believed in God's greatest promise: the promise of a Saviour from sin and death. From the tribe of Judah would come the Son, who would crush the head of that ancient serpent called the devil or Satan. The victory of this Saviour would be proclaimed thus: *"the lion of the tribe of Judah . . . has triumphed"* (Revelation 5:5). The Saviour was coming—and Jacob looked forward to that day, welcoming Him and believing in Him hundreds and hundreds of years before He ever arrived. That was why Jacob said that Judah would be praised; that was how all his father's sons (and his father too) would bow down to Judah—through a Son and a King that would come from him, even Jesus Christ, the Lord of all. About Jesus, Judah's descendent, the angel said: "He will reign over the house of Jacob forever. His kingdom will never end" (Luke 1:33).

Then Jacob continued blessing his sons. He spoke of the land that Zebulun and Issachar would inherit and he spoke of the judges that would come from Dan, whose name means "Judge." Jacob also blessed Gad, Asher and Naphtali.

Jacob had blessed his first ten sons and now he came to Joseph, his darling, to whom he had already given a double portion and whose two sons he had already blessed. Jacob gave Joseph blessing upon blessing upon blessing. Jacob said that Joseph was blessed in all his troubles because of the LORD, "because of the hand of the Mighty One of Jacob, because of the Shepherd, the Rock of Israel, because of your father's God who helps you, because of the Almighty who blesses you with blessings of the heavens above and blessings of the deep that lies below." Joseph would have the LORD's blessing of children; he would be like a fruitful vine. Jacob said, "Your father's blessings are greater than the blessings of the ancient mountains, than the bounty of the age-old hills." All these blessings were for Joseph! Jacob said, "Let all these rest on the head of Joseph, on the brow of the prince among his brothers."

Jacob had one more son, his youngest son, Benjamin—and he blessed him also.

In the middle of these blessings to his sons, Jacob cried out to God, "I look for Your deliverance, O LORD!" That was Jacob's great hope as he faced death. His hope was not in his sons and what they would do, but in God's Son and what He would do. Jacob/Israel was looking for God's salvation! "I look for Your deliverance, O LORD!" What a blessing it was for all the sons of Jacob to hear that cry of faith from the lips of their dying father.

Thus Jacob had the faith and the strength upon his deathbed to bless each of his twelve sons and to proclaim to them one last time that deliverance is from the LORD. They must look to God for salvation. Then he gave them his final instructions: "I am about to be gathered to my people. Bury me with my fathers in the cave . . . in Canaan, which Abraham bought as a burial place . . . There Abraham and his wife Sarah were buried; there Isaac and his wife Rebekah were buried, and there I buried Leah." Jacob gave his sons exact instructions about where the cave was in the land of Canaan. He wanted to rest with his loved ones. He wanted his body to be buried where their bones lay, even though he believed his soul would be gathered to his people in heaven. Jacob had faith in God's promises to the very end. With his last breaths he spoke of the two countries promised by God—the earthly one and the heavenly one. "The mouth of the righteous is a fountain of life . . ." (Proverbs 10:11). Even on his deathbed, Jacob's mouth poured forth words of faith and life.

When Jacob had finished speaking to his sons, he drew his feet up into the bed, breathed his last, and was gathered to his people. Jacob finally went home to his eternal rest.

The teacher's guide for this lesson starts on page 542.

GRIEF AND DEATH WITH FAITH AND HOPE

- **Genesis 50**
- **Hebrews 11:22**

Jacob died. He took his last breath and then lay in the stillness of death. Joseph threw himself upon his dead father and wept over him. He also kissed his father one last time. Then Joseph had his physicians embalm his father. For seventy days Joseph, his brothers, the whole family of Israel and the whole country of Egypt mourned Jacob's death. Then Joseph asked Pharaoh's permission to leave the country to bury his father. He explained that his father made him swear an oath to bury him in the tomb he dug for himself in the land of Canaan. Joseph said, "Let me go and bury my father; then I will return." Pharaoh granted permission. He said, "Go and bury your father, as he made you swear to do." So the body of Jacob was brought back to Canaan for burial. It was an impressive funeral procession that entered the Promised Land. Besides the Israelites, there were a large number of Egyptians too. It was not only the family of Jacob, but also the officials of Pharaoh, that attended the funeral service. Chariots and horsemen were also part of the funeral procession. It was as if a king was being buried, not a simple shepherd. But then, was

not Israel a prince in the kingdom of God? God honoured Jacob in his
death. Many times when he was alive, Jacob had thought he would go down
to the grave in sorrow, bereaved of his children, but God was gracious to
him. Jacob went to his grave in honour, attended by a very large company—
and every one of his children! Jacob went to his grave in peace, with faith
and hope in his God. The ones left behind, were the ones who were grieving. By the Jordan River they lamented loudly and bitterly, observing a seven-
day period of mourning for the father of Joseph. Even the Canaanites who
lived there were amazed and said, "The Egyptians are holding a solemn ceremony of mourning." But at last Jacob was laid to rest. His sons did as he
had commanded them: They had carried him to the land of Canaan and
now they buried him there, in the cave in the field which Abraham had
bought as a burial site so long ago.

Abraham, Isaac and Jacob—the men to whom God had spoken, the
men to whom God had given His promises—they were gone. Their souls
had departed and their bodies had returned to dust. What would happen
now to the sons of Israel? The remains of their forefathers were just grey bones
in the dry ground—and their God, (the God of Abraham, Isaac and Jacob,)
was now silent. He did not speak to the sons of Israel, as they stood by their
father's grave. There was only the sound of the hot wind, as it blew the withered grass about their feet. Where should they go? What should they do?
Their homes and their farms, their flocks and their herds, their wives and
their children, were not here. Only the dead dwelt here. Everything they
owned and everyone they loved were in Egypt. The only thing that belonged
to them here in the Promised Land were bones and graves. Joseph and his
brothers left Canaan and returned to Egypt.

Now that Jacob was dead and the funeral was finished, the brothers of
Joseph feared that he would seek revenge and pay back their evil with evil.
They said, "What if Joseph holds a grudge against us and pays us back for
all the wrongs we did to him?" So they sent word to Joseph, saying that their
father had left him a message before he died: "I ask you to forgive your brothers the sins and the wrongs they committed in treating you so badly." The
brothers themselves also asked for forgiveness: "Now, please, forgive the sins
of the servants of the God of your father." When Joseph heard their message, he wept. Then the brothers came to Joseph and threw themselves down
before him. "We are your slaves," they said. (Once again the dreams that
Joseph had as a boy were fulfilled, as his brothers bowed down to him.)

Joseph must have rejoiced in their repentance, but he was grieved by their lack of faith in him and in God. They still did not understand. So Joseph said to them, "Don't be afraid. Am I in the place of God? You intended to harm me, but God intended it for good! He did it to accomplish what is now being done—the saving of many lives. So then, don't be afraid. I will provide for you and your children." Thus Joseph reassured them and spoke kindly to them.

Joseph and his brothers remained in the land of Egypt for the rest of their lives. Their children and their children's children grew up there, while Joseph and his brothers became withered, whitened, old men there. Joseph became a great-great-grandfather in the land of Egypt. He lived to be 110 years old. Finally the time came for Joseph to leave the land of Egypt and this world. The time had come for him to be gathered to his people. Although God had never spoken to Joseph, he remembered what his father Jacob had spoken on his deathbed: "God will be with you and He will take you back to the land of your fathers." Joseph believed those words, because God Himself had promised: "I will surely bring you back again." Yes, Joseph believed the Word of God! As he lay dying, he too confessed his faith and trust in God. He said to his brothers, "I am about to die. But God will surely come to your aid and take you up out of this land to the land He promised on oath to Abraham, Isaac and Jacob." Joseph trusted the promises of God sworn to his forefathers, although he himself had never heard God's voice. Because he believed in the Word of the LORD and the LOVE of the LORD, because he believed in God's faithfulness to all generations, Joseph made the sons of Israel swear an oath that he too would be buried in the Promised Land. Joseph said, "God will surely come to your aid, and then you must carry my bones up from this place." What faith! Joseph believed that some day God would bring his people out of Egypt into the Promised Land and he was willing to wait for that day to be buried! Joseph's bones waited 400 years for burial—but they were at last laid to rest in the Promised Land! The Bible commends Joseph for this act of faith: "By faith Joseph, when his end was near, spoke about the exodus of the Israelites from Egypt and gave instructions about his bones" (Hebrews 11:22). Joseph's last words in this world were a great proclamation of faith! When Joseph died, he was embalmed and placed in a coffin in Egypt—but he was not buried, for his bones were waiting for another resting place. His bones were waiting for burial in another land—the Promised Land. Joseph's waiting coffin would be a reminder to generation after generation of the children of Israel, that God would surely come to rescue them and take them (with Joseph's bones) out of Egypt and bring them into the land that He Himself had promised to give to them.

Joseph died in faith, even as he had lived in faith. His whole life was a testimony to the LORD, to encourage the faith of God's people for thousands and thousands of years. God was in control of Joseph's life from the day he was born until the day he died. Joseph understood that the Sovereign LORD had caused even the most painful and awful things in his life to be for the glory of God and the good of God's people. Joseph understood that he had been used by God to save his people. Long ago Joseph had told his brothers that it was not they, but God, who had sent him to Egypt. He said, "God sent me ahead of you to preserve for you a remnant on earth and to save your lives by a great deliverance" (Genesis 45:7, 8). Many years later he said, "You intended to harm me, but God intended it for good, to accomplish what is now being done—the saving of many lives" (Genesis 50:20). Joseph understood that he was a saviour of his people—but was he the Saviour whom God had promised from the beginning? No, for Joseph died and was laid in a coffin, from which he did not rise. Another Saviour was still coming, who would lay down His life as a ransom for many. This promised Saviour would die to pay for the sins of His people, but neither death nor the grave could hold Him. He would be resurrected, leaving an empty tomb behind Him. This Saviour would live and reign forever! Who was He? It was Jesus Christ our Lord!

Joseph was a foreshadow of that Saviour. Joseph was a type of Christ, his life being a shadowy preview of what would happen several hundred years later. Joseph's life pointed forward into the future to another Man's life. The events in Joseph's life were like a series of signs, which pointed to the Messiah, even to Jesus Christ our Lord: Joseph was the son, whom his father loved; Jesus was also the beloved Son, who pleased His Father. Twice God's voice came from heaven and declared of Jesus, "This is my Son, whom I love; with Him I am well pleased" (Matthew 3:17 & 17:5). Like Joseph, Jesus was also envied and hated by his brothers, who plotted to kill him. Joseph was sold for some pieces of silver; so was Christ. Joseph was bound and led away by foreigners; so was Christ. Joseph was cut off from his people; so was Christ. Joseph was cast into a dark dungeon; Christ was cast into the darkness of death and laid in a tomb. Joseph was figuratively "raised from the dead"; Christ was literally resurrected. Joseph was exalted to the highest position, becoming the great lord of all the land; so Christ was made King of kings and Lord of lords, "who sat down at the right hand of the throne of the Majesty in heaven" (Hebrews 8:1), "far above all rule and authority, power and dominion, and every title that can be given . . ." (Ephesians 1:21). Joseph became the saviour of his people, forgiving their sins and preserving them from death—and so he pointed to a greater Saviour, to Jesus, who would not only forgive the sins of His people, but would also atone for their sins, and redeem them from death forever. Joseph said of himself, "God sent me ahead of you to preserve for you a remnant on earth and to save your lives by a great deliverance." How much more could that be said of Christ! God sent Him into the world to preserve a remnant on earth and to save His people from their sins by the sacrifice of Himself. God sent Jesus to save our lives by the greatest deliverance of all! Jesus Himself said, "God so loved the world that He gave His one and only Son, that whoever believes in Him shall not perish, but have eternal life" (John 3:16).

How shall we escape the wrath of God, if we neglect so great a salvation? This salvation was proclaimed by God from the beginning! This Saviour was announced again and again by God's servants, the prophets. His life was foreshadowed by the saints of old—that we might recognize the real and true Man when he appeared on the earth. Even Jacob announced the coming of this Messiah and Joseph's whole life bore witness to this coming Saviour. There is no excuse for unbelief. God slowly, but clearly, steadily and wonderfully revealed the eternal gospel of salvation through His Son, Jesus Christ. We must not neglect so great a salvation! We must pay careful attention to what we have heard, so that we do not drift away by unbelief. We must make sure that none of us has a sinful, unbelieving heart that turns away from the living God. We have heard the gospel preached to us, but that message of salvation is of no value to us, if we do not combine it with faith. We must believe in God's Saviour, Jesus Christ. We must believe in God's great salvation, the sacrifice of Jesus Christ on the cross to pay for our sins. We must make sure that we are those who believe and are saved.

❊   ❊   ❊

T he first book of the Bible, Genesis, has come to an end. This book opened with God giving life to the world, but it ends with the fear of sin and the pain of death. It ends with weeping, mourning, grieving and bitter lamenting. It ends with funerals and burials. It ends with tombs and bones. These are the last words in Genesis: "a coffin in Egypt." But death does not have the final word.

There is much hope in the last words of this book, because there is faith and because there is God. There is forgiveness of sin and there are shadows of the Saviour. There are children being born. Little new-born babies are placed on the knees of their great-great-grandfather, Joseph. The family of faith continues. The promises of God are remembered: "God will surely come . . . God will surely come to your aid." There is hope and there is life, because there is God. By His grace, we are saved. In the fullness of time God sent His Son, that we might live through Him. "HEREIN IS LOVE: not that we loved God, but that He loved us and sent His Son as an atoning sacrifice for our sins" (I John 4:10).

The teacher's guide for this lesson starts on page 544.

GENESIS
TEACHER'S GUIDE

Explanation of the Teacher's Guide

I wrote this guide for the teacher who is using the lessons from *Herein Is Love: Genesis*. This manual can be used by any adult involved in teaching children the Bible: Sunday School teachers, Christian School teachers, Home School teachers, Vacation Bible School teachers, camp counsellors and parents. Prayerfully study the Scripture references given at the beginning of each lesson. After that, read the lesson carefully. Find the visual aids you need to use for that lesson. Prepare the memory work handouts. Assemble the craft materials. Practice the Psalm. Plan the route of your field trip . . . and you're ready to go!

If you have only an hour each week with your class of children, (which is all most Sabbath School teachers have,) you cannot possibly do everything suggested for each lesson in this teacher's manual. However, with one hour you will have time to: teach the lesson (which is your first priority), show and discuss the visual aids (while you are teaching), hear the children's memory work, sometimes do a quick craft, ask a few questions, pray, (for there is always the time and the need to pray,) and sing a psalm. If you have a two or three hour block of time, the making of crafts and singing of psalms can be greatly extended. Camp counsellors and parent-teachers will find the field trip suggestions particularly useful.

Many Sabbath School teachers think that the children must have a lesson sheet to take home with them each week. Personally, I do not like those sheets. They are expensive, uninteresting, sometimes damaging, and usually wind up in the garbage can unused anyway. I do agree that it is nice for the children to have something to take home with them, but really it need not be any more than a verse of memory work. What could be more important for the children to take away with them than a jewel from God's Word?! However, if you think a parent page is necessary for a lesson review during the week, you can very simply and cheaply make your own by including:

1. The main Bible text (to be read at home)
2. The memory work (to be learned at home)
3. A craft suggestion (if you didn't make one in class)
4. A copy of the main Psalm (to be sung daily in family worship)
5. The field trip suggestion (for a family outing)

Visual Aids

I am completely dissatisfied with (and sometimes utterly offended by) the illustrations found in most Bible curriculums currently available for children's Sunday School. The pictures that are intended to be visual aids become visual harms, because they represent the Scriptures as little more than fairy tales or comic strips. These pictures cheapen the Holy Word of God. How can the children take seriously their forerunners in the faith, when they are so often represented visually as cartoon characters? I have suggested visual aids for the children, which will connect the Bible to the real world.

Use PHOTOGRAPHS! These are far more interesting for the children, impressing upon them that the study of the Scriptures is serious study. With this approach, there is no concern about pictures being current or relevant, because the pictures are of enduring significance. The wealth of visual aids that the human race has collected since the invention of the camera is overwhelming. Make use of this rich resource. Expose the children to the amazing scenes witnessed and captured by the human eye through the camera. Photography books, National Geographic magazines, old calendars, postcards, etc. is where you will find the necessary pictures. For example, when you are studying the fourth day of creation, go to your local library and find a good book on astronomy. Show the children pictures of the moon and stars taken through telescopes or from satellites. The heavens declare the glory of God—and these photos are evidence of that glory! Photographs can be used as powerful, visual testimony to help the children focus on and believe in the lessons you are teaching from the Scriptures.

Use MAPS! Whenever possible in a lesson use a map by tracing the route of a patriarch's journey, pointing out an important mountain or river, showing the area of a certain country, etc. Let the children see that the accounts in Scripture are historical events that happened in the real world.

Use SPECIMENS! Many of the stories in the Bible have an object in it that is central. It can be something so simple, and yet that object rivets the children's attention to the lesson. An example is the goatskin that Jacob used to deceive his father. Can you locate a goatskin? (I knew a grandmother who had a soft, grey, goatskin coat.) Bring the goatskin to class, blindfold the children and then let them feel for themselves what happened in the Biblical account. Real objects from the real world help to connect the children to the real and true stories of the Bible.

Memory Work

I always impress upon my children the need to store up God's Word like a treasure in their hearts, which can help them in a time of need. I tell the children that the real reward is knowing God's Word, but I also give them a little incentive by making each child a memory work book. This is quite simple:

1) Make booklets by folding 8 x 12 sheets of construction paper in half. (Make them all the same colour with younger children to avoid squabbles.) Make the front cover interesting by pasting on it a slightly smaller rectangle of some sort of picture. (Again, I always make the books identical.) Sometimes I use wrapping paper. Sometimes I recycle attractive church bulletins.

I usually make books to last three months for weekly lessons, changing them with the seasons. For example, the memory work book for the autumn quarter could have a picture of brightly coloured leaves on a yellow background. Often I add a few sparkles to the front cover too. Make sure each child's name is on his/her book.

2) Type out the verse. (I use a 4 x 6 sheet of paper.) Xerox copies for double the number of children in the class. One copy goes into their book, (which you keep until the books are finished!) The other copy is handed out to each child to learn during the week. I try to make the hand-out copies interesting: In autumn I make the children's verses in different shades of brightly coloured paper cut in the shape of leaves. That way, their weekly Bible verses can make a pretty display on their bulletin boards or refrigerators at home. In winter I hand out white "snowballs." It takes just a few extra moments to trace a circle around the verse before cutting it. In spring you can hand out diamond-shaped "kites" or petalled "flowers" in pastel hues. Be creative! There's more than one way to hand out a slip of memory work, giving the children something special to take home.

3) Buy sheets of stickers, continuing the seasonal theme. (There are usually twelve stickers per sheet, four sheets per package, which costs about fifty cents per quarter per child.) Write each child's name on the back of their sticker sheet. For each week's memory work that is learned, they get to choose a sticker from their own sheet to put in their book. At the end of the term, collect all the unearned, unused stickers—but let all the children take their books home.

Craft

For each lesson I suggest one or more crafts that in some way deal with what you have discussed in that lesson. Many of the crafts can be easily modified to fit your required time-frame. I have not described in detail how to make each item, for this is not meant to be a step-by-step craft book; its purpose is to give you some ideas. For example, with the lesson on the fifth day of creation, when God made the birds, I suggest (among several other ideas) to make bird feeders. This can be a simple ten-minute project using pine cones and peanut butter or, if you need something to fill a two-hour craft gap, you can work with hammer and nails on a more difficult bird feeder.

Simply check a children's nature/craft book at your local library and there you will find all kinds of directions on how to make bird feeders. Pick the one that best suits the age level and time allotment of your particular class of children.

Review Questions

For each lesson I ask a few specific review questions. However, there are two very important questions that should be asked with every lesson:

1. What does this lesson teach us about God?
2. How does this lesson help us to live our lives?

Prayer

The application of each lesson to the children's lives is found in the prayer.

Psalms to Sing

I list one Psalm (or part of a Psalm) that is particularly relevant to the lesson, as well as several others that are also related to it. Singing the Psalms is a crucial way, but simple way, for the children to store God's Word in their hearts. "Give thanks to the LORD; call on His Name . . . Sing to Him; sing psalms to Him" (Psalm 105:1, 2). "Let the word of Christ dwell in you richly as you teach . . . and as you sing psalms" (Colossians 3:16). If time permits, I recommend singing the main Psalm for each lesson several times, so that the children have already begun to memorize it. You could also send home a copy of the main Psalm, so that the children can sing it at home during the week with their families. The Psalter I have used is *The Book of Psalms for Singing,* published by the Reformed Presbyterian Church of North America, 1973.

Field Trip

The teaching of the Word of God to our children is not meant to be confined within the four walls of our Christian churches, schools and homes.

Take God's Word outside, into the fresh air and sun shine! Teach it in the open fields and the busy streets! Moses says, "Fix these words of mine in your hearts and minds . . . Teach them to your children, talking about them when you sit at home and *when you walk along the road*" (Deuteronomy 11:18, 19). How will God's Word be fixed in the hearts and minds of our children? It will happen, not only when we read the Scriptures around the family dinner table or when we study the Bible in our Sunday School classrooms, but it will happen when we are walking along the road, when we are looking at the world around us as we discuss the things of God. I will never forget the time our family (with four children, ages 2 through 12) was driving through Sequoia National Park, looking with awe at the largest trees in the world. As we drove along these great green giants we sang a psalm in praise of the Creator: "The trees of the LORD are well watered, the cedars of Lebanon that He planted" (Psalm 104:16). We were in California, U.S.A.—but the same God planted those majestic "cedar" trees too. That Psalm concludes with these words: "I will sing to the LORD all my life; I will sing praise to my God as long as I live . . . Praise the LORD, O my soul. Praise the LORD" (Psalm 104:33, 35). A very important message was communicated to our children that day, as they delighted in those amazing trees—but you don't have to drive across a continent to have that kind of teaching opportunity. It's along every ordinary road, along every little pathway in your life.

For each lesson I have suggested some small outing to a place which will impress that particular Bible teaching upon your children. What a way to review a lesson! If you are setting out with that purpose in mind, "to teach your children . . . when you walk along the road" it will actually happen. You will do it—and they will be blessed!

Please turn the page for the guide to lesson 1.

The Word of God

John 1:1–4, 14

VISUAL AIDS

Bring Greek and Hebrew Bibles for your children to examine or bring each child a sample page of writing from each of these languages. (You could xerox some pages from your pastor's library.) Have the children try to read them! This will stimulate their interest in written words, other languages and the work of translation.

MEMORY WORK

"Thy word I have treasured in my heart . . ."(Psalm 119:11)

CRAFT

You could make treasure chests or jewel cases by covering small cardboard boxes (or heart-shaped boxes) with pretty paper on the outside and felt-like fabric on the inside. A simpler project would be to fold pieces of red construction paper in half and cut out a large heart for each child. Print the memory work on the inside of the heart or make a pocket in which all the Bible verses can be kept. Have the children glue gold and silver sequins and sparkles inside the heart, reminding them as they work that the Word of God is more precious than gold or silver.

REVIEW QUESTIONS

1. Why is the Bible different from all other books in the world?
2. What are three ways that God and people use words?
3. How did God usually speak His Word? What were some special ways that He spoke His Word?

4. How did God usually write His Word? What were some special ways that He wrote His Word?
5. What languages did God use to write the Bible? How did we get the Bible in our own language?
6. God gave us something very precious, more precious than silver and gold. What precious gift did God give us? Why is it worth so much?
7. Where should we keep this treasure? How can we hide it in our hearts?
8. It is not enough to hear God's Word or know God's Word. What else must we do?
9. Who is called "The Word of God"?

PRAYER

LORD, thank You for giving us the precious gift of Your Word. Please, help us to treasure it in our hearts all our days on this earth.

PSALMS TO SING

119B . . . and 19BD; 119F; 119I; 119M; 119N; 119O; 119T; 119WX.

FIELD TRIP

Explore a big library! See if you can find among many special books, the most special book of all.

(This student lesson starts on page 1.)

In the Beginning, Out of Nothing

Genesis 1:1

VISUAL AIDS

You could bring to class an acorn, a sunflower seed and some little ripe puff-balls for the children to touch to produce the "puff" of spores. If you don't have any puffballs at your fingertips, perhaps you could bring a big ripe mushroom from the supermarket; explain that its spores (along the gills) are too tiny even to see. (However, if you place the cap, gill-side-down, on a piece of white paper, cover it with a bowl and leave it for a few hours, you will have a beautiful spore print, made of millions of spores, which the children can see.) There are wonderful pictures available in children's magazines or books, which show the stages of butterflies, frogs and chickens from egg to adult. To see the stages of a developing human being, pro-life groups put out excellent pamphlets and there are many books available too, such as *A Child Is Born or Being Born*, with exquisite photographs by Lennart Nilsson. (If you're on a tight time schedule, watch out! An hour can slip by easily without getting to the real lesson, because the children are fascinated by these "beginnings.")

MEMORY WORK

"In the beginning God created the heavens and the earth." (Genesis 1:1)

CRAFT

Cut out some large, ostrich-sized, oval-shaped "eggs" from plain white paper, two or three for each child in your class. They can then draw the beginnings of some little creatures inside the eggs. They can draw an owl or a turtle, a flamingo or an alligator, a duck-billed platypus or even a dinosaur.

REVIEW QUESTIONS

1. Did you have a beginning?
2. Did the world have a beginning?
3. Did God have a beginning?
4. The things that we see in the world around us—from where did they all come?
5. Out of what did God make the world and everything in it?
6. Who said, "I am the Beginning and the End"?
7. Why is God worthy to receive all our praise?

PRAYER

Heavenly Father, we thank You for beginning and creating everything. We thank You and praise You for making us!

PSALMS TO SING

106G . . . and 90CD (1); 115B (8); 121B (1); 134AB.

FIELD TRIP

Visit some sort of hatchery. It's very exciting for young children to see a little creature emerging from an egg.

(This student lesson starts on page 6.)

The First Day

Genesis 1:1–5

VISUAL AIDS

Show the class a picture of how the world looked in the beginning. You will need a plain black piece of paper!

MEMORY WORK

1. "God is light; in Him there is no darkness at all." (I John 1:5)
2. God said, "I am the LORD and there is no other. I form the light and create darkness." (Isaiah 45:6)

CRAFT

Have each child begin a book called The Days of Creation. You will need different colours of construction paper. The first page should be plain black. The second page should be yellow. Print (or label) "DAY 1" on the top of the light page. On the bottom print: GOD SAID, "LET THERE BE LIGHT." Keep the children's books until all seven days are completed. You could also make paper-plate clocks with movable hands and discuss what we do at different times. Print "GOD MADE TIME" on the back of the clocks. Another craft for this lesson could be making simple candles. Place them in empty tuna-fish cans and write this verse on the side: "You, O LORD, keep my lamp burning; my God turns my darkness into light" (Psalm 18:28). Tin-can lanterns (with holes nailed all around it and a candle inside) could be another craft. Make sure there is adult supervision for any candle-lighting!

REVIEW QUESTIONS

1. How did the world look in the beginning?

2. Who was there? What was He doing?
3. What was God's first good gift to the world?
4. Why did God make light?
5. Who said, "I am the Light of the world"?
6. Where is the "outer darkness"?
7. Why does the heavenly city not need sun, moon or any lamp?

PRAYER

LORD, thank You for making light. Thank You for making both the day and the night. Please take care of us through all our days and nights upon this earth. LORD, we pray, that You would lift up the light of Your face upon us and grant us peace. "O God Almighty, make Your face shine upon us, that we may be saved" (Psalm 80:7).

PSALMS TO SING

27AD (1) . . . and 4B; 36B; 43 (3–5); 77A; 80B (1); 89D; 112AB (1, 2); 119NOR (1); 139B (5, 6).

FIELD TRIP

Experience the dread of darkness and the joy of light by visiting some underground caves. If you have no dark caves in your vicinity, just sitting with small children in a very dark room for awhile and then flicking on a lamp or lighting a candle is fun. If the children made their own candles or lanterns, let their lights shine all together in the darkness! Children also love to go for a flashlight hike on a dark night.

(This student lesson starts on page 10.)

The Second Day

Genesis 1:6–8

VISUAL AIDS

Show the children a photo of the world taken from outer space. What you primarily see is earth's water: the blue of its seas and the white of its clouds. You can also show them beautiful photographs of clouds and the things that come from clouds: snowflakes, raindrops, hailstones, lightning, tornadoes.

MEMORY WORK

"Stop . . . and consider the wonders of God." (Job 37:14)

CRAFT

Continue working on the creation book. This next page should be grey construction paper with the words "DAY 2" at the top, and in the middle of the page print: GOD SAID, "LET THERE BE AN EXPANSE BETWEEN THE WATERS TO SEPARATE WATER FROM WATER." The children can paste cotton clouds above God's Word and draw blue and white waves below it. You can also bring balloons for the children, fill them with what God made on that second day and write "GOD MADE AIR" on them. Besides balloons to float in the air, you could make pinwheels to spin in the wind and streamers to flutter in the breeze. If you want a more difficult project, have the children make kites. Let them feel for themselves the power of the air as it moves.

REVIEW QUESTIONS

1. What were the three ways that God worked?
2. What did God create on the second day? What did God separate? What did God name?

3. What do we call the water above the sky?
4. Is earth's air important? Why? Do other planets have this?
5. Who delighted in God and what He made on the second day?
6. Who should rejoice in the LORD and all His works now?
7. Have you ever thanked the LORD for making the air that you breathe? Have you ever thanked Him for the blue sky and white clouds? Have you ever looked at a beautiful snowflake and said "thank-you" to God?

PRAYER

LORD, we thank You and praise You for the beautiful clouds which we can see and the critical air which we cannot see. Thank You for the rain and the snow, the winds and the storms. LORD, we even thank You for the thunder and the lightening, which remind us of Your power and Your splendour.

PSALMS TO SING

105A (1–3); 108A . . . and 18B; 77C (9–12); 97AC; 104A (1–3); 147B.

FIELD TRIP

Just go outside to an open space and admire the clouds and sky. Feel the wind; breathe the air . . . and thank God for them! You could also visit a weather station to watch the people as they work to understand the clouds, the winds, the air pressure, etc.

(This student lesson starts on page 14.)

The Third Day

Genesis 1:9–13

VISUAL AIDS

Bring a globe or map of the world and show your small pupils how God separated the land from the sea, forming the oceans and continents which we now have named. Point out the different shapes of the countries (like Italy's boot) and remind them that it was God who formed and shaped the earth. Hide the names of large land masses (including their own country) and see if they can identify these areas simply by their shapes. Point out the difference between natural boundaries and man-made ones. Show them beautiful pictures of coastlines, mountains, canyons, deserts, etc. Specimens and/or pictures of rocks, gems, jewels and metals will make this class more interesting too. You could also bring a piece of coal—and don't forget a little box of "ordinary" dirt, for out of this extraordinary substance God would bring forth all manner of marvellous things!

MEMORY WORK

"I worship the LORD, the God of heaven, who made the sea and the land." (Jonah 1:9)

CRAFT

You can continue working on the creation book. At the top of a blue page of construction paper print the words "DAY 3," and at the bottom print: GOD SAID, "LET DRY GROUND APPEAR." Have the children create land forms by cutting out irregular shapes from earth-coloured paper. These can be glued on the sea-blue pages. Rocks and gems can be added by cutting out jewel shapes from bits of shiny foil paper and pasting them onto the land forms. If you want a more difficult project, have the children make papier-mache landscapes with mountains, valleys, oceans, rivers, etc. Let them form the "rising land" with their own fingers!

REVIEW QUESTIONS

1. The earth had light for man to see and air for him to breathe, but what else did it need?
2. What did God separate on the third day?
3. What did God name on that day?
4. The earth was no longer formless. What happened?
5. The earth was no longer empty. What happened?
6. When God saw what He had made, how did He judge His work?
7. When you see what God has made, how do you judge His work?

PRAYER

Our loving heavenly Father, thank You for giving us this beautiful earth as our home. Thank You for allowing us to see it and feel it; thank You that we can walk on it, play on it and live on it! LORD, help us to take good care of this great gift.

PSALMS TO SING

95A . . . and 24A (1), 33A; 57B (5, 7–10), 66A(1); 98AB; 104A; 146AB.

FIELD TRIP

You could visit canyons, coastlines or mountains, but even less spectacular views anywhere in the world display the beauty of what God created on that third day. You could also visit a mineral exhibit at a museum or tour the depths of the earth in a mine or just look at God's gifts in a jewelry store.

(This student lesson starts on page 17.)

Green! Glorious Green!

Genesis 1:11–13

VISUAL AIDS

Photos of badlands and wastelands to contrast with pictures of lush green wood-lands and grasslands would be useful. This class can be enhanced by seeing, smelling and tasting what God has made . . . so bring a bouquet of flowers and a tray of fruit and let the children enjoy the gifts of God! Since you are dis-cussing seeds in this lesson, bring an apple and knife to reveal (by cutting the apple crosswise) the beautiful "star" and the precious seeds of this fruit. The seed cases of plants are fascinating, such as the star-topped poppy pod with its tiny seeds that shake out or a dry crackly milkweed pod with its silky seeds that float away or the long curly pod of a scarlet runner bean with its pretty, pink-and-purple, speckled beans or even an ordinary prickly bur that sticks to your clothes. There are lots of interesting seed-bearing plants. God made millions of them!

MEMORY WORK

"The earth is full of the lovingkindness of the LORD." (Psalm 33:5)

CRAFT

Continue working on the creation book. This page should be made of bright green construction paper. Old seed catalogues are perfect for cutting out pic-tures of flowers, fruits, vegetables, shrubs, trees, etc. and pasting them onto the page. At the bottom print: God said, "let the land produce vegetation." There are many art projects that can be done with plants, such as leaf prints, either by rubbing (with a crayon) or stamping (with ink) or splattering (with paint.) You could also make placemats or bookmarks with pressed flowers. Artists have always been inspired to paint still-life pictures of vases of flowers or bowls of fruit, so . . . bring out the water colours!

REVIEW QUESTIONS

1. What did God make on the third day of creation?
2. Plants usually grow from seeds in the ground, but how did the plants sprout out of the earth on the third day of creation?
3. Why did God make plants?
4. How do plants praise the LORD?
5. People use plants to make clothes, paper, and medicine. How? Can you name some more ways that people use plants?
6. What is your favourite tree? Why? What is your favourite flower? Why? What are your favourite vegetables and fruits?
7. Have you ever thanked God for giving you all these gifts? Why don't you thank Him right now?!

PRAYER

LORD, thank You for Your LOVE, which fills the earth. Thank You for giving us a world filled with plants to see and smell and eat . . . and use in many other good ways.

PSALMS TO SING

96B . . . and 1AB; 23; 65B; 67A; 72C; 85B; 92C; 104B; 111A; 126; 145C.

FIELD TRIP

Visit some gardens, greenhouses or an arboretum. Walk through the fields and the woods, delighting in God's gifts!

(This student lesson starts on page 20.)

The Fourth Day

Genesis 1:14–19

VISUAL AIDS

God has filled the universe with the splendour of the stars and planets and galaxies. Show the children some of the beautiful photographs available to us taken through telescopes and satellites. It would also be useful to bring a globe to this class to demonstrate the movements of the earth. Pictures of spectacular sunrises and sunsets would also be helpful and can often be found in old calendars. You could also bring photographs of glistening dewdrops, sparkling waters, shimmering leaves, interesting shadows, exciting rainbows, etc. They all made their appearance on that fourth day. They all glorify God!

MEMORY WORK

"The heavens declare the glory of God; the skies proclaim the work of His hands." (Psalm 19:1)

CRAFT

This page of the creation book could be pink construction paper, with the children colouring a sunrise or sunset in brilliant colours. Add a silvery crescent moon and some little stars. The top should read: DAY 4. The bottom should read: GOD SAID, "LET THERE BE LIGHTS IN THE EXPANSE OF THE SKY." If you want more difficult projects, your children could make a mobile with sun, moon and stars or a model of our solar system.

REVIEW QUESTIONS

1. What did God make on the fourth day of creation?

2. The sun, the moon and the stars are glorious, but they "speak" and "point" to a glory surpassing their own. Of whom do they speak? To whom do they point?
3. Why did God make the heavenly bodies so beautiful?
4. Give three other reasons why God made the sun, the moon, and the stars.
5. How do the sun and the moon give earth its days, months, seasons and years?
6. Some people worship the sun, moon and stars. Is this right?
7. What should we do from sunrise to sunset? What should we do every day of our lives?

PRAYER

Our loving God, we thank You for Your good, gracious and glorious gifts. Thank You for the bright sunshine, the pale moonlight and the twinkling stars. Thank You for the different seasons and for ordering our time into days and months and years.

LORD, help us to use our days to glorify You!

PSALMS TO SING

19A . . . and 8B (1, 2); 104C (10); 113A (1–3); 147A (1, 3); 148.

FIELD TRIP

Visit an observatory or planetarium. Witness a sunrise or sunset. Stand in an open field on a starlit night and praise the name of the LORD!

(This student lesson starts on page 24.)

The Fifth Day

Genesis 1:20–23

VISUAL AIDS

There are many beautiful books abounding with pictures of this world's incredible fish and birds that you can enjoy with the children. Also, bring to class some shells and feathers, especially a peacock feather. A recording of the songs of birds (played as background music) could also add an interesting note to this class.

MEMORY WORK

1. "He performs wonders that cannot be fathomed, miracles that cannot be counted." (Job 9:10)
2. "The earth is full of his praise." (Habakkuk 3:3)

CRAFT

A piece of white construction paper (with "DAY 5" at the top) would be good for the next page in the creation book. Divide it in half with a horizontal line of waves. At the bottom print: GOD SAID, "LET THE WATER TEEM WITH LIVING CREATURES, AND LET BIRDS FLY ABOVE THE EARTH." The children can draw fish swimming in the lower section and birds flying in the upper section. If you have some spare cockle shells bring them to class. The children can paint them with plain water, either with little brushes or with little fingers, to let their true (underwater) colours show. While they are still wet, hold the shells up to a window to see their full beauty. This is a wonderful activity for small children. They could also colour white shells with magic markers. Two other easy paper crafts would be fish or bird mobiles, letting the children decorate the white, cardboard, fish or bird shapes. If you want more difficult projects, you could build bird feeders or make aquariums.

REVIEW QUESTIONS

1. What did God make on the fifth day?
2. Why did God make them?
3. How did God bless them?
4. What is your favourite fish? Why?
5. What is your favourite bird? Why?
6. How is a nightingale an excellent preacher?
7. How does a peacock feather proclaim the LORD?

PRAYER

LORD, we thank You for the marvellous creatures that swim and fly! We thank You for the songs of the birds and we ask that You would help us, with our lives and our lips, to fill the earth with Your praise.

PSALMS TO SING

104D . . . and 55A (1, 4,5); 84A; 148.

FIELD TRIP

Visit an aquarium and an aviary. Even pet stores usually have selections of tropical fish and birds. You could also take your children for a walk along a seashore to gather shells or a walk through the woods to listen to the birds.

(This student lesson starts on page 28.)

The Sixth Day

Genesis 1:24, 25

VISUAL AIDS

Look in your local library. There are all kinds of books with wonderful photographs of mammals, reptiles and insects. You can also find in children's books or magazines many amusing and exciting pictures of people doing things with animals. A young class will particularly appreciate these. This is also a good lesson to have a "show-and-tell" time. Ask each child to bring for this class a picture of his/her favourite animal. Have the child show the picture to the class and tell why it's his/her favourite animal. You should be prepared to show and tell yours too! This is fun for everyone.

MEMORY WORK

1. "Let everything that has breath praise the LORD. Praise the LORD!" (Psalm 150:6)
2. "Let every creature praise his holy name for ever and ever." (Psalm 145:21)

CRAFT

Use a piece of orange construction paper with "DAY 6" at the top for the next page in the creation book. Have lots of ovals and circles in different sizes cut out of fuzzy grey, brown and white fabric. Have the children glue them onto their pages and make them into animals by drawing legs, ears, tails, etc. At the bottom of the page add the words: GOD SAID, "LET THE LAND PRODUCE LIVING CREATURES." If you need a more difficult craft, what about sewing and stuffing some "furry" animals?

REVIEW QUESTIONS

1. What did God create on the sixth day?
2. From what did God make the animals?
3. How did God make them?
4. Why did God make the animals? Give two reasons.
5. How do animals help us? How can we help the animals?
6. The sixth day was the last day of creation. When all the animals were created, was God's work finished?
7. How do animals praise the LORD?

PRAYER

LORD, thank You for making all the animals.

(Each child might want to thank the LORD for some particular creature that he/she loves.)

PSALMS TO SING

150AB . . . and 104C.

FIELD TRIP

Visit the zoo or a farm! Make sure to use this opportunity to talk about the marvellous creatures that God created for us. Even a trip to a friend's house to see little kittens or hold furry gerbils can be a God-centred, fun-filled, educational experience.

(This student lesson starts on page 32.)

A Creature Is Crowned

Genesis 1:26–28

VISUAL AIDS

You will have several, living, breathing, human specimens right in your class! Bring a little box of dirt so they can see their origins and marvel at the work of God in creating them from the dust of the ground. You could also bring some photography books, such as *The Family of Man* by E. Steichen, which has beautiful photos of human beings.

MEMORY WORK

God said, "Let us make man in our image, in our likeness, and let them rule . . ." (Genesis 1:26)

CRAFT

This is the final page of the creation book. You will need purple construction paper, a royal colour. Cut the outline of a man and a woman for each child. You could use plain brown paper, to represent their earthiness. Use shiny silver paper for their hearts, to represent a mirror and the fact that human beings were to be a reflection of God. Cut gold paper crowns for each child's man and woman. Finish the page with these words: GOD SAID, "LET US MAKE MAN IN OUR IMAGE . . . AND LET THEM RULE." You could also make gold crowns, one for each boy and girl to wear home. Another project could be a collage of people: men and women, boys and girls, of every race.

REVIEW QUESTIONS

1. When were people created? What else was created on that day?
2. Whom did God make to rule all the animals?

3. How are animals and humans alike? How are they different?
4. Do we come from gorillas or from God? How do we know?
5. When the Bible says, "God created man in His own image," does it mean only men or does it mean both men and women?
6. When God said, "Let us make man in our image . . ." to whom was He speaking? Is there more than one God? Who are the Three Persons of God? What does "Trinity" mean? (Can you think of other words that begin with "tri" and refer to "three"?)
7. At the end of the sixth day, what did God see? Was it good?

PRAYER

Our Heavenly Father, thank You for creating us. Thank You for making us in Your image and calling us Your children. Thank You for crowning us with glory and honour. Thank You for making each one of us to be a prince or a princess, sons and daughters of the King. (Perhaps each child would like to thank God in prayer for some of the special people in his/her life.)

PSALMS TO SING

8AB . . . and 21AC; 24ABC; 100ABC; 103D; 113AB.

FIELD TRIP

Have you ever just sat down on a park bench and watched the people walking past? Take your children on a people-watching expedition. As you observe all kinds of people, take the opportunity to teach the children that all people are created in the image of God. Because they are created in the image of God, people are precious. They should not be harmed by us in any way — in thought, word or deed. God commands us to love people, to bless them and to do good to them, even to our enemies.

(This student lesson starts on page 35.)

The Image of God

Genesis 1:26–31

VISUAL AIDS

Before you begin, you want the children to understand the word "image," so bring a fairly large mirror to class with you. Have each child look into it. Who is peering back at them? Whom do they see in the mirror? No, they are not in the mirror. The real person is sitting right there, facing the mirror. What they see is just a reflection or image of themselves. You can also bring a small plastic or china animal, such as a horse. Ask the children, "What is this?" The whole class will probably answer, "A horse!" Then you can instruct them, "No, it is not a horse. It is an image of a horse." The same idea can be illustrated with a photograph. Bring a recognizable photo of yourself. Once again you can ask, "Who is this?" and answer, "No, I'm right here. This is just an image of me." Bring some coins too. When I taught this class, I gave each child a Canadian penny and an American penny. Whose images are on the coins? Queen Elizabeth and President Lincoln! At the end of this discussion time, your children should be interested in the word "image" and this difficult lesson on the image of God.

MEMORY WORK

"God created man in His own image; in the image of God He created him; male and female He created them." (Genesis 1:27)

CRAFT

This is the lesson to bring out the plactecine! The children can make "images" of animals. Suggest creatures with striking characteristics, such as an elephant or a giraffe or a snake. (Bring from the children's section of the library, a Barbara Reid book, such as Two By Two, for interesting examples of little clay creatures.) Examine each child's work and discuss it. "Is this an elephant? No, it's a model or image or likeness of an elephant. It is not an exact representation of an elephant. Only God (or other elephants) can make a real one. How do we know that this is meant to be an image of an elephant? It's grey and has a long trunk and big ears." This little craft time is meant to underline the main points of the lesson: Man, created in God's image, has characteristics of God, but he is not God.

REVIEW QUESTIONS

1. What special gift did God give to human beings, that was given to no other creature on earth?
2. What are three ways that people were made to be like God?
3. There was a Man who was the exact representation of God, a Man who was God. What was His name?

PRAYER

Our Heavenly Father, we thank You for creating us and loving us and giving us Your own image. LORD, help us be holy, even as You are holy. LORD, we thank You that, by faith, we are being conformed to the image of Your Son. We thank You that by Your grace, whenever people turn to the LORD, they "all reflect the LORD's glory . . . being transformed into His likeness with ever-increasing glory" (II Corinthians 3:18). God, we thank You for all these blessings.

PSALMS TO SING

100ABC . . . and 7B (9); 29A (1); 97A; 111A (1–3); 136A (1&2); 138AB; 145A.

FIELD TRIP

There are several places you could go with the children to discuss "images." Art galleries are filled with images—paintings, sculptures, photographs, etc. You could go to a fun house, where there are strange mirrors that distort the images reflected in them. You could go to shrines or temples or even some churches, where people have made images of God, called idols. You could discuss how it is wrong to worship images in the form of anything. The LORD alone, the eternal and invisible God, is worthy of worship.

(This student lesson starts on page 38.)

The Gift of Life

Genesis 2:7

VISUAL AIDS

It's time to make another trip to your local library, where you can find amazing books about our amazing bodies. The children's section will have wonderful picture books on the human body, which you might find helpful for this class. Particularly useful would be photography books with action shots of people doing amazing things. You can show your class pictures of gymnasts, runners, dancers, swimmers, skaters, jumpers, divers, etc. You can show pictures of people playing the piano, riding a bike, crocheting lace, throwing a ball, typing on a computer—anything and everything! It will be more difficult to find pictures of people loving, hoping and trusting, but they are available. Once again, *The Family of Man* is a good source book.

MEMORY WORK

"O LORD . . . I praise you because I am fearfully and wonderfully made." (Psalm 139:14)

CRAFT

Does your classroom have a bulletin board? Self-portraits (with the child's signature on their work) would be a lovely display under this lesson's Bible verse. Does your church/school have a xerox machine? Just for fun, take a little trip to the office and xerox each child's hand. Human hands are a wonderful creation of God's, that are able to do so many things. You might point out that human hands made xerox machines! There are many amazing machines made by human hands and planned by human minds, but the hands and the minds of human beings are God's creation! Or you could make unique presents to send home for the parents—fingerprint bookmarks. All you need are an ink pad, strips of cardboard and little willing fingers. Don't forget to tell the children that their fingerprints are unique and that they are unique. There are no two fingerprints and there are no two people in all the world which are identical, not even "identical" twins!

REVIEW QUESTIONS

1. Man was not created out of nothing. What did God use to form man's body?
2. How did God make man a living being?
3. God gave you life. What should you give God?
4. Why did God make man?
5. What is your favourite activity? Have you thanked God for that ability?

PRAYER

Our heavenly Father, thank You for the gift of life.

(Perhaps each child would like to thank God for some ability or activity, which they particularly enjoy. You, the teacher, could also thank the LORD for each precious person that is in your class. Mention them by name! Give thanks to God for creating each one of them!)

PSALMS TO SING

139B . . . and 71A; 100ABC; 119J.

FIELD TRIP

You can go almost anywhere to see people doing amazing things. Watch some boys playing hockey or some girls jumping rope. Watch a man twirling a pizza or a grandma knitting some socks. Go to a musical concert or a ballet recital. Watch a track meet or a gymnastics demonstration. As you watch, teach the children about the LORD and the good gift of life, which He graciously gave to us.

(This student lesson starts on page 41.)

The Gift of A Garden

Genesis 2:4–17

VISUAL AIDS

What you need for this lesson are pictures of cultivated lands throughout the world: wheat fields in Canada, vineyards in France, orange groves in U.S.A., flower gardens in England, rice terraces in China, potato crops in Ireland, olive trees in Israel, tulip beds in Holland, etc., etc.

MEMORY WORK

"Believe in the Lord Jesus, and you will be saved." (Acts 16:31)

CRAFT

A simple craft would be to cut a large circular "garden" out of green construction paper for each child. In the centre of the garden the memory work could be glued in a smaller white circle. Then the children can surround God's Word in the centre with all kinds of delicious fruits and gorgeous flowers. Those old seed catalogues would come in handy again. If you want to tackle a more complicated project, each child could plant a real little garden (or terrarium.) You will need pie plates (or large glass jars,) earth, mosses, plants, pebbles, etc. — and lots of patience!

REVIEW QUESTIONS

1. Where did God place the man whom He had made?
2. What did God plant in the centre of the garden?
3. What did God plant in the rest of the garden?
4. What command did God give to the first man?
5. What would happen if he disobeyed that command?

6. What command does God give to us now?
7. What will happen if we disobey that command? What does God promise to give us if we obey that command?

PRAYER

LORD, we thank You for Your LOVE in sending Your one and only Son to die for our sins. Help us obey Your Word and believe Your Son and trust Your promises. LORD, we pray that each child here might have faith in the Lord Jesus Christ, and so be saved.

PSALMS TO SING

119F . . . and 3 (5); 13 (5); 25AB; 119ABCE.

FIELD TRIP

People have planted beautiful gardens! Take a trip to one of them. Even in the middle of winter, there are public greenhouse gardens that are especially enjoyable to visit in the cold bleak months. For several years I lived in a little cottage on an estate near New Hope, Pennsylvania. The two old ladies who owned the property had spent almost their entire ninety years planting exquisite trees and flowers. There were pink magnolia trees, yellow forsythia bushes, white dogwoods, purple lilacs, red azaleas, and many other shrubs whose names I did not even know. These spinster sisters had planted fields of daffodils, beds of tulips, borders of irises, and every summer flower imaginable. Don't underestimate the abilities of the little old ladies in your congregation or neighbourhood. A trip to one of their flower gardens could prove to be a worthwhile visit. Remember to impress upon your young students: If these are the gardens that people can make, just imagine the garden that the LORD made!

(This student lesson starts on page 45.)

The First Wedding

Genesis 2:15–25

VISUAL AIDS

Pictures of couples and pictures of weddings and pictures of families from all around the world will stimulate interest in this lesson. Once again, *The Family of Man* by Edward Steichen has excellent photographs. (See pages 182 and 183: "We two form a multitude.")

MEMORY WORK

1. "Marriage should be honoured by all." (Hebrews 13:4)
2. "For this reason a man will leave his father and mother and be united to his wife, and the two will become one flesh." (Ephesians 5:31)

CRAFT

Have the children draw pictures of a bride and groom. If there are no children with single parents or divorced parents in your class, perhaps the assignment could be to draw pictures of their fathers and mothers on their wedding days. If you want to enhance the project, mount the drawings on a large piece of bright construction paper. Smear glue around this frame and scatter it with confetti, sparkles, or rice. If you have a bulletin board, set up a display of their wedding pictures by decorating the board with white paper bells and twisted streamers. Afterall, weddings are a celebration!

REVIEW QUESTIONS

1. What work did God give the man?
2. What did God say was not good?
3. What did man need?

4. How did God make the woman?
5. What did the man say when he saw her?
6. Was it good, how God made people male and female?
7. Was it fair, the place God gave to each of them?

PRAYER

Our loving heavenly Father, thank You for making human beings in two genders. Thank You for making men and women, fathers and mothers, boys and girls. LORD, we thank You for marriages and for families. We ask that at the right time You would provide the right partner for each boy and girl here, a person who will love them and who will love You for the rest of their lives. May these children know the joy of a godly marriage.

PSALMS TO SING

128B . . . and 21AC, 45C, 111A, 127A.

FIELD TRIP

It would be wonderful if you could take your children to a real wedding, but if an invitation to one is not so providentially arranged, you might see one on a Saturday afternoon in the city, especially in the month of June. Just to see a bride and groom descending the church steps and being showered with confetti from well-wishers and driving off in a decorated car with horns blaring is all very exciting to young children!

(This student lesson starts on page 49.)

The Seventh Day, A Holy Day

Genesis 2:1–3

VISUAL AIDS

Show the children an ordinary calendar. Thousands of years later, people still recognize the seven-day week. Although the names given to the days are pagan names honouring pagan gods, the seven-day week honours the one true God. Most people now think of the week beginning on Monday (and some calendars even begin the week there,) but they are wrong. The first day of the week is Sunday, the LORD's Day, the New Covenant Sabbath.

MEMORY WORK

"The LORD blessed the Sabbath day and made it holy." (Exodus 20:11)

CRAFT

We wish one another a "Merry Christmas" or a "Happy Birthday" and we send cards for these special days, but there is only one day that the LORD set apart and blessed. It is the Sabbath! Surely on this day we should greet one another with a "good sabbath," as well as a "good morning." Your class could make cards to take home to their families. The children could draw pictures of happy people praising God and inside the cards could be this greeting: HAPPY LORD'S DAY!

REVIEW QUESTIONS

1. What did God do on the seventh day?
2. Why was the seventh day special? Who made it special?
3. For whom was this day made?
4. Did the man and the woman begin their life on the earth with rest or work? Why?

5. Did God rest from every kind of work when He finished making the world? What other work did He still have to do?
6. What is the common name of the first day of the week? Why was the Sabbath changed from the seventh day to the first day? Who made this change?
7. Where can we find rest and peace for our souls?

PRAYER

LORD, we thank You for the Sabbath day! We thank You for the work that You have finished for us. Thank You for creating the world and redeeming the world. Thank You for making us and saving us. We thank You for Jesus, for the rest and the peace that we have in Him, which is found nowhere else in world. LORD, help us to remember the Sabbath Day by keeping it holy. Help us to delight in this holy day, that we might find our joy in You.

PSALMS TO SING

118C (14–17) . . . and 72D; 96A; 100ABC; 121ABC; 134AB; 150AB.

FIELD TRIP

It used to be in this country that on a Sunday afternoon you could drive down the main street of your town and the stores would all be closed. You could drive along the side streets and everything would be quiet. Sadly, what you now can show your children is how the LORD's Sabbath is ignored and despised. People are mowing their lawns and doing their chores; they are selling their wares and buying their goods on a day meant for rest and peace and worship. If there is a religious Jewish community nearby, you could show your children how they still keep the seventh-day Sabbath. Their shops and stores are closed on Saturday and they attend the synagogue to worship the Creator.

(This student lesson starts on page 54.)

War in Heaven

Revelation 12:1–17

VISUAL AIDS

Alas! We have no photographs of the angels; no, not a single one. (However, if people have entertained angels unawares, then they may have taken their pictures also, thinking they were ordinary human beings.) There is no photo you can show your children of the war in heaven. These spirits have left no physical evidence of their appearances on earth and we must rely on the infallible testimony of Scripture that they have been seen and heard by human witnesses. But you could show the children the sad photo documents of the recent wars on earth.

MEMORY WORK

"Be self-controlled and alert. Your enemy the devil prowls around like a roaring lion looking for someone to devour. Resist him, standing firm in the faith . . ." (I Peter 5:8, 9)

CRAFT

Any Christmas craft book from a public library is sure to have ideas for making angels. Also available is *A Christmas Angel Collection* by Catherine Stock, (Random House, New York). Angels can be made quite simply from gold, silver, or white paper doilies. Use one half to make cone-shaped robes. Use the other half to make wings. You will need gold, silver or white painted styrofoam balls or wooden beads for the heads, tinsel for halos, and pipe cleaners for arms.

REVIEW QUESTIONS

1. Before God created people, had He created anyone else?

2. There was war in heaven. Who fought? Who won?
3. There is an evil angel roaming and prowling through the earth. He has several names   What are they?
4. Who is more powerful, God or the devil?
5. Why did Satan rebel against God? What did he want?
6. Why did Satan want to destroy the man and woman?
7. What should angels and people everywhere, both in heaven and on earth, be doing?

PRAYER

LORD, we thank You for Your truth and goodness in a world filled with lies and wickedness. Please, deliver us from evil and protect us from the devil. Strengthen us, that we may stand firm in the faith, resisting every temptation.

PSALMS TO SING

103D . . . and 27B; 34AC; 35AB, 91A, 148.

FIELD TRIP

There is no place on this earth where we can go to view the heavenly host. Jacob's ladder, with the angels of God ascending and descending on it, were for his eyes alone. However, if there is a field of soft white snow, take your children there to make "snow angels." A little friend of mine on a winter walk was observing the different tracks that the animals had made when he came across the clear outlines of angels. Not knowing that these imprints were made by children, he thought it was a place where some angels had landed. Explain to your children, that the angels come and go without a trace. They leave no footprints, nor do they drop shimmering feathers from heavenly wings.

(This student lesson starts on page 58.)

The Day of Evil

Genesis 2:25

VISUAL AIDS

Pictures of the armour and weapons mentioned in this passage of Scripture, (such as a breastplate, helmet, shield, sword, arrows, etc.) would be useful for this lesson.

MEMORY WORK

"Be strong in the LORD and in His mighty power. Put on the full armour of God, so that you can take your stand against the devil's schemes . . . Put on the full armour of God, so that when the day of evil comes, you may be able to stand your ground, and after you have done everything, to stand" (Ephesians 6:10, 11, 13). Emphasize standing as opposed to falling.

CRAFT

This is the lesson to line up your little soldiers and arm them for battle. (Of course, you have been doing just that as you study the Bible with them, but now they can know that the Word of God is the Sword of the Spirit.) Have your favourite Bible verses printed in profusion and cut into strips for the children to paste in a collage onto cardboard swords. In bold red letters write the words: SWORD OF THE SPIRIT = THE WORD OF GOD.

REVIEW QUESTIONS

1. Which day was the evil day?
2. What did Satan want to stop?
3. How could he do this?
4. What was Satan from the beginning?

5. What protection did the man and woman have against the devil's schemes?
6. What weapon did God give to them?
7. How must we fight against Satan's attacks?

PRAYER

O LORD, we thank You for Your LOVE and Truth and Grace, by which we are able to stand against our adversary, the devil. LORD, keep us from slipping or stumbling or falling. Deliver us this day and every day from the Evil One. Please, LORD, plant our feet firmly upon the Rock, even Christ Jesus, our Lord.

(Pray for each child, by name, that he/she would not waver in faith, but be strong in the LORD, in His mighty power.)

PSALMS TO SING

18A . . . and 3; 11; 28A (1, 2,6–8); 33C; 35A; 44A; 45A; 46ABC; 59B (7, 12, 13); 91A; 144A; 149.

FIELD TRIP

If you are fortunate enough to have a museum nearby, where shining armour has been left by knights of old, that would be an excellent place to review our God-given armour and weapons.

(This student lesson starts on page 69.)

The Serpent

Genesis 3:1–5

VISUAL AIDS

Pictures of different kinds of snakes, with their many patterns and poisons, would be useful for this class.

MEMORY WORK

1. "Submit yourselves, then, to God. Resist the devil, and he will flee from you. Come near to God and He will come near to you." (James 4:7, 8)
2. Jesus said, "I have given you authority to trample on snakes and scorpions and to overcome all the power of the enemy; nothing will harm you." (Luke 10:19)

CRAFT

Colourful serpents can be made easily by small children with multicoloured plasticine. Coiled snakes can also be made by cutting paper in a spiral. The children can paint them in bold bright colours.

REVIEW QUESTIONS

1. How did Satan disguise himself?
2. Why did the devil choose the serpent for his wicked work?
3. How did the serpent strike at the woman? What did the devil use as his flaming arrows?
4. What did Satan ask the woman? What was her answer? Did she add anything to God's Word?
5. What did Satan tell the woman? Was it true? What did he hope his lies would accomplish?

6. What should the woman have done when she heard God's Word contradicted? To whom should she have turned for help?
7. When you are being tempted where should you turn for help?

PRAYER

LORD, You are our help, our strength, our shield, our Saviour! Thank You for the truth of Your Word. Please give us discernment, that we would not be deceived by the lies of Satan. Oh Lord, lead us away from temptation and deliver us from evil.

PSALMS TO SING

120 (1); 140A . . . and 5AB; 12AB; 36A; 52AB; 62A; 91A; 119P.

FIELD TRIP

If there is a natural history section at a local museum, which has a snake display, or if there is a snake pit at your local zoo, or if you happen to have a friend whose hobby it is to charm snakes, this would be the appropriate time to visit them! Or perhaps, (if you live anywhere in the world except Ireland,) you could take your children on a snake hunt, looking for specimens of harmless serpents.

(This student lesson starts on page 72.)

The First Temptation

Genesis 3:4–6

VISUAL AIDS

What you need for this class are a variety of lures. Do you know a fisherman who would lend you his fishing tackle for this class? Watch out for the hooks as you examine them. Show the children how the fish are fooled by the shining, spinning bits of metal that look like swimming minnows and how they are then caught by the hooks. Teach the children that Satan's words were lies, similar to those lures.

MEMORY WORK

"The fear of the LORD is the beginning of wisdom, and knowledge of the Holy One is understanding." (Proverbs 2:6)

CRAFT

To make a lure is a simple project. Have cardboard or paper fish-shapes ready for the children to colour. They can also paste strips of silver paper onto them. Attach to the lures a harmless "hook" (made of bent wire) and tie them onto the ends of long pieces of string. Sticks may be added to make fishing poles, but make sure no one gets poked. This is a very popular project, as small children love to pretend to fish.

REVIEW QUESTIONS

1. What were the three lures that Satan used to tempt the woman to eat the forbidden fruit?
2. Whose words should the woman believe, God's or Satan's?
3. If anyone lacks wisdom, what should they do?

PRAYER

LORD, we thank You for the opportunity to study the Bible, which is the Word of God and which is able to make us wise. LORD, we ask You for wisdom concerning everything that is good. We ask You for knowledge concerning the LORD and his Law.

PSALMS TO SING

119E . . . and 19B (5–7); 111B (9), 119CDJMQR.

FIELD TRIP

A little fishing expedition could be fun and, as the hooks and baits and lures are used to catch the unsuspecting fish, remind the children of this lesson: Satan used lies to lure the woman to sin.

(This student lesson starts on page 77.)

The Fall

Genesis 3:6

VISUAL AIDS

To stimulate interest in this lesson, you may wish to discuss * WARNING * signs. Bring some labels that warn of poisonous, corrosive and flammable products. Discuss the flashing red lights at intersections and railway crossings. Show the children some of the many road signs that warn of danger. Discuss fire alarms and air-raid sirens. Then you can teach your class that God has made each person with an inner warning mechanism, called a conscience, that alerts us to danger. Our conscience does not ring an alarm for us to hear or flash a red light for us to see, but nonetheless it makes us aware of what is right and wrong (Romans 2:14, 15). We know when we are about to sin and our conscience warns us not to do it! God's Word is also a warning. Hold up a Bible before the class and say, "There are many words of warning in this book. Pay attention to them! They will keep you from danger and from death."

MEMORY WORK

"Sin entered the world through one man, and death through sin, and in this way death came to all men, because all sinned . . ." (Romans 5:12)

CRAFT

Make red-and-white, warning, octagon, stop signs. On them in bold letters print the words: STOP! DANGER! DON'T SIN! The sign posts can be made from drinking straws and the bases from plasticine. Your class can also make warning flags. Use small squares of red material glued to sticks or straws. The object of the lesson: Be on guard against sin!

REVIEW QUESTIONS

1. The serpent was tempting the woman to eat, but what three things were advising her and warning her not to eat?
2. What was the woman's first step towards the fall?
3. What was her next step?
4. What was the final step, when she fell into sin?
5. What was the first thing she did as a sinner?
6. The man also fell into sin. How?
7. What happened to the whole human race when the man sinned?

PRAYER

Our heavenly Father, give us ears to hear the warnings of Your Word. Please, LORD, deliver us from harm, evil and temptation. Bless us and keep us for Your name's sake. And God, we do thank You for Your LOVE, mercy and forgiveness, for we have all sinned and rebelled against You.

PSALMS TO SING

19B . . . and 5B; 26A; 92A; 119E; 145B.

FIELD TRIP

Go for a walk along any city street, noting all the warning signs and sounds, such as flashing lights, bicycle bells, stop signs, honking horns, red flags, screaming sirens, etc.

(This student lesson starts on page 81.)

The Word Fulfilled

Genesis 3:7

VISUAL AIDS

A friend sent me a large fig leaf from Israel. The children in my class, who have only lived in cold northern climates, had no idea what kind of leaf it was. They were very interested to see a real fig leaf, the very kind that Adam and his wife used to sew clothes for themselves. However, if it is not possible to bring such a leaf to class, you could bring pictures of fig trees and leaves. You could also bring some dried figs or fig cookies for them to eat. Now men and women sew cotton and linen fabrics for clothing, some samples of which you could show the children, along with the plants from which they come.

MEMORY WORK

"There is no one righteous, not even one . . . There is no one who does good, not even one." (Romans 3:10, 12)

CRAFT

You will need a needle and some thread for each child. If you have a supply of fig leaves—great! Your children can try sewing real fig leaves together. (If you live in Canada, you will have to substitute some maple leaves.) However, people don't make clothes out of leaves now. We use fabrics, often made from plant fibres. Involve the children in a simple sewing project with cotton or linen material.

REVIEW QUESTIONS

1. Satan promised the man and woman that their eyes would be opened. Were they? What did they see? What did they do?

2. Satan promised that they would be like God. Were they?
3. Satan promised they would gain knowledge. Did they?
4. God promised they would die. Did they?
5. What are the three kinds of death?
6. How was God's LOVE demonstrated on that evil day? Did the man and woman die immediately? Did they die completely?
7. Jesus promises to restore what Satan destroyed. Can we trust this promise of God? Can we trust every promise of God?

PRAYER

LORD, we thank You for Your promises to us, which You always keep. We thank You for Your Word, which is always true. Thank You for the promise of eternal life through Christ Jesus.

PSALMS TO SING

96B . . . and 5AB; 6; 18D; 107B; 119FGPQSTUVW.

FIELD TRIP

Take the children to a garment or fabric factory. People are still making clothes to cover their nakedness.

(This student lesson starts on page 86.)

Division, Division, Division, Division

Genesis 3:8–19

VISUAL AIDS

There is no shortage of pictures to illustrate this lesson. Open any newspaper or magazine. (Again, *The Family of Man* has excellent photographs of the human condition.) You will want all kinds of photos showing man's misery—the bleaker, the better. You will need pictures depicting people's toil, grief, pain and death. You can show your class people worshipping idols, people fighting and killing each other, people starving, people cursing, people crying, etc. You will also want pictures of natural disasters and man's environmental blunders.

MEMORY WORK

"Your sins have separated you from your God . . ." (Isaiah 59:2)

CRAFT

Let us make a collage of misery. This can be a group project. On a large piece of poster board, paste both pictures and words of human suffering. A terrifying (but true) picture of man's misery should emerge. You can entitle your project: "The Result of Sin."

REVIEW QUESTIONS

1. What brought about the separation between man and God?
2. Can we see that God and people are separated now? Give some examples.
3. What proof do we have in the Bible, in the Garden of Eden, that the relationship between God and people was broken immediately after they sinned?
4. What brought about separation between people?
5. Can we see that people are separated now? Give some examples.

6. What proof do we have in the Bible, in the Garden of Eden, that the relationship between people was also broken?
7. What brought about the separation between man and his world?
8. Can we see the war man has with the world? Give examples.
9. Is a man sometimes separated even from himself? Explain.

PRAYER

O LORD, we are fallen people, living in a fallen world. There is suffering all around us. We thank You for Your LOVE, in spite of our sin, and ask for Your mercy upon many.

(Pray about the current problems in the world and the present sorrows of each child. Ask for God's help.)

PSALMS TO SING

38A; 39B . . . and 2; 5AB; 6; 7AB; 9AB; 10AB; 13; 14ABC; 18AG; 25D; 27C; 30AB; 31BF; 55A; 107BC.

FIELD TRIP

One doesn't have to go very far afield to see the suffering of man. Perhaps your class can be involved in some ministry to your community, such as singing psalms of hope to lonely people in an old-age home or sick people in a hospital, who often don't have little visitors. They could also bring these people small bouquets of flowers or baskets of fruit—and children's smiles!

(This student lesson starts on page 94.)

Hope

VISUAL AIDS

In all my years of teaching, the visual aids for this lesson were the most fun. I brought animal skins to class—all kinds of them! From a friend I borrowed a big bear-skin rug, with a grizzly head and scary claws. That I placed in the centre of our circle. Then, from an old alligator bag, I brought out all sorts of leather and fur. There were enough hats and collars for each child to wear something. "What is the teacher going to wear?" asked one child. I wrapped a large, soft, deer skin around my shoulders like a cape. I saved the sheep skin to show the class at the end of the lesson. It wasn't the softest or the prettiest, the thickest or the scariest, but it was given special attention as the skin that God probably used to clothe the first man and woman.

MEMORY WORK

1. "The wages of sin is death, but the gift of God is eternal life in Christ Jesus our LORD." (Romans 6:23)
2. "May the God of hope fill you with all joy and peace as you trust in Him, so that you may overflow with hope . . ." (Romans 15:13)

CRAFT

Cut out a large cardboard doll or two for each child. Bring a bag of scrap material—all different kinds and colours. Let the children cut and paste "clothes" of their own creation onto the dolls. You could also sew some real clothes, using a simple pattern for a child's hat or mittens. Real fur is difficult to sew, but fake fur is a very easy fabric with which to work. Let each child think of some little person, who would like a gift of a warm hat and matching mitts. Fringed polar-fleece scarves can be made without any stitching, just cutting.

REVIEW QUESTIONS

1. Sin and pain and death fill the world. Where is our only hope?
2. How did God show that He still loved human beings?
3. God gave the man and woman a very great promise. What was it?
4. Do you think Adam and Eve believed God's promise? Why?
5. What is the great hope and promise that God has given to us?
6. How did God guard the tree of life? Will anyone ever eat the fruit of that tree? How?
7. An animal (probably a lamb) was slain on the day that the first man and woman ate the forbidden fruit. Why?

PRAYER

LORD, we thank You that, although we are wretched sinners, You have given us hope in Your great LOVE. Thank You, LORD, for providing a covering for our sin. Thank You for the Lamb of God, who was slain before the foundation of the world, even Jesus Christ, our Lord.

PSALMS TO SING

62A (1, 4,5); 119T . . . and 31D; 42ABC; 43; 52B (3);71A (1–3); 71C; 119GK (1); 119P; 130AB; 131 (3); 141B (9).

FIELD TRIP

People still use animal skins for clothing. Visit a factory where sheep-skin garments are made or a store where fur coats are sold.

(This student lesson starts on page 101.)

The Stand

Matthew 3:16–4:11

You may wish to divide this lesson into four lessons.

VISUAL AIDS

You need photos to show the kind of place where each temptation occurred: an empty wasteland, the pinnacle of a temple, the top of a mountain, a place of death littered with bones and sculls.

MEMORY WORK

1. "Man does not live on bread alone, but on every word that comes from the mouth of the LORD." (Deuteronomy 8:2, 3)
2. "Do not put the LORD your God to the test." (Deuteronomy 6:16)
3. "Worship the LORD your God and serve Him only." (Deuteronomy 6:13)
4. "Thanks be to God! He gives us the victory through our LORD Jesus Christ." (1 Corinthians 15:57)

CRAFT

You can have the children draw the four places of Christ's worst temptations. You could divide a large sheet of paper into four sections or use separate sheets for each picture.

REVIEW QUESTIONS

1. There is another Adam in the Bible, called the last Adam. Who was he?
2. When Jesus was baptized, a voice spoke from heaven. Whose voice was it? What did He say?

3. Where did the first temptation take place? What did Satan say? What did Jesus answer?
4. Where did the second temptation take place? What did Satan say? What did Jesus answer?
5. Where did the third temptation take place? What did Satan say? What did Jesus answer?
6. Where did the final temptation take place? What did people say? What did Jesus do? Why?
7. The first Adam fell into sin. Did the last Adam?

PRAYER

LORD, we thank You for the great victory that we have through Jesus Christ. We thank You for Jesus, who stayed on the cross and died on the cross, that the serpent might be crushed and we might be saved. LORD, help us also to stand against the Evil One.

PSALMS TO SING

98AB (1–4) . . . and 22ABCDEFGHI; 32C; 59B (7, 12, 13); 118C.

FIELD TRIP

Is there a wilderness you can visit, where all you can hear is the moaning of the wind and the howling of the wolves? Can you look at the ground far below you from the top of a high tower? Can you view distant landscapes from a mountain height? If you have no access to such places, don't worry. What the children really need to know is that they can be tempted anywhere, in the most ordinary of places—at home, at school, at church.

(This student lesson starts on page 108.)

Grace & Faith

John 3:1–18

VISUAL AIDS

There are no visual aids for faith. We believe in a God whom we cannot see. There is no picture or image on earth that will help us believe in Him.

MEMORY WORK

"For God so loved the world that He gave his one and only Son, that whoever believes in Him shall not perish, but have eternal life." (John 3:16)

CRAFT

The children could make something very important today, something that could save a person's life. Faith comes by hearing (or reading) the Word of God. The children could proclaim God's life-giving Word in a poster that they make. This could be a large group project or each child could make his own small poster. Print the words from John 3:16 and then decorate the poster however you want. If it's a group poster, you might want to put the hand-print of each person involved, to be seals of testimony of people who believe, or you might want to put stars on it because we "shine like stars in the universe as we hold out the word of Life" (Philippians 1:15, 16).

REVIEW QUESTIONS

1. God said, "You shall surely die." How can we escape death?
2. What is the work of God that we must do?
3. We are born dead in sin. How can we be born again?
4. What is the gospel message? Do you believe it?
5. We cannot save ourselves. How are we saved?

6. What is the victory that overcomes the world?
7. Do you believe in Jesus, the Son of God?

PRAYER

Heavenly Father, thank You for sending Your one and only Son to die for our sins, so that we might have life . . . forever. Thank You for the gift of faith. LORD, you know each person's heart; if there are any children here who do not believe, we ask that You would grant them faith also, that they too might have eternal life.

(Ask each child if there are any people whom he/she loves, who does not believe in Jesus. Then, pray! Pray for each person mentioned, that they would believe!)

PSALMS TO SING

32C; 67A . . . and 4B; 9A (1, 5); 13; 16AB; 18A; 25AB; 27E; 31EF; 33C (9, 10); 38D; 62ABC; 63B; 67A; 71A (1–3); 86A; 143B; 145B; 145C (10–13).

FIELD TRIP

The world is filled with dying people, who need the Word of Life. Take the poster you made and find a public bulletin board where you can display it, where people can read it.

(This student lesson starts on page 124.)

Grace & Peace

Romans 5:1

VISUAL AIDS

You may wish to introduce this lesson and stimulate interest in this topic by showing some pictures of people in this world searching and striving for peace. You can show pictures of gurus meditating, protestors marching, soldiers fighting, vacationers retreating—all in their quest for peace.

MEMORY WORK

1. "Having been justified by faith, we have peace with God through our Lord Jesus Christ." (Romans 5:1)
2. "Grace and peace to you from God our Father and from the Lord Jesus Christ." (Romans 1:7)

CRAFT

The children could make peace banners with "peace" verses from the Bible. (Check the end of Lesson 26 for appropriate references.) Then they can have their own peace march right in your classroom: Onward Christian soldiers, marching for God's peace, with the gospel of His grace; it will never cease!

REVIEW QUESTIONS

1. There is only one mediator, who can restore the peace between man and God. Who is this mediator?
2. How does Jesus make peace between God and men?
3. What does the word "justification" mean?
4. What does God credit to us (or count for us) as righteousness?
5. What does God promise that He will do, if we confess our sins?

6. What did the first Adam bring?
7. What did the last Adam bring?

PRAYER

LORD, thank You for Your grace and peace to us. What wonderful gifts they are!

PSALMS TO SING

85B . . . and 4B; 29A (1, 6); 32AC; 35E; 38D (10, 11, 13); 128B.

FIELD TRIP

Is there a war museum or a war memorial in your community? That would be a good place to visit with the purpose of teaching the children about the horror of war and the blessing of peace. The only true and lasting peace in this world is in Christ. Jesus said: "In Me you may have peace. In this world you will have trouble. But take heart! I have overcome the world" (John 16:33).

(This student lesson starts on page 128.)

A Child Is Born, A Son Is Given

Genesis 4:1–5

VISUAL AIDS

Can you find pictures of boys playing, of brothers hugging, of friends laughing? Cain and Abel were the first two brothers in the world, the first two boys upon this earth. You might also find these pictures useful: a flock of sheep, some lambs, and a bountiful, beautiful, harvest arrangement of fruits and vegetables.

MEMORY WORK

"Behold the Lamb of God, who takes away the sin of the world!" (John 1:29)

CRAFT

Abel offered God a firstborn lamb from his flock of sheep. Each child can make a lamb. Cut sheep-shapes out of black cardboard and then cover the bodies (not the faces or legs) with white wool or cotton. Add eyes and maybe a real bell on a ribbon.

REVIEW QUESTIONS

1. What was the name of the first child ever born in this world?
2. What was his brother's name?
3. They brought offerings to God. What did each one bring?
4. Was Cain's offering accepted by God? Why not?
5. Was Abel's offering accepted by God? Why?
6. Does God accept us? Why? Do we have an offering for sin?
7. Who is the Lamb of God, who takes away the sin of the world?

PRAYER

LORD, we thank You for showing us the way to be accepted in Your sight. We thank You for the sacrifice, which You provided, to pay for our sin. Thank You for sending Your Son to die for us, that we might have eternal life.

PSALMS TO SING

96A . . . and 4A (1–5); 20AB; 27BE; 50A; 51ABC; 54AB; 66B (11–14); 107C; 116C; 118C.

FIELD TRIP

Visit a sheep farm! If it is springtime, all the better. Then your children can see the firstborn lambs, leaping for joy and racing with life. They will see what a sacrifice it was for Abel, the shepherd, to offer God the finest lambs from his flock. Sin has a terrible price. Without the shedding of blood there is no forgiveness. The Lamb of God, even Jesus our Lord, poured out his blood for us, to save us from sin and death.

(This student lesson starts on page 134.)

Cain's Choice:
Life Or Death

Genesis 4:1–16

VISUAL AIDS

The face of a murderer—what does it look like? I lived in the U.S.A. for a few years and in the post offices there, the faces of wanted men are posted. For some reason I found these facial photos very interesting and I used to study them whenever I picked up our mail. There was something strange in the "look" on all the faces of these criminals, but what exactly it was, would be hard to describe. Perhaps for this class you could show the children photographs of faces— both happy faces and angry faces. Show them the famous and infamous faces of the world. Is there any difference? Is there such a thing as an evil look?

MEMORY WORK

"If you do what is right, will you not be accepted?" (Genesis 4:7)

CRAFT

God said to Cain, "Why is your face downcast?" Have the children make faces (or paper-plate masks!)—some that are angry and some that are happy, some that have eyes and mouths that are turned down and some that have eyes and mouths lifted up. Remind the children that, if we do what is right before God, we will be blessed by Him; inside ourselves we will be happy and on the outside it will show on our faces. But if we don't do what is right we will be unsettled, angry and sad—and our faces will show it.

REVIEW QUESTIONS

1. Cain had a choice. What was it? What did he choose?
2. What is a martyr? Who was the first martyr in the world?

3. Why did Cain murder his brother Abel?
4. How can Abel still speak, even though he is dead?
5. Cain was under a double curse. Explain.
6. God was merciful to Cain. How?
7. Cain lost many blessings. What were they?

PRAYER

Heavenly Father, we thank You for Your LOVE and mercy to all people. Please forgive our sins and accept us through the sacrifice of Your Son, Jesus Christ.

PSALMS TO SING

52AB . . . and 1AB; 5AB; 7AB; 10AB; 11; 14ABC; 26B; 31G; 37B; 54AB; 94AB; 116C; 119KU; 140AB; 142.

FIELD TRIP

Is there a memorial for martyrs in your community? If there is, you could take the children there for a visit.

(This student lesson starts on page 139.)

Two Kinds of People, Two Races of Men

Genesis 4:16–5:32

VISUAL AIDS

Cain built the first city, but now the cities of man cover the earth. Find photographs of the world's great cities—New York, London, Paris, Tokyo, Moscow, etc. Here you will find man's greatest achievements in technological progress and cultural advance. However, these places are not known for righteousness or faithfulness!

MEMORY WORK

"As surely as I live," declares the Sovereign LORD, "I take no pleasure in the death of the wicked, but rather that they turn from their ways—and live!" (Ezekiel 33:11)

CRAFT

As a group project, you could make a large family tree, showing the different branches (both godly and ungodly) that proceeded from the first parents, Adam and Eve. You could also make individual and personal family trees for each child, showing their siblings, parents, grandparents, etc.—but make sure in the trunk of the tree are carved the names Adam and Eve, from whom comes every human being.

REVIEW QUESTIONS

1. Cain was condemned to be a wanderer. What did he do instead?
2. What did Cain name his first son and the first city?
3. For what were the children of Cain renowned?

4. God gave to Adam and Eve another son, to take the place of Abel. What was his name?
5. What was the name of Seth's son and what did he do?
6. Adam and his sons after him lived long lives, but then they died . . . except for the seventh "son of god." What was his name and what happened to him?
7. What did this show/demonstrate to the people of God?

PRAYER

LORD, we thank You for being patient with us and our sin. Heavenly Father, we ask that You would help us live like "children of God" in a wicked generation. We pray that we might be like Enoch, who "walked with God" and was commended for his faith. We pray that we might be used in the building of God's kingdom on earth, during the short time that we are here.

PSALMS TO SING

90CD . . . and 12AB; 17C; 22E; 31D; 34BD; 48B; 71C; 73C; 78A; 100BC; 103C; 112A; 127A; 128AB; 146AB.

FIELD TRIP

Every community has a cemetery, for the generations of man come and go. Take your children to visit a cemetery—the bigger, the better. Let them see how death spreads to all men in all generations. Let them see how man's days and years are numbered. God said, "Dust you are, and to dust you shall return." As you look over the tombstones, remind the children of Enoch, the seventh son from Adam, who did not die. God took him to heaven. That same hope of eternal life is ours in Jesus Christ our LORD, who is the Living One and the first-born from the dead. Enoch's hope was in God—and our hope must also be in God.

(This student lesson starts on page 144.)

Only Evil, All the Time

Genesis 5:25–6:8

VISUAL AIDS

You will need two pieces of fruit for this class, such as two apples. One should be an appetizing apple—firm and round and red. The other apple should be disgustingly rotten—mouldy and smelly and squishy. Let the children sense what the word "corrupt" means. Of what use is the rotten apple? It is just garbage to be thrown away. Think about that word "corrupt" and what the Bible says: "The earth was corrupt in God's sight." The world was rotten, rotten to the core—and the core was man's heart, which was only evil, all the time. That was why God was going to destroy the world. It was no longer good for anything.

MEMORY WORK

"Oh righteous God, who searches minds and hearts, bring to an end the violence of the wicked—and make the righteous secure." (Psalm 6:9)

CRAFT

Here is a group project, which can extend through the next few lessons: Put a large, brown, paper, ark (which has a ramp and an open door) onto the classroom wall. Have some of the children draw Noah and his wife, along with his three sons and their wives. These "people pictures" should be coloured and cut, then stuck onto the ark. Next, assign a pair of animals to each child to draw, colour and cut. When these pairs of creatures are ready, they can also be stuck onto the wall. The procession of animals has begun! As the lessons continue about Noah's ark, assign new creatures. You can have hundreds of different kinds, that can extend in a long line around the four walls your classroom.

REVIEW QUESTIONS

1. In the beginning, when God created the earth, it was good. What did it become?
2. The LORD was grieved that He had made man. Why?
3. The godly line became corrupted and polluted. How?
4. Who found favour in the eyes of the LORD? Why?
5. Who lived longer than any other man? How long did he live? What year did he die? Who was his grandson?
6. What does the name Noah mean?
7. Enoch and Noah were "types of Christ." What does this mean? How did they prefigure or foreshadow the Messiah?

PRAYER

LORD, we thank You for Your mercy in preserving a faithful remnant in every age. Thank You that Your truth and praise and word endure forever. Merciful heavenly Father, we ask You to keep us from corruption and to create in us a pure heart.

PSALMS TO SING

53 (1–3) . . . and 1AB; 5AB; 7AB; 12AB; 14ABC; 34BDE; 36AB; 37ABC; 52AB; 55ABC; 56; 75; 92ABC; 139C; 140AB.

FIELD TRIP

Can you go some place, such as a stadium, where thousands upon thousands of people can be viewed? Imagine what it would be like to be the only person left, who loved God.

(This student lesson starts on page 150.)

By Faith, An Ark!

Genesis 6:9–7:5

VISUAL AIDS

For this lesson, a wooden hammer would be useful, to bang out Noah's warning: "Repent!" You could also bring photos of ships being built in shipyards.

MEMORY WORK

1. "Faith is being sure of what we hope for and certain of what we do not see." (Hebrews 11:1)
2. "The righteous will live by his faith." (Habakkuk 2:4)

CRAFT

Continue the animal art-work around your meeting-room. There were thousands of creatures that entered the ark: mammals, reptiles, birds, insects, etc. You shouldn't run out of assignments for the children to continue the procession of animals, two by two, into the ark. An alternate project would be to have the children make pairs of animals from plasticine. Set them up on a table, along with a toy ark. At your local library, in the children's section, find Barbara Reid's *Two By Two* (North Winds Press) and use this book for inspiration in plasticine creatures! Our church is located in the world's coldest capital: Ottawa, Canada. Sub-zero temperatures last for many weeks of the year. At the annual mid-winter outdoor carnival, "Winterlude," there are all kinds of ice and snow sculptures. One year there was Noah's ark! If you need an outdoor activity and the climate is right, that is another craft idea for this lesson. Another project would be making model arks out of wood or cardboard.

REVIEW QUESTIONS

1. God told Noah that He was going to destroy the world. What words of hope did God give to Noah?
2. How did Noah respond to God's Word?
3. What was Noah's work in this world? What made it difficult?
4. What great sign did the people of the world have, to show them that a flood was coming?
5. What else warned them about the flood?
6. When did Noah enter the ark? Why?
7. We also live in a wicked generation. What is the work that we must do?

PRAYER

LORD, we thank You for Your mercy to the human race. Please, help us with our work—the work of believing Your Word and proclaiming Your Truth.

PSALMS TO SING

37AF . . . and 1AB; 3 (5); 4AB; 5AB; 7A (5); 9A; 18C; 25AB; 31A; 71ABC; 109B (9); 119FW.

FIELD TRIP

If you live near the ocean, make a trip to the harbour, where the large ships are anchored. Perhaps you can have a tour aboard one of them. Is there a shipyard, where large boats are built? That would be an interesting excursion. If you live inland, then you may have to settle for a trip to a sawmill, where the children can see the huge logs being hauled and stripped, sawed and stacked. Imagine the work that Noah and his sons had to do, without the help of machines!

(This student lesson starts on page 155.)

The Flood

Genesis 7

VISUAL AIDS

There are many photographs available in magazines (such as National Geographic) which show the devastations caused by tidal waves, floods, monsoons, hurricanes, storms, typhoons, etc. Altogether, these disasters would not equal the world-wide destruction caused by the flood in Noah's day.

MEMORY WORK

"Fear God and give Him glory, because the hour of His judgement has come. Worship Him who made the heavens, the earth, the sea and the springs of water." (Revelation 14:7)

CRAFT

Continue the procession of animals into the ark. Make sure that there are more than two sheep! Seven entered the ark!

REVIEW QUESTIONS

1. When did Noah and his family move into the ark?
2. Who closed the door of the ark? Why?
3. How did Noah find all the animals for the ark?
4. Why did God save two of every creature, a male and its mate?
5. Why did God save more than one pair of sheep?
6. What were other people in the world doing, until the flood came and swept them away?
7. How long did it take God to create the world? How long did it take God to destroy the world?

8. How will the world be destroyed in the end on the final Day of Destruction?
9. How can we be saved?

PRAYER

LORD, we thank You for providing a way of escape for us. We thank You for Your great plan and promise of salvation. We rejoice that "what God opens no one can shut, and what He shuts no one can open" (Revelation 3:7). We rejoice that our salvation is in the hands of God! We praise You and Thank You, O LORD.

PSALMS TO SING 2

9A (1, 2,6); 93A . . . and 9A; 18BH; 32A; 33C; 36B; 46ABC; 47A; 69C (11, 12); 90ABCD; 93A; 124A; 130AB; 135A (2).

FIELD TRIP

I still remember the day, although I was a very young age, when my father took me to see some flood damage after Hurricane Hazel. What a sight to see! Parts of the road were under water and fields were filled with stranded, flopping fish. Even a small flood is very impressive for a child. However, a flood may not be available for your children to witness, (for which you can be thankful.) Perhaps you can show them some floodgates. Imagine what would happen, if they were suddenly opened! Perhaps there is a large dam in your vicinity. Imagine what would happen if it cracked and burst! Remind the children that God ripped open the dams of the earth and the gates of the sky, so that all the world would be destroyed by water. It is a terrifying thought, but the fear of the LORD is a good thing. It is an incentive for obedience and reverence to God!

(This student lesson starts on page 159.)

A Journal of Praise

Genesis 7:6–8:19

VISUAL AIDS

Do you have a personal, hand-written, day-by-day diary? Do you have a journal in which you recorded the many days of a long trip? Bring them to show the children.

MEMORY WORK

"This I recall to my mind and therefore I have hope: Because of the LORD's Great LOVE, we are not consumed, for His compassions never fail. They are new every morning. Great is Your faithfulness!" (Lamentations 3:21–23)

CRAFT

Have each child work on his/her own "Journal of Praise." The daily entries need not be long, but they should record at least one small thing that gave them joy or made them smile. I have done this in Sabbath School, with a large class of six-and-seven-year-olds. I handed each child a small book to take home. There were eight xeroxed pages, beginning with a decorated title page: JOURNAL OF PRAISE. At the top of the next seven pages was the date and this question: What happened today? At the bottom of each page was this declaration: PRAISE THE LORD, FOR HE IS GOOD!

The space in between was left for the children to fill with good things. The following week they brought their books to share with the class. This was a wonderful project!

REVIEW QUESTIONS

1. What is a journal? (What French word is found inside this English word?)
2. Who wrote about the flood in the Bible? How did he know what happened?
3. What dating system is used in the account of the flood?
4. Who steered the ark through the raging waters of the flood?
5. How did God get rid of the water that covered the earth?
6. One day the ark stopped moving on the waters. Why?
7. What was the first creature to leave the ark?
8. What gift did the dove bring to Noah?
9. What happened on Noah's birthday?
10. When did Noah, his family and the animals leave the ark?

PRAYER

LORD, we thank You for all the days that You give us! LORD, help us to count our days and redeem the time.

PSALMS TO SING

107D . . . and 13 (1, 3,5); 27C (15, 16); 28AB; 29A (1, 2,6); 31CDEG; 34ACDE; 36B; 42B (8, 9,12); 46C; 66B; 90CD (6–8); 93A; 100ABC; 105A (1, 2,3, 5); 106A; 118C (14, 17); 121ABC; 130AB.

FIELD TRIP

Since we live near Ottawa, the capital of Canada, we have at our disposal the National Archives. There you can take children to see the carefully kept journals of many explorers. However, every community keeps records and every library has journals. Perhaps you can find some interesting ones to study.

(This student lesson starts on page 165.)

A New Beginning

Genesis 8:15–22

VISUAL AIDS

Season has followed season, year after year, century after century, according to the kind promise of our LORD. The unchanging change of the seasons—is it not wonderful? Bring calendars with photographs displaying the beauty of each season: spring's flowers, summer's fields, fall's forests, winter's frost. Show them pictures of our work and play in each season: swimming on hot summer days or sledding on cold winter nights, planting on a sunny spring morning or harvesting on a chilly fall evening. There are so many marvellous pictures!

MEMORY WORK

"As long as the earth endures, seedtime and harvest, cold and heat, summer and winter, day and night will never cease." (Genesis 8:22)

CRAFT

It is easy to make a "clock" for the seasons. Take a round paper plate and divide it in quarters, with each season's name printed on top. The children can then illustrate each section. Add a moveable hand to the centre of the clock. Move it round and round, showing the children how season has followed season, uninterrupted, for thousands of years. God promised never again would he stop everything because of man's sin—and God has kept that promise! Another craft idea is this: Divide a piece of white art paper into four sections, labelling each with the name of a season. Then have the children draw a picture of the same scene, (such as a person standing under an apple tree,) four times. The only thing changing in each picture is the season!

REVIEW QUESTIONS

1. What was the first thing that Noah built in the new world?
2. What did Noah kill and burn on this altar? Why?
3. Was God pleased with Noah's offering? Why?
4. What did God promise?
5. Has God kept that promise?

PRAYER

LORD, we thank You for Your loving words and faithful promises, which You have kept through all generations. Thank You, LORD, for the seasons, in which we have such joy. Thank You for not cursing the ground or killing all life again because of man's sin. We give thanks to You, O LORD; Your mercy endures forever!

PSALMS TO SING

104A . . . and 26A; 30AB; 54AB; 66C; 72C; 74B; 96AB; 100ABC; 104E; 117B; 119L; 136B.

FIELD TRIP

One need not travel very far to view the change of seasons. Look out over a field or a forest, a park or your front lawn—and there with your eyes you can see one season and with your minds you can "see" all the seasons. Talk about what you see now and what changes there would be in the other seasons. Use all your senses. What would you feel, smell, taste or hear in each season?

(This student lesson starts on page 176.)

A Sign In the Clouds

Genesis 9:1–17

VISUAL AIDS

Bring "rainbow-makers" (glass prisms) for your children to use. Explain how the sun shining through millions of raindrop prisms creates a rainbow in the sky. You should also bring photographs of all kinds of rainbows: full arcs, half arcs, double ones, fading ones, etc. Man has captured many beautiful rainbows on film!

MEMORY WORK

"God said . . . I have set My rainbow in the clouds, and it will be the sign of the covenant between Me and the earth." (Genesis 9:13)

CRAFT

Using paints, crayons, coloured pencils or glitter glue—have the children make rainbows.

REVIEW QUESTIONS

1. God said, "Be fruitful and multiply and fill the earth." To whom was this blessing given? When was it given?
2. What food did God give to man in the beginning? What food did God give to man after the flood?
3. How did God show that human life was different than animal life? How was human life protected?
4. What did God say in the beginning about man, that He repeated after the flood?
5. What is a covenant?

6. What promise did God make in this covenant?
7. What was the sign of this covenant?
8. At the end of the world, there will be another sign in the clouds. What (or whom) will all people see in the sky?
9. How can we escape that terrible Day of the LORD, when God will destroy the heavens and the earth? How can we be saved?

PRAYER

LORD, we thank You for all Your blessings to us, especially for Your Word, Your promise and Your covenant—which endure through all generations. God, we thank You for rainbows, the sign of Your covenant with the earth. LORD, thank You for providing a way of escape from that final day of destruction.

PSALMS TO SING

111A . . . and 25C; 50A; 65B; 103C; 105A (1–3, 5).

FIELD TRIP

If you live in Ireland, no doubt you can go for a walk and see a rainbow, but for the rest of us it may be difficult to see God's sign of the covenant set in the clouds. If you live near Niagara Falls (or even a waterfall of lesser magnificence) you can view something similar. You can see a "spraybow" of colours, which you can also make on your own front lawn by turning on a sprinkler and standing between the water and the sun.

(This student lesson starts on page 180.)

A Divided Family

Genesis 9:18–11:32

VISUAL AIDS

Find pictures of the world's great towers, such as the C.N. Tower in Toronto, The Eiffel Tower in Paris, the Leaning Tower of Pisa, the Empire State Building of New York, etc. A political map of the world would also be useful, to show how people have spread over the entire earth and how they have been divided into nations. Bring books in different languages, especially those using different alphabets, and let the children try to read them. It will give them a real experience of Babel!

MEMORY WORK

"I am God and there is no other; I am God and there is none like Me . . . I say: My purpose will stand, and I will do all that I please . . . What I have said, that will I bring about; what I have planned, that will I do." (Isaiah 46:9–11)

CRAFT

Perhaps your children can build a tall tower (with blocks or sticks, boxes or bricks—anything!) Build a tower that "reaches to the heavens" and then watch it collapse!

REVIEW QUESTIONS

1. What were the names of Noah's three sons?
2. Which son was cursed? Which son was blessed? Why?
3. Who was Canaan? Which people came from him?
4. Which people came from Shem?
5. Who is called the father of faith?

6. Who was the most important person born in the line of Shem?
7. The sons of men decided to build a city with a tower reaching to the heavens. Why?
8. God divided people into many different languages. Why?
9. What does "Babel" mean?
10. Why did God pour out the Holy Spirit on His children, causing them to speak in other tongues or languages?
11. How can we share the gospel with people of another language?
12. Which tribes, peoples, nations and languages will be praising God forever in heaven?

PRAYER

LORD, thank You that we can trust You and Your Word, that what You say, You do. God, we praise You that Your plans and purposes never fail. We thank You for the great gift of the Holy Spirit, poured out upon all Your sons and daughters, that we might proclaim the good news of the Saviour to all people. We pray for the work of missionaries and translators, as they bring the gospel to every tribe and people and nation—in their own language. And LORD, we thank You for the good gift of speech! May we ever use our voices to bless one another and glorify You.

PSALMS TO SING

9A; 33B . . . and 2; 12A; 18AG; 34BDE; 55B (1); 49B (7–10); 61; 64AB; 102B; 112AB; 144A; 145A.

FIELD TRIP

Is there a tower in your community? This would be the time to visit it! Is there a construction site? Listen to the men talk as they build. Imagine the confusion, if they all spoke different languages. They would have to abandon their work.

(This student lesson starts on page 186.)

The City of God

Genesis 12:1–9

VISUAL AIDS

Ruins! There are many pictures of the ruins of ancient cities, citadels, civilizations, etc. (Check magazines, like National Geographic.) What man builds, eventually falls; what God builds, lasts forever. Also useful for this lesson would be photographs or specimens of the precious stones used in the walls of the City of God, (as described in Revelation 21:19, 20.)

MEMORY WORK

"Trust in the LORD forever, for the LORD, the LORD, is the Rock eternal." (Isaiah 26:4)

CRAFT

For this lesson you could have the children make name plaques for themselves. This can be done by painting or "glittering" their names onto cardboard, burning or carving their names into wood, scratching their names onto stones or metal, chalking their names onto walls or sidewalks, pressing their names into sand or cement, etc. While the children are working, make sure to emphasize the only way their names will last: If they believe in Christ Jesus, the Lamb of God, their names are written in the Lamb's Book of Life—forever!

REVIEW QUESTIONS

1. Why did Abram leave his country, his city and his family?
2. What was the great promise that God made to Abram?
3. Who went with Abram on this journey of faith?

4. God promised to make Abram into a great nation, but what two things were missing?
5. Where did God lead Abram? To whom did this land belong? Why was this country called "The Promised Land"?
6. What did Abram build in this land? Why?
7. Why did Abram not build a city or find a country for himself? For which city/country was Abram waiting and longing?
8. Describe that city. How do we know what it looks like?
9. For whom has God prepared this city?

PRAYER

LORD, we thank You for Your precious promises to us, which we can trust with all our hearts! Thank You, LORD, for the gift of faith, because by faith we can follow You (wherever You lead us) and by faith we can obey You (whatever You tell us.) God, we thank You for the men and women of old, who lived by faith, that we might imitate them. We thank You their stories, revealed to us and recorded for us in the Bible, for our great benefit. We rejoice in You, O LORD, and in the City of God, which You have prepared for us. In this world, in the cities and countries in which we live, we have trouble—but You, O LORD, have prepared a place for us, where there is no more grief or pain. For this we thank You, O merciful God, and for the time when You will wipe away every tear from our weary eyes.

PSALMS TO SING

48B . . . and 31DG; 46ABC; 72C; 84B; 90C; 107A; 135C.

FIELD TRIP

Perhaps you live in a country that has ruins of castles or cathedrals, where you can view the slow decay of ancient dreams. Or perhaps you can take a tour in any town or city, looking for the ways men try to make their names last. There are names carved into tree trunks and sprayed onto rocks; there are names printed on books and signed on paintings; there are names in gold letters beneath massive monuments; there are names flashing in neon lights; there are names everywhere, but the only important place to have your name is the one place no one can see it—in the Lamb's Book of Life!

(This student lesson starts on page 194.)

The God Who Guides and Guards and Gives

Genesis 12, 13

VISUAL AIDS

Tragic pictures of starving nations, which show the effects of drought and the ravages of famine, would be appropriate for this lesson. Show the children how a famine looks with the carcasses of cattle lying shrivelled on land which is hard, bare, cracked and parched. Show them pictures of desperate people, who hold out withered hands for a crust of bread. Show them the dying children, just frail little skeletons, who sadly clasp the only thing they own—an empty bowl. Famine! That was what Abram faced in the land of Canaan. You might also show the children pictures of the world's wandering shepherds, the nomads who dwell in tents.

MEMORY WORK

"O God . . . I long to dwell in your tent forever and take refuge in the shelter of your wings." (Psalm 61:4)

CRAFT

You can make various kinds of tents with your children, depending on their ages. If it's a young class, bring sheets to drape over chairs. The children can sit in their "tents," while they listen to the lesson. You can make tiny "teepees" too, by having the children paint bright designs on half-circles of brown paper. (Tent poles can be glued on the inside and door flaps cut on the straight edge.) Fold them into cones and secure with tape.

REVIEW QUESTIONS

1. Abram lived by faith, trusting God to guide him, guard him and give to him. Give examples to show that Abram lived by faith.
2. Was there any time when Abram lived by fear, instead of faith?
3. How was it possible that Abram became so rich?
4. Where did Lot choose to live? Why? Was it a good choice?
5. What did God give to Abram?

PRAYER

LORD, thank You that You are a God whom we can trust. Thank You for taking care of us, for guiding us and guarding us and giving to us.

(Each child can also give thanks for specific ways in which God has cared for him.)

PSALMS TO SING

33C . . . and 27B; 28A (6–8); 31ADE; 32D; 34AC; 37CD; 40DF; 61; 62A (1, 4,5); 73C; 91A; 121ABC.

FIELD TRIP

Sleeping in a tent can be a scary experience. I have heard coyotes howling as they ran by my tent. I have heard bears sniffing around the campsite. I have imagined mountain lions screaming in trees overhead, (which turned out to be raccoons fighting) and I have imagined rattle snakes slithering under the canvass. When darkness descends, you suddenly realize how thin the walls of your tent really are! To sleep over-night in a tent would be an excellent outing to teach your children about Abram, who by faith lived in a foreign land . . . in a tent . . . trusting God to guard him all through the night.

(This student lesson starts on page 200.)

An Account of Kings

Genesis 14

VISUAL AIDS

Pictures of war would be useful for this lesson, especially those photographs that depict the anguish of people taken prisoner.

MEMORY WORK

1. "It is God who arms me with strength and makes my way perfect." (Psalm 18:32)
2. "You give me Your shield of victory, and Your right hand sustains me; You stoop down to make me great!" (Psalm 18:35)

CRAFT

Perhaps for this lesson your children could work on a mathematical as well as a theological concept: the tithe! Bring paper plates divided into ten equal wedges. Have the children colour (or cut out) one tenth to show the tithe. Also, if your class isn't too large, bring small bags, each with ten pennies in them. There are nine pennies for each child to keep, but the tenth one belongs to God, which can be put in the church collection plate. You can also make xeroxed sheets for each child, showing fifty "loonies" (the one-dollar Canadian coin) or fifty of whatever currency you use. Work out with the children what one tenth would be and colour (or cut out) the appropriate number of coins. The pharisees tithed on their herbs and spices, so bring a jar of pepper-corns, nutmegs or cloves and figure out what the tithe on them would be. You can tithe on anything—lines of sheep, baskets of apples, bags of gold, etc.

REVIEW QUESTIONS

1. There was a war in the land of Canaan. How many wicked kings with their armies were involved in this war?
2. What happened to Lot? Why? How was he rescued?
3. What does Melchizedek mean? Who was he?
4. What did Abram give to Melchizedek?
5. Melchizedek was a living "shadow" to help us see . . . whom?
6. Did Abram receive anything from the king of Salem? What?
7. Did Abram receive anything from the king of Sodom? Why not?

PRAYER

LORD, we thank You for the great King of Righteousness, even Jesus our LORD, who has blessed us in the heavenly realms with every spiritual blessing!

PSALMS TO SING

47A; 110 . . . and 2; 10B; 18EJ; 28AB; 33C; 37B; 44AD; 54AB; 56; 59AB; 62C; 68A; 72B; 89D; 96A; 136A (1, 2); 138AB; 145A; 149.

FIELD TRIP

Is there somewhere you can go to see the glory of earthly kings? The crown jewels are on display in the Tower of London, the Louvre in Paris, the Kremlin in Moscow. Vanity of vanities! Abram despised the wealth of such earthly kings, taking not even one jewel from their crowns, not even one thread from their robes. What Abram treasured was the blessing, which he received from heaven's only King.

(This student lesson starts on page 206.)

A Very Great Reward

Genesis 15:1–6

VISUAL AIDS

There are wonderful photographs of the starry heavens. A picture of the millions of stars in the Milky Way would be particularly useful. Look in any astronomy book.

MEMORY WORK

"Consider Abraham: He believed God, and it was credited to him as righteousness." (Galatians 3:6)

CRAFT

You can make a starry sky in your classroom by hanging hundreds of stars large and small from the ceiling. Among these many stars there should be a star for each child with his/her name on it. If they believe in Jesus, if they have the faith of Abraham, then they are among his children, like stars in the sky.

REVIEW QUESTIONS

1. Why did Abram not accept the king of Sodom's reward?
2. Afterwards, what did God say about what Abram had done?
3. Abram spoke to God about something that was troubling him. What was it? How did God reassure Abram? What did God say?
4. Why did the LORD take Abram outside his tent at night?
5. What did God promise Abram? How did Abram respond?
6. How is any person made righteous in the sight of God?
7. What was the very great reward that God had for Abram?

PRAYER

LORD, I pray that each child here might have the same faith as Abram, that each one might also believe in You. Thank You, God, for crediting our faith as righteousness, for not holding our sins against us. LORD, thank You for Your most precious gift to us—Jesus, "The Bright Morning Star," who enables us to shine like stars in the universe, as we hold forth the Word of Life! Thank You that, although we may miss many of the rewards in this life, You have given us the greatest reward of all, which is Your Son, Jesus Christ, in whom we have eternal life. May we praise Your Holy Name forever and ever.

PSALMS TO SING

127A . . . and 5AB (1, 5); 8AB; 18C; 20B (1–3); 31DG; 32AC; 34BD; 37A; 62C; 71C; 128AB.

FIELD TRIP

Take the children out on a clear night to view the Milky Way and all the other stars. Try to count them! Remind the children of God's promise to Abram.

(This student lesson starts on page 211.)

Know For Certain

Genesis 15:7–21

VISUAL AIDS

A picture of vultures circling in the heat of the day would illustrate the setting for this lesson. Also, a metal box with a lock containing legal documents (such as property deeds) would be a very useful visual aid. Remind the children that what Abram kept locked in his heart, which was God's Word, was more valuable than any deed to the promised land.

MEMORY WORK

"Praise the LORD . . . He remembers His covenant forever." (Psalm 111:1, 5)

CRAFT

The children could make decorated folders or envelopes for their important papers. Of course, they won't have legal documents to place in them, but they may have important letters or pictures or reports that they wish to keep in a safe place.

REVIEW QUESTIONS

1. What question did Abram ask God?
2. What did God tell Abram to do?
3. How long did Abram have to wait for God's answer?
4. When Abram fell into a deep sleep, what did He see?
5. What did God tell Abram was going to happen in the future?
6. God made a covenant promise to Abram. What was it?
7. God has made a covenant promise to us. What is it?

PRAYER

LORD, thank You for Your promises, in which we can hope and trust—especially Your promise of eternal life in Jesus Christ. Thank You for the New Covenant in the precious blood of Your Son, by which we can "know for certain" that there is everlasting life for all who believe.

PSALMS TO SING

111B . . . and 25C; 32D (5); 37B (6–8); 47A; 50A; 62B (1, 2); 89E; 97AC; 105A; 111A; 130AB.

FIELD TRIP

Can you take the children somewhere to see a blazing fire and billowing smoke? "Our God is a consuming fire" (Hebrews 12:29). God often presents Himself to men in fire and smoke, as He did that night when He came to Abram in a vision.

(This student lesson starts on page 215.)

God Hears! God Sees!

Genesis 16

VISUAL AIDS

X-ray pictures of bones and ultrasound photos of unborn babies (both boys and girls) would be useful for this class. Modern technology allows us to see inside the human body, but God alone can see into the future.

MEMORY WORK

"Trust in the LORD with all your heart and lean not on your own understanding; in all your ways acknowledge Him, and He will make your paths straight." (Proverbs 3:5, 6)

CRAFT

You can all work together to make two collage-type posters. In magazines find pictures of old women, whose faces are wrinkled and whose bodies are withered. For the other poster find pictures of smooth-skinned, straight-backed, young women—especially ones who are expecting a baby or holding a baby. You can also clip from newspapers and magazines some appropriate words for each poster. To which group did Sarah belong? To which group did Hagar belong? (This craft prepares the way for the miracle described in Genesis 21:1–7— the birth of Isaac.)

REVIEW QUESTIONS

1. Sarah had a plan to get a baby for herself and Abram. What was the plan? Was it a good plan? Why or why not?
2. How old was Abram when he got married to his second wife?

3. After Hagar became pregnant, did Abram have a happy family? Why not? Who was having difficulties with whom? Why?

4. Why did Hagar run away from home? Was that a good solution to the problem?

5. Who found Hagar in the desert? What did He tell her to do? 6. What did the LORD tell Hagar about her unborn baby?

7. Why was Hagar supposed to call her baby Ishmael? What does that mean?

8. Was there a happy ending to this story? What was it?

9. Do you think Ishmael was the child that God promised to Abram?

PRAYER

LORD, we thank You for always hearing us and seeing us, even when we are hiding from everyone else. Thank You, God, for helping us when we are in terrible situations. LORD, thank You that our hope in You is never disappointed. Help each one of us to always turn to You in our distress. Help us to turn to You before we bring trouble and travail into our lives.

PSALMS TO SING

139A . . . and 5AB (1, 5); 27C; 28A (1, 2,6, 7,8); 31E; 32BD; 34ACD; 86A; 102A (1); 116A; 119T; 121ABC; 130A; 139B.

FIELD TRIP

Perhaps you can arrange for your class to minister to two groups of women. Young women who are pregnant often need help, as do old women who are lonely and needy.

(This student lesson starts on page 220.)

The Covenant Confirmed

Genesis 17

VISUAL AIDS

For this lesson you need pictures of old men with wrinkled faces and weary eyes and snowy beards, for Abraham was almost 100 years old when God appeared to him again. Also, a world map would be useful for this lesson, when you are discussing the greatness of the world's nations. Make sure to point out the little land of Israel in contrast to the vast land of Russia. You could also bring some legal documents or diplomas to show the children the seals affixed to them. Circumcision was the sign and seal of God's covenant.

MEMORY WORK

"Against all hope, Abraham in hope believed . . . He did not waver through unbelief regarding the promise of God, but was strengthened in his faith and gave glory to God, being fully persuaded that God had power to do what He had promised."

(Romans 4:18, 20)

CRAFT

For this lesson, type out Genesis 17 and xerox enough copies for all the children in your class to have their own page. Have them read it and highlight the word *covenant*, which is found fourteen times in this passage. Now you need a craft to reinforce the idea of "a sign and a seal." Have the children write their signatures on their piece of work and then add their thumb prints in sealing wax. Their work is now authenticated by a sign and a seal—their signature and their finger-print.

REVIEW QUESTIONS

1. What are the four new names to consider? What do they mean? Why did God give those names?
2. In the covenant with Abraham, what did God promise?
3. In the covenant with Abraham, what did God require?
4. What was the sign of the covenant? What did it mean? To whom was this sign supposed to be given?
5. Was Sarah included in the covenant? How do we know?
6. When was Abraham made righteous? Was it before or after he was circumcised? What did God count as righteousness?
7. How is a person purified from sin?
8. Abraham would soon have two sons. With which one would God establish His covenant?
9. How old was Abraham when he was circumcised? How old was Ishmael? How many days passed before Abraham did what God commanded?
10. Circumcision was the sign of the Old Covenant. What is the sign of the New Covenant?
11. God promised Abraham and Sarah that kings would come from them. Who were s some of those kings? Which son of theirs was known as the King of kings?
12. How did this Son of Abraham purify God's people from sin?

PRAYER

LORD, we thank You for Your great covenant promise, which You first spoke to Abraham, so very long ago: "I will be their God." LORD, we thank You and praise You for being our God, for "blessed are the people who have the LORD to be their God" (Psalm 144:15). We thank You and praise You for making us Your people and for saving us from our sins through Jesus Christ. We thank You for the great peace and joy which we have in Him. We exult in You, O LORD, for You have fulfilled all Your covenant promises to Abraham and to us . . . in Jesus.

PSALMS TO SING

71C . . . and 25C; 32D (5); 67AB; 92C (5); 100ABC; 105A; 111AB;

FIELD TRIP

There are two ceremonies by which children are entered into the covenant. Perhaps your class can witness a baby's baptism in a church, whereby he/she receives the sign of the New Covenant. Male babies eight-days old, who are in Jewish families, receive circumcision, the sign of the Old Covenant. To witness this "cutting of the covenant," even if it were possible, might not be advisable, for it remains a sign of blood and tears.

Note: This lesson deals with a sensitive topic: circumcision. If your class does not know what circumcision is, you may wish to deal with it linguistically first: circum = around (e.g. circumference & circumvent) and scission = cutting (e.g. scissors & incision). Circumcision is, therefore, a "cutting around." Then you may wish to deal with the topic medically by explaining what doctors sometimes do in the hospital to new-born baby boys. On the part of his body, which makes a baby boy a boy, there is an extra piece of skin, (called the foreskin,) which the doctor removes . . . sometimes. Not all baby boys have their foreskins removed. It used to be that only Jewish boys were circumcised, because it was a religious ceremony for them. When Jewish boys were eight days old they received the sign of the Old Covenant: circumcision!

(This student lesson starts on page 225.)

Please turn the page for the guide to lesson 44

Three Visitors

Genesis 18

VISUAL AIDS

Lush green river valleys have always attracted people. Farmers are excited by their bounty; painters are inspired by their beauty. Alas! There are no pictures of that area, which the Bible claims was like the "Garden of God." What Abraham saw that day, can never be seen again. One day later, it was destroyed and that whole area vanished forever. It became a sterile wasteland of smoking sulphur, salt and sand. Today it is still a wasteland. Show your class photographs of the area around the Dead Sea. Contrast those pictures with ones showing lush, green river valleys.

MEMORY WORK

1. "Nothing is impossible with God." (Luke 1:37)
2. "Will not the Judge of all the earth do right?" (Genesis 18:25)

CRAFT

In this lesson we have angelic beings appearing in the form of human beings. Perhaps the small humans in your class would like to masquerade as angels! Masks are always fun to make. I have no idea how an angel's face looks, since I have never seen one, so your imagination is as free as mine in this area. Paper plates (sprinkled with sparkles) or foil pie plates would make an easy base for the mask.

REVIEW QUESTIONS

1. Who were the three visitors? How did Abraham treat them? What did he do for them?

2. Why had these three visitors from heaven come to earth? What was their mission?
3. The LORD said, "Sarah will have a son." How did ninety-year-old Sarah respond to this promise?
4. Did Sarah finally have faith in the Word of God?
5. Why were the angels going to Sodom?
6. Abraham began pleading with God to spare Sodom. Why was Abraham so concerned about that wicked city?
7. The LORD promised not to destroy the city of Sodom, if He found how many righteous people in it?

PRAYER

LORD, we thank You that nothing, not even the sin of unbelief, could stop Your great plan of salvation! LORD, we believe Your Word. Please help us when we lack faith. LORD, thank You for preserving the righteous and destroying the wicked. LORD, we thank You that Your mercy and justice fill the earth. We rejoice in You, the Righteous Judge of all the earth.

PSALMS TO SING

113A . . . and 1AB; 7A (3–5); 7B; 9AB; 36B; 37E; 50A; 71C; 94AB; 96B (4, 6); 98AB.

FIELD TRIP

Have a picnic under the shade of some trees. Pack a lunch of freshly baked bread, slices of veal or beef, cheese curds and milk drinks. Recall the meal that Abraham served his heavenly visitors . . . and keep an eye open for angels!

(This student lesson starts on page 235.)

A Day of Destruction, A Day of Salvation

Genesis 19

VISUAL AIDS

You may not wish to show the children the pictures of present-day Sodomites, as they display themselves and their sin in their "Gay Pride Parades." (However, such photographs are available.) There are also pictures of destroyed cities from World War II, such as Hiroshima. Although there were survivors from these disasters, the children will get a sense of the awful and total destruction that can befall a city. Also of interest for this lesson, would be some of the excellent photographs of the Dead Sea area in modern Israel—the wasteland, which testifies to the catastrophe which God brought upon the cities of that plain, although once it was like the "Garden of the LORD."

MEMORY WORK

1. "The LORD knows how to rescue godly men from trials and to hold the unrighteous for the day of judgement . . ." (II Peter 2:9)
2. "Hallelujah! Salvation and power and glory belong to our God, for true and just are His judgements." (Revelation 19:1, 2)

CRAFT

The children could make a picture called *destruction*: First paint bright flames of fire. When the paint is dry, add charcoal swirls of black smoke. Then put streaks of glue over the whole picture, shaking salt onto it before the glue dries. To this chaos of raging flames and billowing smoke and swirling salt, you might want to add the horror of grey faces or words from newspaper clippings—ripped and burned around the edges, as if these are scraps of debris from that day of destruction.

REVIEW QUESTIONS

1. How many righteous people did the two angels find in Sodom?
2. How did Lot try to protect the two strangers in Sodom?
3. How did these strangers, who were angels, protect Lot?
4. What happened to Lot's wife? Why?
5. What did God do to Sodom, Gomorrah, and the whole plain?
6. Why were these people without excuse?
7. Sodom and Gomorrah are a warning for the whole world! What is God's warning to everyone?
8. What is the great and dreadful Day of the LORD? When is it? How can we escape it?
9. What happened to Lot? How did he end his days on this earth?

PRAYER

We give thanks to You, O God, that Your judgements are true and just. We rejoice, that salvation and glory and power belong to our God. LORD, thank You for rescuing the godly from trials, for saving Your people from sin and death. We praise You, LORD, for Your mercy to us. God, grant to us Your help and strength to be a holy people, living before You—a God who is Holy, Holy, Holy. Our God, we know You are a consuming fire; grant us the proper fear and love before You. We pray for these children, that they might have faith, that they might never turn back in unbelief—and thus, by God's grace, that they might be spared and saved from that great and dreadful Day of the LORD.

PSALMS TO SING

11; 97C; 140B . . . and 1AB; 2; 9A; 18BH; 21B; 28AB; 37ABEF; 50A; 68A (1, 2); 69D; 73C; 83B; 94AB; 98AB; 104E.

FIELD TRIP

I suppose you could attend a "Gay Pride Parade"—but I wouldn't view such a detestable display of sin, much less expose children to it. Instead, perhaps there is a place of destruction near you, such as a bombed-out block or a burned-out house. Perhaps there is a place where nothing grows, a waste area. There are pockets of destruction all over the earth. Perhaps you can find one, even a little one, to be the sober reminder of what happened to Sodom and Gomorrah.

(This student lesson starts on page 242.)

The Serpent Strikes, But Fails

Genesis 20; 21:1–7, 22–34

AUDIO AIDS

For this lesson you will need to collect some laughter. You can make a recording of all the different kinds you find—giggles and chortles and guffaws. Perhaps you can include the laughter of your class on the recording, both the individuals and the group. Let the children listen to the laughter and remind them that when Isaac was born, Sarah said: "God has brought me Laughter, and everyone who hears about this will laugh with me."

MEMORY WORK

"Our mouths were filled with laughter, our tongues with songs of joy . . . The LORD has done great things for us, and we are filled with joy." (Psalm 126:2, 3)

CRAFT

Make a collage. Have the children collect pictures of laughing, smiling faces and happy, joyful words.

REVIEW QUESTIONS

1. Why did Abraham move? Where did Abraham move?
2. Why did Abraham say that Sarah was his sister?
3. What promise of God did Satan attack?
4. For awhile it seemed that the child God promised to Abraham and Sarah could not be born. Why?
5. Who was Abimelech? Was he a good king? Did he fear God?
6. How did God speak to Abimelech? What did God say? Did the king listen?

7. There were several things that happened to give this story a happy ending. What were they? What was the happiest event?
8. Did God keep His promise to Abraham and Sarah?
9. Can we also trust God, to keep His promises to us?

PRAYER

LORD, we rejoice that Your Word prevails, against the schemes of demons and the sins of men. We rejoice, that all the promises of God are fulfilled in Jesus Christ our Lord. Please help us to always fear God, rather than men. Deliver us from the Evil One. Be with us, O God, as we take our stand, by faith, against all the schemes of the devil.

PSALMS TO SING

126AB . . . and 66C (1, 3,5); 67AB; 100ABC; 104E; 106A; 113A; 138AB; 145A.

FIELD TRIP

Go on a little expedition and look for laughter. Hint: Where you find the blessing of children, there you will find the blessing of laughter.

(This student lesson starts on page 253.)

The Lord Gives and the Lord Takes Away

Genesis 21:1–21

VISUAL AIDS

Pictures of parties, especially birthday parties, would be useful for this lesson.

MEMORY WORK

"The LORD gave and the LORD has taken away; blessed be the name of the LORD." (Job 1:21) NAS

CRAFT

Help celebrate someone's birthday, especially a younger child's birthday. Perhaps your class could make birthday cards and/or birthday hats. Plan a simple party for some little person. Don't forget to sing and shout: "Happy Birthday!"

REVIEW QUESTIONS

1. Isaac was not born in the ordinary way. How was he born?
2. What did Ishmael do to his little brother, Isaac?
3. Why was Abraham greatly distressed?
4. How did God settle the matter? What did God say to do?
5. Why were Hagar and Ishmael crying in the desert? Who heard them? How did God help them?
6. Were the prophesies about Ishmael fulfilled? Did he become a "wild" man? Did he become a nation of people? Who were they?

PRAYER

LORD, it comforts us to know that You hear and see everything. Deliver us from our enemies, from those who hate us and mock us, from those who ridicule us and persecute us. Help us, God, to be a people marked by kindness and gentleness towards one another.

PSALMS TO SING

71A ... 34D; 70C; 107A; 123; 131; 145C.

FIELD TRIP

Attend a small child's birthday party to bring him/her gifts, laughter, good wishes, smiling faces and congratulations!

(This student lesson starts on page 257.)

The Lord Will Provide

Genesis 22

VISUAL AIDS

Genesis 22:17 is the first time God promises Abraham "descendants as numerous . . . as the sand on the seashore." Bring a jar of sand and try to count the individual grains of sand. Imagine how many grains of sand are on a seashore! Maps and photos showing the mountains of Moriah would also be useful for this lesson.

MEMORY WORK

1. "God Himself will provide the lamb . . ." (Genesis 22:8)
2. "Behold the Lamb of God, Who takes away the sin of the world." (John 1:29)

CRAFT

Your class can make Bible bookmarks from pretty flowered paper glued on cardboard and cut in the shape of a cross. On the cross beam add their verse of memory work: *God himself will provide the lamb.*

REVIEW QUESTIONS

1. How did God test Abraham? Why did God test Abraham?
2. Abraham was going to sacrifice his son, as God commanded, but he said to his servants, "We will come back to you." What did Abraham believe God was going to do?
3. What did Abraham carry up the mountain? What did Isaac carry?
4. What did Isaac ask on the way? What was Abraham's answer?
5. How did God rescue Isaac?
6. Tell two ways that God provided a lamb as a substitute?

7. Two thousand years later, what was built on Mount Moriah?
8. Who was the Lamb of God, who takes away the sin of the world?
9. God swore an oath to Abraham. Why? By whom did He swear?
10. What did God promise? Had He made this promise before that day? When?
11. What were the results of Abraham's obedience?
12. How was Abraham a prophet? How did he "speak" about Jesus?

PRAYER

LORD, thank You for providing all our needs, especially our greatest need—the Lamb for the sacrifice! Heavenly Father, thank You for loving us and for sending Your Son as a substitute, to die on the cross to pay for our sins.

PSALMS TO SING

118C . . . and 22C; 34DE; 40E; 61; 66B; 106A; 111A; 150A.

FIELD TRIP

Visit a farm (or zoo) that has rams, with long curly horns—the kind of horns that could get caught in a bush.

(This student lesson starts on page 262.)

A Loved One Lost, A Loved One Gained

Genesis 23, 24

VISUAL AIDS

Photographs of camel caravans and veiled women, would be useful for this lesson. Look in National Geographic and books about the Middle East.

MEMORY WORK

"Charm is deceitful and beauty is vain, but a woman who fears the LORD, she shall be praised." (Proverbs 31:30) NAS

CRAFT

Have your class make a camel caravan. If each child makes one camel, you will have a caravan to display on your classroom wall. (Make sure all the heads are facing the same direction.) Camels can be drawn on white paper, painted, and then cut. They could also be made from brown construction paper. The children can load the camels by pasting onto them whatever cargo they choose — little boxes wrapped in gold or silver paper, little cloth bags filled with stuffing, bales of fabric tied with string, etc. Don't forget to have each child draw a self-portrait, to ride on top of his/her camel!

REVIEW QUESTIONS

1. How old was Sarah when she died? How long did Isaac have his mother?
2. What was the first piece of property that Abraham owned in the promised land?
3. Abraham wanted a godly wife for his son. How could he find one? What was his plan? Who would help him?
4. Did God lead Abraham's servant? Where did God lead him?

5. How did Isaac and Rebekah meet each other? Did Isaac like the woman God chose for him? What does the Bible say?
6. The LORD had a very great plan and purpose for Rebekah's life. What was it?
7. How is this lesson a double love story?

PRAYER

LORD, we thank You for the stories of our lives. We thank You for surely leading us and loving us. Heavenly Father, we pray for these children, that at the right time You will provide the right person to be their marriage partners.

PSALMS TO SING

45C ... and 13; 32D (5); 52A (7, 8); 57B (5, 9,10); 106A; 108A; 117A.

FIELD TRIP

Most of us can not go to a place to see a camel caravan walking along the desert sands. However, maybe there is a zoo, where at least you can view a live specimen and perhaps even ride on one!

(This student lesson starts on page 270.)

God Blesses Isaac

Genesis 25:1–26; 26

VISUAL AIDS

Do you have ultrasound pictures of any of your children before they were born? Do you have a friend with twins, who has their ultrasound photo before they were born? Such pictures would be an excellent visual aid for this lesson.

MEMORY WORK

1. "Blessed are those who hear the Word of God and obey it." (Luke 11:28)
2. "The LORD bless you and keep you; the LORD make His face shine upon you and be gracious to you; the LORD turn His face toward you and give you peace." (Numbers 6:24–26)
3. "The LORD remembers us and will bless us . . . He will bless those who fear the LORD." (Psalm 115:12, 13)

CRAFT

You have probably seen those old-fashioned, cross-stitch samplers that say: God Bless This House. The children could make such a sampler, making bright X's with yarn or pen on cardboard.

REVIEW QUESTIONS

1. Abraham remarried. What was his new wife's name? How many more sons did Abraham have? Who was the son of promise, through whom his children were counted?
2. How was Abraham's faith tested? How was Isaac's faith tested?
3. How many years passed before Rebekah became pregnant?
4. At first Rebekah was delighted; then she became alarmed. Why?

5. Whom did Rebekah ask what was happening? What did God say?
6. What were the names of the twins? Why?
7. How long did Abraham live in the Promised Land?
8. What trouble did Isaac face in Canaan? How did God help him?
9. Where did God speak to Isaac? What did He say?

PRAYER

LORD, we thank You for all Your blessings to us!

PSALMS TO SING

67AB; 134AB . . . and 1AB; 3 (5); 5AB (1, 5); 21AC; 33B (6); 34AC; 40ABE; 41BC; 65A; 72D; 84AB; 89I; 106AG; 112AB; 115D; 116A; 119A; 128AB; 146AB.

FIELD TRIP

You can take the children to watch a well being dug. It is a lot of work, even with machines. Remind them of what happened to Isaac. Time after time his servants would dig a well—and the Philistines would steal it from him!

(This student lesson starts on page 280.)

God Chooses Jacob; Jacob Chooses God

Genesis 25:19–34

VISUAL AIDS

For this lesson pictures of identical twins (and triplets, quadruplets, quintuplets, etc.) would be interesting for the children to see and to contrast with the twins, Jacob and Esau, who were not identical. You could also bring some red lentils for your children to see.

MEMORY WORK

1. "Let us hold firmly to the faith we profess." (Hebrews 4:14)
2. "Let us hold unswervingly to the hope we profess, for He who promised is faithful." (Hebrews 10:23)

CRAFT

Your children could make a lentil mosaic. You will need cardboard, glue, and different kinds of many-coloured lentils. If you have access to a kitchen, you could also supervise a cooking project. Each child could make a small loaf of bread and all together the class could make a big lentil stew. (Put tomato sauce in it to give it a bright red colour, and lots of vegetables and spices for taste.)

REVIEW QUESTIONS

1. Were Jacob and Esau identical twins? How were they different?
2. What was the most significant difference between these twins?
3. When did God choose Jacob?
4. Did God choose Jacob because he was good or because he had faith? Is anyone saved because of their own righteousness? How then are people saved?
5. Did Esau live by faith? Did Esau hope in God's promises?

6. How did Jacob show that he believed the Word of God?

7. What did Esau do that showed he was a godless man?

PRAYER

LORD, we thank You for Your grace to us and choice of us and love for us. We humbly ask for Your help that we might always cling fast to Your precious promises. Help us to seek first Your kingdom and Your righteousness. May we never be foolish and godless like Esau, trading heavenly treasures for earthly pleasures. O LORD, lead us not into temptation, but deliver us from evil this day . . . and all the days of our lives.

PSALMS TO SING

135AB (1); 65A (2) . . . and 4AB; 14C; 33B (6); 47A; 53; 95B (5, 6); 105A; 119WX; 146AB.

FIELD TRIP

Do you know some identical twins? I know some elderly ladies, (over ninety years old) who still look exactly alike and who still enjoy confusing people. I know other younger sets of twins too. Invite these people to your class for a visit and ask them to dress in their "twin" clothes—just for fun.

(This student lesson starts on page 286.)

First the Birthright, Then the Blessing

Genesis 26:34–27:40

VISUAL AIDS

Photos of blind people, walking with white canes or guide dogs, would be useful to stimulate discussion for this class. Does your church have a braille Bible? Bring it (or some other samples of braille writing) for your children to examine. Borrow a blind person's watch to show your students.

MEMORY WORK

"The word of the LORD stands forever." (I Peter 1:25)

CRAFT

Your children can make pictures for a blind person by gluing bits of yarn and scraps of cloth onto cardboard. Since this is a picture to feel rather than to see, the children will have to think about making their artwork interesting by using different textures, instead of different colours.

GAME

Blindfold your children and have them identify different things by using:

1. just their ears (e.g., the sound of a zipper or car keys)
2. just their nose (e.g., the smell of crayons or spices)
3. just their tongue (e.g., the taste of fruit or cheese)
4. just their hands (e.g., the feel of a clothespin or pinecone)

REVIEW QUESTIONS

1. What did Esau do with his birthright?
2. What else did Esau do that troubled and angered his parents?

3. What did Isaac decide to do before he died? Why? Was he right or wrong in what he planned to do?
4. What did Rebekah decide to do? Why? Was she right or wrong in what she planned to do?
5. What were four things that Jacob did to deceive his father?
6. What blessings did Isaac give to Jacob?
7. When Esau knelt before his father weeping and pleading, why did Isaac not change his mind and give him the blessing?
8. What "blessing" was given to Esau by his father?
9. How was the blessing to Jacob finally and eternally fulfilled? What Son of Jacob rules this very day, as the King of kings and LORD of lords?

PRAYER

LORD, we are thankful that it is not our plans, but Your great plan, that prevails. We praise You, O God, that Your Word stands firm. We rejoice that Your blessings to us, in Jesus Christ, are forever sure.

PSALMS TO SING

115D . . . and 67AB; 119F; 119I (1); 134AB.

FIELD TRIP

Take your class to visit a blind person. Bring the special pictures that the children made. You could also bring other things that a blind person would enjoy: a bouquet of fragrant flowers, a song your class has learned, a tasty treat you have made together. Your blind friend will have many interesting things to show and share with your children also.

(This student lesson starts on page 292.)

Jacob Blessed and Blessed Again!

Genesis 27:41–28:22

VISUAL AIDS

The dust of the earth—it is everywhere! Show your children a shaft of sunlight shining through a window—and how it illuminates the dust of the earth, which is even in the air.

MEMORY WORK

"Be strong and courageous. Do not be afraid or terrified . . . for the LORD your God goes with you; He will never leave you nor forsake you." (Deuteronomy 31:6)

CRAFT

The children could each draw a picture of Jacob's dream or you could all work together on a classroom display. Make a large, floor-to-ceiling, cardboard ladder on one of the walls. Then have the children draw and colour (from top to bottom on pieces of white art paper) one angel, their own guardian angel. They can also decorate their angels with sparkles and sequins. Cut out the angels (making sure each child's name is somewhere on it) and place this heavenly host all along the ladder. You might want to put a large stone at the bottom of the ladder, where the children can rest their heads, while they look up the ladder.

REVIEW QUESTIONS

1. Did Esau repent of his unbelief? How do we know?
2. What was Rebekah's plan to save Jacob's life?
3. What did Isaac command Jacob to do? How did he bless him?

4. Where did Jacob spend the first night of his journey?
5. What did Jacob dream? What did he see? What did he hear?
6. What did God promise Jacob when He spoke to him in the dream?
7. Why was Jacob afraid when he awoke from his dream?
8. What did Jacob do to remember the spot where God visited him?
9. God made promises to Jacob and Jacob made promises to God. What were they?
10. Why do you think Jacob would return to the promised land?

PRAYER

LORD, we thank You for Your promise that You will never leave us, nor forsake us.

PSALMS TO SING

3; 27C; 55A . . . and 4AB; 7A; 11; 31AE; 46ABC; 52B; 54AB; 56; 57AB; 59AB; 62A; 73C; 86B; 91AB; 118C; 142; 143C; 146.

FIELD TRIP

Take your children to a safe place where they can lie down in the night with a stone for a pillow and the sky for a ceiling, where they can hear the wind moaning in the trees and see shadows moving in the dark. Let each child experience the loneliness and scariness of Jacob's situation. Remind the children that God is with them too.

(This student lesson starts on page 301.)

Deceiver Is Deceived

Genesis 29:1–30

VISUAL AIDS

Show some photographs of refugees to the children. Discuss how these people have had to leave their homes and flee for their lives, bringing little or nothing with them. Jacob was a refugee in a foreign land. All he brought with him was his shepherd's crook. You could also bring a shepherd's crook to show your children Jacob's only possession, his only visible, tangible possession. All he had was a staff in his hand, but in his heart he possessed a great treasure—the promises of God!

MEMORY WORK

"The LORD disciplines those He loves, and He punishes the child in whom He delights." (Hebrews 12:6)

CRAFT

Jacob had a staff for his journey. When people in Japan hike up Mount Fuji they buy special walking sticks, which are branded with a sign at each level of the journey. These sticks are also adorned with bright ribbons and tinkling bells. Perhaps your children could each make one of these sticks. Visit your local lumber store and pick up some 1x1 sticks of the appropriate length. Each child's name can be burned into the wood. Then the children can decorate their own staffs as they please.

REVIEW QUESTIONS

1. What is a fugitive? Was Jacob a fugitive?

2. What did Jacob take with him on his journey? What did he hold in his hand? What did he hold in his heart?
3. Name one river that Jacob had to cross.
4. Whom did Jacob hope to find in this foreign land? How did he find them?
5. With whom did Jacob fall in love?
6. How did Jacob's uncle trick him? Why did Laban do this?
7. Do you think Jacob learned a very important lesson when he was deceived? What do you think he learned about treating people?

PRAYER

LORD, thank You for being with us wherever we go. Thank You for always being fair and just, even when people cheat us and harm us. LORD, we thank You for not giving us what we deserve, for not giving us what we have earned by our sins—which is death and hell. Thank You, LORD, for lovingly and graciously giving us eternal life in Jesus Christ. Help us never to cheat other people, but to always be fair with them. Help us to obey Your Law: "Do unto others, as you would have them do unto you."

PSALMS TO SING

119P . . . 36A; 37A; 62AB; 101; 119M; 120 (1); 140AB; 141A.

FIELD TRIP

I'm sure the children would like to go for a long hike over rugged terrain, using the walking sticks they made.

(This student lesson starts on page 309.)

The Stars Begin to Shine

Genesis 29:31–30:24

VISUAL AIDS

Show your class some pictures of happy mothers with several children. Then show a picture of a sad woman, a childless woman, who is all alone.

MEMORY WORK

"Behold, children are a gift of the LORD; the fruit of the womb is a reward." (Psalm 127:3)

CRAFT

Have each child draw a picture of his/her family. Perhaps these family portraits could be signed by the artists, framed and then wrapped up as presents to give to the mothers.

REVIEW QUESTIONS

1. Why did the LORD open Leah's womb, so that she could have many children?
2. What were the names of Jacob's first three sons?
3. What was the name of Jacob's fourth son? What did his name mean? What special place did Judah have in God's plan for the world?
4. Jacob loved his wife Rachel, but she was very unhappy. Why?
5. How did Rachel get two little boys for herself? What were their names? Were they really her children? Leah got two more sons in the same way. What were their names?
6. Then Leah gave birth to two more sons. What were their names?
7. Finally a daughter was born for Jacob. What was her name?

8. Then God remembered Rachel. He heard her prayers and opened her womb. She gave birth to a son in Jacob's old age. What was the name of Jacob's eleventh son?
9. Why are these children like stars in the sky? Which son of Abraham, Isaac and Jacob is called the "Bright Morning Star"?

PRAYER

LORD, thank You for the gift of children. Thank You, LORD, for always hearing and answering our prayers. Please give us the grace to wait for Your proper time and Your good answer to our prayers. May we rejoice always in Your great LOVE for us.

PSALMS TO SING

147A (1–4, 7) . . . and 8AB; 22H; 34BD; 113AB; 127A; 128AB; 144D (7, 8); 148.

FIELD TRIP

It's time to view the stars again. Late in the evening watch the stars come out one by one. Perhaps you can name them in the order of Jacob's children. Note how some stars are brighter than others. What Biblical names could you give these bright stars? Then perhaps you could arise before dawn and find the bright morning star, which has been honoured above all the stars with the name of Jesus. Christ Himself said, "I am . . . the Bright Morning Star" (Revelation 22:16).

(This student lesson starts on page 313.)

Time to Go Home

Genesis 30:25–31:55

VISUAL AIDS

You will need photographs of all kinds of animals with their look-alike offspring. Show the children plain, spotted, patched, speckled and striped animals with their young ones of identical shadings and markings.

MEMORY WORK

Jesus said ". . . Do not worry, saying, 'What shall we eat?' or 'What shall we drink?' or 'What shall we wear?' For the pagans run after all these things, and your heavenly Father knows that you need them. But *seek first His kingdom and His righteousness*, and all these things will be given to you as well. Therefore, do not worry . . ." (Matthew 6:31–34)

CRAFT

Have the children produce sheep and goats for Jacob's flocks. Hand each child a few from Laban's flock—that is, fairly large, white, sheep-or-goat shapes already cut and ready to paint. Remind the children that Jacob's animals must be dark, spotted or speckled. Use old tooth brushes to spatter on the spots or bits of sponge to splotch on the speckles. You should have a large, lovely flock to display on a green background on your classroom wall. The children can also make small bright flowers to add to this pastoral scene.

REVIEW QUESTIONS

1. Why did Jacob want to go home? Why did Laban want him to stay?
2. What were the wages that Jacob proposed for his hard work?
3. How did Laban try to cheat Jacob out of those wages?

4. No matter what Laban did, Jacob still prospered. Why? Who was helping Jacob?
5. Why did Jacob leave suddenly, without even telling Laban?
6. What crime did Laban suspect and accuse Jacob? Who really stole his silver and gold idols?
7. Why was there almost a war between Jacob and Laban? Who stopped it? How?
8. What was the sign of the peace treaty (or covenant) between Jacob and Laban? What did they each promise not to do?
9. What promise did God make to Jacob at the beginning of his journey? Did God keep His promise?

PRAYER

LORD, thank You for being our Help and our Shield. Thank You for guarding us, when people are trying to harm us; thank You for giving to us, when people are trying to cheat us; thank You for blessing us, when people all around may be cursing us. LORD, we thank You and praise You for your LOVE!

PSALMS TO SING

35A . . . and 3; 4AB; 5AB; 7AB; 18ADGIJ; 20AB; 23ABCD; 27ABDE; 28AB; 30AB; 31ABCDEFG; 33C; 34AC; 37A; 43; 59AB; 121ABC; 140A; 142; 143BC; 144AD.

FIELD TRIP

Visit a zoo or a farm where you can see animals with their offspring. Especially try to find a place that has spotted goats with cute, little, spotted, bottle-fed kids. Your "kids" will love them and rejoice in what God gave Jacob!

(This student lesson starts on page 317.)

Jacob Returns to the Promised Land

Genesis 32, 33

VISUAL AIDS

Pictures or x-rays showing ball-and-socket joints, especially the hip joint, would be helpful for this lesson.

MEMORY WORK

"The Angel of the LORD encamps around those who fear Him, and He delivers them." (Psalm 34:7)

CRAFT

Your children could make a model of Mahanaim. Set up the tents of Jacob, (using folded squares of coloured paper), small plants for trees, piles of tiny twigs for campfires, etc. Then encircle this camp with a host of angels, (which the children can simply draw, cut and tape upright or make from white cones and balls, decorated with gold wings, halos, sequins, etc.) Another craft idea for this lesson would be to make gift bags, (having each child decorate a plain white paper bag,) or gift boxes with matching gift tags. These can be made simply by folding and gluing pretty wrapping paper to cover the tops and bottoms of small cardboard boxes. Using cardboard and the same paper, make some tags. A bow can be added to the top of each child's box.

REVIEW QUESTIONS

1. Who met Jacob on his way to the promised land?
2. What did Jacob name that place? Why? What did the name mean?
3. Who else was coming to meet Jacob?

4. Jacob was in great distress. Why? What did he do to deal with these difficulties? What did he pray? What was his plan?
5. What very strange thing happened in the middle of the night? Who wrestled with Jacob? What did He do to him? What did He give to him? Why wouldn't Jacob let go of the Man? What was Jacob's new name? What did it mean?
6. How did God answer Jacob's prayer and rescue him from his brother Esau?
7. Jacob went on his way . . . limping. Why?

PRAYER

LORD, thank You for watching over us and for commanding Your angels to guard us in all our ways. We thank You for Your daily protection and provision. We ask that even this day You would mercifully deliver us from evil and supply all our needs. LORD, we thank You for the new name that You have waiting for us! (See Revelation 2:17.)

PSALMS TO SING

34AC; 41B . . . and 17C; 25D; 27BE; 35A; 46ABC; 72D; 85A; 91A; 103D; 106G; 121ABC; 124AB; 140A; 143ABC; 148.

FIELD TRIP

Is there a hill, which overlooks a campground? As you view the tents below, remind the children of Mahanaim, Two Camps. The children can look into the clouds too, but, alas, they will not see God's host of angels. Imagine, though, how exciting it was for Jacob to see them surrounding his tents!

(This student lesson starts on page 325.)

Jacob's Refuge

Genesis 34, 35

VISUAL AIDS

Jacob set up a stone pillar at the place where God talked to him, but people everywhere through the ages have used stone pillars as markers. Most of them did not glorify God, but you could show the children photographs of these famous memorials, such as Stonehenge in England. Jacob also set up a stone to mark Rachel's tomb. The children could also be shown pictures of graveyards and tombstones, where "pillars" mark the place where loved ones lie.

MEMORY WORK

"God is our refuge and strength, an ever-present help in trouble. Therefore, we will not fear . . ." (Psalm 46:1)

CRAFT

Find smooth round stones that the children can paint and use to mark some special spot where a pet is buried or a treasure is hidden or a prayer was made. They could also use these stones as paper-weights.

REVIEW QUESTIONS

1. Where did Jacob buy some land? What did Jacob build on it?
2. What was Jacob offered by the king of Shechem? Why was this a temptation from Satan?
3. What did Jacob's sons do to the people of Shechem? Was Jacob pleased? Why not?
4. What did God tell Jacob to do? Why was this difficult?

5. How did Jacob's family get ready to worship the LORD? What happened to the gold and silver idols that his sons stole?
6. What did Jacob do at Bethel?
7. What did God say to Jacob there?
8. Jacob's life was filled with sorrow. What griefs did he face?
9. What (or Who) was Jacob's refuge in all his difficulties?

PRAYER

LORD, we thank You for being our help, refuge and strength in all our troubles. Help us not to be afraid, but to trust in You and Your LOVE for us.

PSALMS TO SING

37F (25, 26); 46ABC . . . and 17B (1–3); 28A; 31E; 34DE; 43; 57A (1–3); 59B (12, 13); 71A; 73C; 91A (1); 142.

FIELD TRIP

Is there somewhere you can visit that has interesting stone markers? Is there a Stonehenge-type place that the children could see? Large stones with a plaque are often used as memorials. In Japan, I once saw a large, moss-covered stone on a mountainside, upon which was carved in oriental characters a poem by Basho, their most famous poet. The stone marked the spot where he wrote the poem. That was a very interesting stone to me! However, if no such marker stones are nearby, you can always visit a cemetery and point out all the tombstones that mark people's graves.

(This student lesson starts on page 332.)

Joseph Loved and Hated

Genesis 37

VISUAL AIDS

Do you have a brightly coloured, richly ornamented robe that you could bring to show your class? Perhaps you could find pictures of royal robes worn by kings and queens to contrast with pictures of plain robes worn by peasants and shepherds. You could bring samples of material: cheap, brown, rough fabrics and rich, bright, smooth fabrics.

MEMORY WORK

"Many are the plans in men's hearts, but it is the LORD's purpose that prevails." (Proverbs 19:21)

CRAFT

Sew some small, plain, brown, burlap bags—enough for each child in your class. Transform them into brightly coloured, richly ornamented bags by weaving bright yarns into the fabric and sewing sequins or trinkets onto it. (Each child will need his own large needle and you should insert a piece of cardboard into his bag to keep him from sewing the two sides together.) Keep one bag unadorned to remind the children how their bags looked before they began working on them. If you prefer a group project, you could sew a simple tunic from a burlap sack—and then everyone could have the fun of turning it into a brightly coloured, richly ornamented robe.

REVIEW QUESTIONS

1. What were the twin sins in Jacob's family?
2. What did Joseph do that made his brothers angry?

3. What did Joseph have that made his brothers angry?
4. What did Joseph dream that made his brothers angry?
5. Which brother tried to rescue Joseph from the others?
6. What terrible thing did nine of the brothers do to Joseph?
7. How much money did they get for selling their brother as a slave?
8. How did the brothers hide their sin?
9. Was all this part of God's plan?
10. How do we know that Jacob loved Joseph? How do we know that God loved Joseph?

PRAYER

LORD, thank You for loving us, especially when others are hating us. Thank You, LORD, for always hearing our prayers and always answering them. Thank You for causing all things to work for the good of those who love You. Help us, O LORD, to remember Your LOVE through all our days.

PSALMS TO SING

88A . . . and 5AB; 33B; 35B; 37D (13); 40ABE; 57B; 69C; 70ABC; 71A; 119K; 140A; 143BC.

FIELD TRIP

Do you know where there is an old well or a deep hole or a dark pit? Take the children there, to see the kind of place where Joseph's brothers threw him. Remind the children that God is with us everywhere, even if we are cast into the deepest, darkest place in all the world.

(This student lesson starts on page 340.)

The Lord Was With Joseph

Genesis 39

VISUAL AIDS

Photographs of Egypt (showing pyramids, sphinxes, camel caravans, etc.) would be useful for this lesson. Also, pictures of the treasures excavated from the tombs of ancient Egyptian kings, would help to arouse interest in this foreign land, the land where Joseph was sold as a slave.

MEMORY WORK

"Who shall separate us from the love of Christ? Shall trouble or hardship or persecution or famine or nakedness or danger or sword? No, in all these things we are more than conquerors through Him who loved us! For I am convinced that neither death nor life, neither angels nor demons, neither present nor future, nor any powers, neither height nor depth, nor anything else in all creation, will be able to separate us from the love of God that is in Christ Jesus our Lord." (Romans 8:35, 37–39)

CRAFT

Cut out post-card-size pieces of white cardboard (one or two for each child in your class) and have the children make "postcards" of scenes from Egypt. Their cards could show pyramids in the desert, crocodiles by the Nile River, camels by some palm trees, etc. The children could also write a message on the back of their postcard. If they had been sold as a slave and sent to Egypt, what would they write to their family at home?

REVIEW QUESTIONS

1. What had Joseph's brothers robbed from him? What precious things did Joseph still have?
2. Joseph's brothers had separated him from his family, but can any person or any power in all creation separate us from the LOVE of God in Christ Jesus our Lord?
3. Joseph was a slave in Egypt. Was his life blessed there? Why?
4. What wicked thing was Joseph commanded to do? Did he obey?
5. What must Joseph not forget or forsake in his new life in this strange land?
6. How did Joseph's coat/cloak get him into trouble again?
7. How did God rescue Joseph from that house of sin and death? Was it part of God's good plan for Joseph?

PRAYER

LORD, thank You for loving us, with a LOVE that can never be taken from us. Please deliver us from all the traps and snares of sin that the Evil One sets for us. Deliver us from all temptation and give us the strength, wisdom and endurance that Joseph had—enabling him by the power of God to flee from sin! LORD, help us to remember Your Law and Your LOVE forever.

PSALMS TO SING

119B . . . and 119AEGHIJLMNPQRST.

FIELD TRIP

Is there a museum in your community with an exhibit on ancient Egypt? Take your children to see it.

(This student lesson starts on page 346.)

Dreams Come True

Genesis 39:20—40:23

VISUAL AIDS

Pictures of prisoners, bound with ropes or chains, and pictures of old-fashioned prisons, with barred windows and barbed wire, are what you need for this lesson. Also, show the children pictures of stocks and irons, rings and shackles, and other ways of confining prisoners. Bring some heavy chains to show the children, the kind used to chain up large animals. It says about Joseph, in Psalm 105:18, that they "bruised his feet with shackles and his neck was put in irons."

MEMORY WORK

"The LORD is good to those whose hope is in Him, to the one who seeks Him; it is good to wait quietly for the salvation of the LORD." (Lamentations 3:25, 26)

CRAFT

If you have access to a kitchen, a good craft for this lesson would be to knead dough to bake breads and squeeze grapes to make juice. You will need small foil pans (one for each child) and some little goblets. If time or space does not permit this activity, you could make paper chains. Have strips of coloured paper ready for each child to make his own "necklace" to take home or you could link them all together, when each child has finished his own section, to form one large chain. If you pick colours appropriate for the season, you can use it to decorate your classroom.

REVIEW QUESTIONS

1. Why would Joseph be tempted to despair?
2. What must Joseph remember in prison? What must he do?

3. How did the LORD show kindness to Joseph in prison?
4. Two important officials of Pharaoh were thrown into prison with Joseph. Who were they? What was their work? Why were they in prison?
5. These two men had dreams, but they were sad because no one could interpret them. What did Joseph say about that?
6. What was the cupbearer's dream? What did Joseph say it meant?
7. What was the baker's dream? What did Joseph say it meant?
8. Were Joseph's interpretations right? What happened?
9. Joseph asked his friend for help when he was with Pharaoh again? Did he? On whom must Joseph depend for help?

PRAYER

LORD, thank You that we can always depend upon You for help. You have promised never to leave us, never to forget us, never to disappoint us. Our hope and trust are in You, O LORD. Help us to wait patiently for Your answers to our prayers. We praise You, O LORD, for You are our God, a God of deliverances!

PSALMS TO SING

142; 146AB . . . and 17A; 25ABCD; 27CF; 35D; 37ABC; 42ABC; 43; 44C; 68A; 69E; 77A; 79B; 86AB; 119K; 119X; 138AB.

FIELD TRIP

Is there a prison the children can view? Even a small jail house, with bars on the window, would be interesting to visit. Remind the children of Joseph, a good man, who was unjustly imprisoned for many years.

(This student lesson starts on page 351.)

From the Prison to the Palace

Genesis 41:1–52

VISUAL AIDS

We store our crops in barns, silos and grain elevators. Pictures of these things, especially the huge grain elevators from the prairie provinces, would be useful for this class. Joseph must have ordered large storage places to be built in all the cities all over Egypt, but we don't know how they looked.

MEMORY WORK

"The LORD, the God of Israel, declares . . . Those who honour Me I will honour."
(II Samuel 2:30)

CRAFT

Have your children draw some dreams. They can use large sheets of white paper cut in the shape of the profile of a person's head, with an almond-shaped hole for the eye. (This unique art paper will make the project more interesting.) They can fill their heads with whatever dreams they want. The children could also make mosaics by gluing grain, seeds and corn onto cardboard.

REVIEW QUESTIONS

1. How many years passed before Joseph's friend remembered him? Who did not forget Joseph, even for a moment?
2. How did God warn Pharaoh about the coming famine?
3. When Joseph stood before Pharaoh, what was the first thing he said to him?
4. Describe Pharaoh's two dreams. What did they mean?
5. Joseph had a plan. What was it? Did Pharaoh like the plan?

6. Pharaoh recognized that Joseph was a man in whom was the Spirit of God. How did Pharaoh honour Joseph? What were some of the things that Pharaoh gave to Joseph?
7. In one day, Joseph woke up as a prisoner and went to bed as a prince. Who caused this to happen? Do you know why?
8. What were the names of Joseph's sons? What did they mean?

PRAYER

LORD, thank You for blessing us beyond what we ask or even imagine. LORD, thank You for remembering us, even if everyone else forgets us and forsakes us. Please help us as we live our lives, to give You honour and glory in everything.

PSALMS TO SING

105C . . . and 18I; 30AB; 66C (1, 3,5); 77B; 89D; 113A; 116AC; 119F; 138B.

FIELD TRIP

For this lesson a trip to some grain elevators would be interesting. Perhaps you can watch them being filled. You could also visit a barn with its loft filled with hay, its silo filled with corn and its rooms filled with grain. Imagine what Joseph did in Egypt! He stored up such huge quantities of food, that it was beyond measure.

(This student lesson starts on page 357.)

The First Journey to Egypt

Genesis 41:53–42:38

VISUAL AIDS

You will need photos of famine. Show the children the effects of drought on land and crops, livestock and people. There are many sad pictures of starving children holding out their empty bowls to receive a little food.

MEMORY WORK

"O LORD, the Law from Your mouth is more precious to me than thousands of pieces of silver and gold." (Psalm 119:72)

CRAFT

Bring various coins for the children to make rubbings. Gold or silver pencils would be best, but lead pencils will do the job too. You could also make coin rubbings with gold and silver foil paper. Have the children cut out their coins and paste them on a piece of coloured construction paper, with their written in the centre of it.

REVIEW QUESTIONS

1. Where did Abraham, Isaac and Jacob go to buy food during famines in the land of Canaan?
2. Why did Jacob not send Benjamin with his ten brothers?
3. Did Joseph recognize his brothers? Did they recognize him? Why not?
4. How did Joseph's dreams from his childhood come true?
5. Why did Joseph accuse his brothers of being spies and throw them into prison?
6. What shows you that the brothers still felt guilty about the sins they committed against Joseph years earlier? What did they say?

7. What had the governor of Egypt told them to do? What would happen to them if they didn't do it? What did Jacob say?

PRAYER

LORD, we thank You, that even when everything seems to be against us, You are for us, causing all things to work together for the good of those who love You. LORD, we thank You for sparing us from famine and for giving us our daily bread. LORD, please keep us from harm and sin throughout our lives, and even through this day. Amen.

PSALMS TO SING

32A . . . and 19B; 33C (9, 10); 71D; 105A; 119IQ.

FIELD TRIP

I am fortunate living near the city of Ottawa, the capital of Canada. The national mint is located here, which is a perfect place to visit for this lesson. There the children will see bins of money, but the LORD's Law and God's Word are more precious than all of this wealth!

(This student lesson starts on page 363.)

The Second Journey to Egypt

Genesis 43

VISUAL AIDS

Bring two bags filled with "some of the best products of the land." Begin with a bag of products from your own country. (If you live in Canada, you could use a bottle of maple syrup, maple sugar, a tin of salmon, wheat crackers, etc.) Then show the children what was in Jacob's bag—honey, balm, spices, myrrh, pistachio nuts and almonds.

MEMORY WORK

"O Lord . . . how sweet are Your words to my taste, sweeter than honey to my mouth!" (Psalm 119:103)

CRAFT

If you have access to a kitchen, bake a batch of cookies (or baklava!) using the honey, nuts and spices. Here is a recipe for some easy honey-nut cookies that do not require baking:

Mix 1/2 cup honey, 1/2 cup peanut butter (or other nut butter), 1 cup powdered milk, 1/2 cup raisins, 1/4 cup sunflower seeds. Roll into balls. Then roll these balls in coconut or wheat germ.

REVIEW QUESTIONS

1. Why would Jacob's sons not return to Egypt without Benjamin?
2. Why did Jacob not want Benjamin to go with them?
3. Which brother promised to be personally responsible for him?
4. What gifts did Jacob send with his sons to Egypt? What else did he send with them?

5. Why were the brothers terrified when they were lead to the governor's house? What did they think would happen to them?
6. When they sat down to eat with the governor, what amazed them?
7. Why did the brothers consider their second journey to Egypt a great success?

PRAYER

LORD, we thank You that we can entrust our lives and the lives of our loved ones to You. We thank You that even in difficult or dangerous times, we can trust You to guard us and guide us. Even this day, LORD, we ask You to deliver us from evil, from every harm and every sin.

PSALMS TO SING

119M . . . and 19B; 25D; 31AD; 76AB.

FIELD TRIP

Visit an apiary or, if the time and place are right, a maple bush and sugar shack.

(This student lesson starts on page 370.)

Hidden Things Revealed

Genesis 44:1–45:15

VISUAL AIDS

Your children may not know what a "goblet" is. If you can get a large, richly-ornamented, silver goblet to set before the children as you teach, it would be a very effective visual aid. Use pictures of royal goblets and kings' cups too.

MEMORY WORK

"And we know that God causes all things to work together for good to those who love God, to those who are called according to His purpose." (Romans 8:28)

CRAFT

Bring out the clay and let each child make his own cup fit for a king!

REVIEW QUESTIONS

1. In whose sack was the governor's goblet found?
2. How did it get there?
3. Which of the brothers stood up and spoke to the great governor of Egypt? What did he offer to do? Why?
4. How did the lord of the land respond? What did he do and say?
5. Why were the brothers *terrified* to learn the truth about who the governor really was? How do you know they were terrified?
6. What did Joseph say to reassure his brothers? What did he do?
7. Who really was the One who sent Joseph to Egypt? Why?

PRAYER

Heavenly Father, we thank You for being a loving and forgiving God. We pray that You would forgive our sins, as we forgive those who sin against us. LORD, we thank You for causing all things to work together for the good of those who love You. By Your grace, O LORD, may we ever love You.

PSALMS TO SING

130A . . . and 25CD; 32C; 51ABDE; 103A; 107C; 116C.

FIELD TRIP

A gallery of governors' goblets would be great, but I doubt if such an exhibit exists. Perhaps though you could arrange a visit to watch silver smiths at work and view a display of various silver artifacts.

(This student lesson starts on page 375.)

Israel Goes to Egypt

Genesis 45:16–46:27

VISUAL AIDS

You need photographs of people on the move—with carts, animals, cars, people, trucks, etc. loaded with the bags, bundles and boxes of a family's belongings. It is a big job to move even one family with only a few people and pets. Imagine what it was like moving Jacob's family with all those people and all their flocks and herds!

MEMORY WORK

"With the LORD a day is like a thousand years, and a thousand years are like a day. The LORD is not slow in keeping His promise . . ." (II Peter 3:8, 9)

CRAFT

Your children could make toy carts—either simple ones made from the bottom of small cardboard boxes with cardboard wheels glued to the sides or more complicated ones built with wood and moveable wheels. Show the children pictures of different kinds of carts such as two-wheeled, large-wheeled ox-carts or simple, four-wheeled farm carts or brightly-painted, gaily-decorated parade carts, etc. The children can paint their carts too and fill them with little gifts for someone or you can have a cart parade on display in your classroom.

REVIEW QUESTIONS

1. What did Joseph give to each of his brothers? Why was that so interesting? What had they stolen from him?
2. What did Joseph give to his father Jacob?

3. Why did Jacob not believe the good news that he heard? What finally convinced him that Joseph was really alive?
4. Why might Jacob be afraid to go to Egypt?
5. What did Jacob do at Beersheba?
6. How did God speak to Jacob? What did God say to him?
7. Where was God going to fulfil His promise to make Israel into a great nation?
8. Who went with Jacob to Egypt? How many people were there? Who else promised to go with him?
9. Is the LORD slow in keeping His promises? Why does it often seem slow to us?

PRAYER

LORD, we thank You for Your Word, which comforts us in our fears, and we thank You for Your promise: "Lo, I am with you always, even to the end of the age" (Matthew 28:20). LORD, help us to live by faith, not by fear, trusting in You all our days.

PSALMS TO SING

73C . . . and 16A (6, 7); 23; 33C; 34AC; 46ABC; 48B (10); 71C; 139A.

FIELD TRIP

Do you know a family who is moving? Perhaps you can take the children to help pack boxes, clean rooms or load trucks. If their "help" isn't needed, perhaps you could just watch the big moving van being loaded with all the family's possessions.

(This student lesson starts on page 381.)

Jacob's Last Years

Genesis 46:28–49:33

VISUAL AIDS

Do the children know what a sceptre is? Bring them some pictures of royal sceptres. You will also need a map showing Canaan as it was divided among the twelve
tribes of Israel. Ask the children, "Where is the tribe of Joseph?" They will not
find it. Point out that Joseph was given a double portion of the inheritance in
his two sons Ephraim and Manasseh.

MEMORY WORK

1. "The sceptre will not depart from Judah . . ." (Genesis 49:10)
2. The angel said . . ." You are to give him the name Jesus . . . and He will reign
   over the house of Jacob forever; His kingdom will never end." (Luke 1:33)

CRAFT

The lion is often used as a symbol on a country's coat-of-arms, even in countries where there are no lions, such as Great Britain. Show the children some
examples of these lion symbols—and then have them make their own shields.
Give each child a shield-shaped piece of white, silver or gold cardboard, on
which he/she can paint a bright red lion. The Scriptures speak of the LORD being our shield and He is "The lion of the tribe of Judah" (Revelation 5:5).

REVIEW QUESTIONS

1. What happened to the Egyptians during the famine? What happened to the
   Israelites during that time?
2. Jacob was a very old man, hardly able to stand, but what did he do as he
   leaned on t the top of his staff?

3. As the end of Jacob's life drew near, what did he do that showed he had faith in the promises of God?
4. Jacob gave his beloved Joseph a double blessing, and blessing upon blessing, but which of Jacob's sons did God choose?
5. In the last book of the Bible someone is called "The lion of the tribe of Judah." Who is it?
6. For what (or whom) was Jacob looking, as he lay dying? What words did he cry out, as he was blessing his sons?
7. Where did Jacob want to be buried? Why?

PRAYER

O LORD, we thank You that in life and in death we can look to You for deliverance. We thank You for Your Word, spoken so long ago by Your servants, which You fulfilled in Jesus Christ. Thank You that our hope Jesus is never disappointed.

PSALMS TO SING

80AB (1) . . . and 24A; 45B (6, 7); 47A; 48B; 60B (6); 68DE; 69E; 71C; 76AB; 78H; 97B; 105A; 108B; 114 (2).

FIELD TRIP

For this lesson you could visit a museum, where royal treasures such as crowns and sceptres are exhibited. If that is not possible, perhaps there is a place where provincial flags or coats-of-arms are on display. Look for the lions!

(This student lesson starts on page 386.)

Grief and Death
With Faith and Hope

Genesis 50

VISUAL AIDS

Photographs of skeletons, skulls and bones, funerals, tombs and graves—these are the kinds of powerful pictures that you need for this lesson.

MEMORY WORK

1. "Even in death the righteous have hope." (Proverbs 14:32)

2. "For it is by grace you have been saved, through faith—and this is not from yourselves; it is the gift of God." (Ephesians 2:8)

3. "How shall we escape if we ignore such a great salvation?" (Hebrews 2:3)

CRAFT

Your class could make sympathy cards. Children tend to like bright colours, so you might want to show them some examples of tasteful, white-on-white cards. A Scripture verse could be written on the inside of the card, such as their memory work: even in death the righteous have hope. Is there someone grieving to whom these offerings made by little hands could be a blessing? Send them, if it is appropriate. As a group project, your children could also make a wreath for someone's grave. If you feel really ambitious, grave-stone rubbings are a good idea too.

REVIEW QUESTIONS

1. Where was Jacob buried?
2. What did Joseph say on his deathbed that showed he believed in the promises of God?

3. Joseph was placed in a coffin in Egypt, but he was not buried. Why not? How long did Joseph's bones have to wait for burial?
4. Many terrible things happened to Joseph in his life. Why? What was God's purpose in all these things?
5. How was Joseph a type of Christ? How did Joseph's life foreshadow the life of Jesus?
6. How is hearing the message of salvation of value to us? Our hearing must be combined with . . . what?
7. What must we not neglect to escape the wrath of God?
8. How does Genesis end? What are the last words of this book?
9. Are there any glimmers of happiness at the end of this book?

PRAYER

LORD, we thank You for conquering death through Jesus Christ. Thank You for Your Grace in revealing to us Your great salvation. LORD, thank You for the gifts of faith, life and hope.

PSALMS TO SING

116A . . . and 3 (5); 13; 30AB; 40F (8); 51AD; 70C; 96A (1); 98AB (1–3); 106A; 118C.

FIELD TRIP

Don't underestimate the children's interest in death. You could watch a funeral procession by a graveyard, with its hearse and long line of cars. You could also point out funeral homes, crematoriums and the cold storage "sheds," where bodies await burial until the ground thaws in the spring. Remind them that we have the hope of eternal life in Christ Jesus.

(This student lesson starts on page 395.)

About the Author

N ancy Ganz has spent the last twenty years in her native land of Canada, helping her husband, Dr. Richard Ganz, in church-planting work and home-schooling their four daughters. She received her formal theological training from the University of Toronto prior to her conversion to Christ at L'Abri in the Netherlands. However, it has been the many years of Bible study since that time which has produced her *Herein Is Love* commentaries on the Old Testament. Currently, most of her time is spent studying the Scriptures, writing various books, and taking long walks along the country roads and woodland paths near her home.